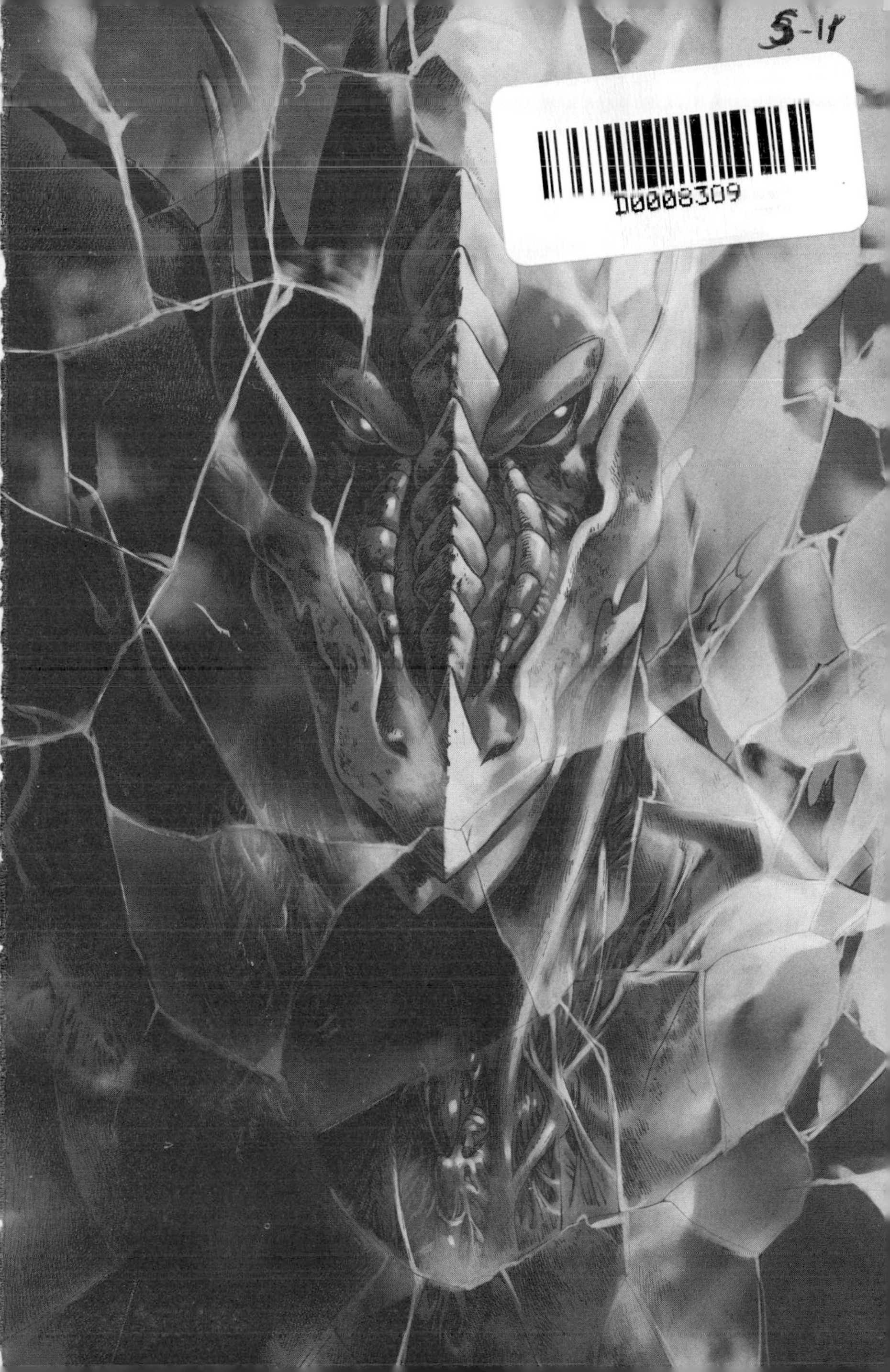

Warcraft®: The Sunwell Trilogy™
Written by Richard A. Knaak
Illustrated by Jae-Hwan Kim

Lettering and Layout - Rob Steen
Copy Editors - Peter Ahlstrom & Hope Donovan
Production Artists - James Dashiell and Jason Milligan
Artist Liaison - Eddie Yu
Cover Artist - Jae-Hwan Kim
Cover Design - James Lee

Editor - Rob Tokar
Digital Imaging Manager - Chris Buford
Pre-Production Supervisor - Lucas Rivera
Art Director - Anne Marie Horne
Managing Editor - Lindsey Johnston
Production Manager - Elisabeth Brizzi
Editorial Director - Jeremy Ross
VP of Production - Ron Klamert
Editor-in-Chief - Rob Tokar
Publisher - Mike Kiley
President and C.O.O. - John Parker
C.E.O. and Chief Creative Officer - Stuart Levy

A  Manga

TOKYOPOP Inc.
5900 Wilshire Blvd. Suite 2000
Los Angeles, CA 90036

E-mail: info@TOKYOPOP.com
Come visit us online at www.TOKYOPOP.com

Special thanks to Chris Metzen, Lisa Pearce, Brian Hsieh, Gloria Soto, and Matt Kassan.

ISBN: 1-4278-0003-0

First TOKYOPOP printing: August 2006
10 9 8 7 6 5 4 3 2 1
Printed in the USA

Warcraft®
The Sunwell Trilogy™

Volume 2

Shadows of Ice

Written by
Richard A. Knaak

Illustrated by
Jae-Hwan Kim

TOKYOPOP®

HAMBURG // LONDON // LOS ANGELES // TOKYO

HISTORY OF THE WORLD OF

The world of Azeroth has long been plagued by the misuse of magic. Originally, only dragons and night elves were able to practice the mystic arts, though eventually, even humans began to wield the unstable energy. Unfortunately, the unrestrained spell-casting eventually caught the attention of a malevolent, extra-dimensional force known as the Burning Legion.

The Burning Legion's first attempt to invade Azeroth, known as the War of the Ancients, was only thwarted after many lives were lost and the world's sole continent was shattered. With their second attempt, the Burning Legion used the Orcs from the world of Draenor as their pawns.

Twisted and corrupted by the Burning Legion's influence, the Orcs invaded Azeroth through the Dark Portal. After many ferocious battles, this Second War ended with the Orcs' defeat and imprisonment. Still determined to conquer Azeroth, the Burning Legion created one of its most twisted servants, the Lich King, to weaken Azeroth's defenders.

The Lich King spread a plague of death and terror across Azeroth that was meant to snuff out human civilization. All those who died from the dreaded plague would arise as the undead, and their spirits would be bound to the Lich King's iron will forever.

The army of the dead swept across the land, and Quel'Thalas, the glorious homeland of the high elves which had stood for thousands of years, was no more. The undead Scourge then moved south to Dalaran, and then to Kalimdor, home of the night elves.

Though the undead Scourge was stopped at Kalimdor, they had essentially transformed Lordaeron and Quel'Thalas into toxic Plaguelands. Grieving for the loss of their homeland, most of the high elves have adopted a new name and a new mission. Calling themselves blood elves, they now seek out and siphon magic from any available source, including demons.

Meanwhile, half of the undead forces staged a coup for control over the undead empire. Eventually, the banshee Sylvanas Windrunner and her rebel undead--known as the Forsaken--claimed the ruined capital city of Lordaeron as their own and vowed to drive the Scourge from the land.

Currently the Lich King resides in Northrend; he is rumored to be rebuilding the citadel of Icecrown. His trusted lieutenant, Kel'Thuzad, commands the Scourge in the Plaguelands. Sylvanas and her rebel Forsaken hold only the Tirisfal Glades, a small portion of the war-torn kingdom, while the humans, orcs, and night elves are trying to rebuild their societies

WarCraft

The Sunwell Trilogy

The story thus far...

Kalecgos, a young blue dragon, was sent by his master to investigate a strange surge of magical power. Before he could reach his destination, Kalec was shot down by the dragon hunter known as Harkyn Grymstone. Grymstone was a twisted, bitter dwarf who lost his loved ones in a dragon attack. He and his ragged band of hunters were only too happy to serve those who would enable them to slay all the dragons they could find.

Transforming into a humanoid form to escape the hunters' nets, a wounded Kalec was aided by Anveena, a kind, innocent maiden who lived nearby. Kalec tried to warn Anveena away, but she seemed unconcerned about the pursuing hunters. Even more remarkably, the young woman seemed unfazed by Kalec's true nature, though most people's reaction to meeting a dragon would be to flee or try to kill it.

Anveena's parents were equally welcoming to Kalec, and they maintained their friendly dispositions even when Grymstone kicked down their door. Kalec and Anveena used a hidden escape tunnel under the house to avoid the hunting party,

BUT THEY WERE DISCOVERED AND FORCED TO FLEE. KALEC TRANSFORMED BACK INTO A DRAGON AND FLEW AWAY WITH ANVEENA, BUT HIS WOUNDS AND GRYMSTONE'S ATTACKS DROVE HIM FROM THE SKY ONCE AGAIN.

UNABLE TO CONTROL HIS DESCENT, KALEC CRASHED INTO A NEARBY LAKE. ANVEENA SWAM TO SHORE AND FEARED THE WORST UNTIL SHE FOUND KALEC LYING AT THE WATER'S EDGE. LUCKILY, THE YOUNG DRAGON WAS ABLE TO TRANSFORM AGAIN AND WASH ASHORE BEFORE HIS BULKIER DRAGON FORM CAUSED HIM TO DROWN.

RETURNING TO ANVEENA'S HOME, KALEC AND ANVEENA FOUND ONLY BURNING WRECKAGE...AND THE UNDEAD SCOURGE. FIGHTING THE SHAMBLING CORPSES, KALEC AND ANVEENA WERE EASILY CAPTURED BY THE RENEGADE ELF KNOWN AS DAR'KHAN. DAR'KHAN PLACED PAIN-INDUCING MYSTICAL COLLARS AROUND KALEC AND ANVEENA'S NECKS, AND OFFERED THEM RELATIVELY PAINLESS DEATHS IN EXCHANGE FOR INFORMATION ABOUT THE SUNWELL.

THE SUNWELL WAS A POOL OF MYSTICAL ENERGY THAT WAS THE ESSENCE OF THE HIGH ELVES' LIVES. LOCATED IN THE ELVEN CITY OF QUEL'THALAS, THIS SOURCE OF MAGIC WAS AS

Kalecgos
A young blue dragon. Though trapped in humanoid form by a mystical collar Dar'Khan placed around his neck, Kalec retains many of his magical talents, including the ability to create a sword out of nothingness.

IMPORTANT TO THE ELVES AS EATING OR BREATHING.
THEY USED ITS VAST POWER TO BUILD THEIR CITIES,
MOLD THE LANDSCAPE AND MAKE WHATEVER THEY
DESIRED. UNFORTUNATELY, DAR'KHAN DESIRED MUCH
MORE THAN THE REST OF HIS BRETHREN, LEADING HIM
TO AN UNHOLY PACT WITH ARTHAS, THE CORRUPTED
HUMAN KNIGHT WHO BECAME THE LICH KING.

DAR'KHAN ENABLED THE UNDEAD SCOURGE TO BYPASS
QUEL'THALAS' FABLED DEFENSES WHILE HE DRAINED THE
SUNWELL'S ENERGIES. WHILE HIS PROUD HOME WAS
OVERRUN BY VICIOUS, ZOMBIFIED CORPSES, AND
DAR'KHAN FOUGHT HIS FELLOW ELVEN SORCERERS FOR
CONTROL OF THE WELL, SOMETHING WENT HORRIBLY
WRONG. THE SUNWELL'S POWER EXPLODED
SPECTACULARLY, RAVAGING WHAT LITTLE REMAINED

Anveena
A caring, innocent young maiden. Anveena
helped a wounded Kalecgos escape from
dragon hunters, though her home and
parents were destroyed.

UNTOUCHED BY THE SCOURGE.

DAR'KHAN WAS SAVED BY THE POWER
OF HIS DARK LORD, AND SENT ACROSS
THE CONTINENT IN SEARCH OF THE
SUNWELL'S ESCAPED MAGIC...WHICH
WOULD SEEM TO BE THE SAME POWER
THAT KALEC'S MASTER SENSED.
DAR'KHAN TRIED TORTURING KALEC
FOR INFORMATION, BUT HE WAS
INTERRUPTED BY THE ARRIVAL OF
TYRYGOSA, A FEMALE BLUE DRAGON
WHO IS ALSO KALEC'S INTENDED.
TOGETHER, TYRI AND KALEC MANAGED
TO WIPE OUT DAR'KHAN'S UNDEAD
SERVANTS AND DRIVE THE ELF AWAY...
BUT THEY COULD NOT REMOVE THE
COLLARS HE PLACED ON HIS TWO
CAPTIVES.

Tyrygosa
A female blue dragon and Kalec's
intended. When forced to assume a
humanoid shape, she refuses to look
merely human. In her words, "At least
elves are aesthetically pleasing."

SIFTING THROUGH THE SHATTERED TIMBERS OF ANVEENA'S
HOME IN SEARCH OF HER PARENTS, THE TRIO INSTEAD
DISCOVERED A STRANGE EGG, WHICH HOUSED AN EVEN
STRANGER WINGED SERPENT. ANVEENA NAMED HIM RAAC
(FOR THE NOISE HE MAKES) AND KALEC AND TYRI
SUSPECTED THAT THE BIZARRE CREATURE MIGHT HAVE
SOMETHING TO DO WITH THE SUNWELL ENERGY THAT
ATTRACTED THEM AND DAR'KHAN.

SINCE KALEC'S COLLAR PREVENTED HIM FROM
TRANSFORMING, TYRI CARRIED HER COMPANIONS TO THE
TOWN OF TARREN MILL IN SEARCH OF BOREL, A MAN WHO
ANVEENA'S PARENTS SPOKE OF OFTEN. THOUGH SHE NEVER
MET HIM, SHE BELIEVED HE MIGHT BE ABLE TO HELP
THEM REMOVE DAR'KHAN'S COLLARS. THE GROUP

Jorad Mace

A human paladin whose loyalty was sworn to Arthas...before Arthas betrayed his father, his homeland and his species. Mace is continually haunted by his terrible loss.

ATTRACTED A LOT OF ATTENTION IN THE SMALL TOWN, INCLUDING THAT OF JORAD MACE. MACE RECOGNIZED BOREL'S NAME, THOUGH HE WAS MORE INTERESTED IN HELPING ANVEENA ESCAPE THE TOWN THAN AIDING KALEC AND TYRI AGAINST A SURPRISE ATTACK BY HARKYN GRYMSTONE AND HIS FELLOW DRAGON HUNTERS.

GRYMSTONE HAD THE DRAGONS CORNERED WHEN HE SUDDENLY FOUND THAT HE, TOO, WAS SURROUNDED BY THE UNDEAD SCOURGE AND DAR'KHAN. DAR'KHAN REVEALED THAT HE HAD DISGUISED HIMSELF AS A HUMAN PRINCE TO PROVIDE THE VENGEFUL DWARF WITH THE RESOURCES NEEDED TO KILL ANY DRAGONS THAT MIGHT BE DRAWN TO THE AREA BY THE SUNWELL'S POWER. AS DAR'KHAN PREPARED TO TAKE RAAC FROM ANVEENA, A SURPRISE ATTACK FROM JORAD MACE HELPED THE DRAGONS AND DRAGON HUNTERS TURN THE TIDE.

WITH THEIR COMBINED EFFORTS, THE UNDEAD WERE WIPED OUT AND DAR'KHAN WAS CONSUMED IN A BLAST OF TYRI'S DRAGON

FIRE. WHEN MACE INFORMED THE OTHERS THAT THEY MIGHT FIND BOREL ON AERIE PEAK, AN APOLOGETIC HARKYN GRYMSTONE ADVISED THEM TO SEEK HIS COUSIN, LOGGI, WHO LIVES IN THE MOUNTAINS NEAR THERE.

HOPING THAT LOGGI MIGHT BE ABLE TO REMOVE THE MAGICAL COLLARS, KALEC, ANVEENA, TYRI AND JORAD MACE SEARCH NOT ONLY FOR THE DWARF, BUT ALSO FOR THE MYSTERIOUS BOREL, WHO MAY KNOW MORE ABOUT THE SUNWELL THAN ANYONE. HOWEVER, REACHING AERIE PEAK MAY BE HARDER THAN IMAGINED, EVEN WITH A DRAGON TO FLY THEM THERE...

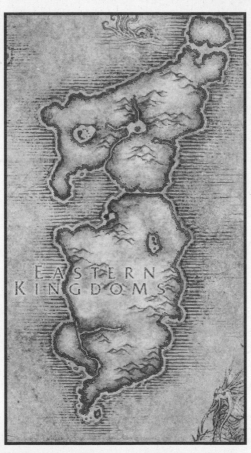

CHAPTER ONE
Terror on the Mountain

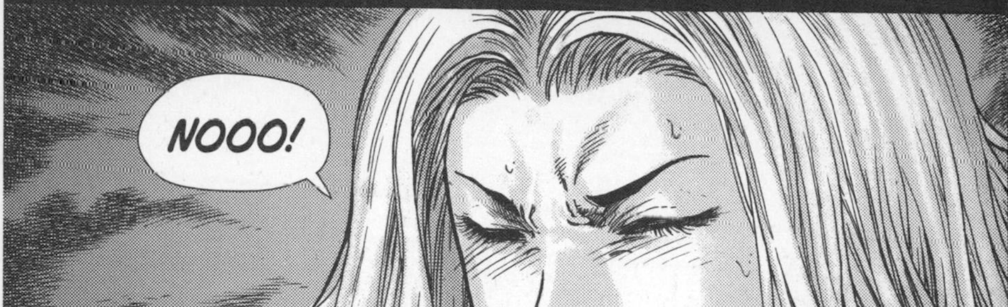
NOOO!
RRRAUGH!!

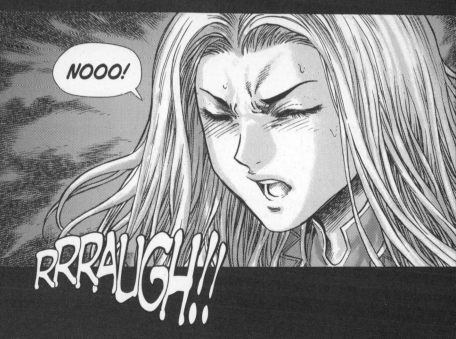

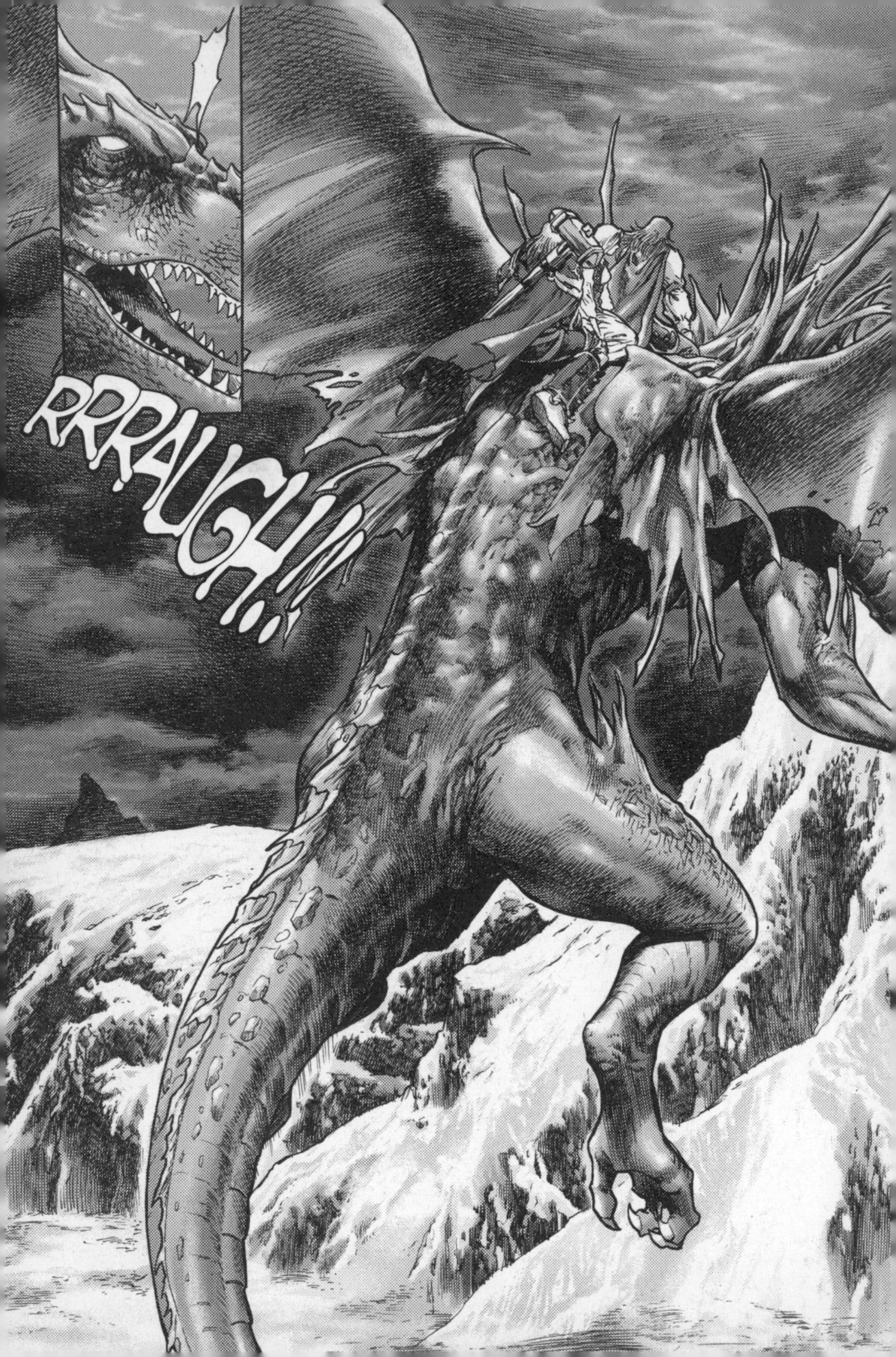
RRRRAUGH!!!

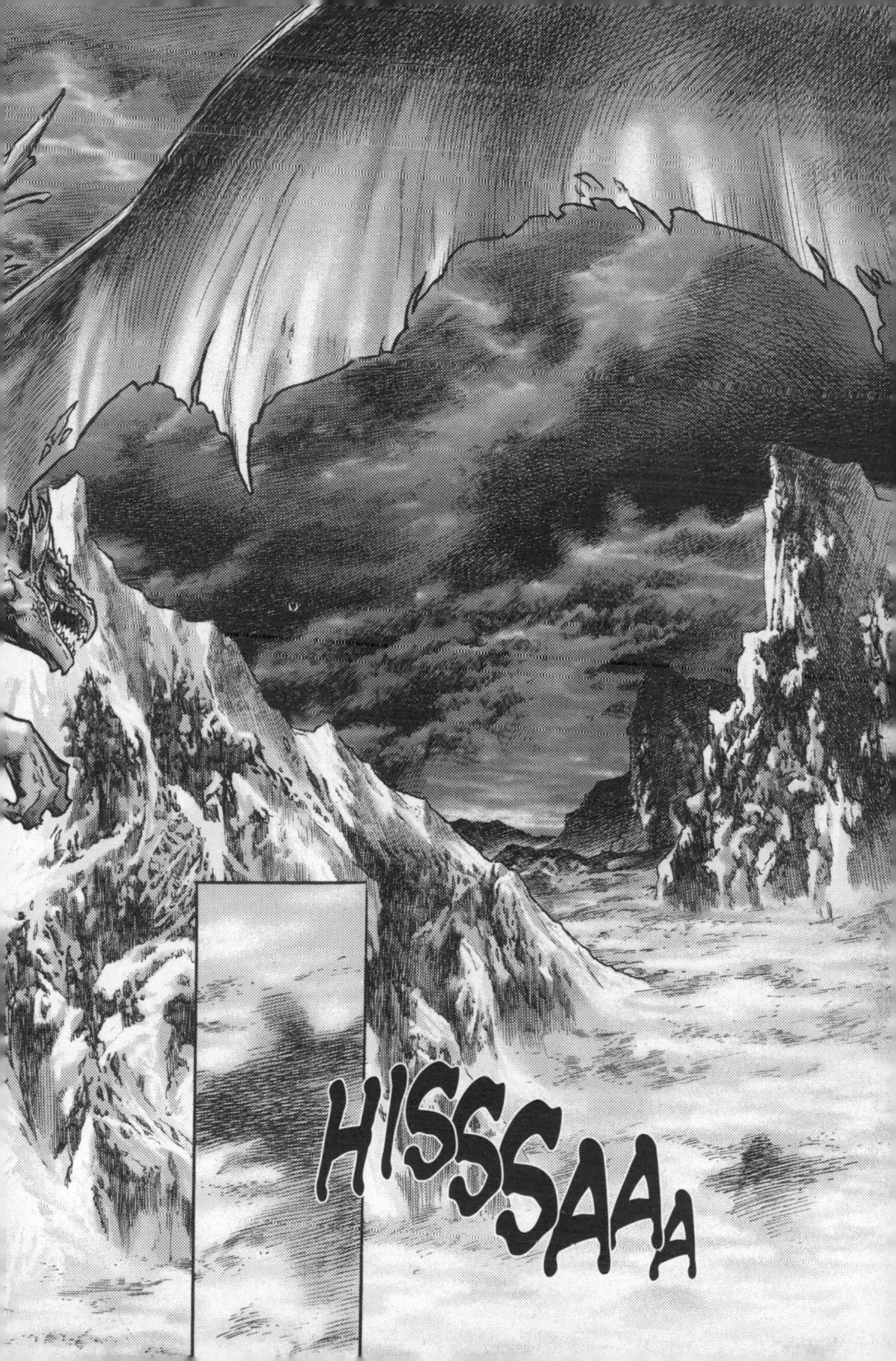
HISSSAAA

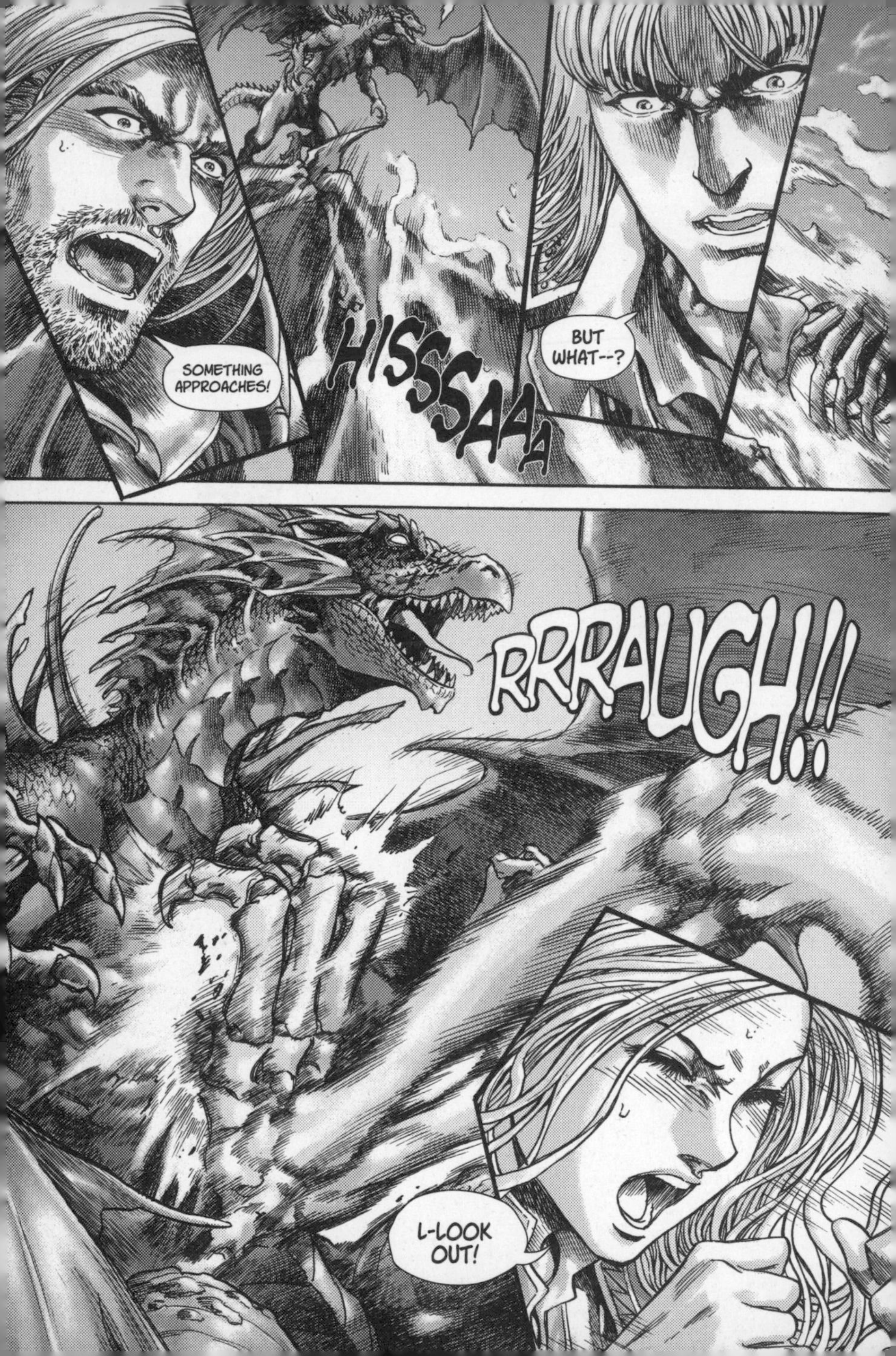
SOMETHING APPROACHES!
HISSSAAA
BUT WHAT--?
RRRAUGH!!
L-LOOK OUT!

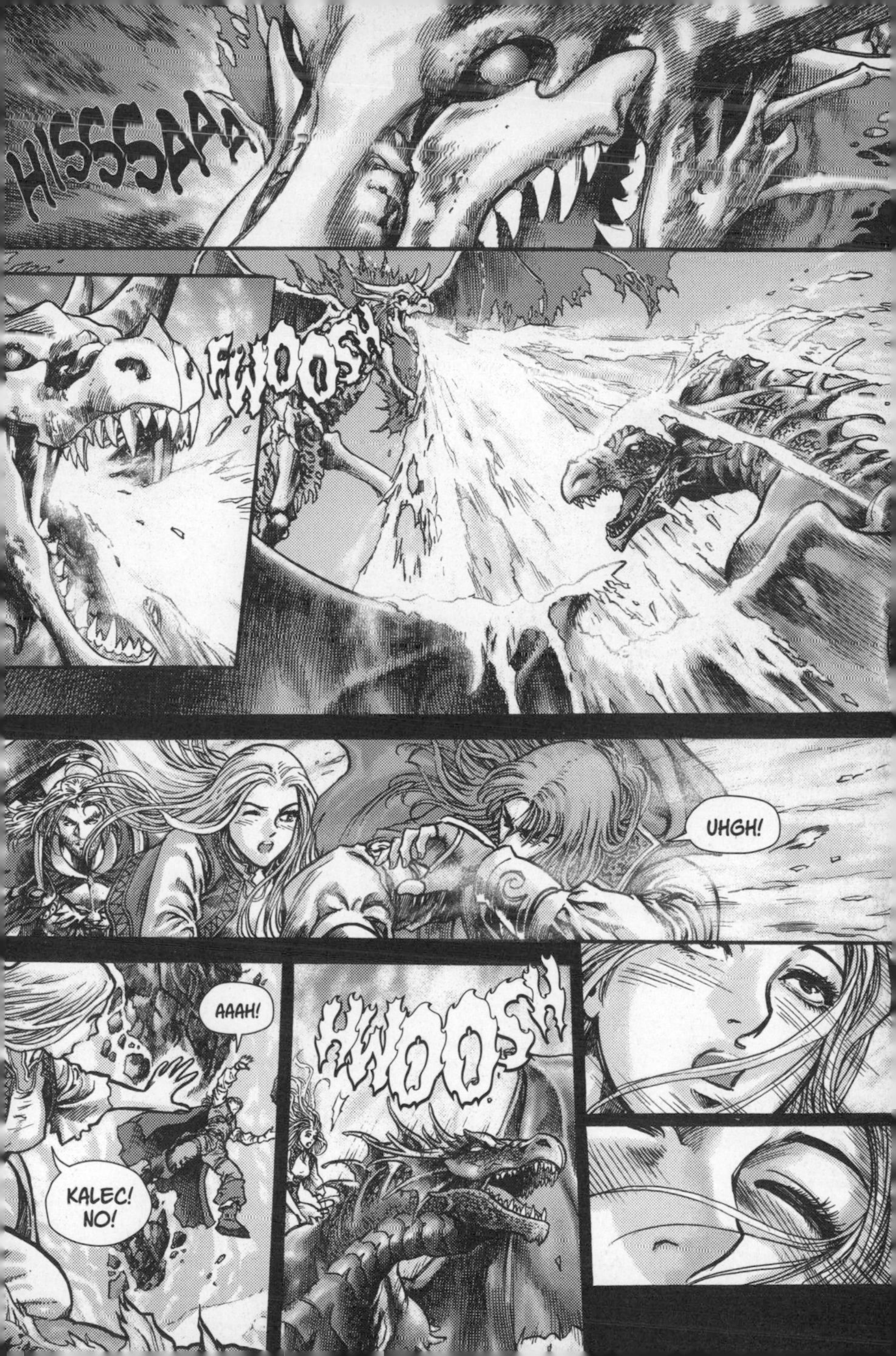
HISSSAAA
FWOOSH
UHGH!
AAAH!
KALEC! NO!
FWOOSH

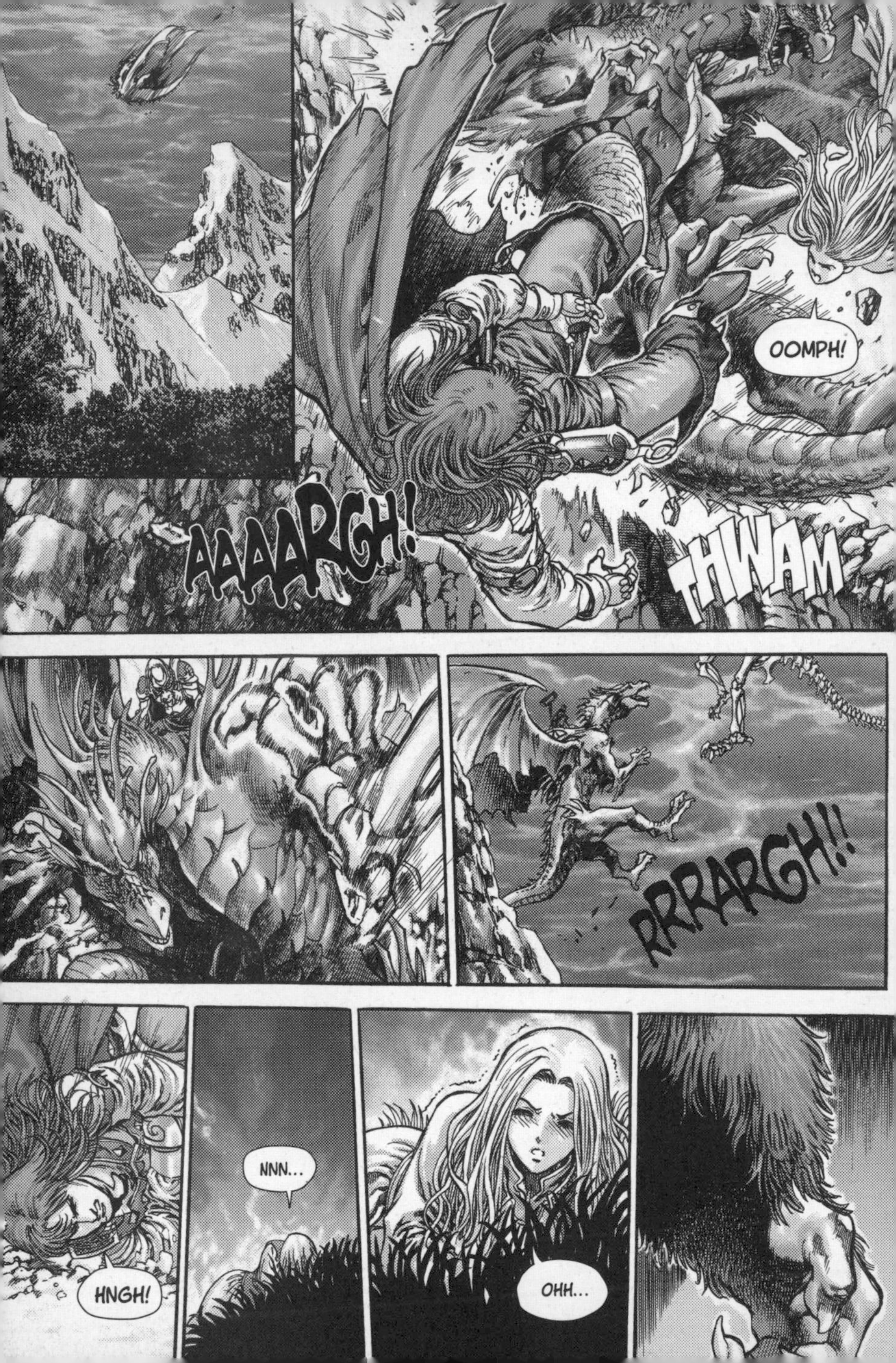
OOMPH!
AAAARGH!
THWAM
RRRARGH!!
HNGH!
NNN...
OHH...

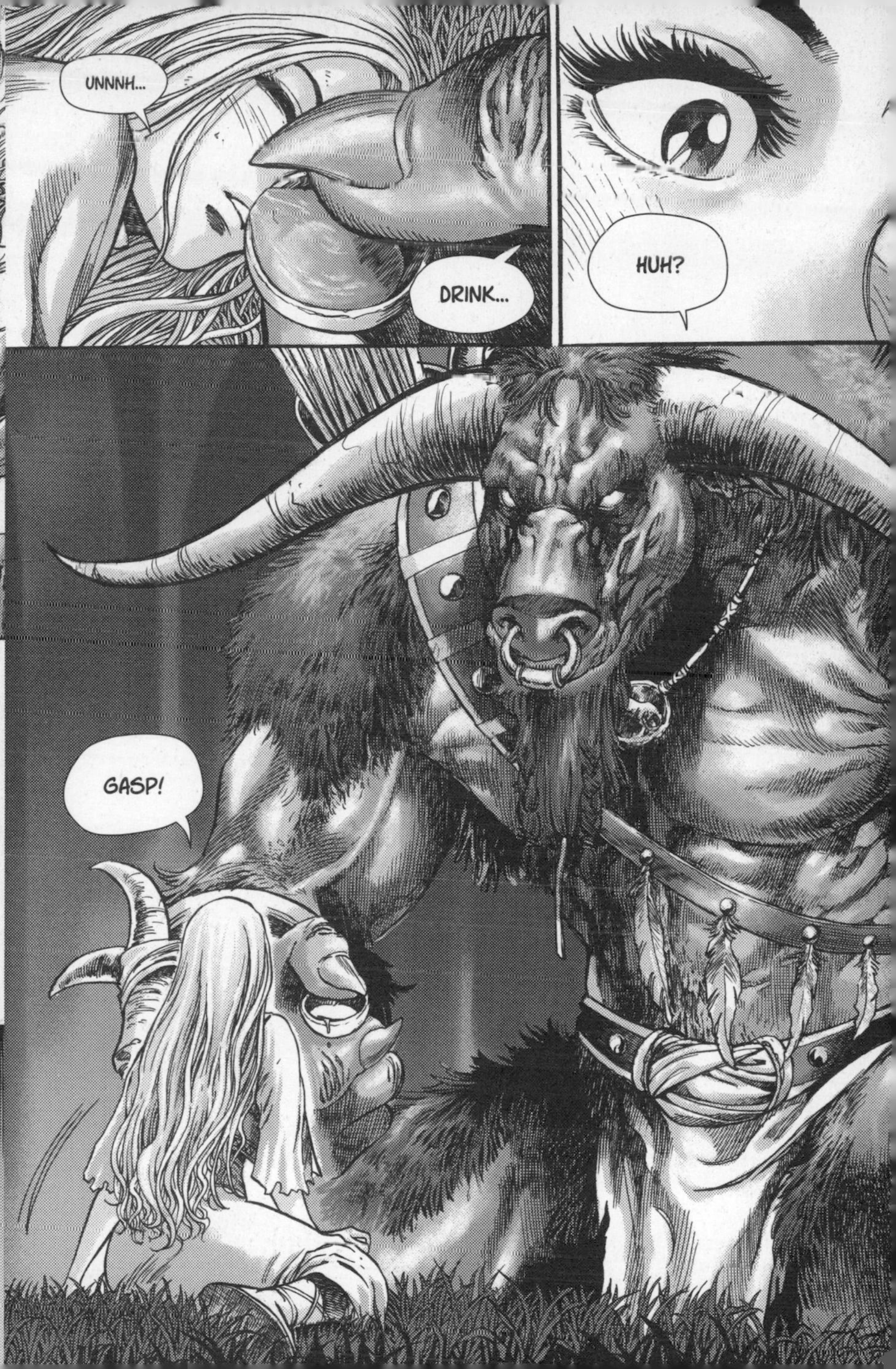
UNNNH...
DRINK...
HUH?
GASP!

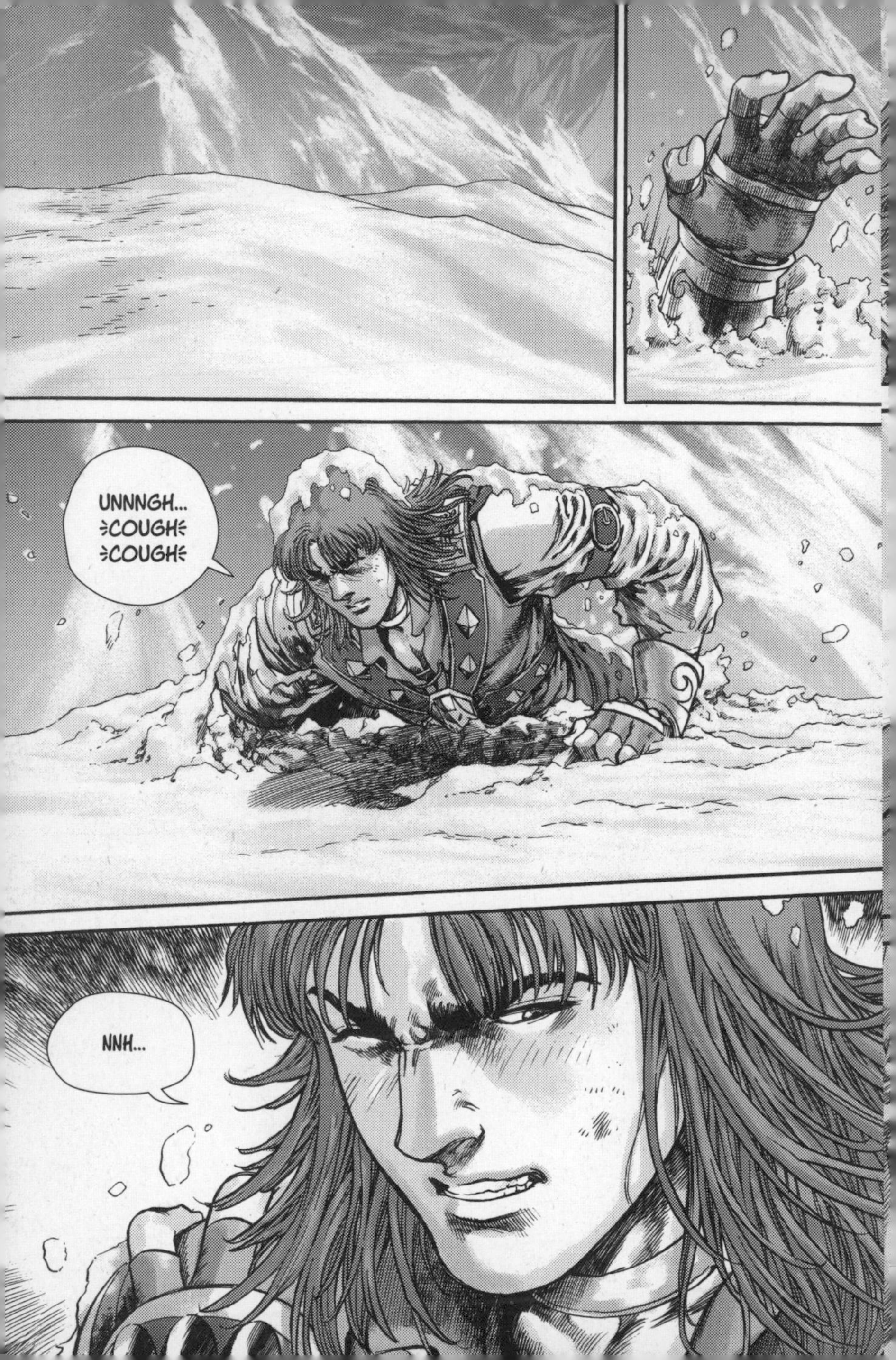
UNNNGH... ≑COUGH≑ ≑COUGH≑
NNH...

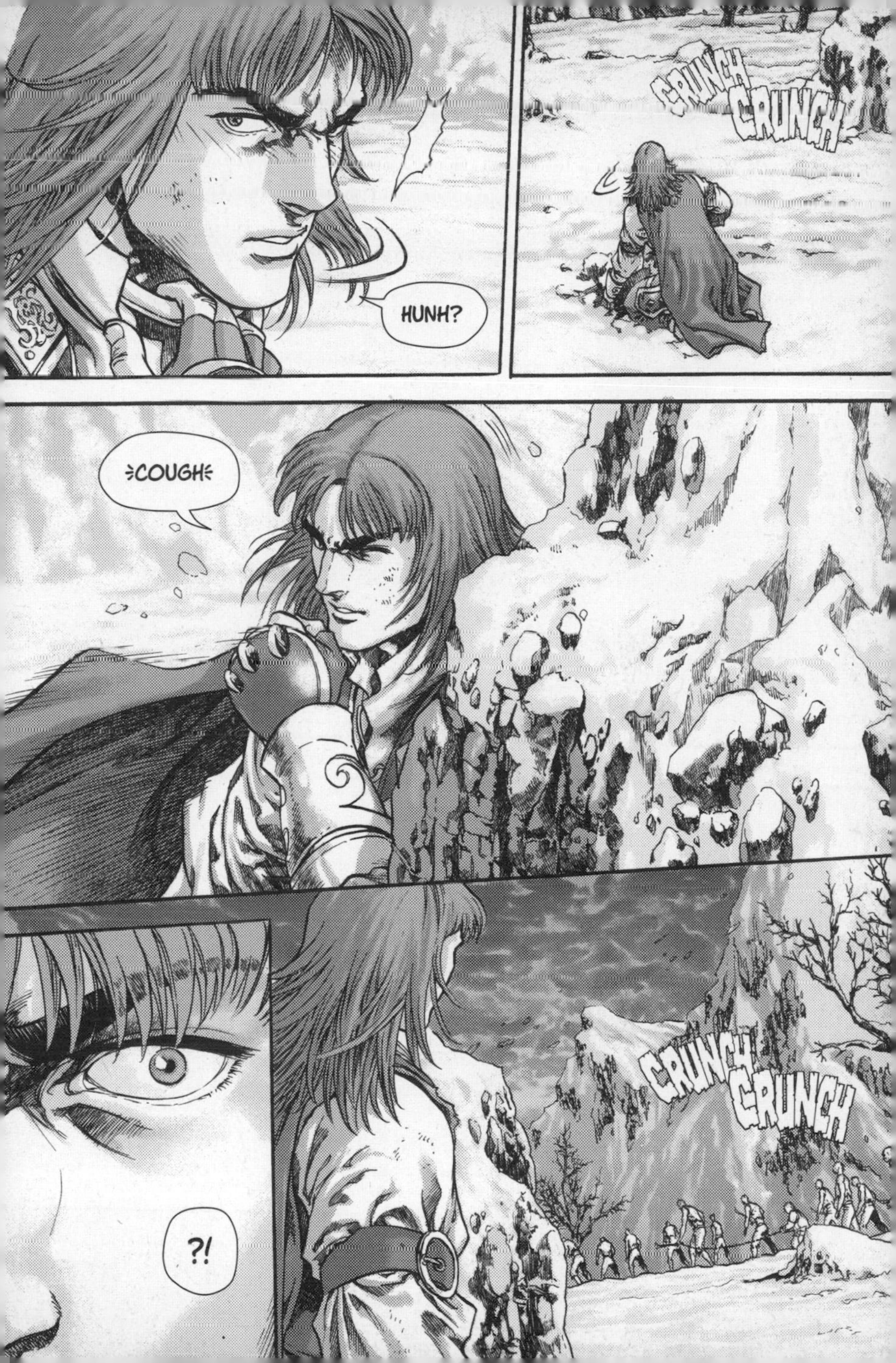
HUNH?
CRUNCH CRUNCH
COUGH
?!
CRUNCH CRUNCH

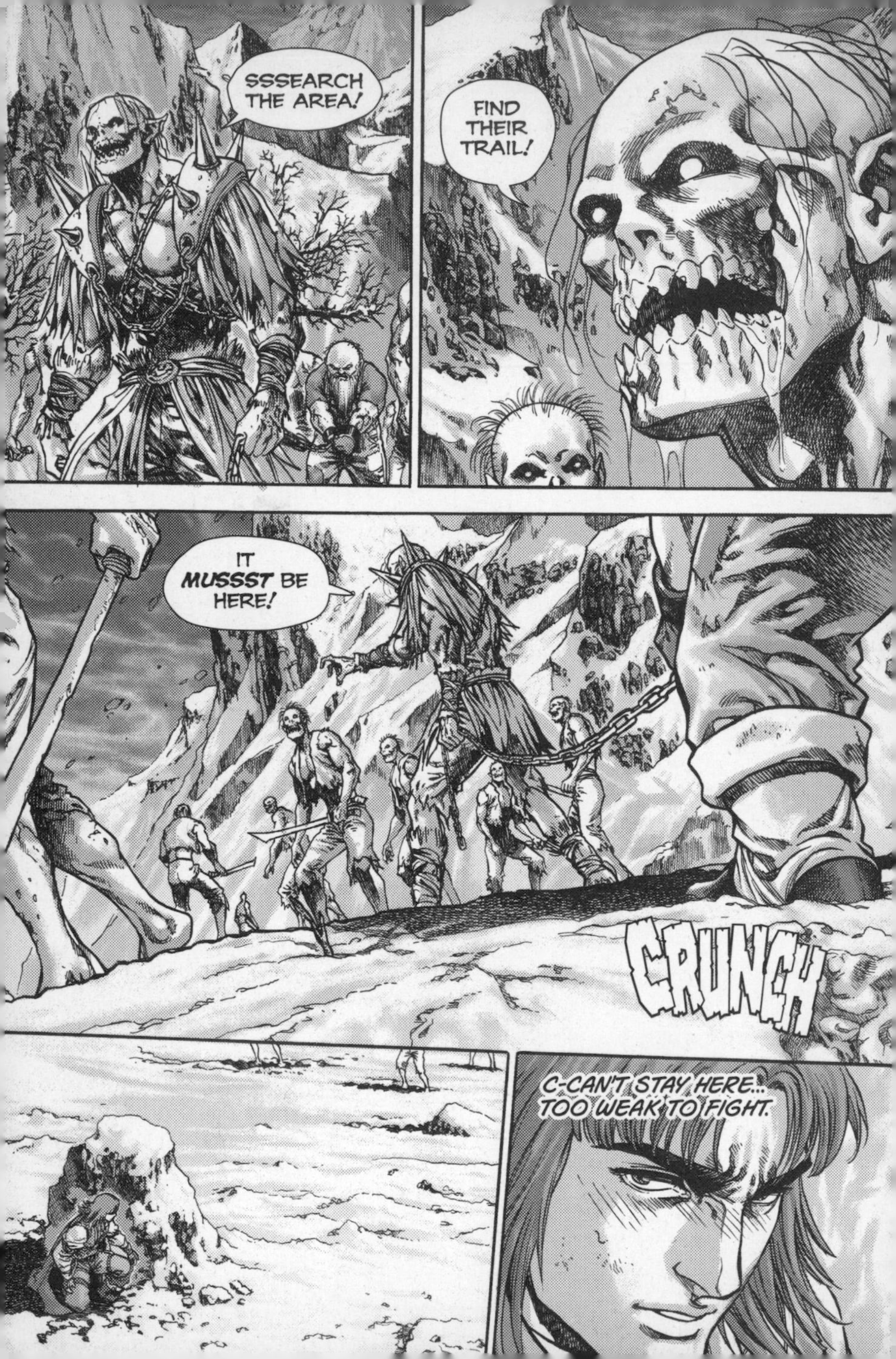
SSSEARCH THE AREA!
FIND THEIR TRAIL!
IT MUSSST BE HERE!
CRUNCH
C-CAN'T STAY HERE... TOO WEAK TO FIGHT.

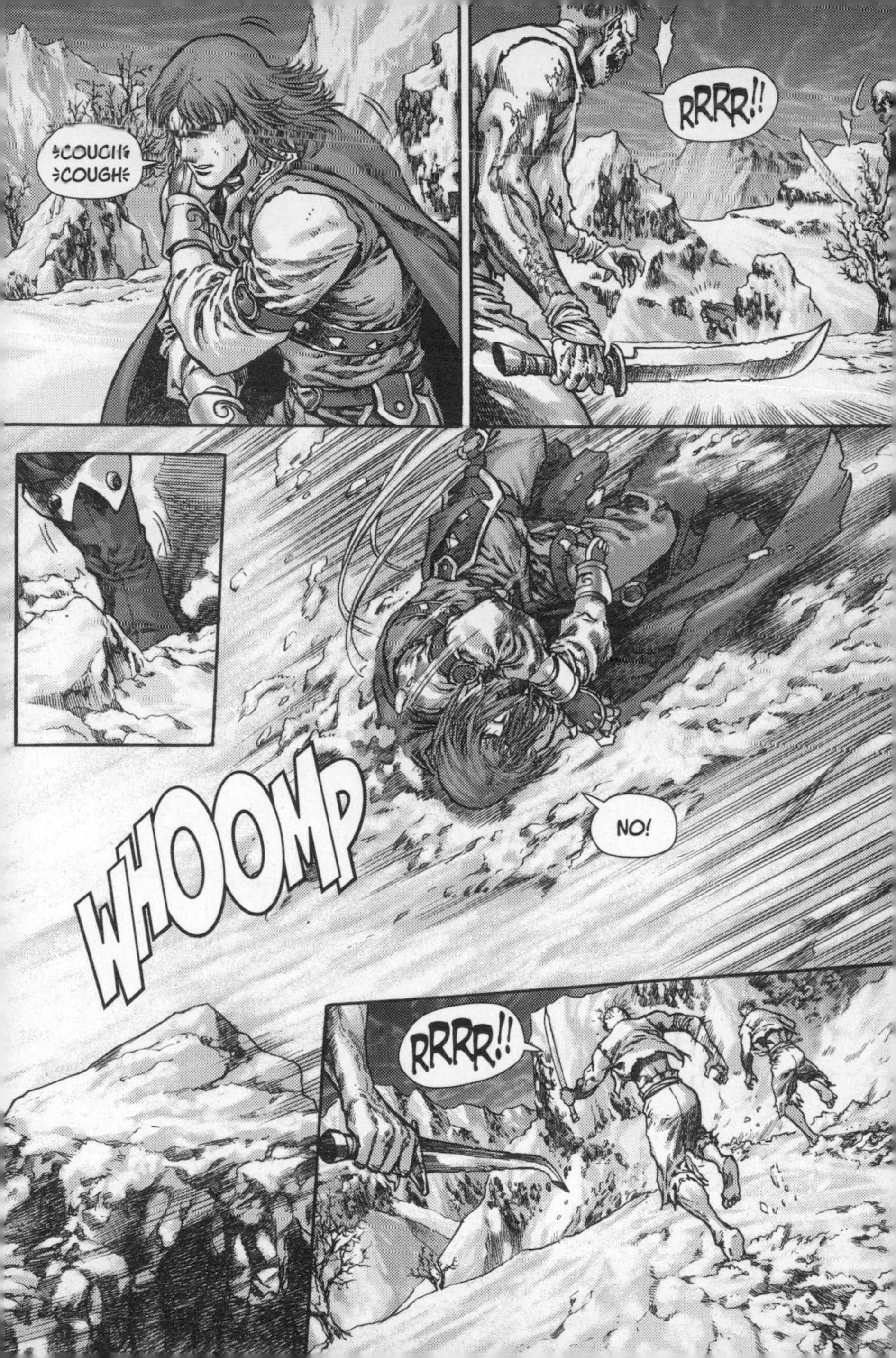
COUGH
COUGH
RRRR!!
WHOOMP
NO!
RRRR!!

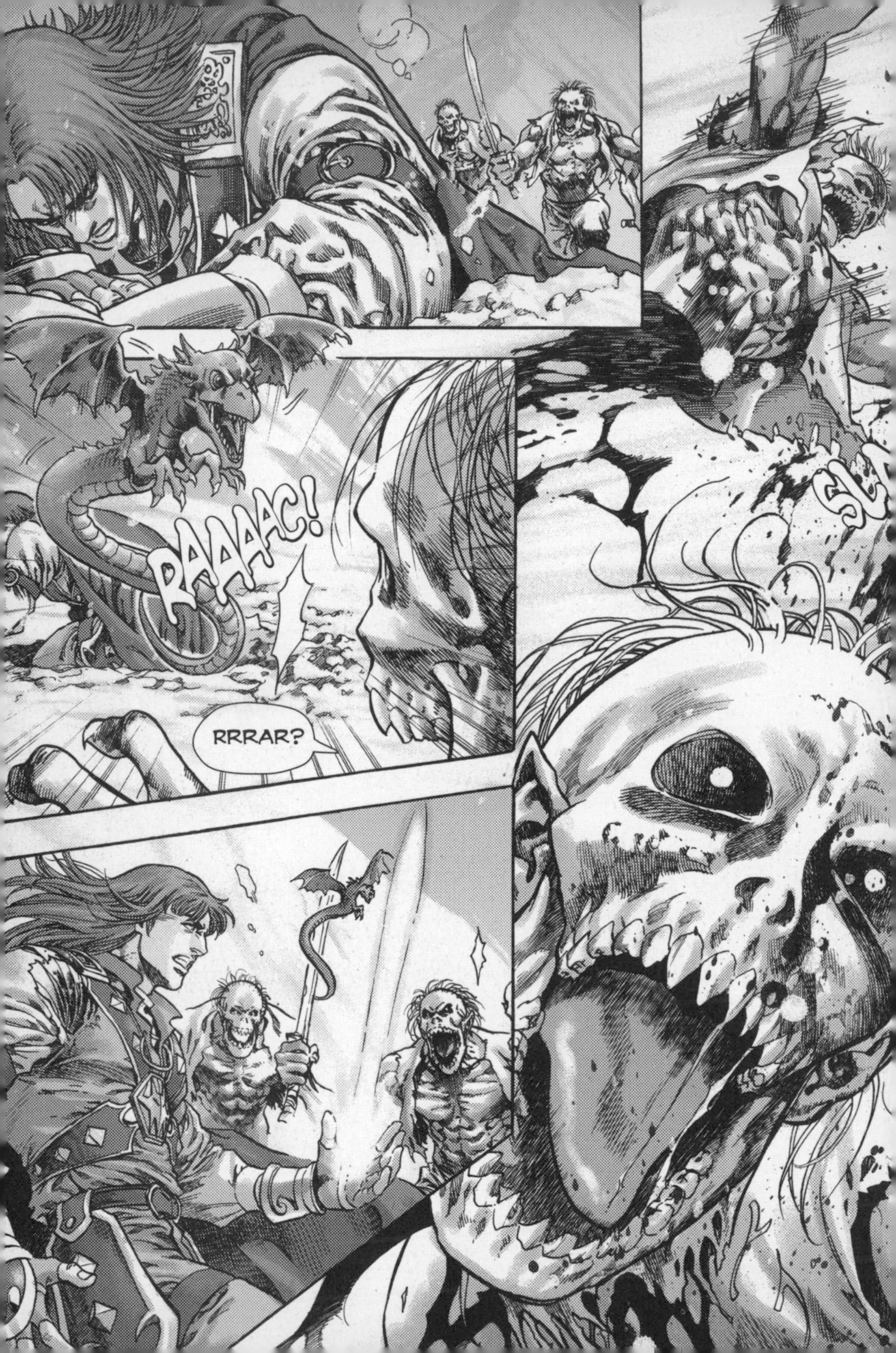
RAAAAC!
RRRAR?

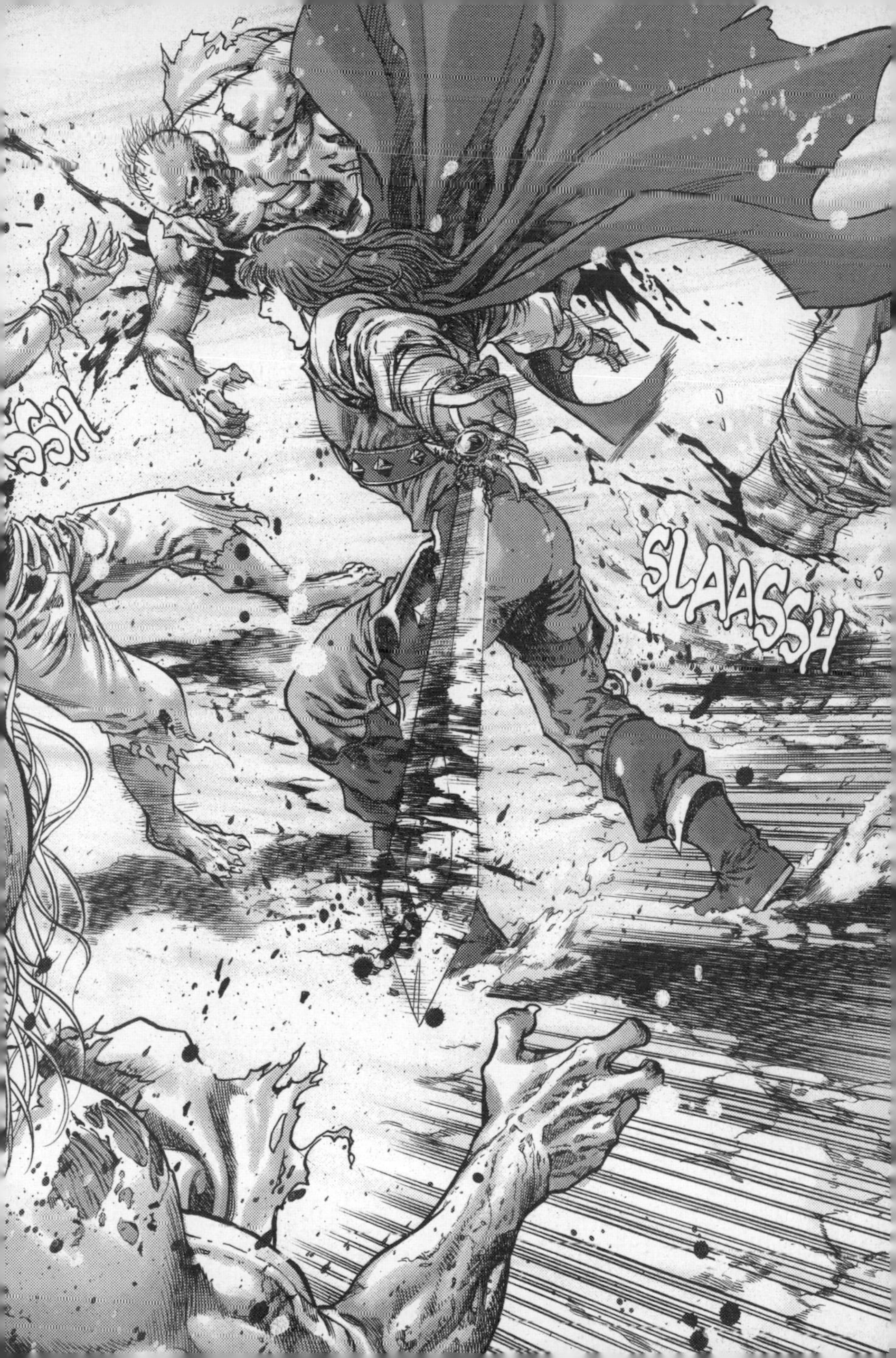
SLAASSH

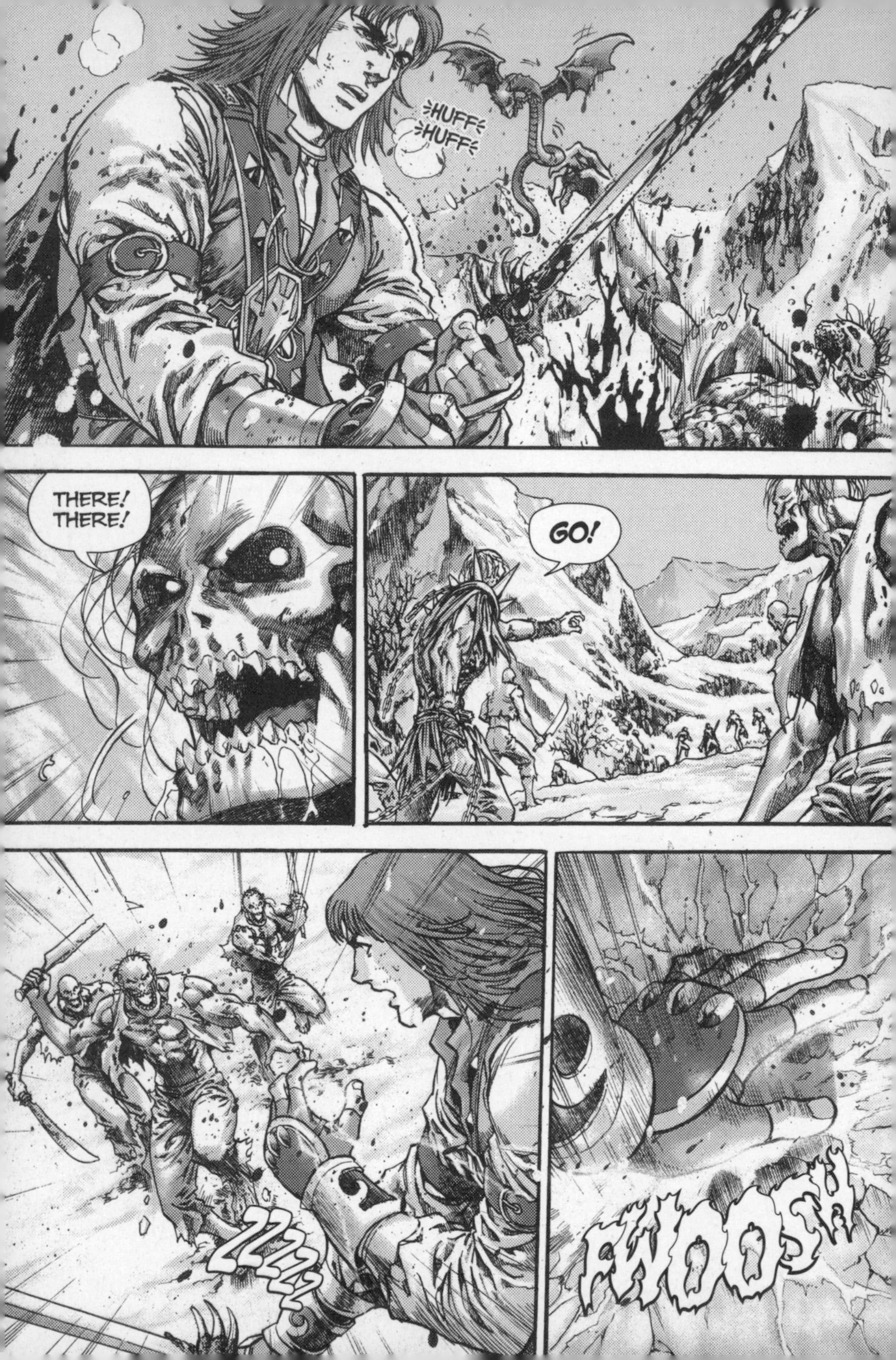
HUFF
HUFF
THERE! THERE!
GO!
ZZZZZ
FWOOSH

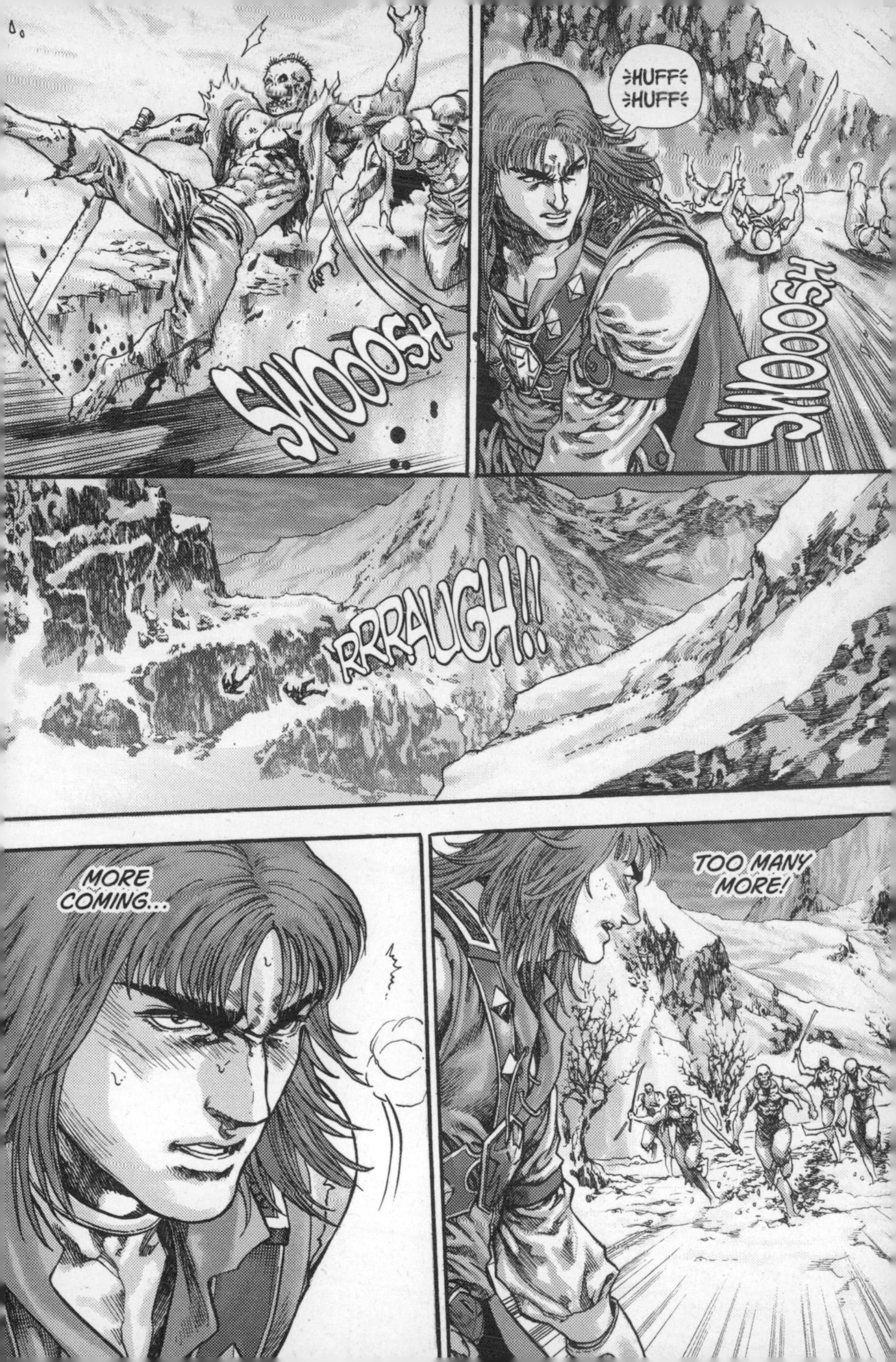
SWOOSH
HUFF HUFF
SWOOOSH
RRRAUGH!!
MORE COMING...
TOO MANY MORE!

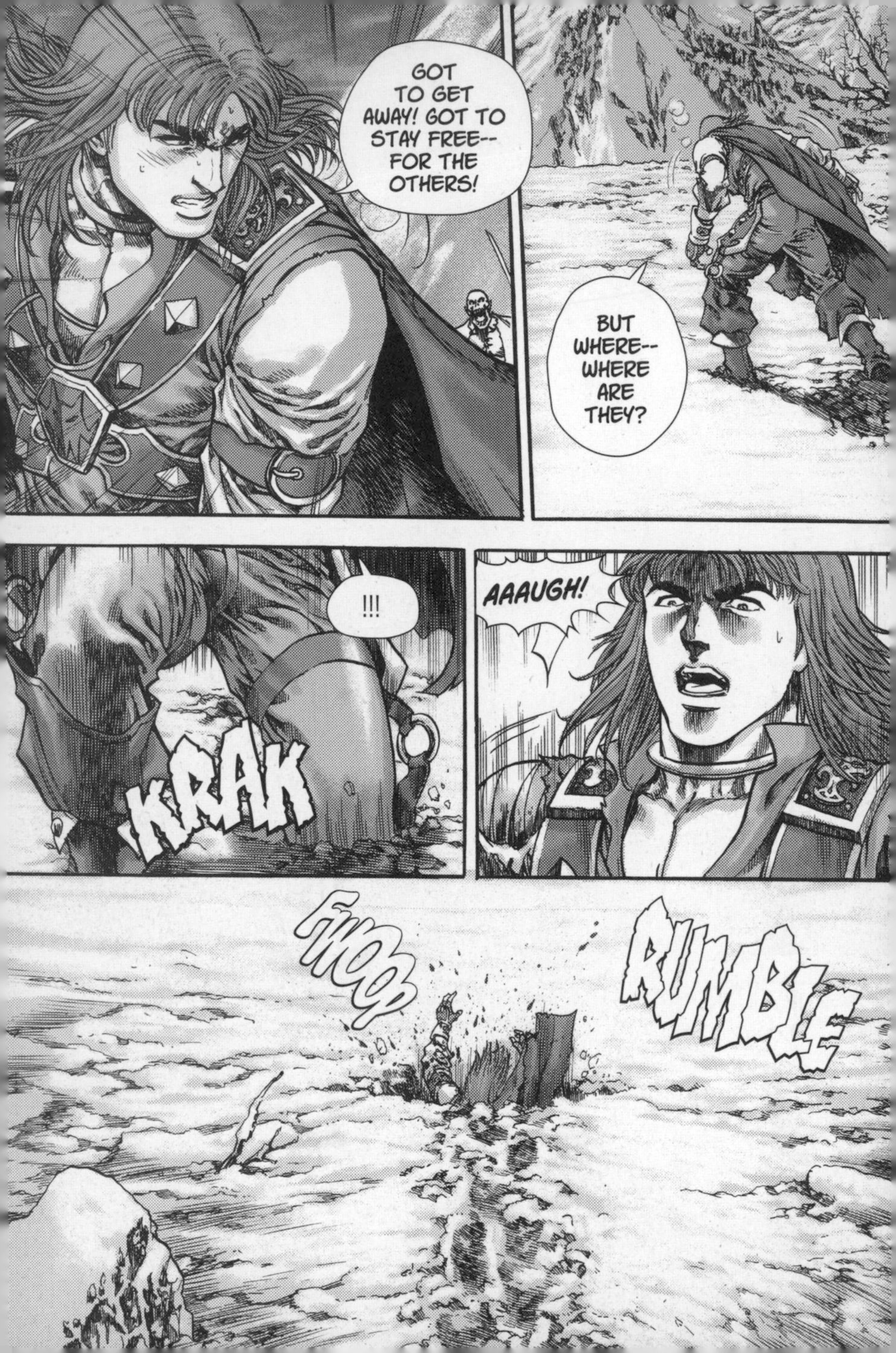
GOT TO GET AWAY! GOT TO STAY FREE-- FOR THE OTHERS!
BUT WHERE-- WHERE ARE THEY?
!!!
KRAK
AAAUGH!
FWOOM
RUMBLE

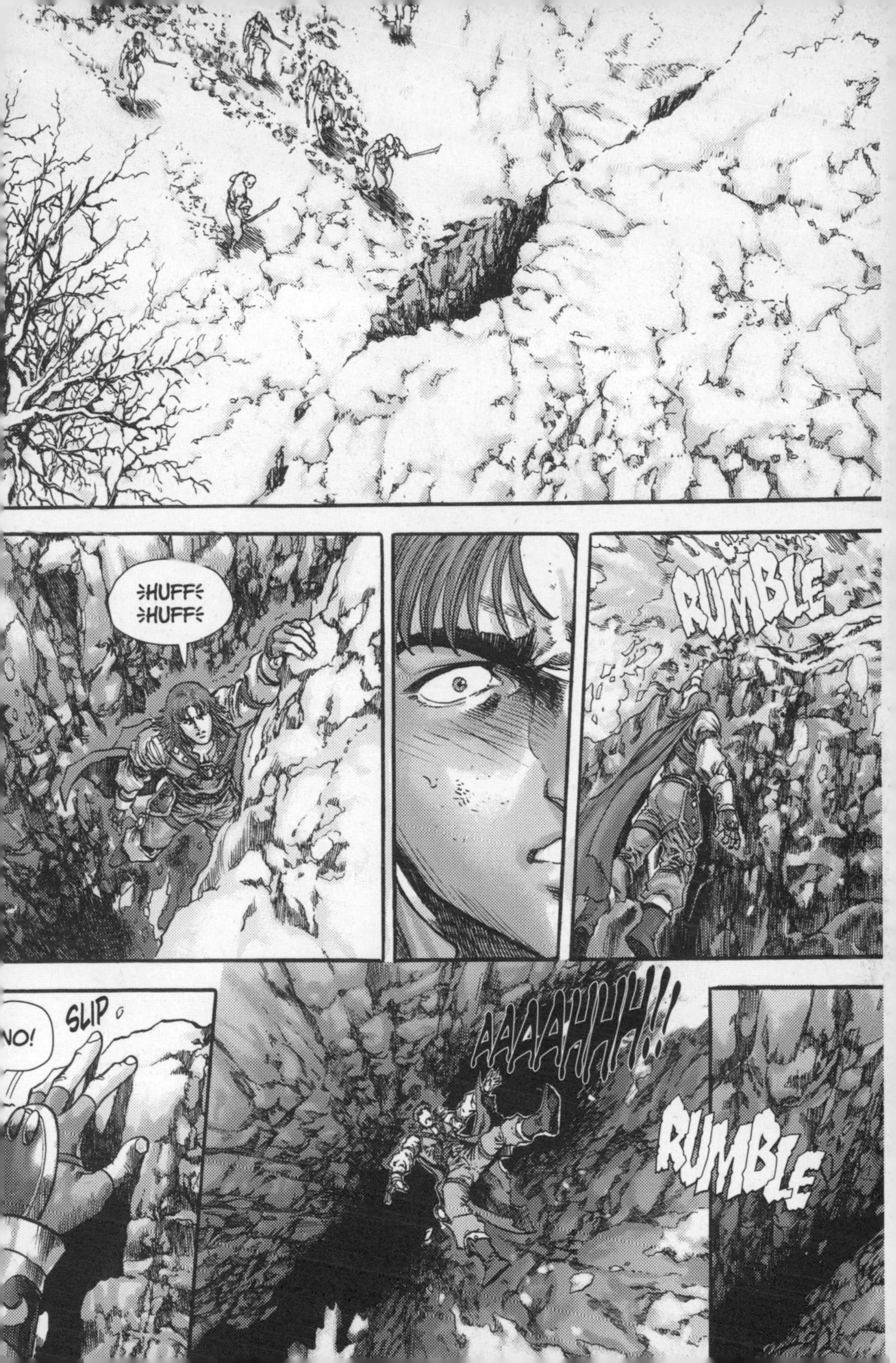
HUFF HUFF
RUMBLE
NO!
SLIP
AAAAHHH!!
RUMBLE

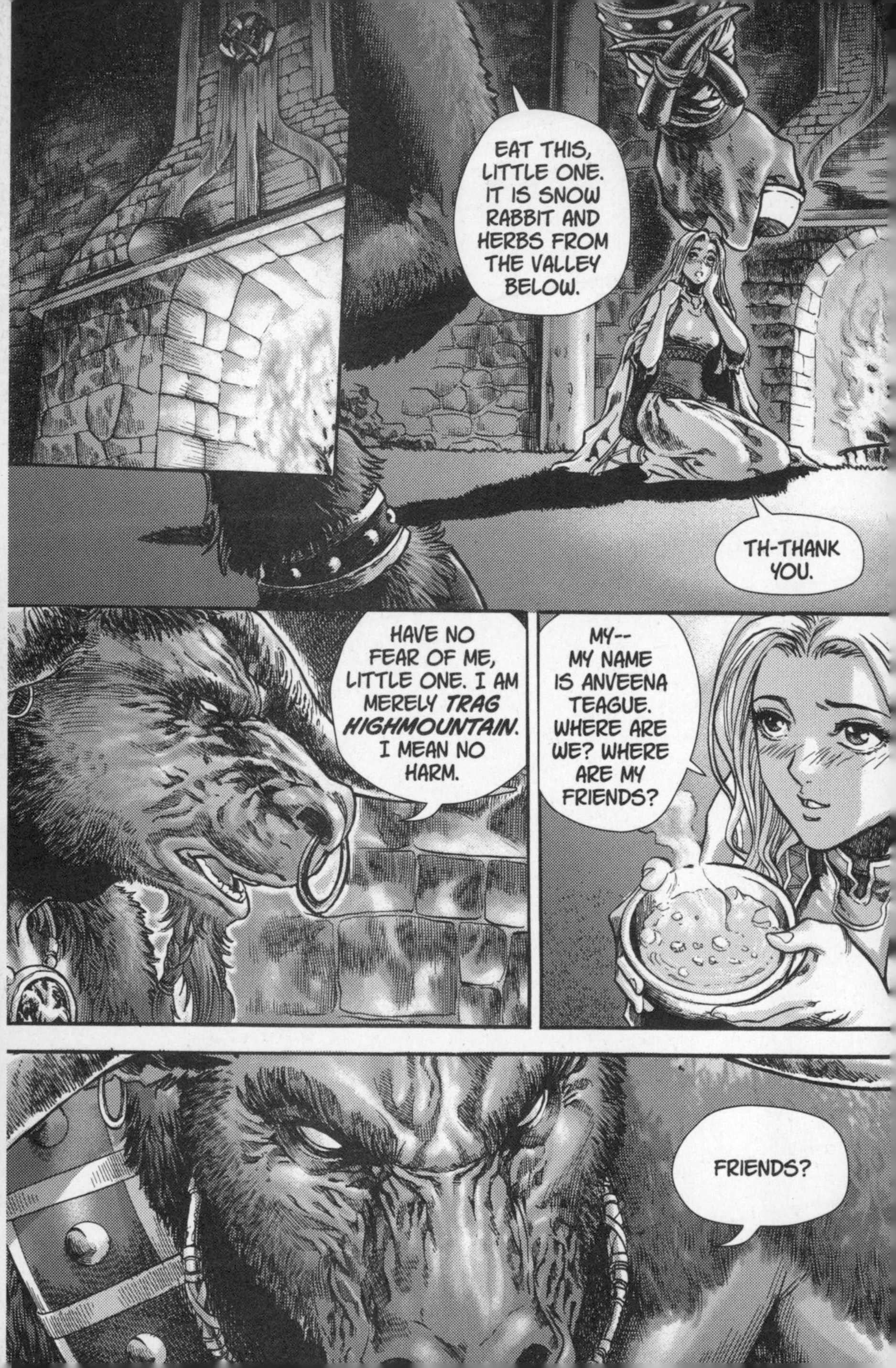
EAT THIS, LITTLE ONE. IT IS SNOW RABBIT AND HERBS FROM THE VALLEY BELOW.
TH-THANK YOU.
HAVE NO FEAR OF ME, LITTLE ONE. I AM MERELY *TRAG HIGHMOUNTAIN*. I MEAN NO HARM.
MY-- MY NAME IS ANVEENA TEAGUE. WHERE ARE WE? WHERE ARE MY FRIENDS?
FRIENDS?

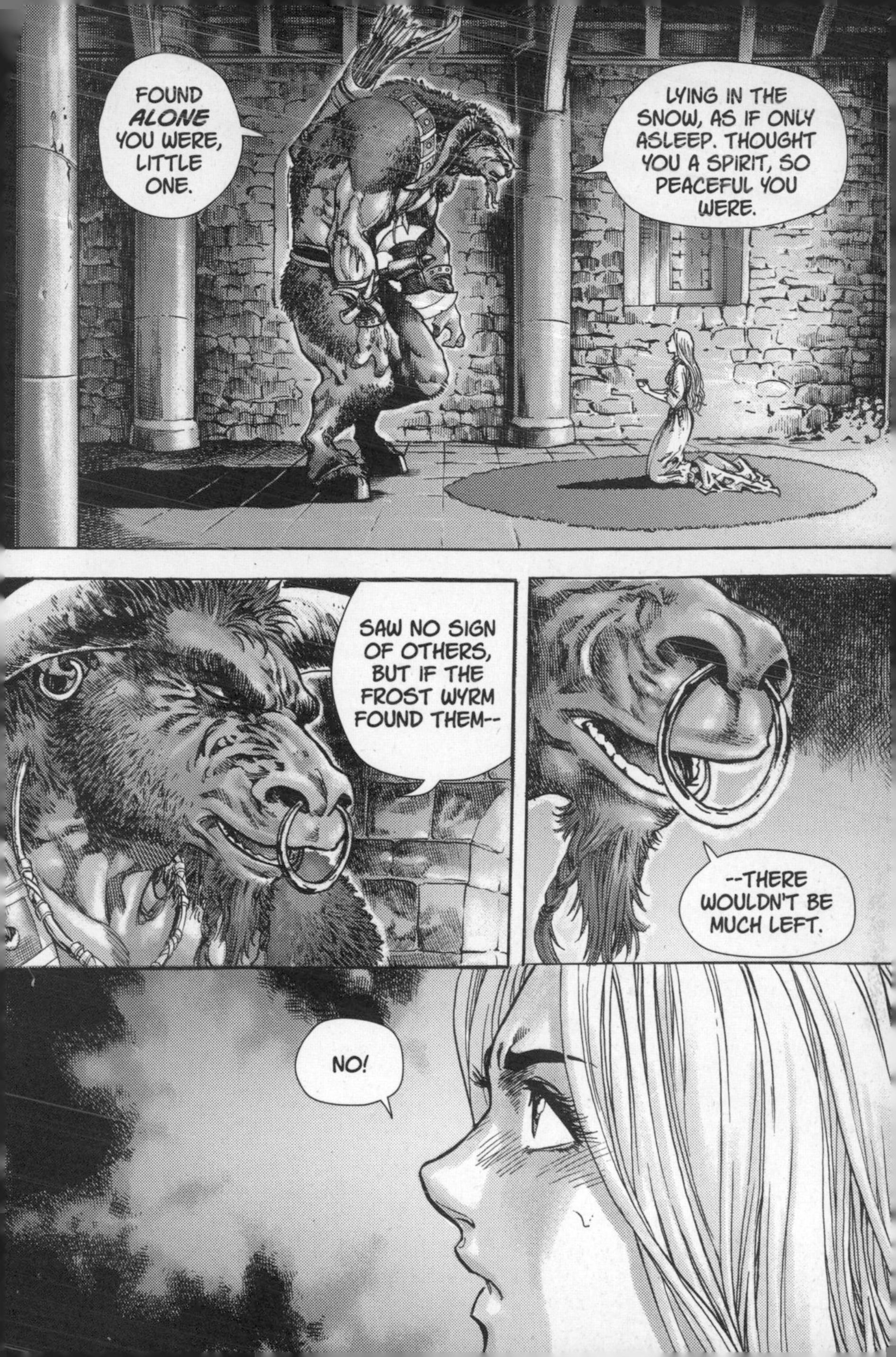
FOUND ALONE YOU WERE, LITTLE ONE.
LYING IN THE SNOW, AS IF ONLY ASLEEP. THOUGHT YOU A SPIRIT, SO PEACEFUL YOU WERE.
SAW NO SIGN OF OTHERS, BUT IF THE FROST WYRM FOUND THEM--
--THERE WOULDN'T BE MUCH LEFT.
NO!

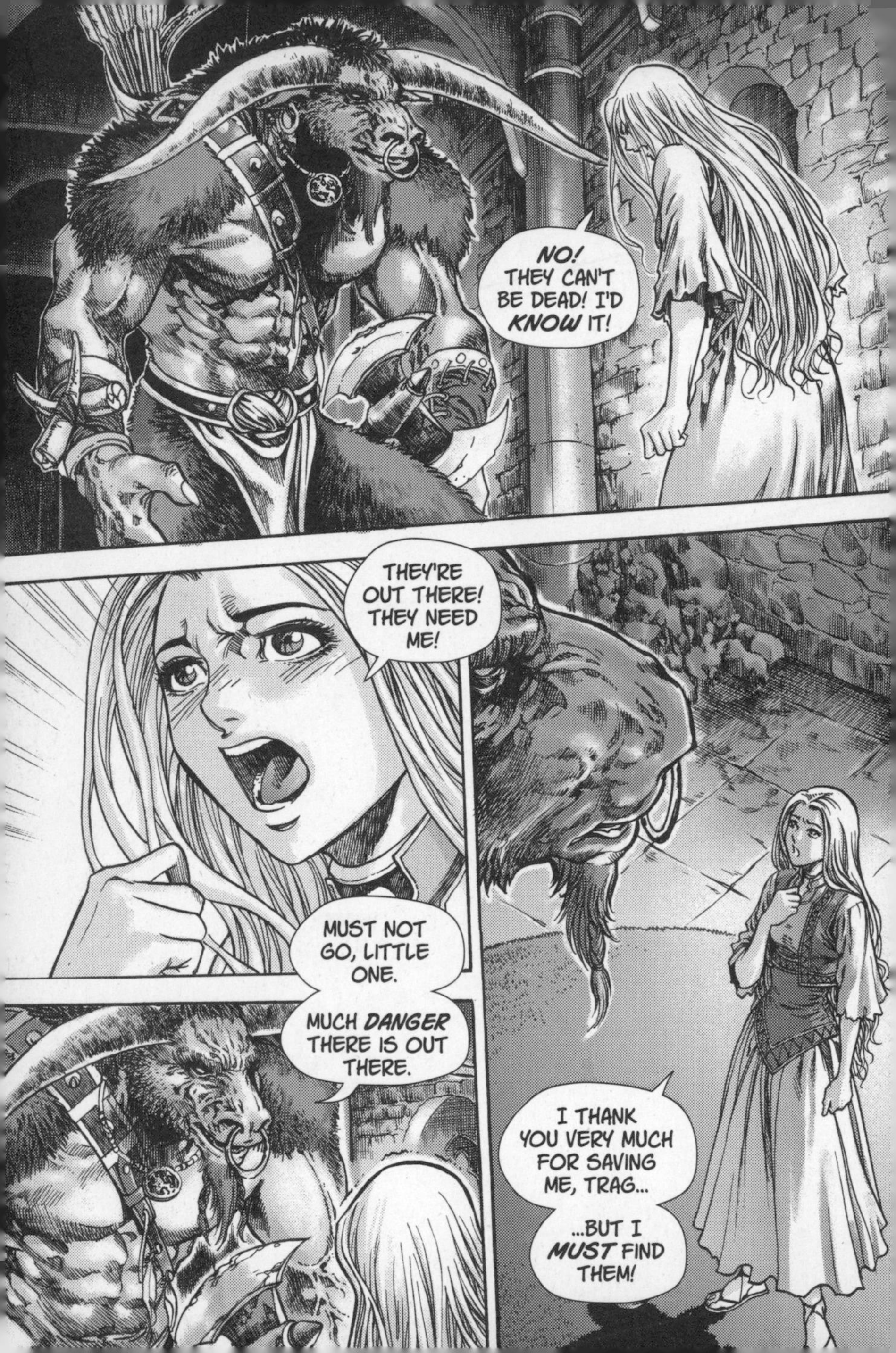

NO! THEY CAN'T BE DEAD! I'D ***KNOW*** IT!
THEY'RE OUT THERE! THEY NEED ME!
MUST NOT GO, LITTLE ONE.
MUCH ***DANGER*** THERE IS OUT THERE.
I THANK YOU VERY MUCH FOR SAVING ME, TRAG...
...BUT I ***MUST*** FIND THEM!

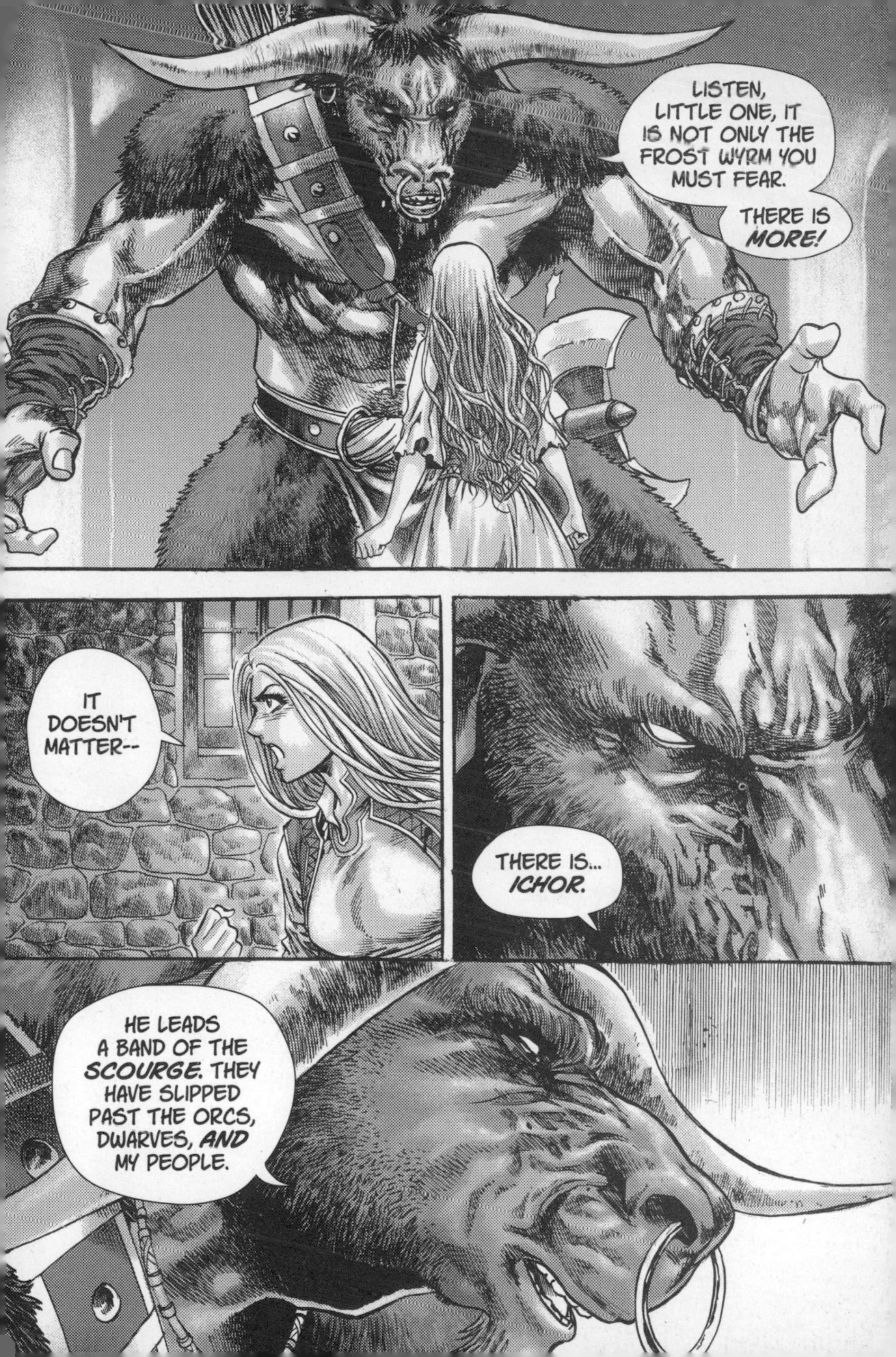
LISTEN, LITTLE ONE, IT IS NOT ONLY THE FROST WYRM YOU MUST FEAR.
THERE IS *MORE!*
IT DOESN'T MATTER--
THERE IS... *ICHOR.*
HE LEADS A BAND OF THE *SCOURGE*. THEY HAVE SLIPPED PAST THE ORCS, DWARVES, *AND* MY PEOPLE.

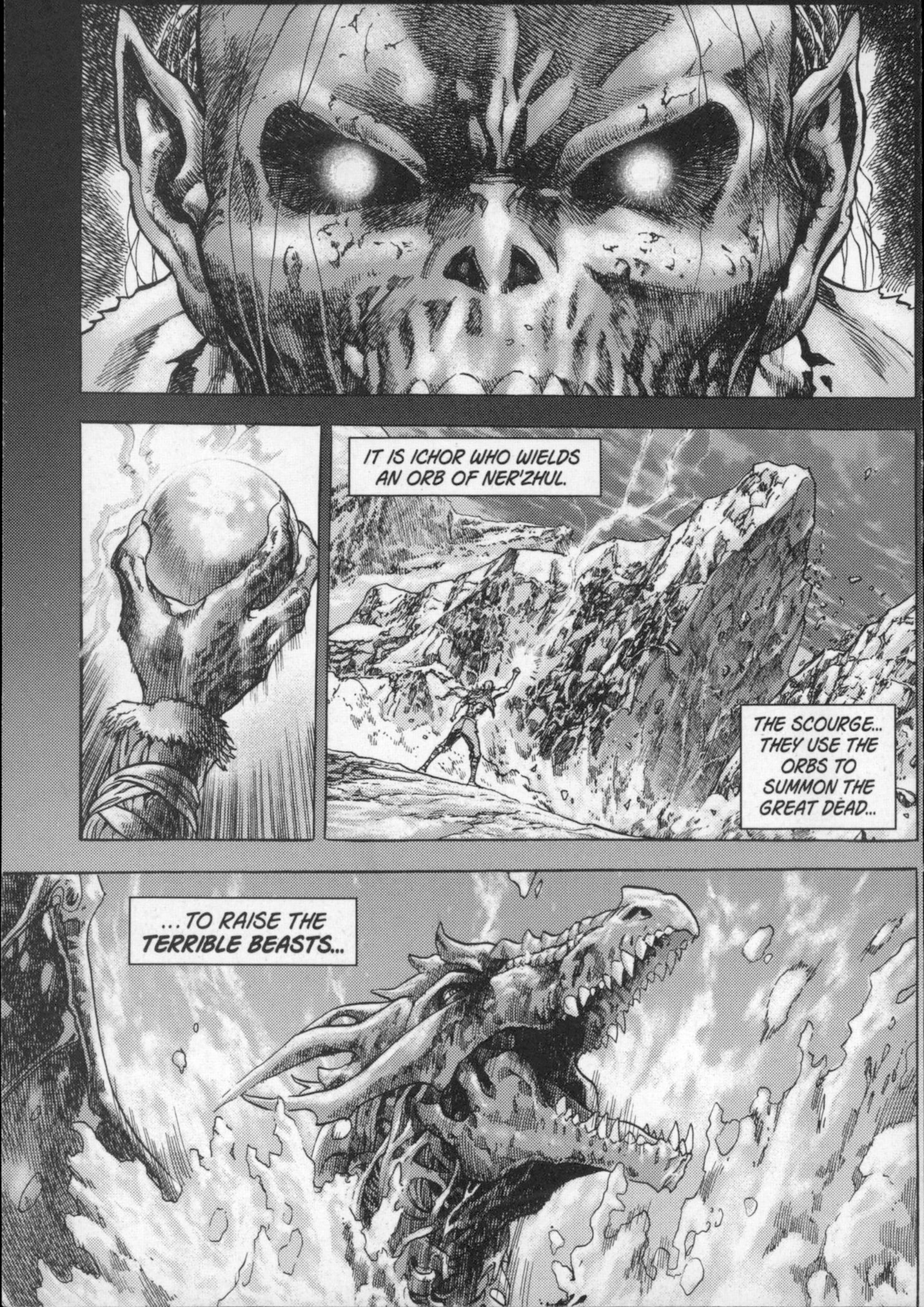
IT IS ICHOR WHO WIELDS AN ORB OF NER'ZHUL.
THE SCOURGE... THEY USE THE ORBS TO SUMMON THE GREAT DEAD...
...TO RAISE THE TERRIBLE BEASTS...

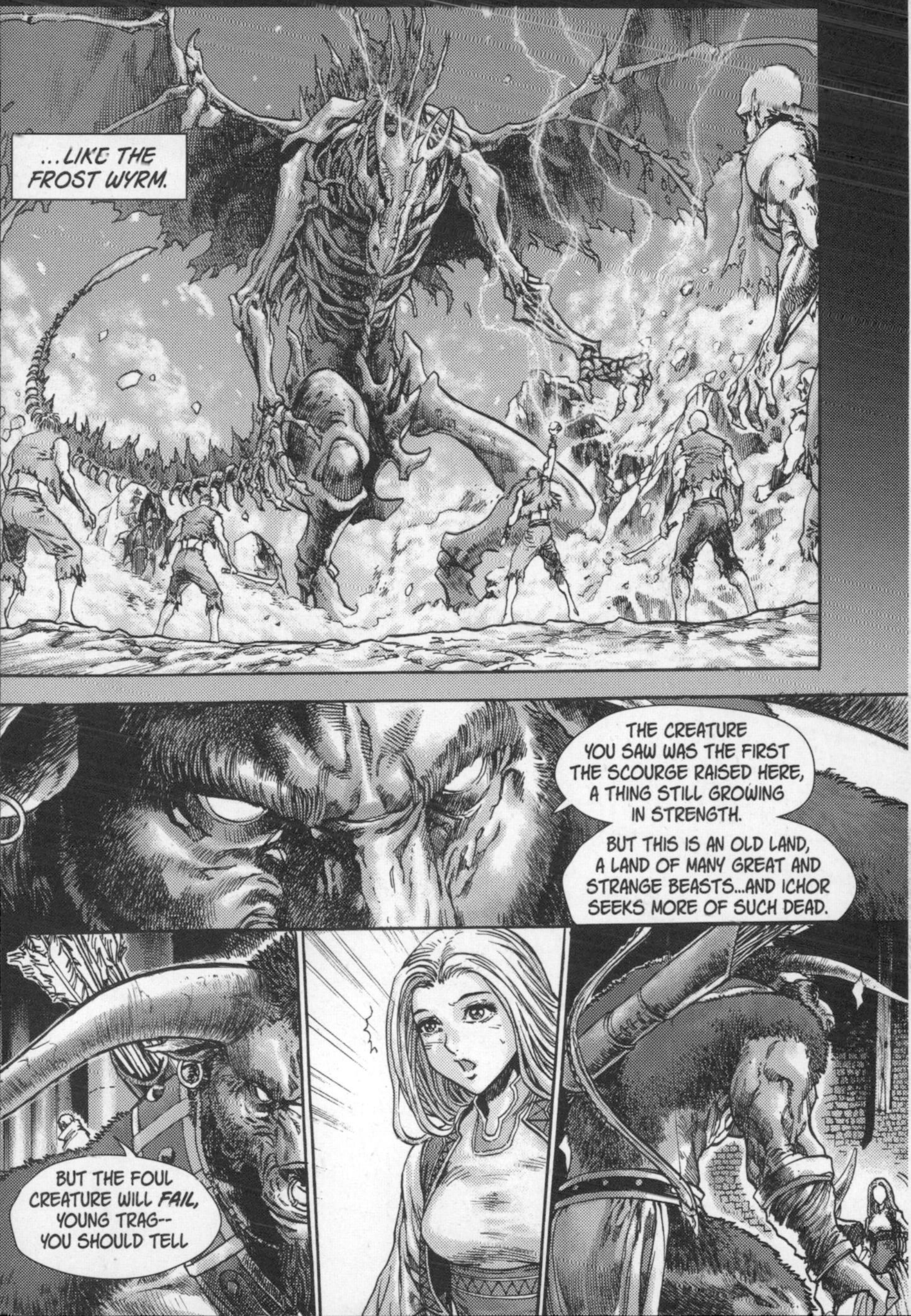
...LIKE THE FROST WYRM.
THE CREATURE YOU SAW WAS THE FIRST THE SCOURGE RAISED HERE, A THING STILL GROWING IN STRENGTH.
BUT THIS IS AN OLD LAND, A LAND OF MANY GREAT AND STRANGE BEASTS...AND ICHOR SEEKS MORE OF SUCH DEAD.
BUT THE FOUL CREATURE WILL *FAIL*, YOUNG TRAG-- YOU SHOULD TELL

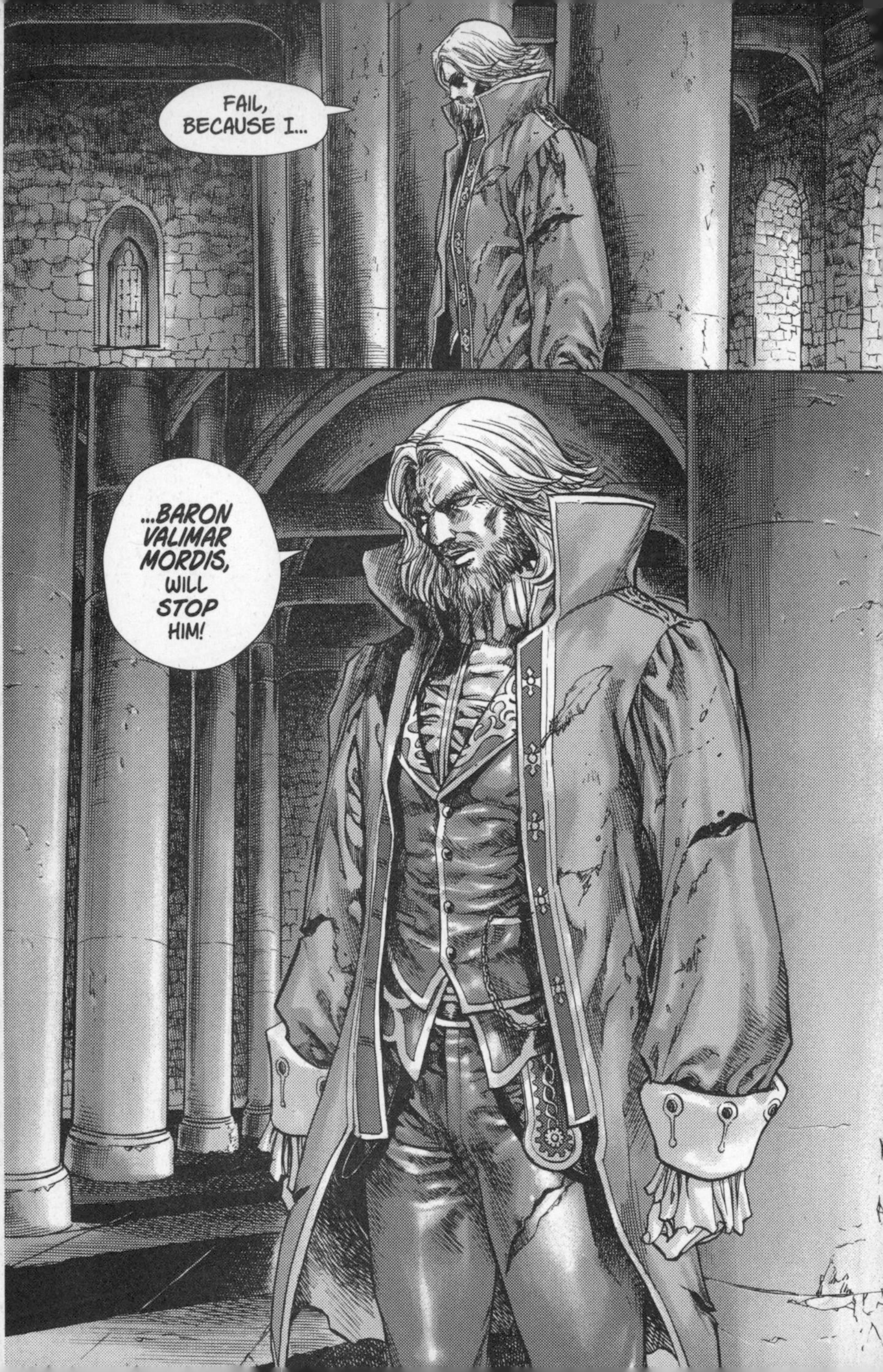
FAIL, BECAUSE I...
...BARON VALIMAR MORDIS, WILL STOP HIM!

CHAPTER TWO
BARON MORDIS

B-BOREL...

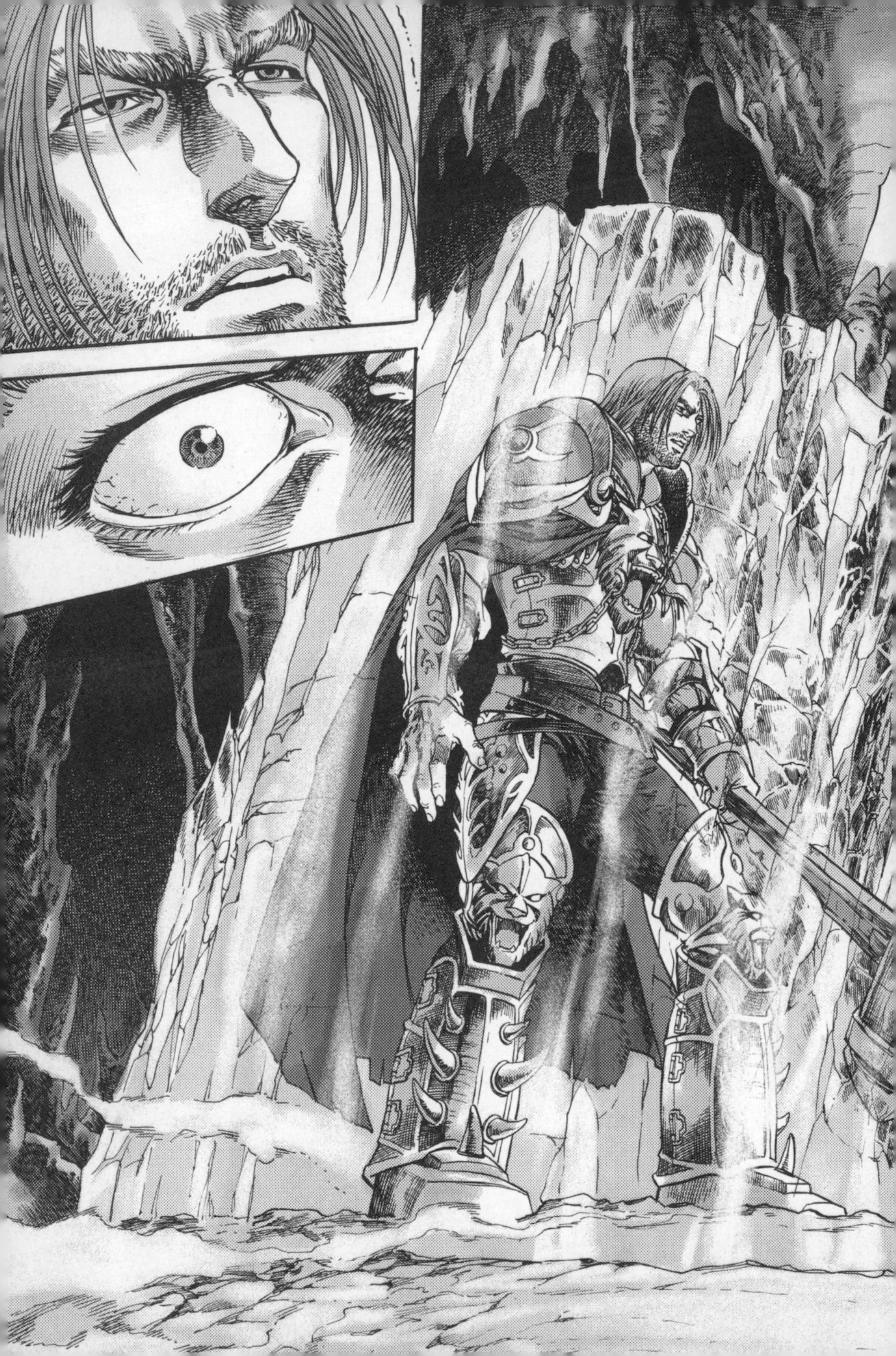

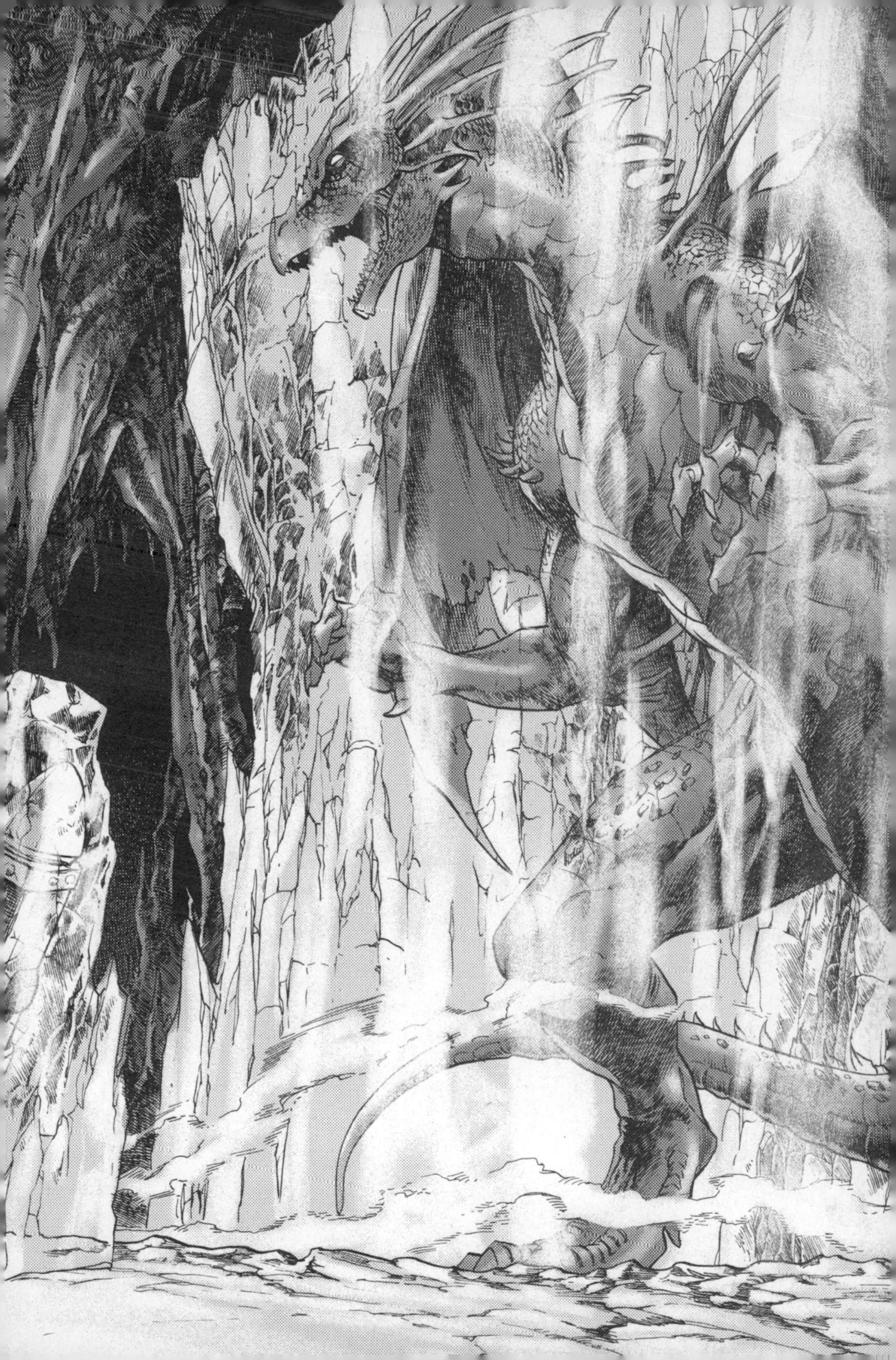

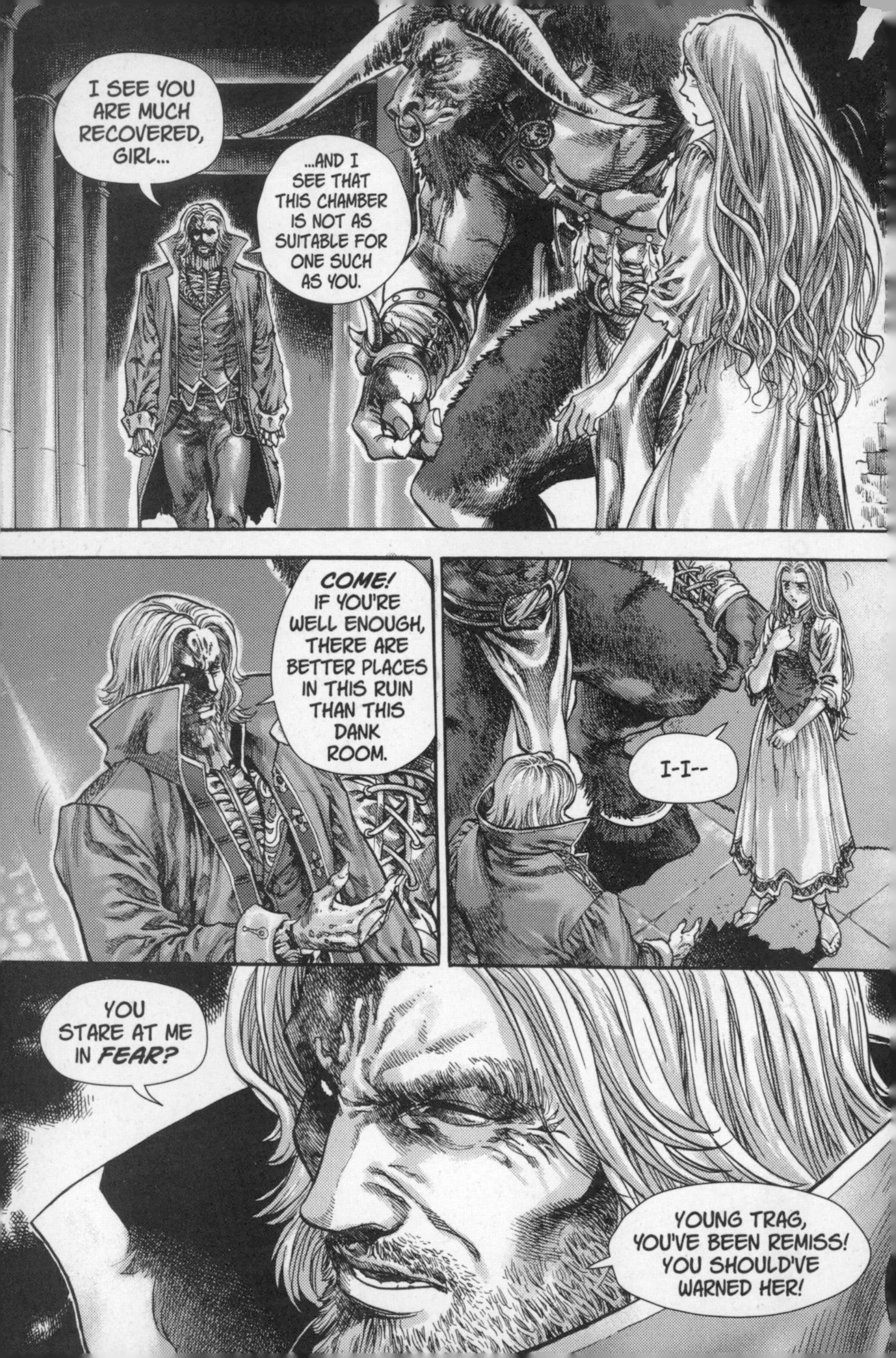
I SEE YOU ARE MUCH RECOVERED, GIRL...
...AND I SEE THAT THIS CHAMBER IS NOT AS SUITABLE FOR ONE SUCH AS YOU.
COME! IF YOU'RE WELL ENOUGH, THERE ARE BETTER PLACES IN THIS RUIN THAN THIS DANK ROOM.
I-I--
YOU STARE AT ME IN FEAR?
YOUNG TRAG, YOU'VE BEEN REMISS! YOU SHOULD'VE WARNED HER!

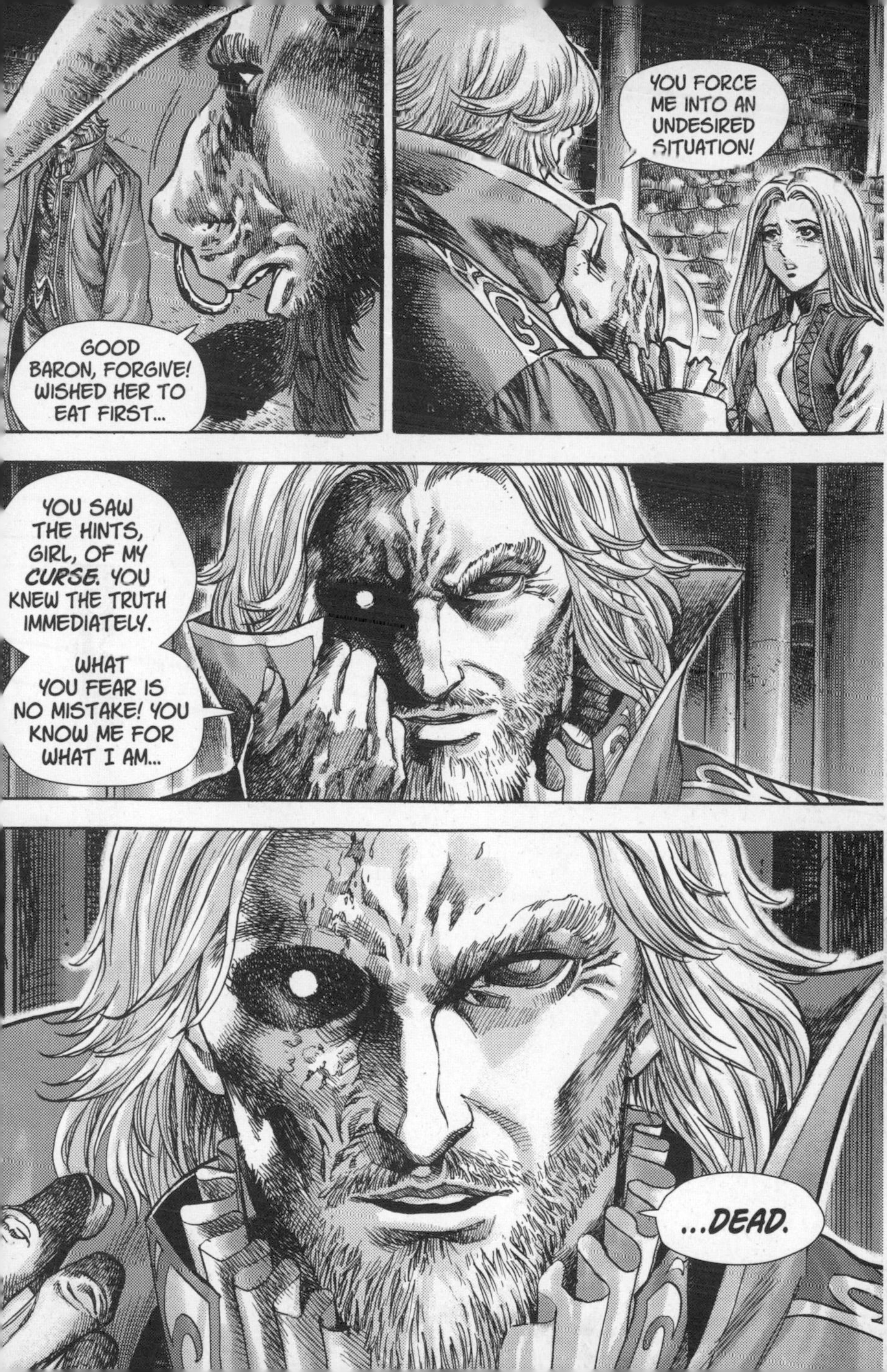
GOOD BARON, FORGIVE! WISHED HER TO EAT FIRST...
YOU FORCE ME INTO AN UNDESIRED SITUATION!
YOU SAW THE HINTS, GIRL, OF MY *CURSE*. YOU KNEW THE TRUTH IMMEDIATELY.
WHAT YOU FEAR IS NO MISTAKE! YOU KNOW ME FOR WHAT I AM...
...*DEAD.*

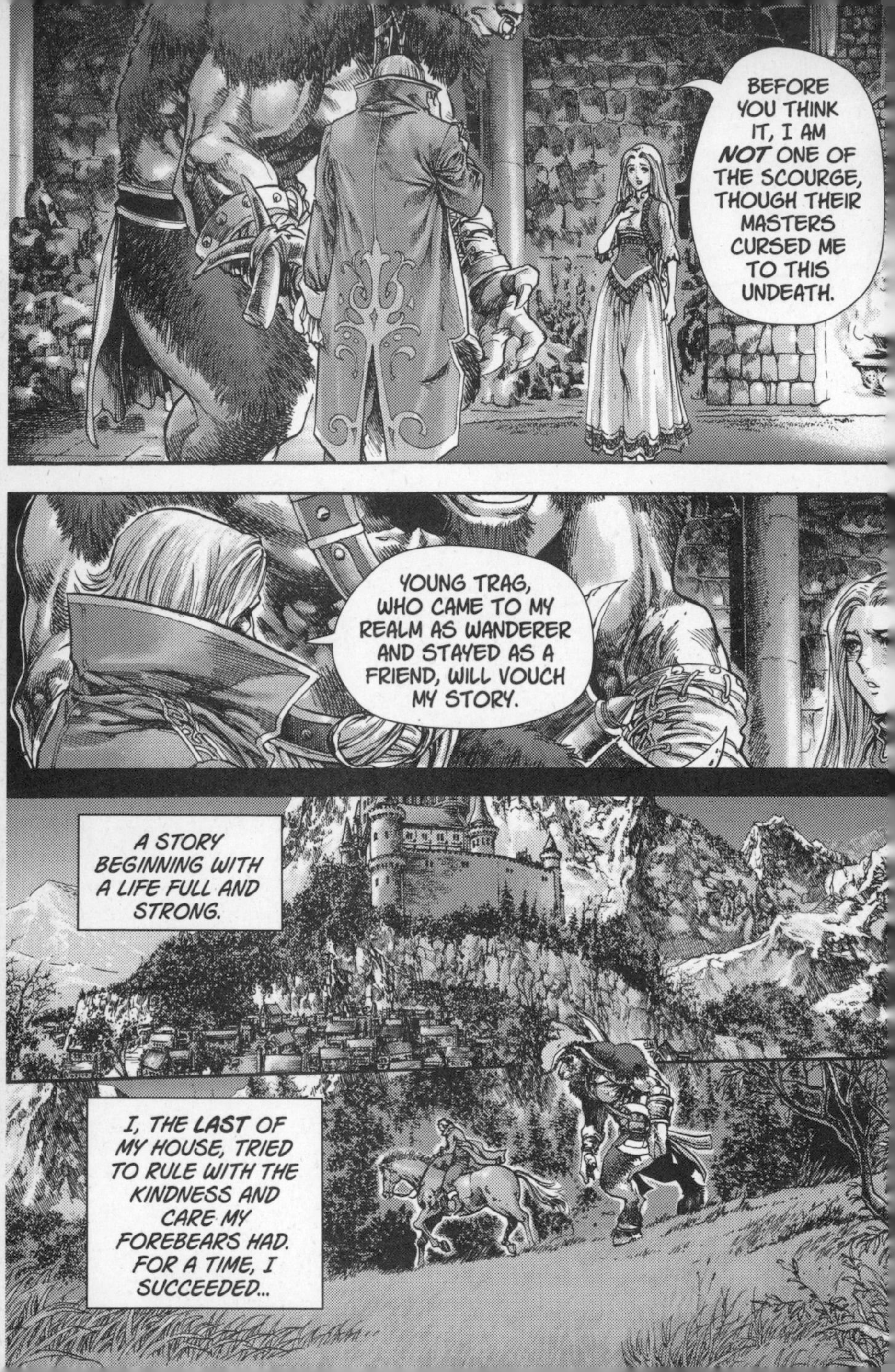
BEFORE YOU THINK IT, I AM NOT ONE OF THE SCOURGE, THOUGH THEIR MASTERS CURSED ME TO THIS UNDEATH.
YOUNG TRAG, WHO CAME TO MY REALM AS WANDERER AND STAYED AS A FRIEND, WILL VOUCH MY STORY.
A STORY BEGINNING WITH A LIFE FULL AND STRONG.
I, THE LAST OF MY HOUSE, TRIED TO RULE WITH THE KINDNESS AND CARE MY FOREBEARS HAD. FOR A TIME, I SUCCEEDED...

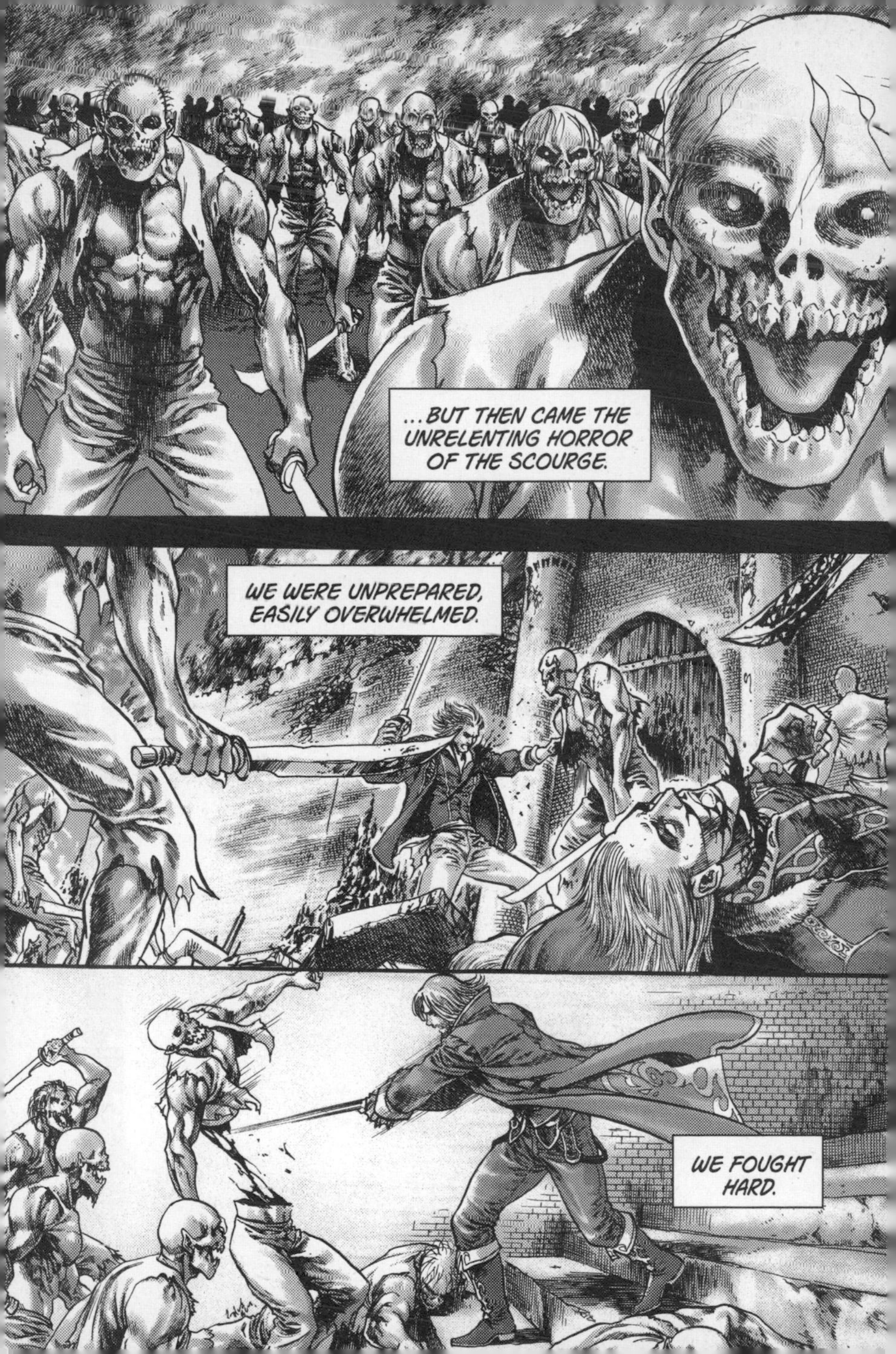
...BUT THEN CAME THE UNRELENTING HORROR OF THE SCOURGE.
WE WERE UNPREPARED, EASILY OVERWHELMED.
WE FOUGHT HARD.

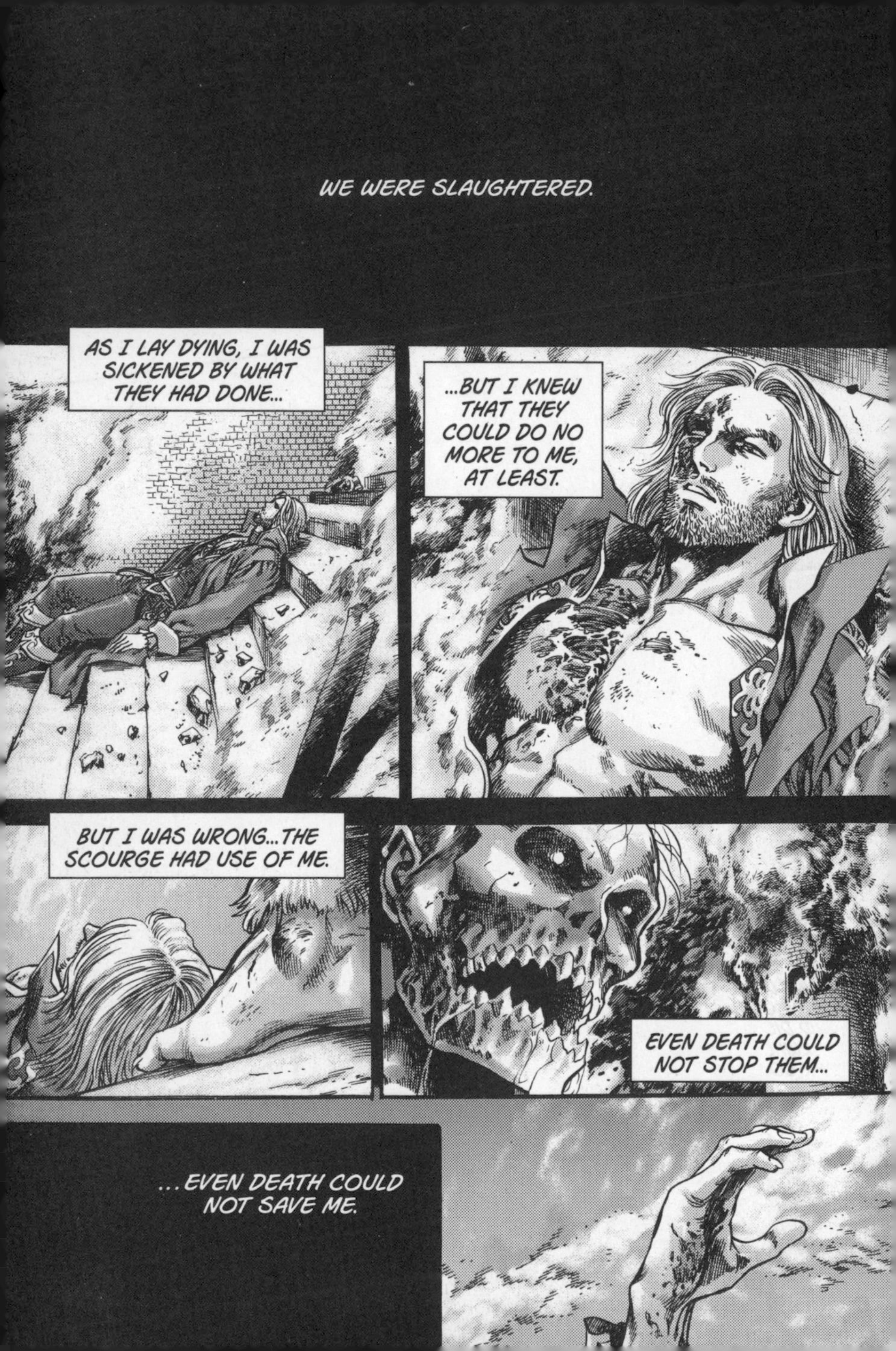
WE WERE SLAUGHTERED.
AS I LAY DYING, I WAS SICKENED BY WHAT THEY HAD DONE...
...BUT I KNEW THAT THEY COULD DO NO MORE TO ME, AT LEAST.
BUT I WAS WRONG...THE SCOURGE HAD USE OF ME.
EVEN DEATH COULD NOT STOP THEM...
...EVEN DEATH COULD NOT SAVE ME.

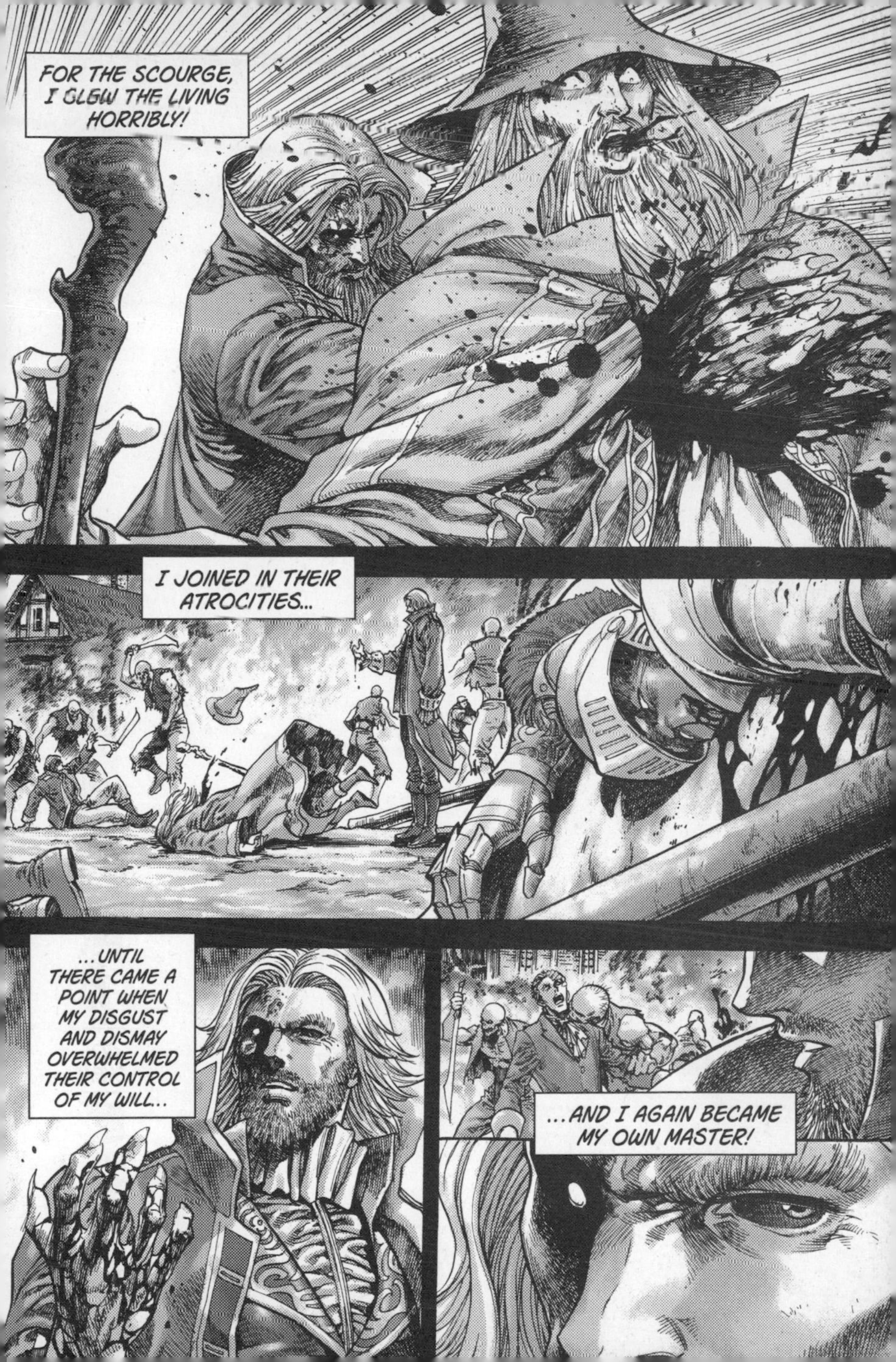
FOR THE SCOURGE, I SLEW THE LIVING HORRIBLY!
I JOINED IN THEIR ATROCITIES...
...UNTIL THERE CAME A POINT WHEN MY DISGUST AND DISMAY OVERWHELMED THEIR CONTROL OF MY WILL...
...AND I AGAIN BECAME MY OWN MASTER!

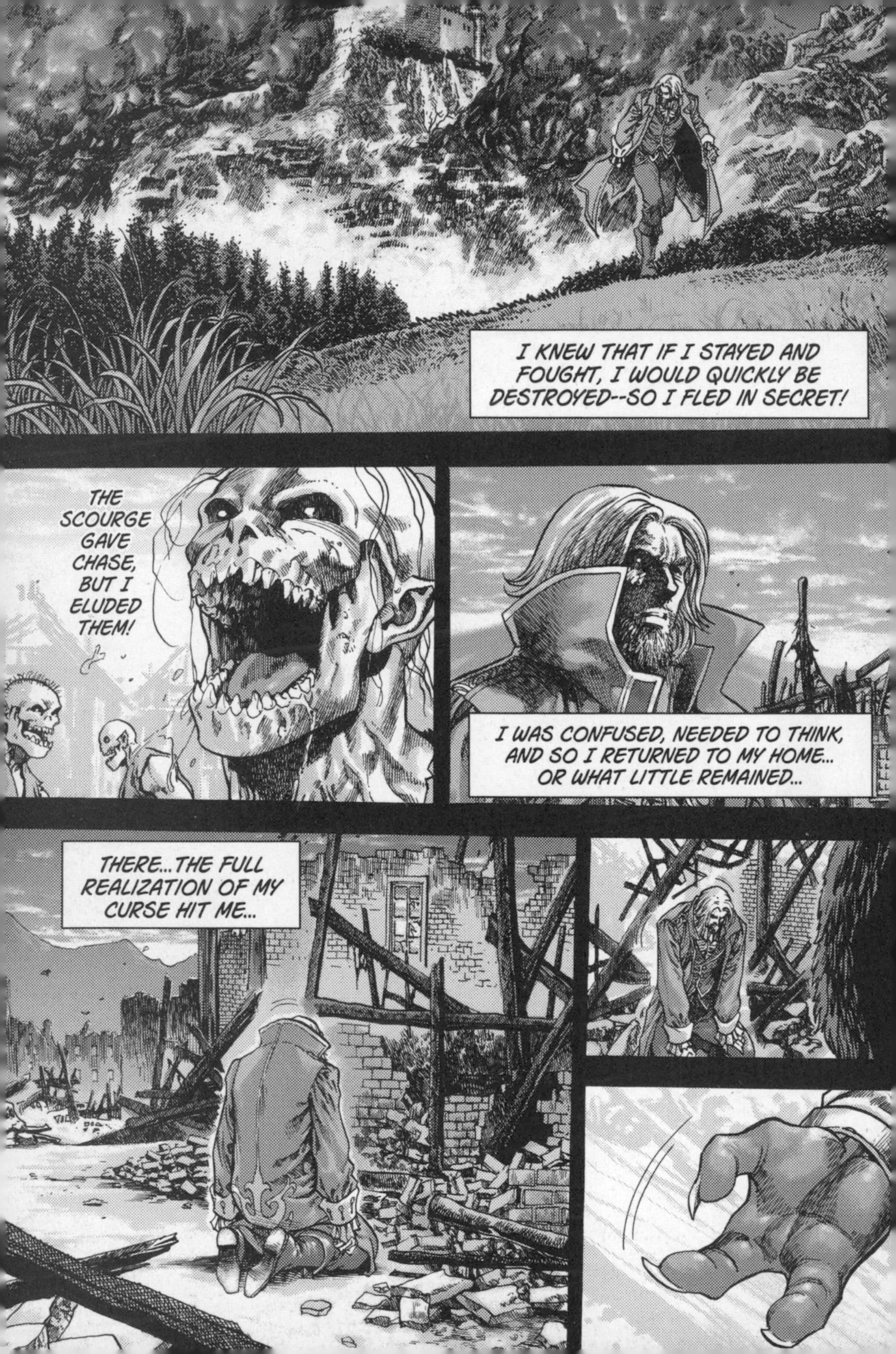
I KNEW THAT IF I STAYED AND FOUGHT, I WOULD QUICKLY BE DESTROYED--SO I FLED IN SECRET!
THE SCOURGE GAVE CHASE, BUT I ELUDED THEM!
I WAS CONFUSED, NEEDED TO THINK, AND SO I RETURNED TO MY HOME... OR WHAT LITTLE REMAINED...
THERE...THE FULL REALIZATION OF MY CURSE HIT ME...

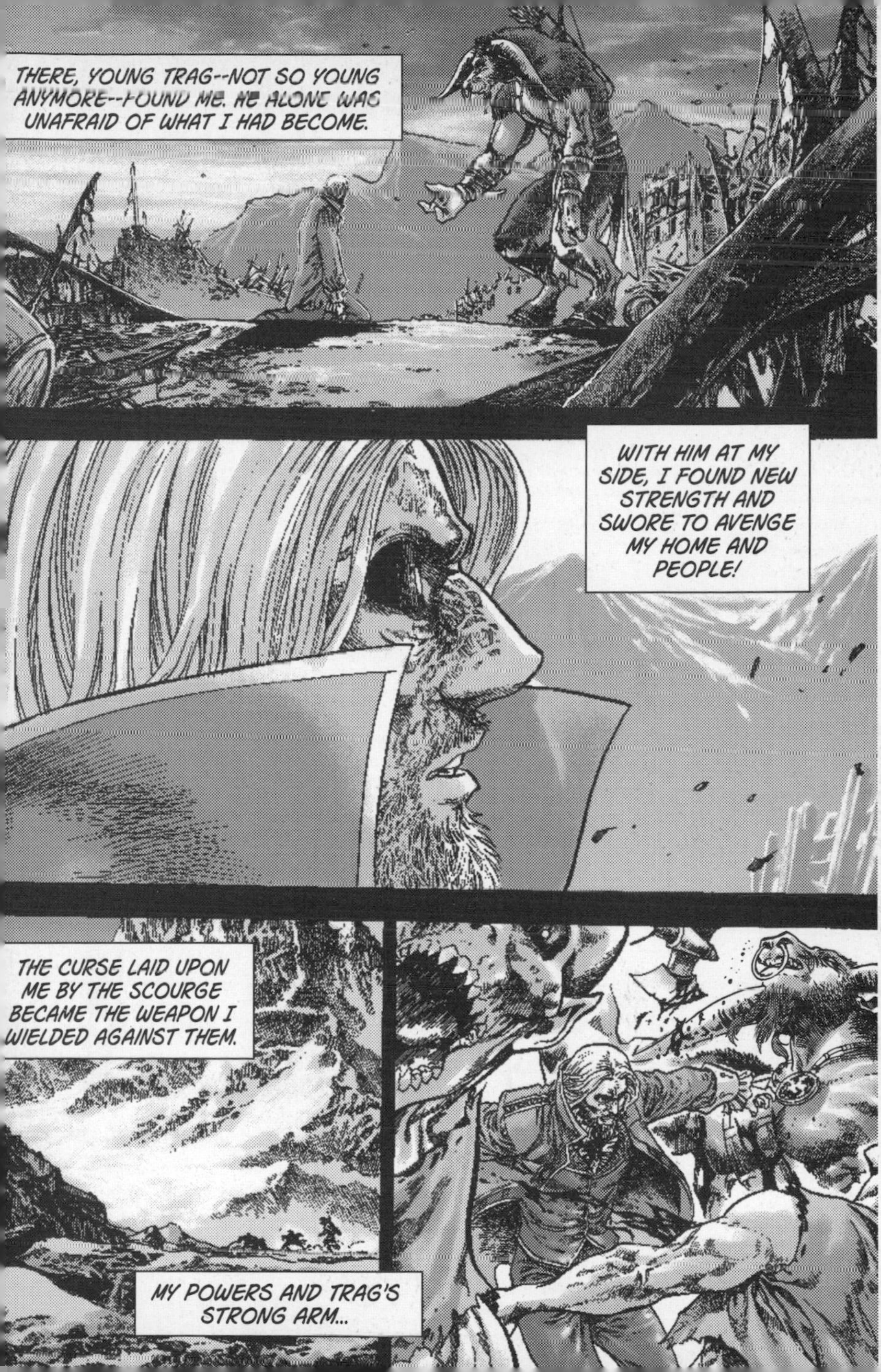
THERE, YOUNG TRAG--NOT SO YOUNG ANYMORE--FOUND ME. HE ALONE WAS UNAFRAID OF WHAT I HAD BECOME.
WITH HIM AT MY SIDE, I FOUND NEW STRENGTH AND SWORE TO AVENGE MY HOME AND PEOPLE!
THE CURSE LAID UPON ME BY THE SCOURGE BECAME THE WEAPON I WIELDED AGAINST THEM.
MY POWERS AND TRAG'S STRONG ARM...

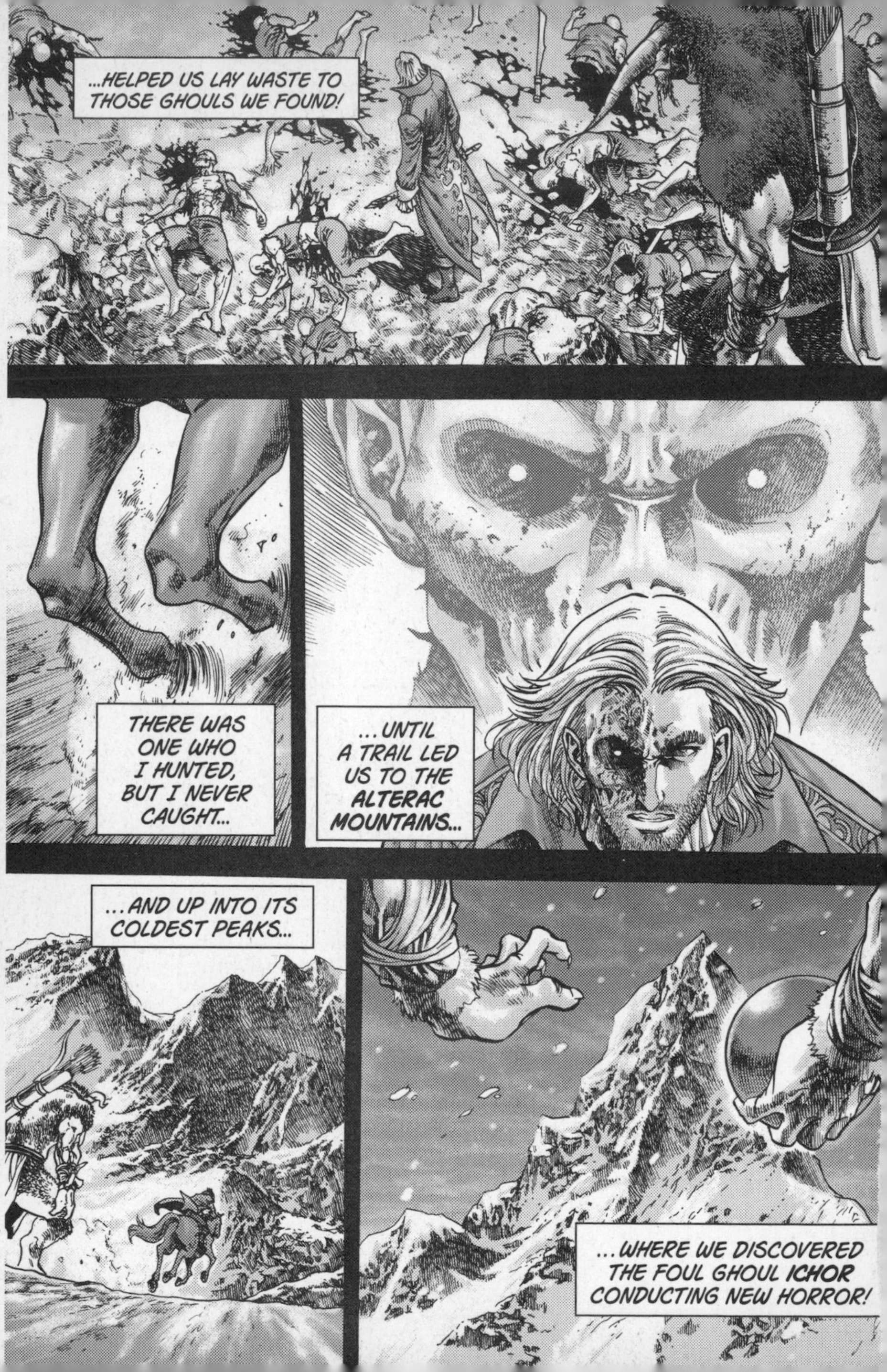
...HELPED US LAY WASTE TO THOSE GHOULS WE FOUND!
THERE WAS ONE WHO I HUNTED, BUT I NEVER CAUGHT...
...UNTIL A TRAIL LED US TO THE ALTERAC MOUNTAINS...
...AND UP INTO ITS COLDEST PEAKS...
...WHERE WE DISCOVERED THE FOUL GHOUL ICHOR CONDUCTING NEW HORROR!

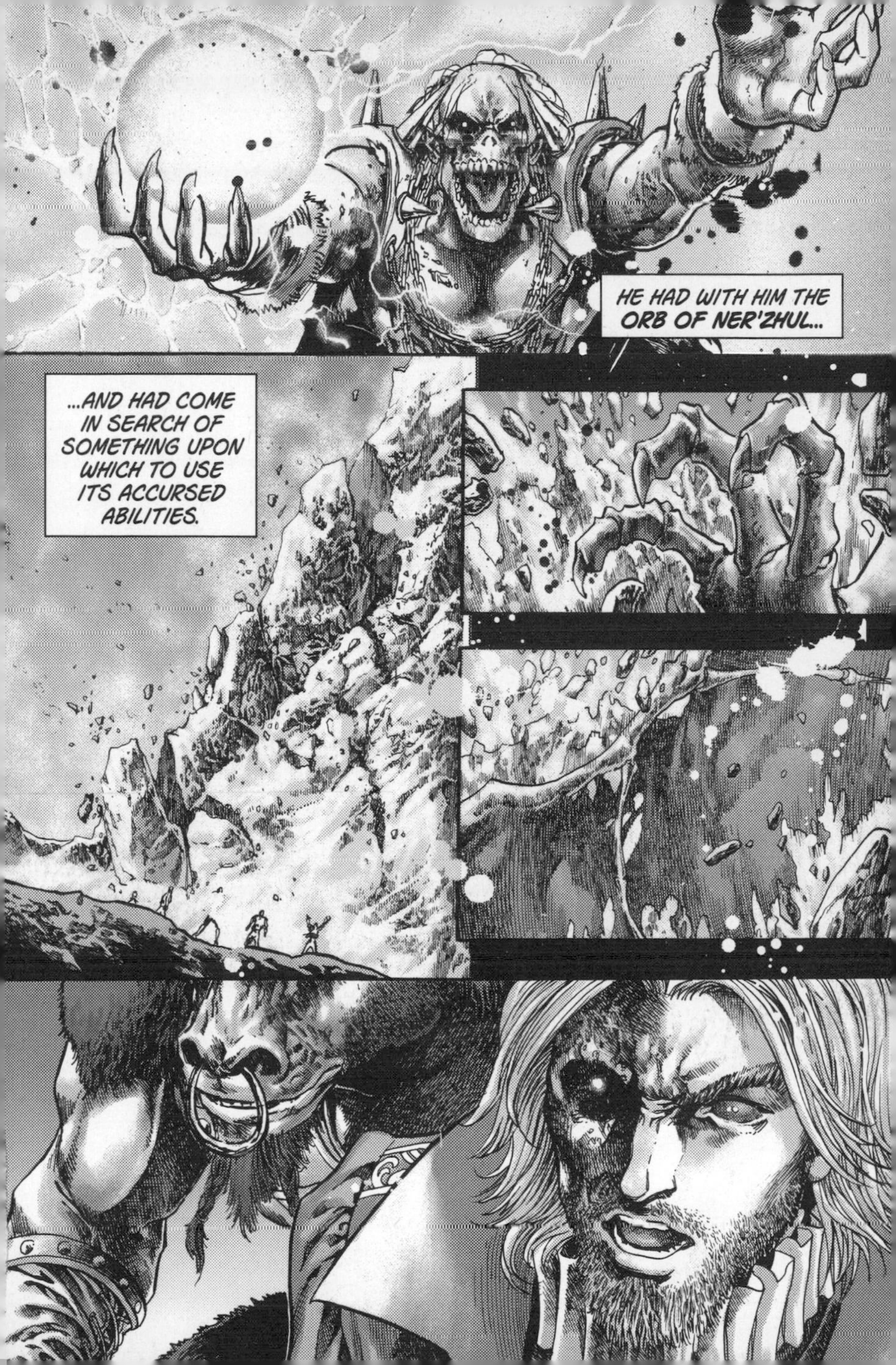
HE HAD WITH HIM THE ORB OF NER'ZHUL...
...AND HAD COME IN SEARCH OF SOMETHING UPON WHICH TO USE ITS ACCURSED ABILITIES.

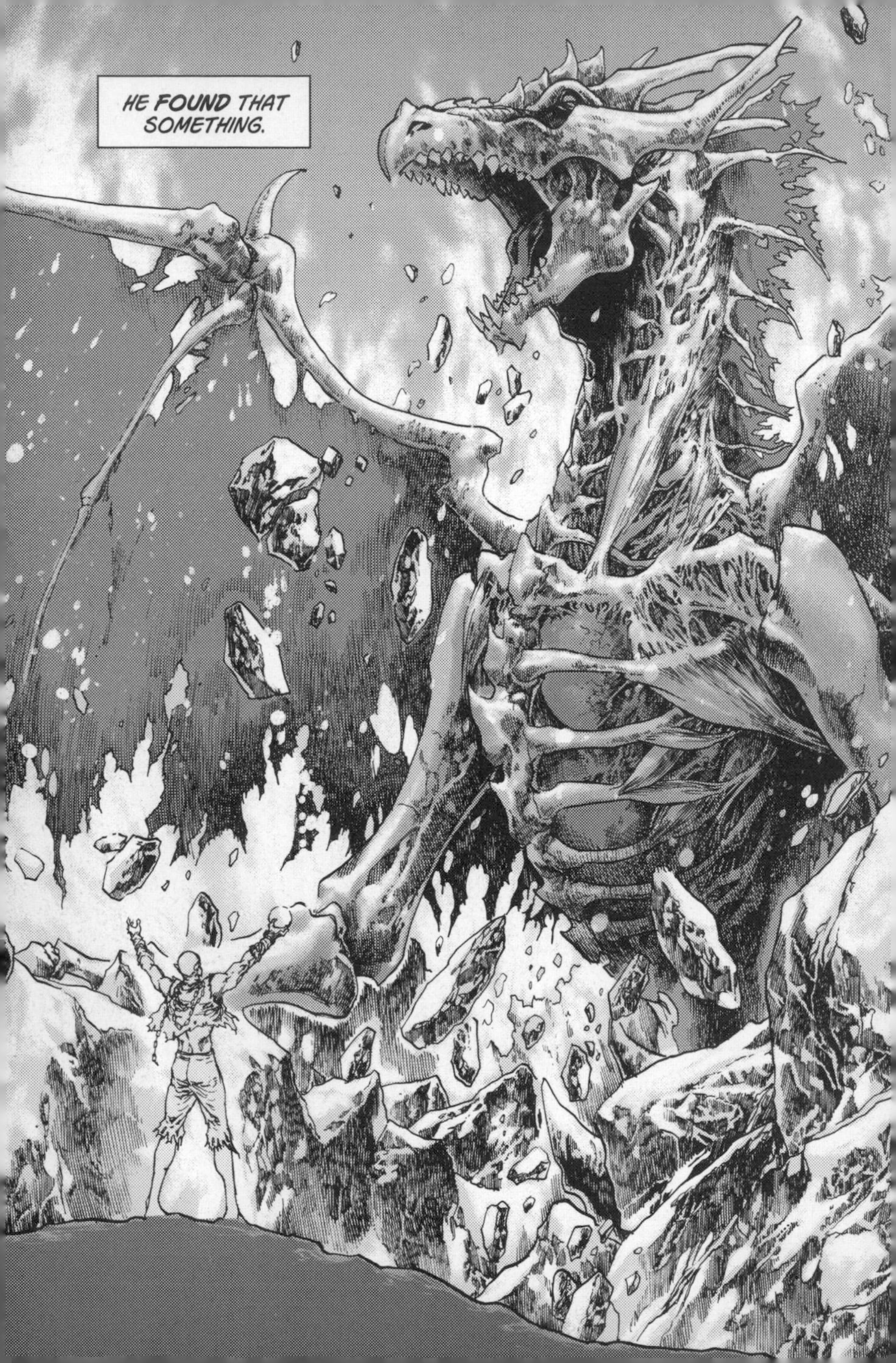
HE FOUND THAT SOMETHING.

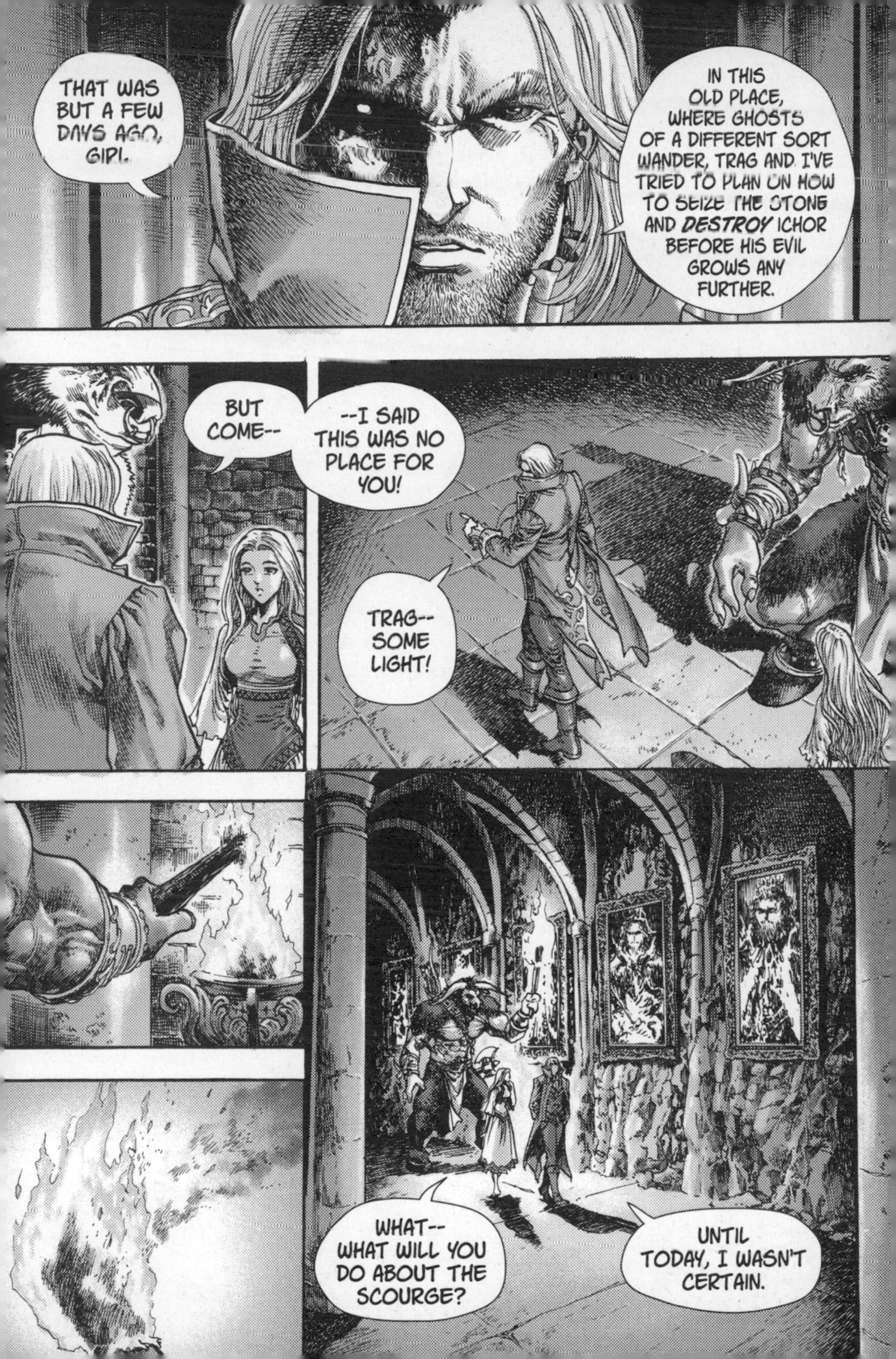
THAT WAS BUT A FEW DAYS AGO, GIRL.
IN THIS OLD PLACE, WHERE GHOSTS OF A DIFFERENT SORT WANDER, TRAG AND I'VE TRIED TO PLAN ON HOW TO SEIZE THE STONE AND DESTROY ICHOR BEFORE HIS EVIL GROWS ANY FURTHER.
BUT COME--
--I SAID THIS WAS NO PLACE FOR YOU!
TRAG-- SOME LIGHT!
WHAT-- WHAT WILL YOU DO ABOUT THE SCOURGE?
UNTIL TODAY, I WASN'T CERTAIN.

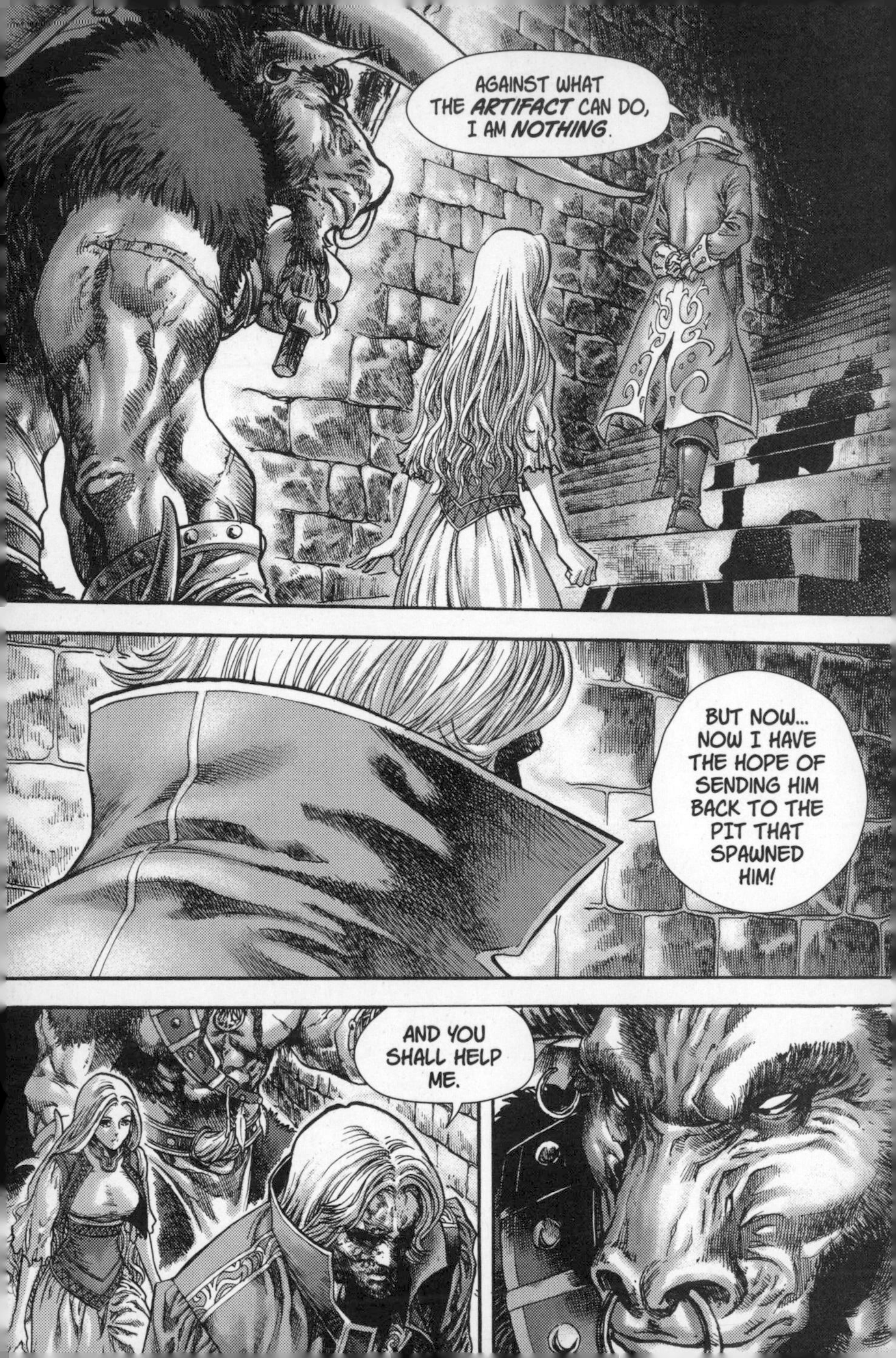
AGAINST WHAT THE ARTIFACT CAN DO, I AM NOTHING.
BUT NOW... NOW I HAVE THE HOPE OF SENDING HIM BACK TO THE PIT THAT SPAWNED HIM!
AND YOU SHALL HELP ME.

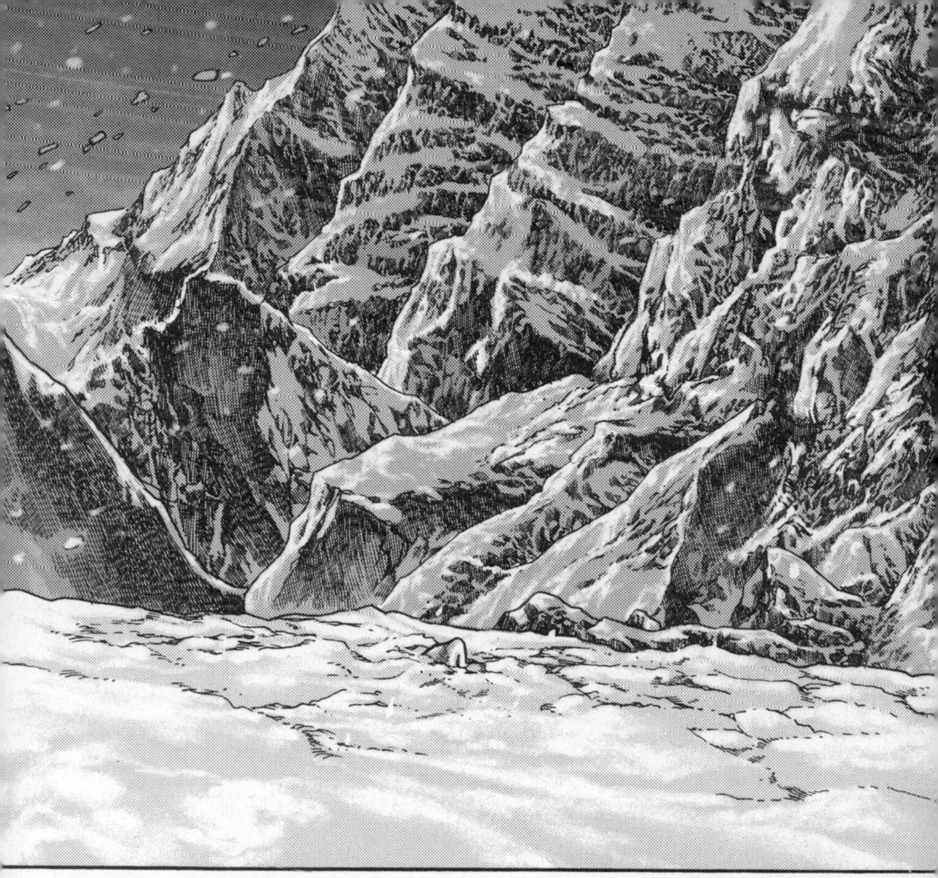

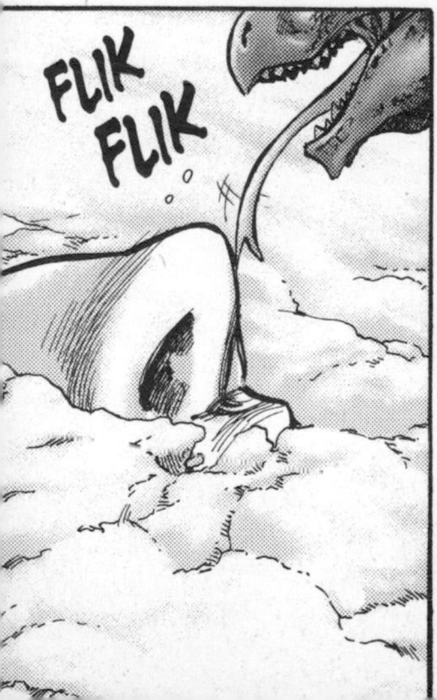
FLIK
FLIK

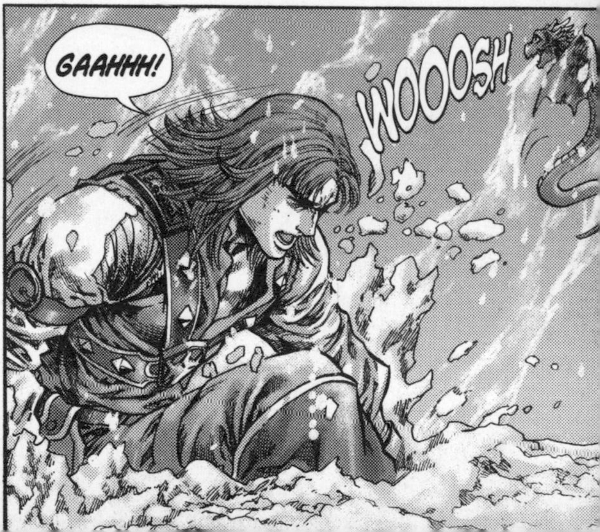
GAAHHH!
WOOOSH

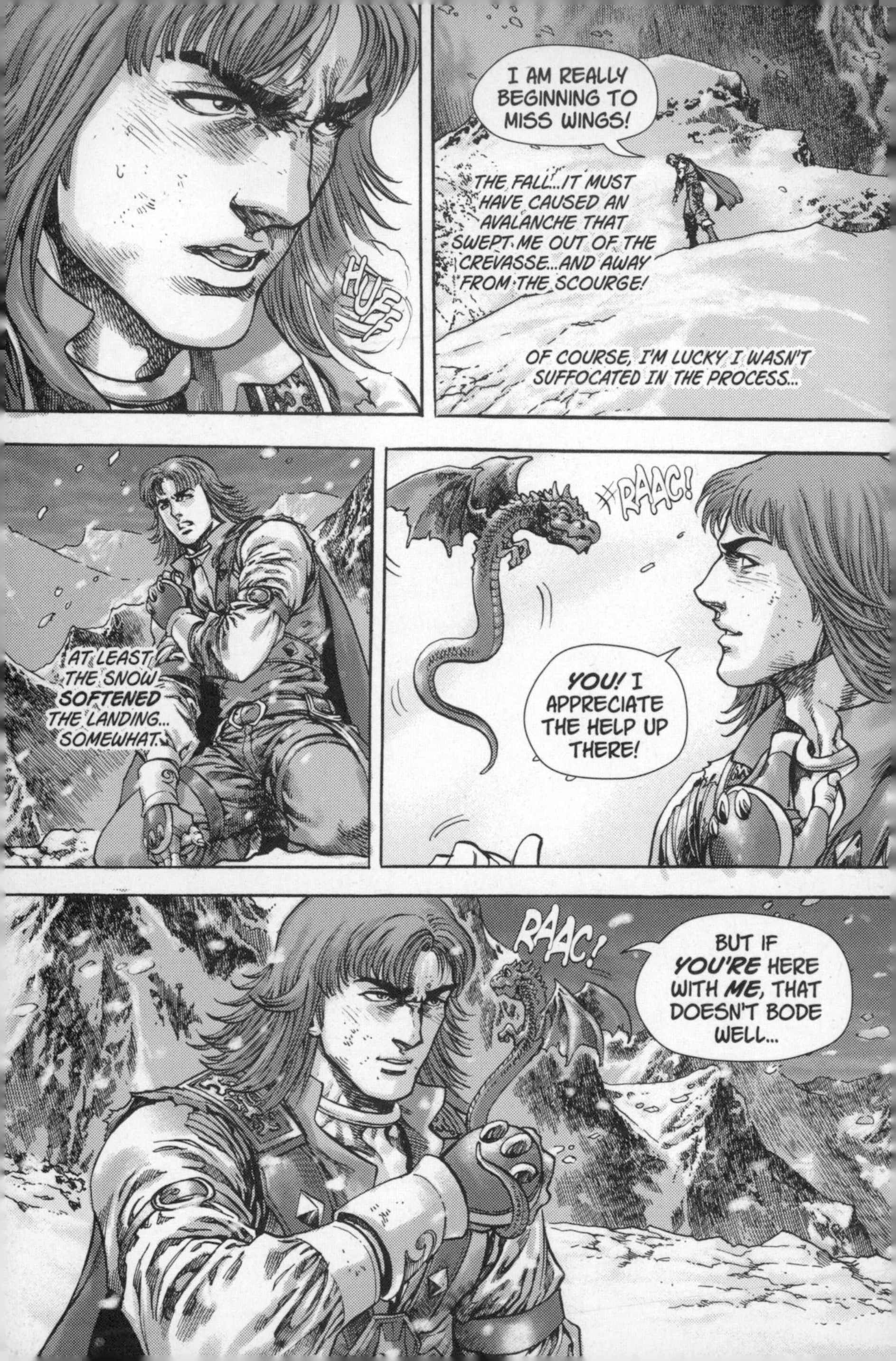
HUFF!
I AM REALLY BEGINNING TO MISS WINGS!
THE FALL...IT MUST HAVE CAUSED AN AVALANCHE THAT SWEPT ME OUT OF THE CREVASSE...AND AWAY FROM THE SCOURGE!
OF COURSE, I'M LUCKY I WASN'T SUFFOCATED IN THE PROCESS...
AT LEAST THE SNOW SOFTENED THE LANDING... SOMEWHAT.
RAAC!
YOU! I APPRECIATE THE HELP UP THERE!
RAAC!
BUT IF YOU'RE HERE WITH ME, THAT DOESN'T BODE WELL...

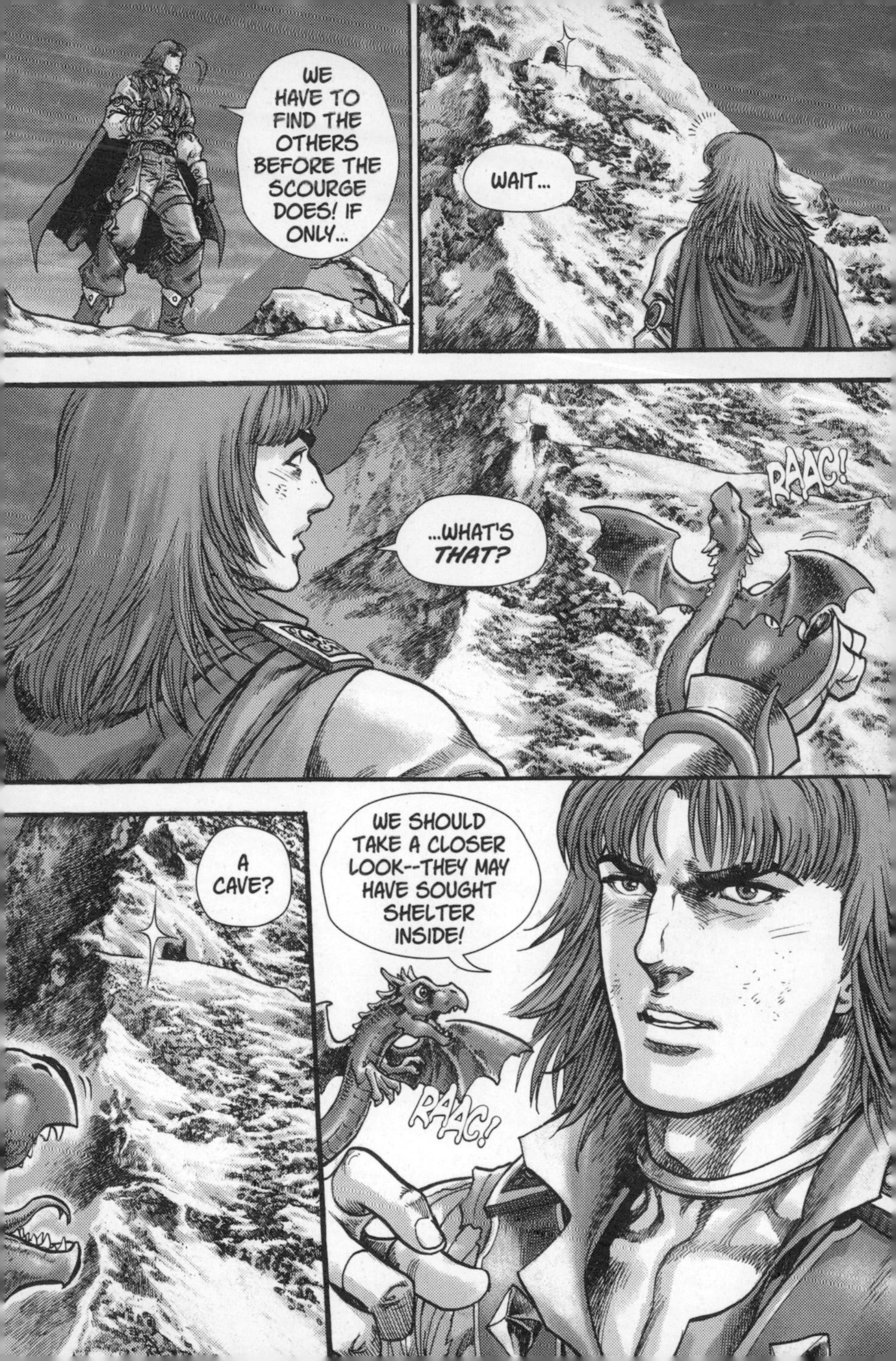
WE HAVE TO FIND THE OTHERS BEFORE THE SCOURGE DOES! IF ONLY...
WAIT...
...WHAT'S *THAT?*
RAAC!
A CAVE?
WE SHOULD TAKE A CLOSER LOOK--THEY MAY HAVE SOUGHT SHELTER INSIDE!
RAAC!

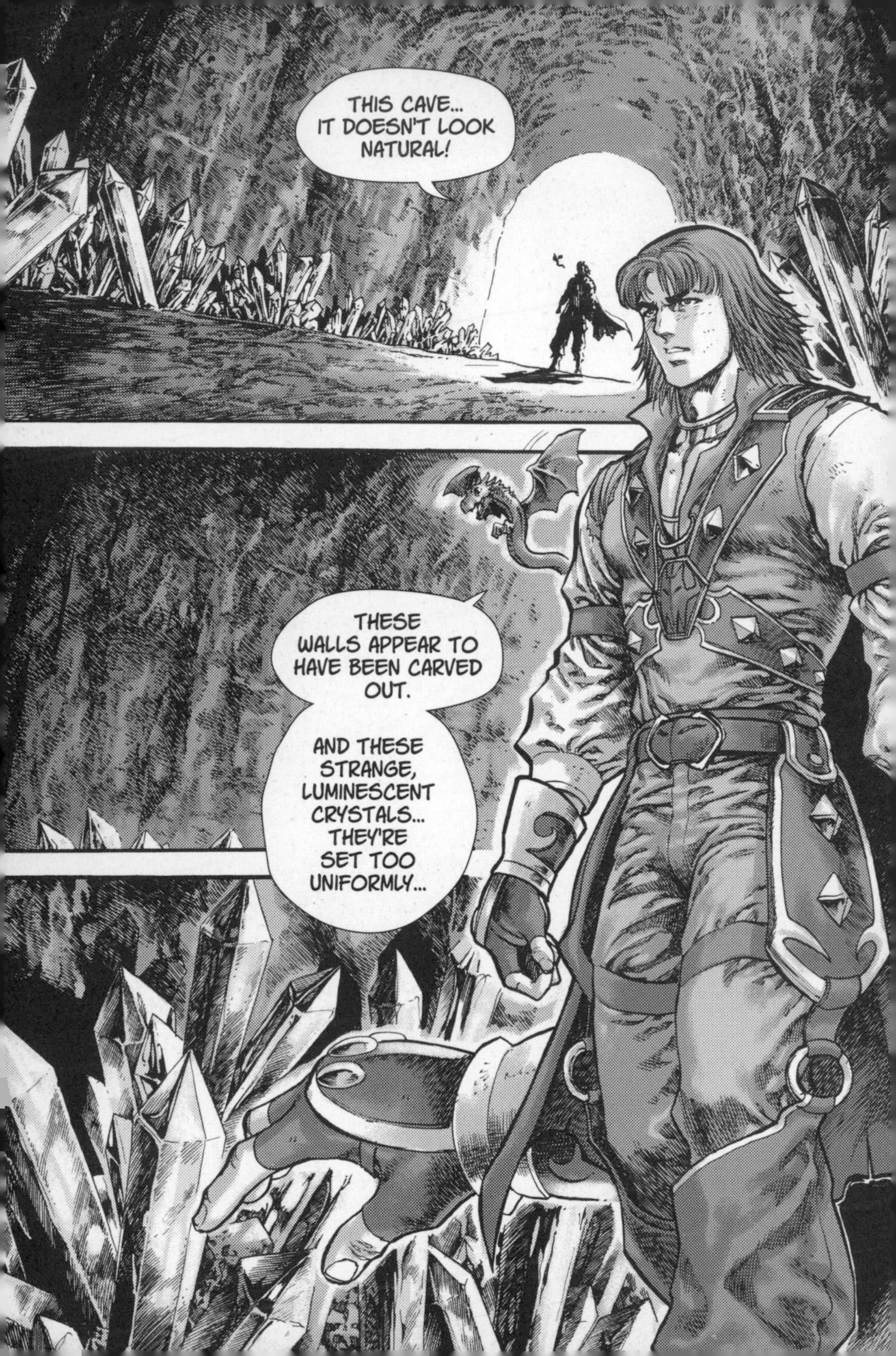
THIS CAVE... IT DOESN'T LOOK NATURAL!
THESE WALLS APPEAR TO HAVE BEEN CARVED OUT.
AND THESE STRANGE, LUMINESCENT CRYSTALS... THEY'RE SET TOO UNIFORMLY...

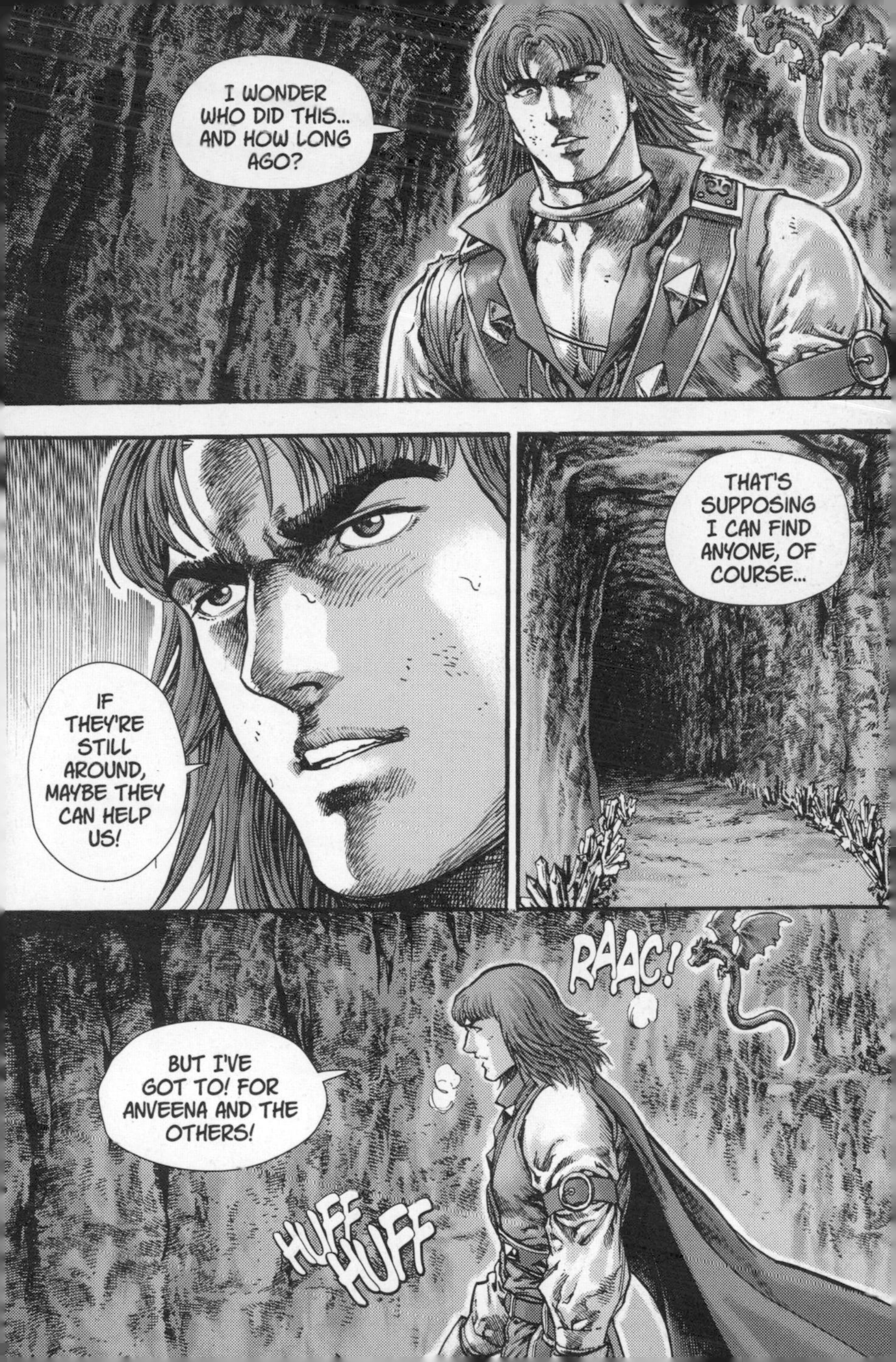
I WONDER WHO DID THIS... AND HOW LONG AGO?
IF THEY'RE STILL AROUND, MAYBE THEY CAN HELP US!
THAT'S SUPPOSING I CAN FIND ANYONE, OF COURSE...
BUT I'VE GOT TO! FOR ANVEENA AND THE OTHERS!
RAAC!
HUFF HUFF

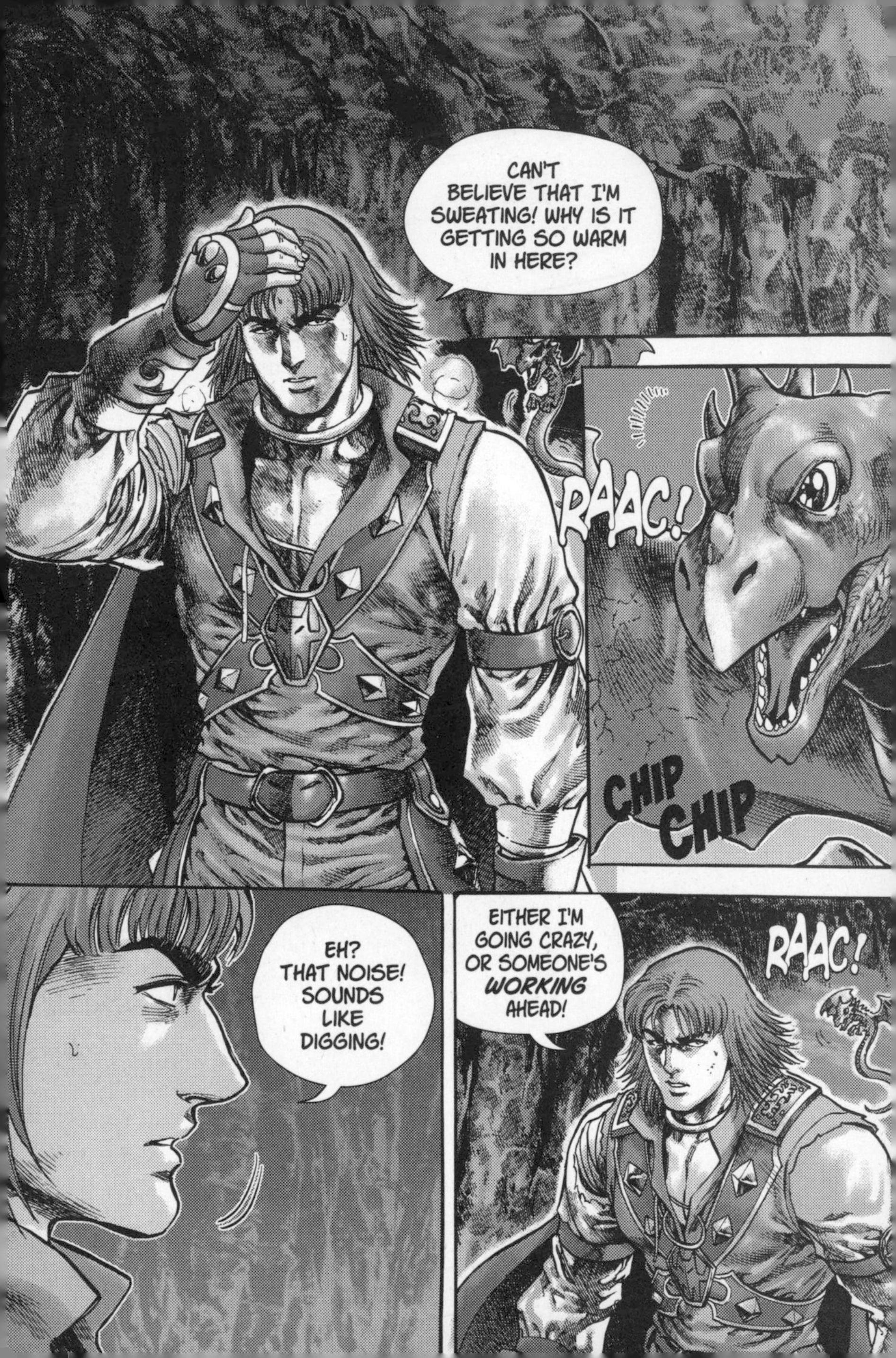
CAN'T BELIEVE THAT I'M SWEATING! WHY IS IT GETTING SO WARM IN HERE?
RAAC!
CHIP CHIP
EH? THAT NOISE! SOUNDS LIKE DIGGING!
EITHER I'M GOING CRAZY, OR SOMEONE'S WORKING AHEAD!
RAAC!

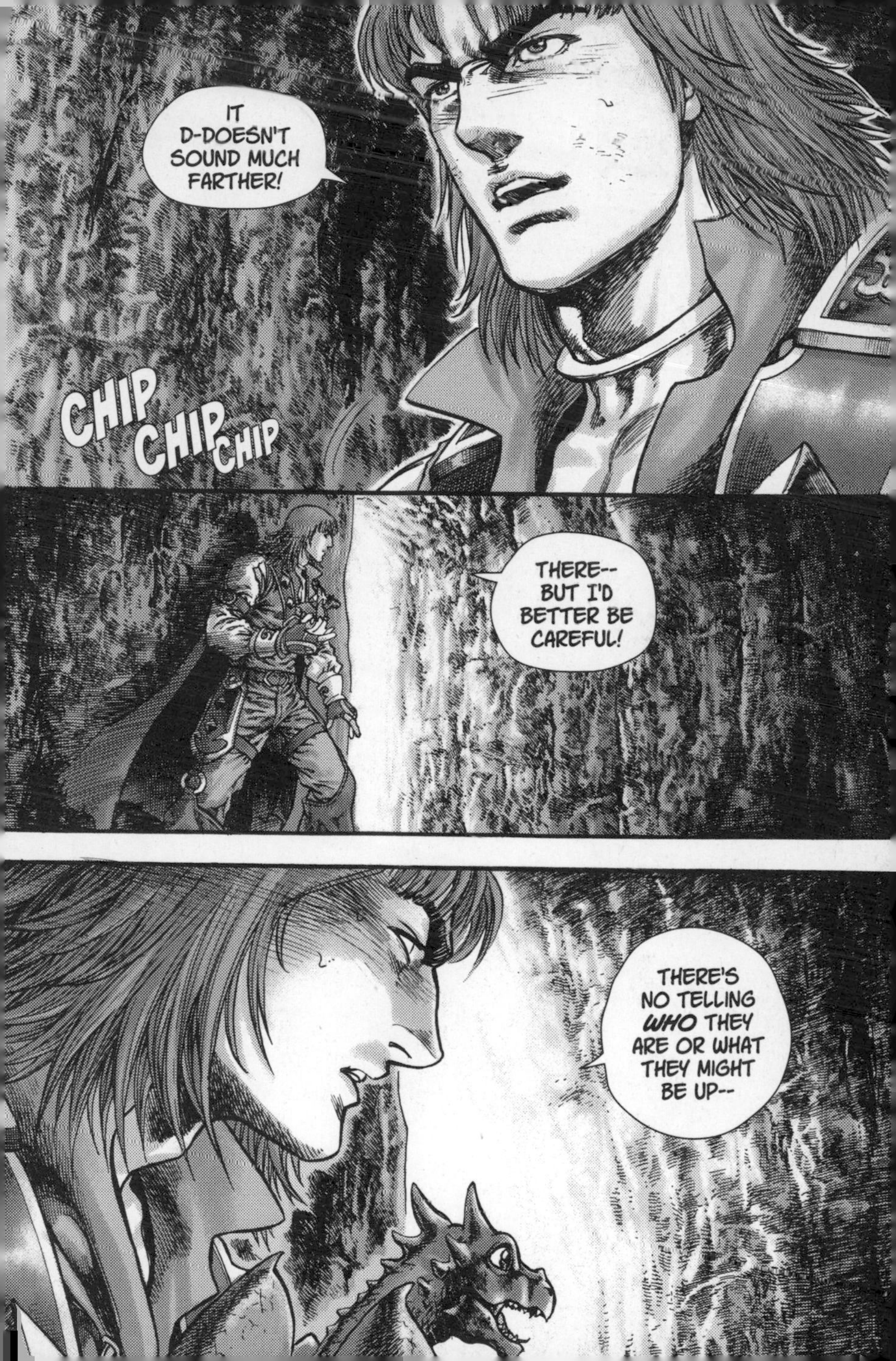
IT D-DOESN'T SOUND MUCH FARTHER!
CHIP CHIP CHIP
THERE-- BUT I'D BETTER BE CAREFUL!
THERE'S NO TELLING *WHO* THEY ARE OR WHAT THEY MIGHT BE UP--

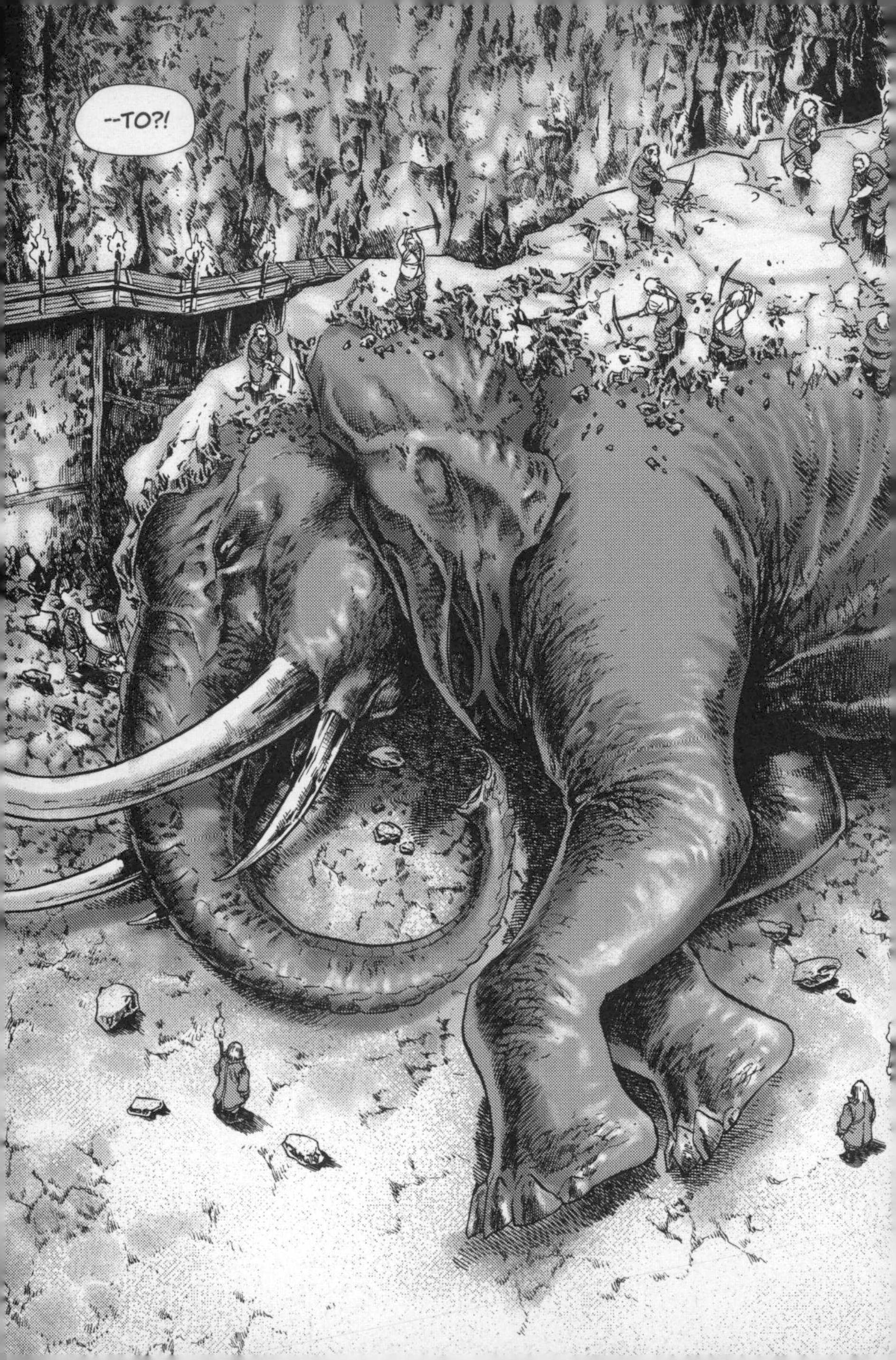
--TO?!

CHAPTER THREE
CAVERNS OF THE DEAD

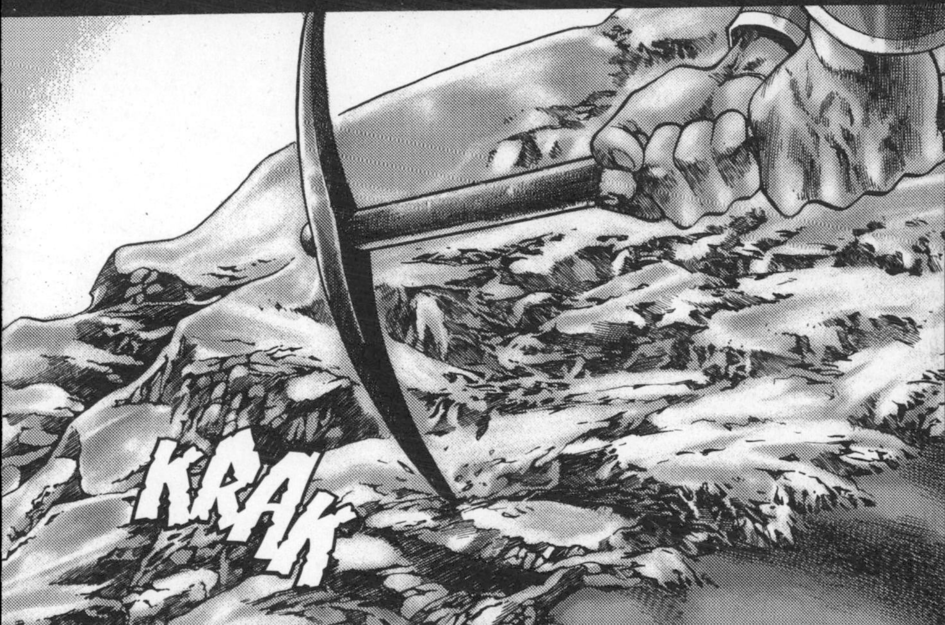
KRAK

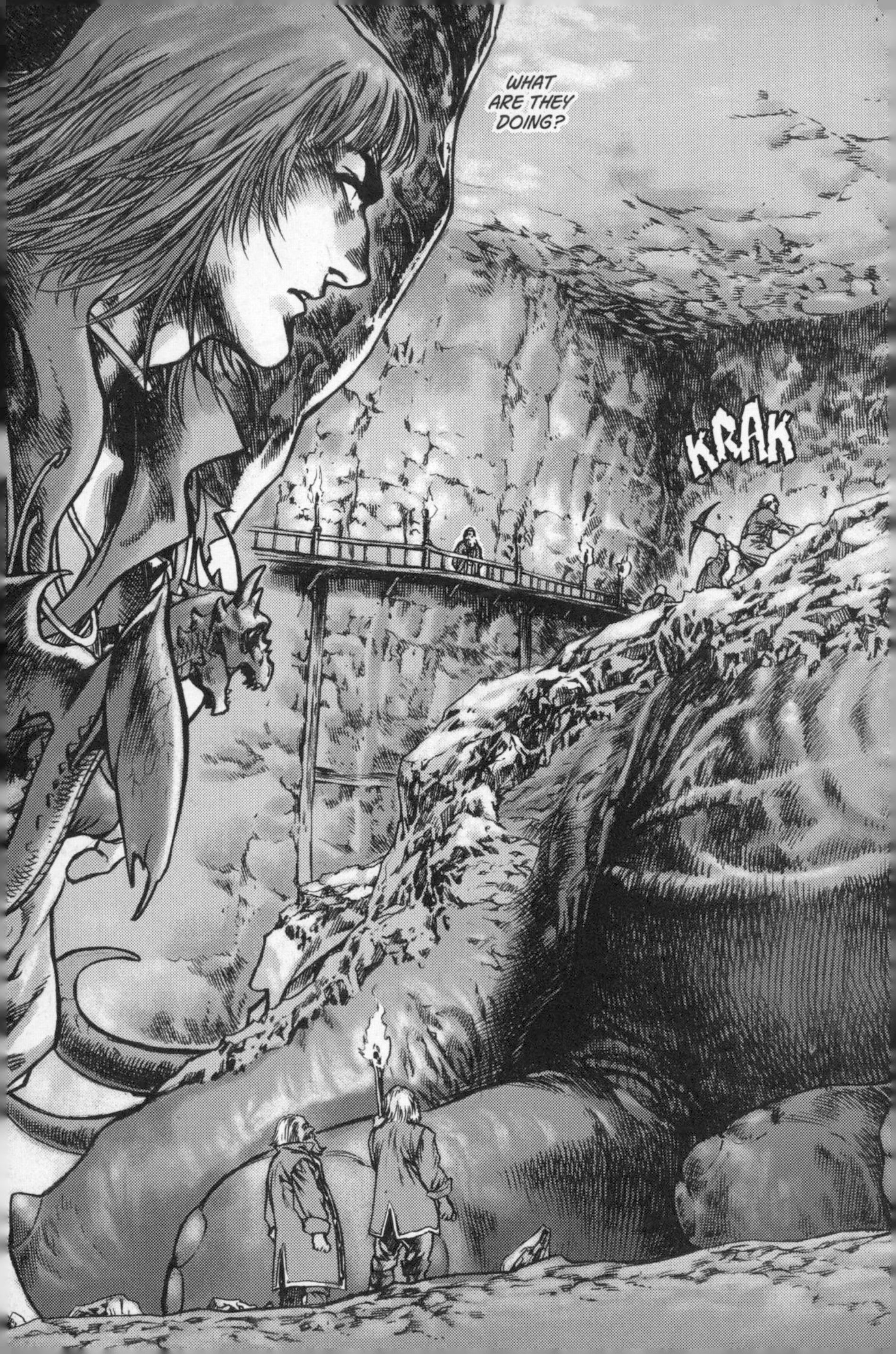
WHAT ARE THEY DOING?
KRAK

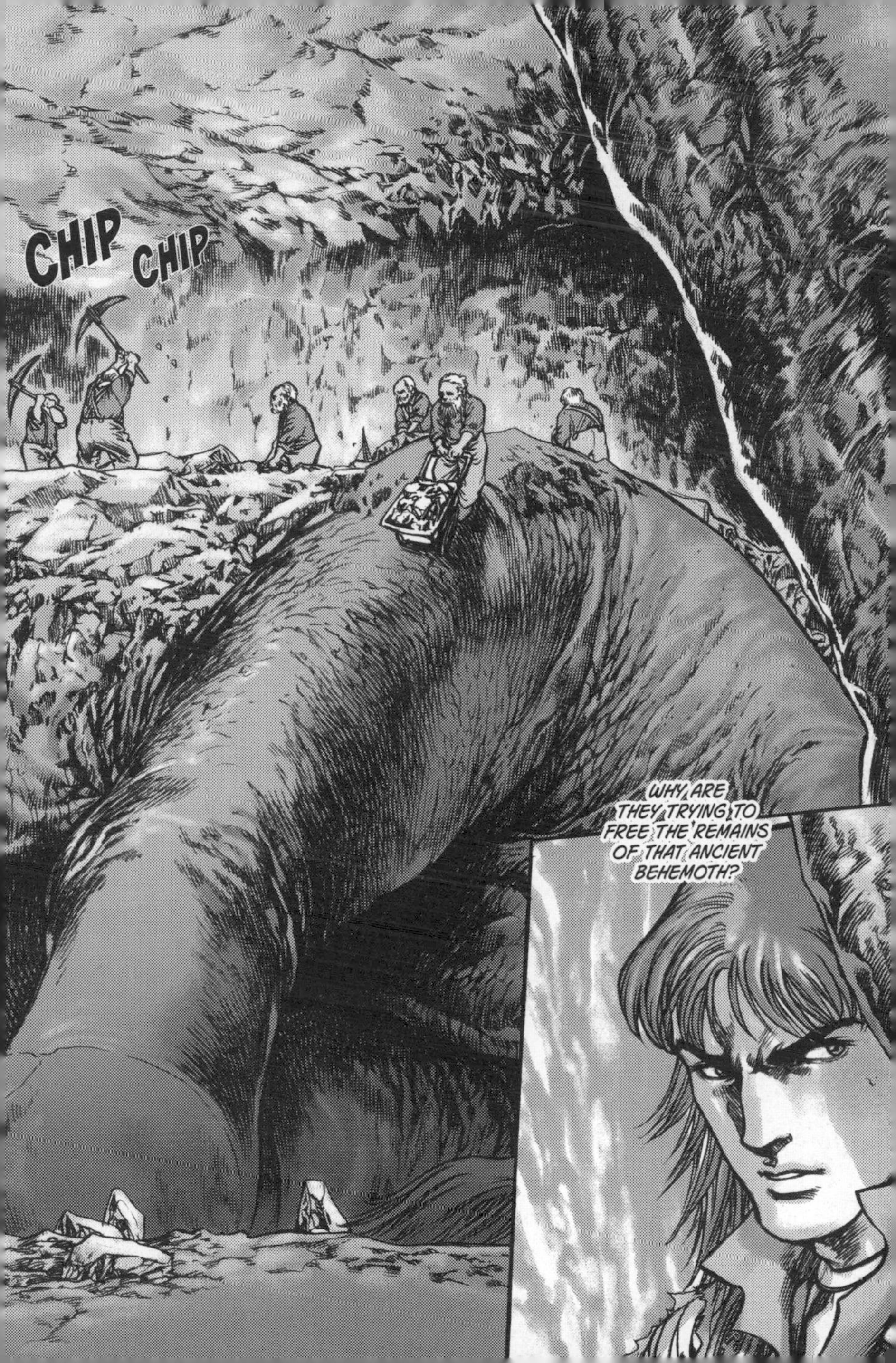
CHIP CHIP
WHY ARE THEY TRYING TO FREE THE REMAINS OF THAT ANCIENT BEHEMOTH?

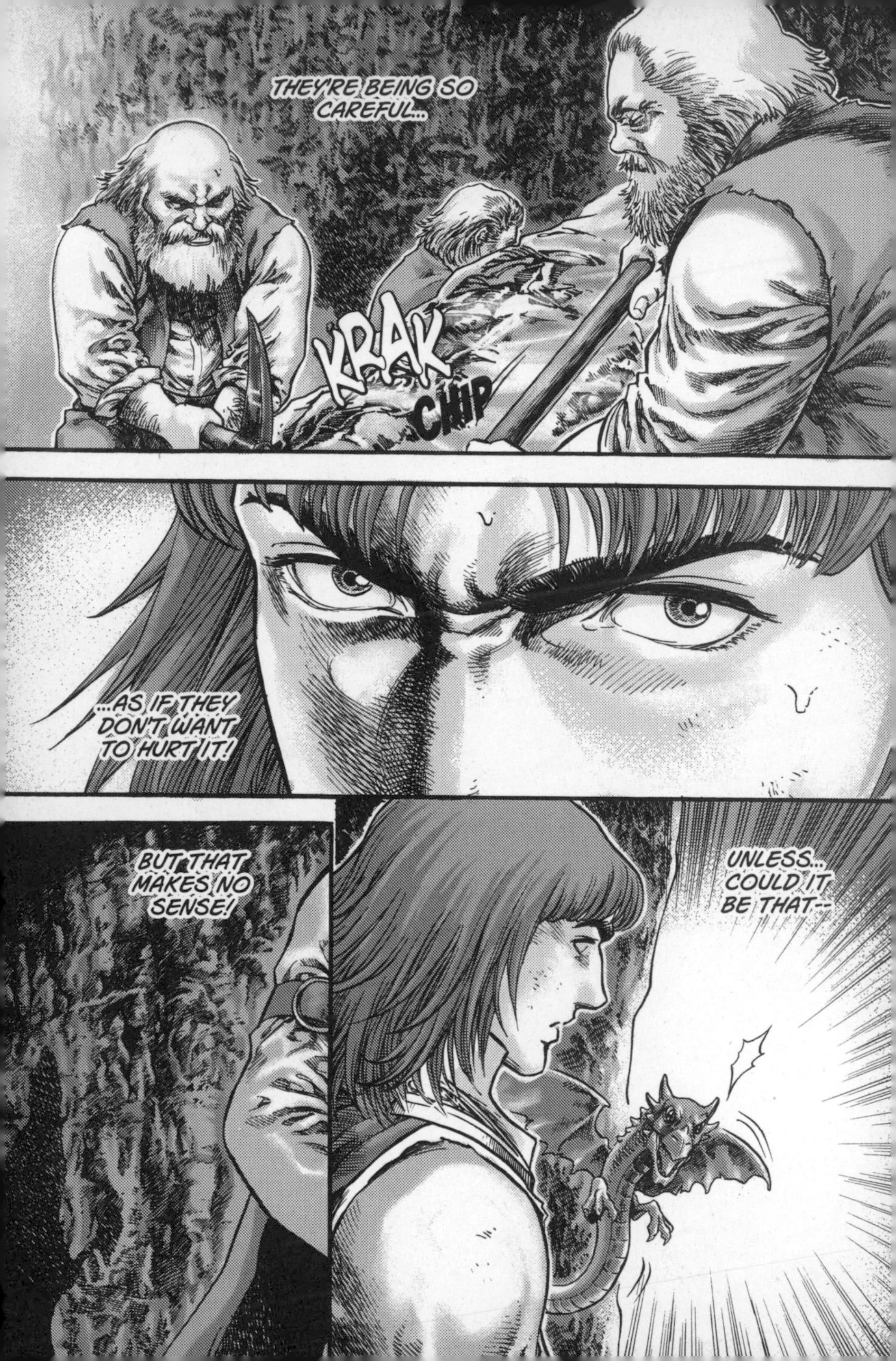
THEY'RE BEING SO CAREFUL...
KRAK
CHIP
...AS IF THEY DON'T WANT TO HURT IT!
BUT THAT MAKES NO SENSE!
UNLESS... COULD IT BE THAT--

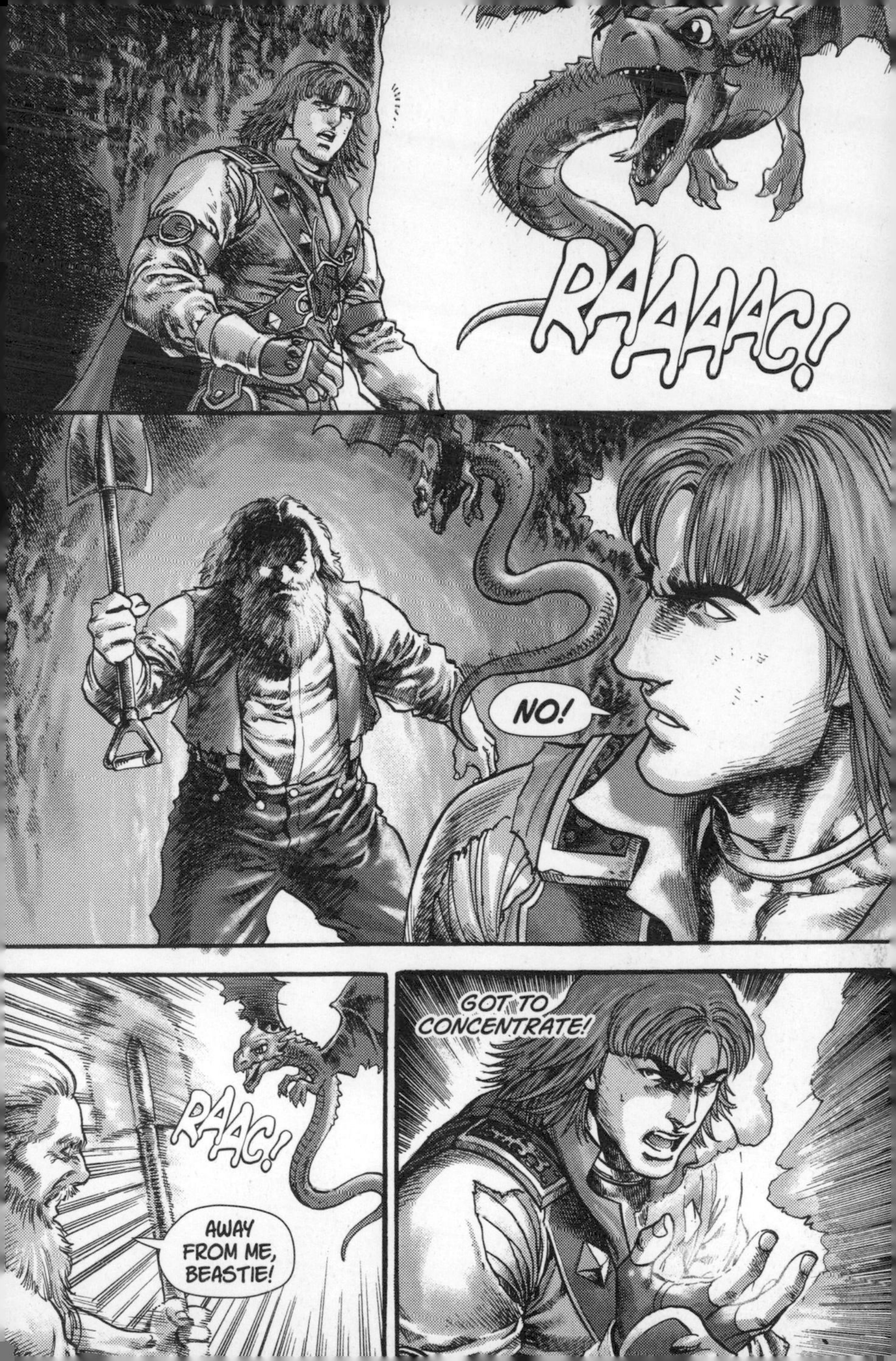
RAAAAAC!
NO!
RAAAC!
AWAY FROM ME, BEASTIE!
GOT TO CONCENTRATE!

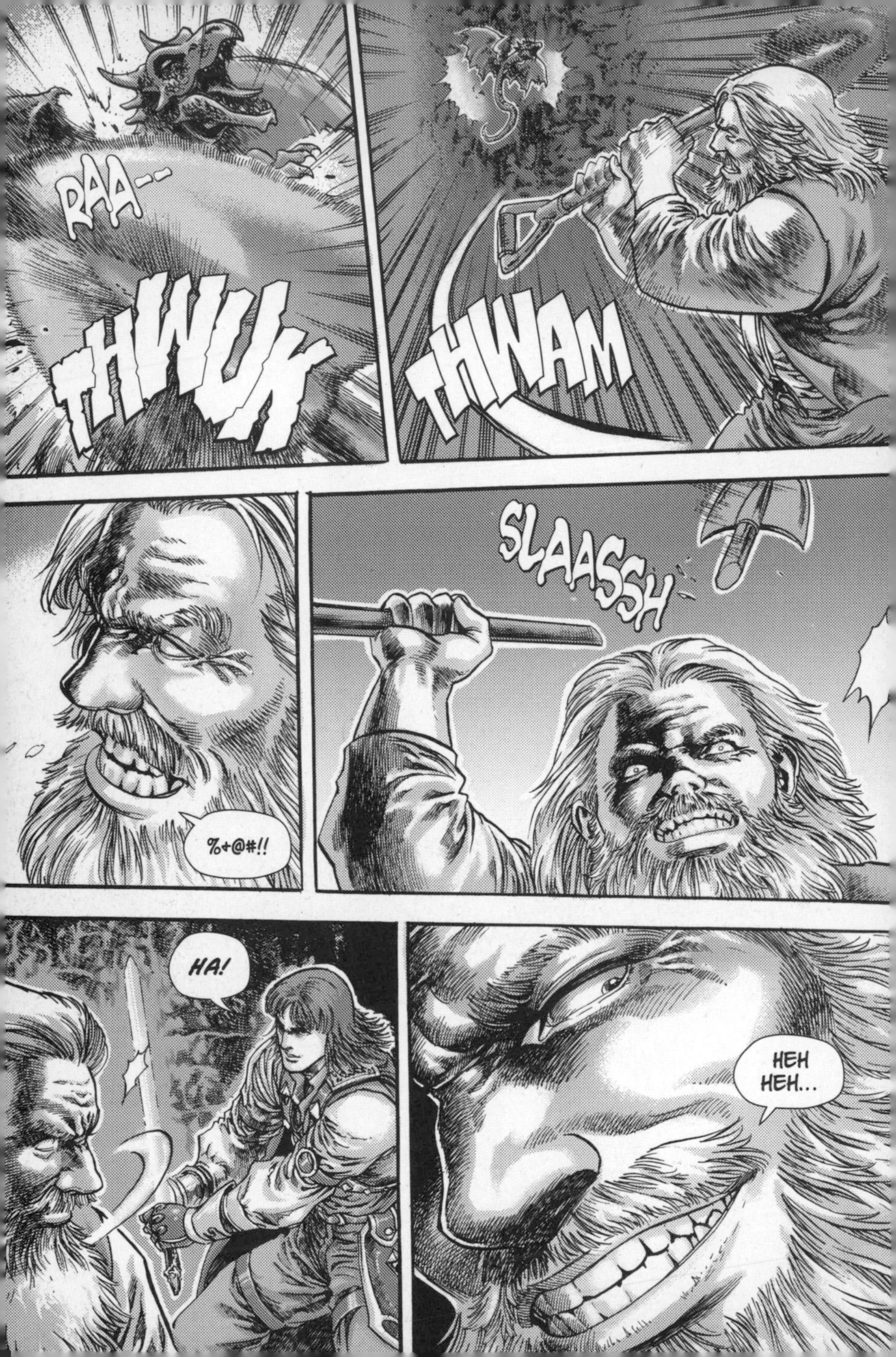
RAA--
THWUK
THWAM
%+@#!!
SLAASSH
HA!
HEH HEH...

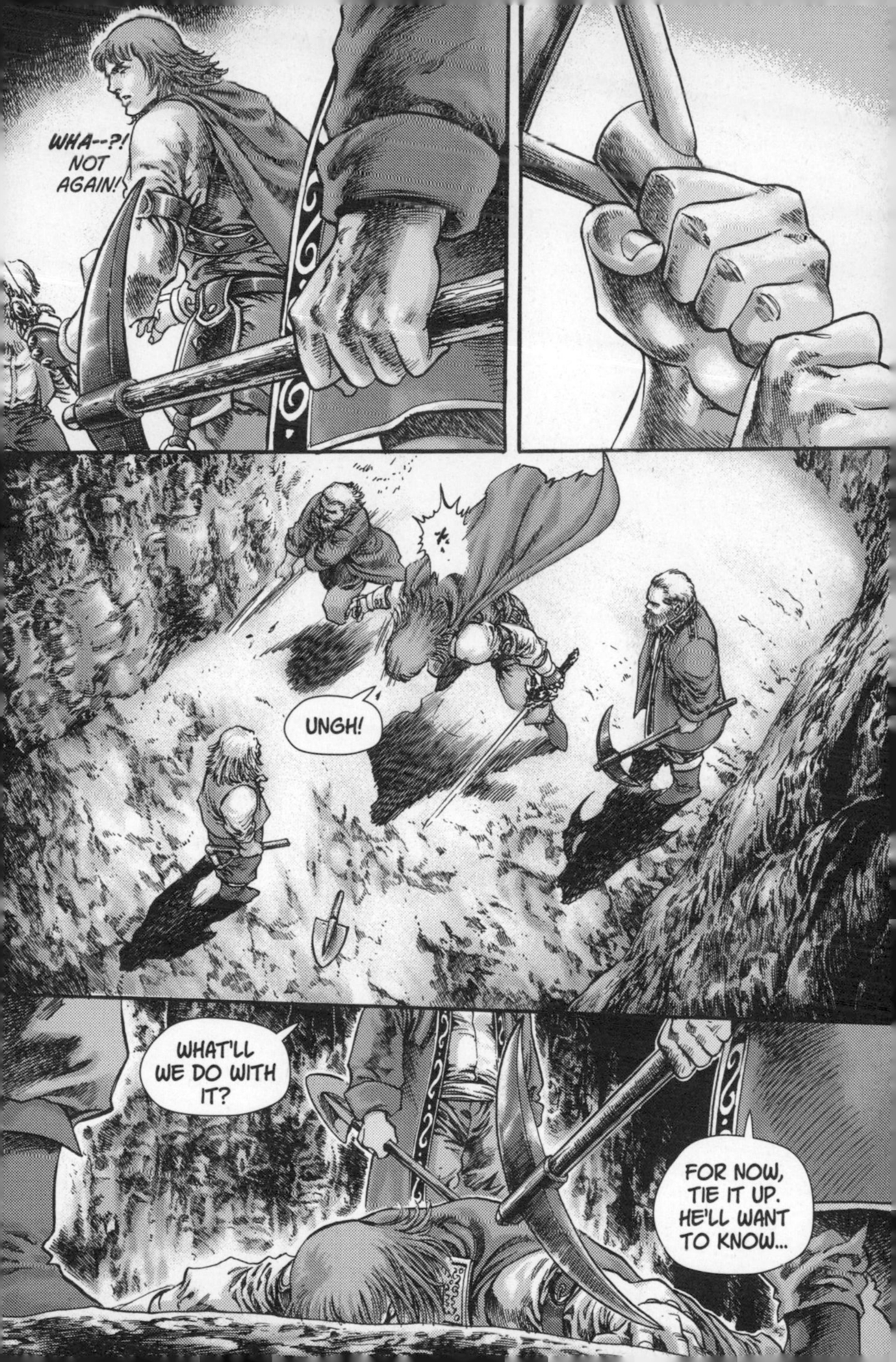
WHA--?! NOT AGAIN!
UNGH!
WHAT'LL WE DO WITH IT?
FOR NOW, TIE IT UP. HE'LL WANT TO KNOW...

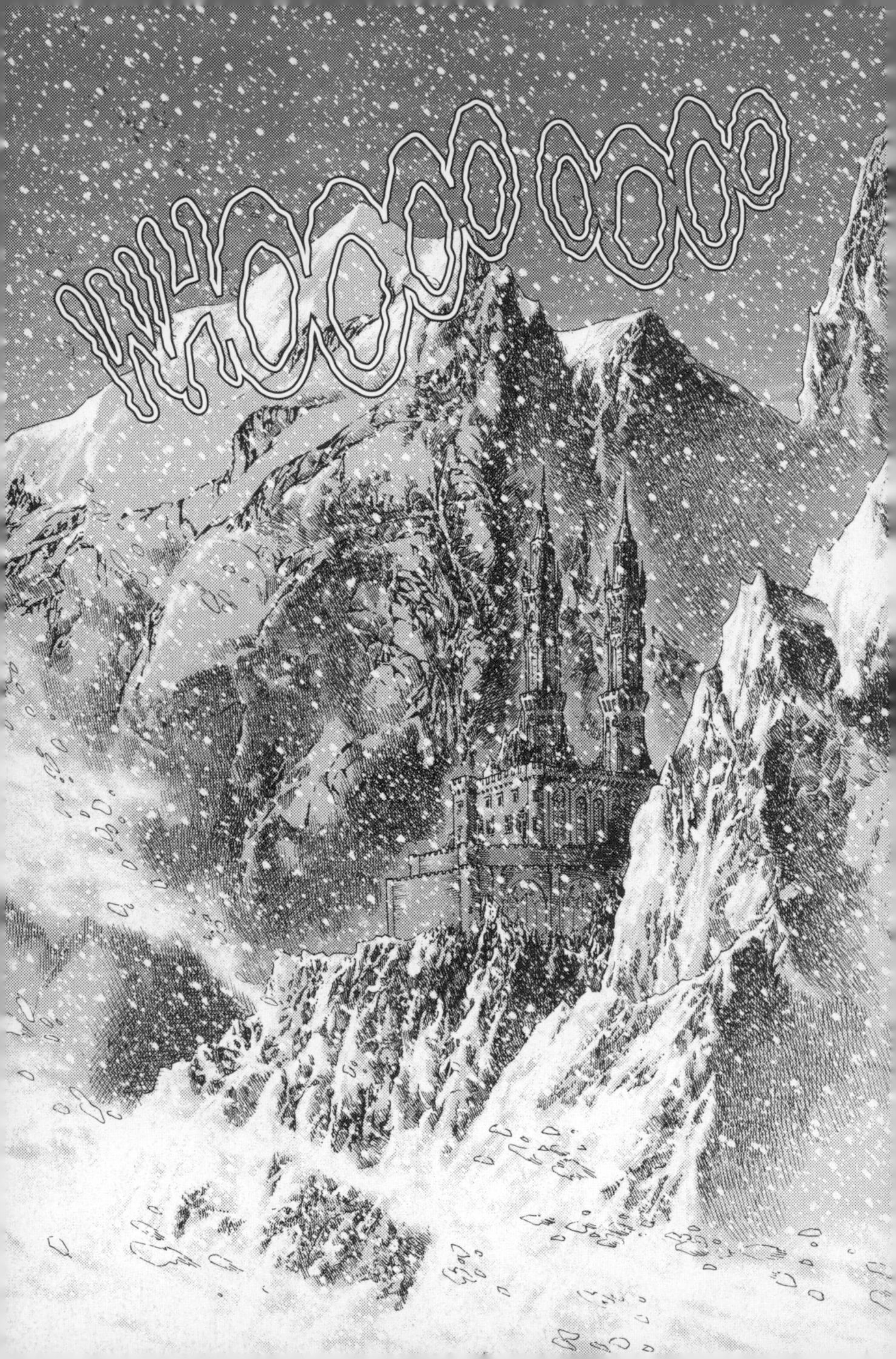
WHOOOO OOOO

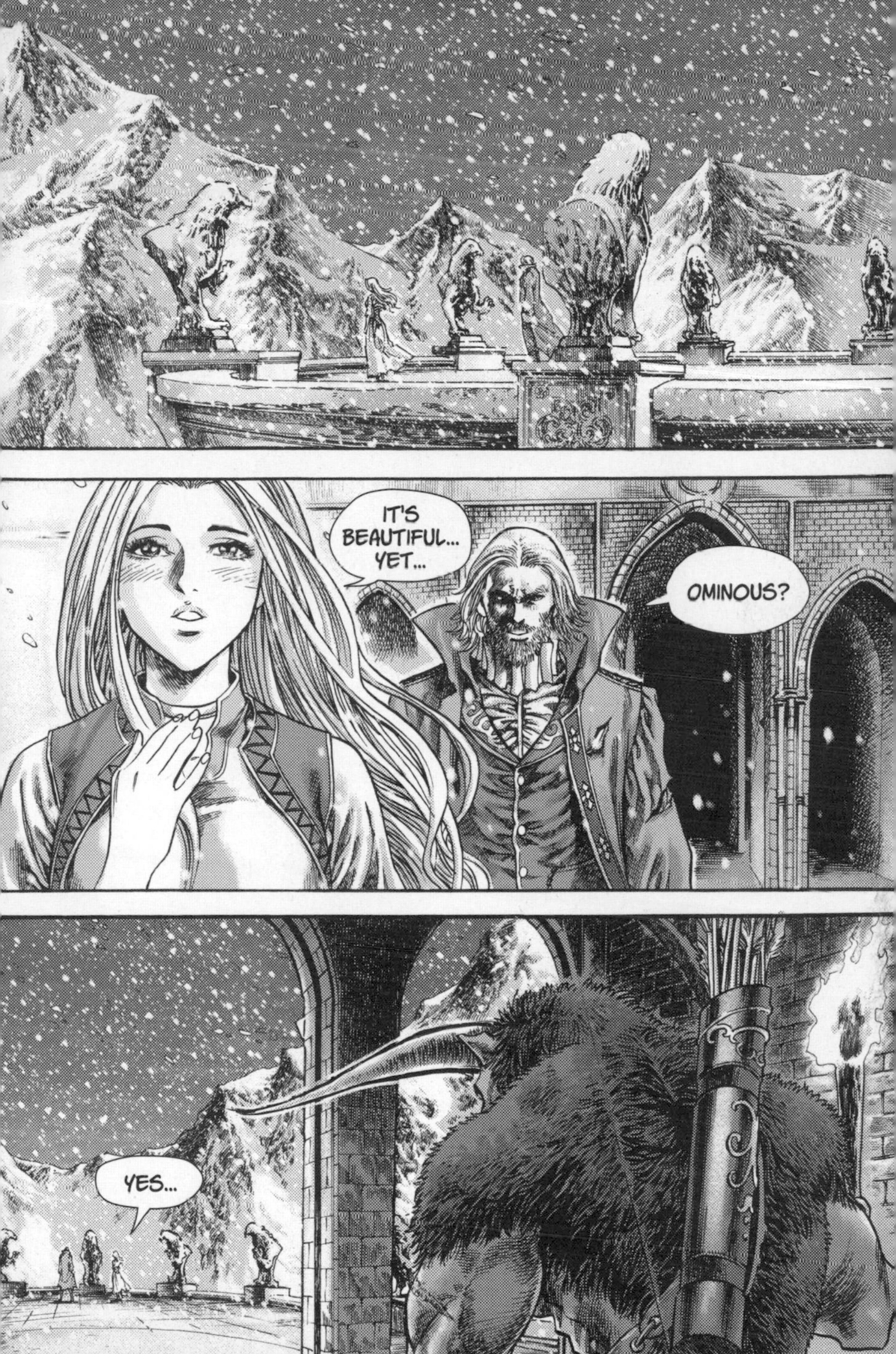
IT'S BEAUTIFUL... YET...
OMINOUS?
YES...

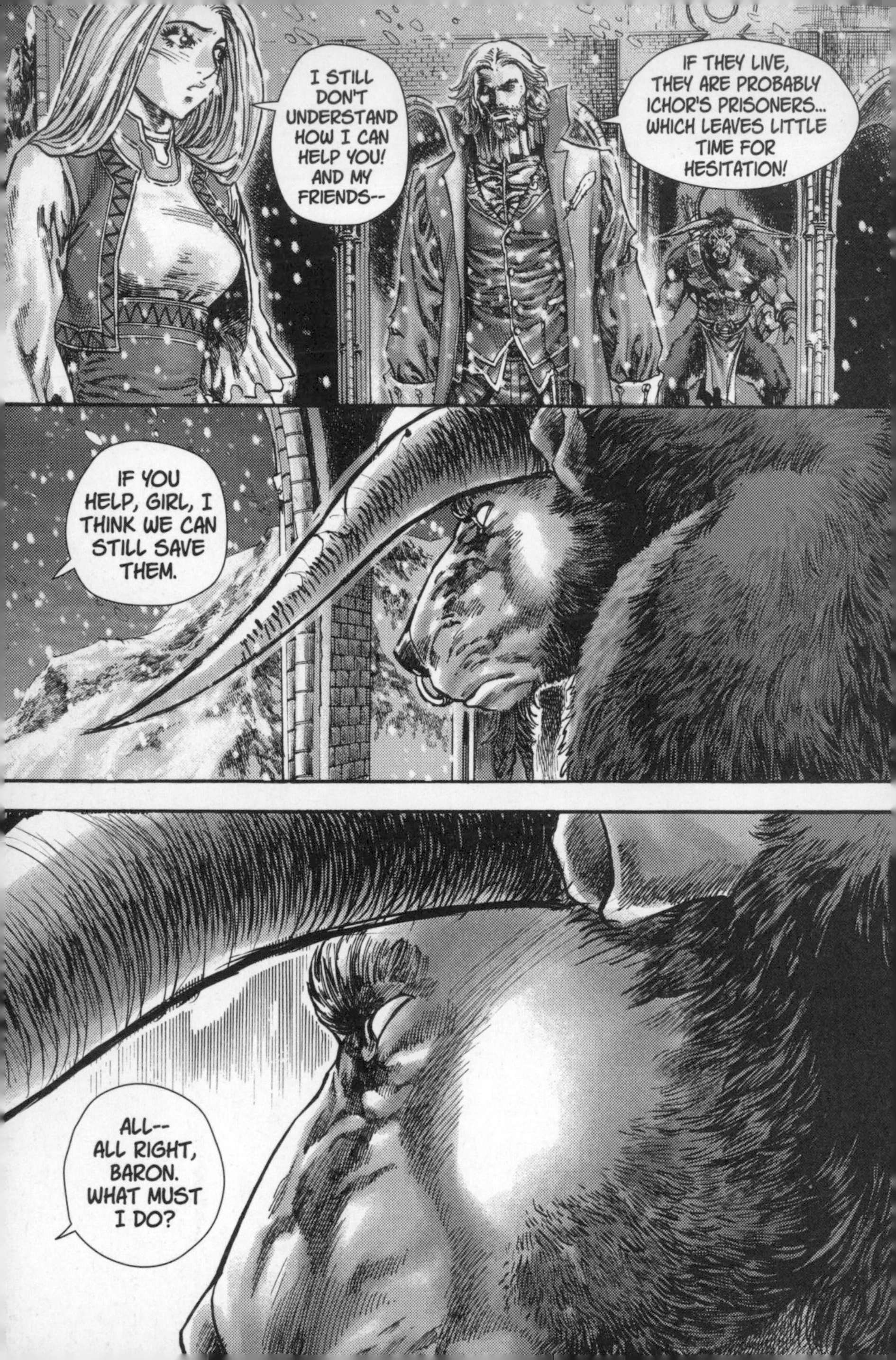
I STILL DON'T UNDERSTAND HOW I CAN HELP YOU! AND MY FRIENDS--
IF THEY LIVE, THEY ARE PROBABLY ICHOR'S PRISONERS... WHICH LEAVES LITTLE TIME FOR HESITATION!
IF YOU HELP, GIRL, I THINK WE CAN STILL SAVE THEM.
ALL-- ALL RIGHT, BARON. WHAT MUST I DO?

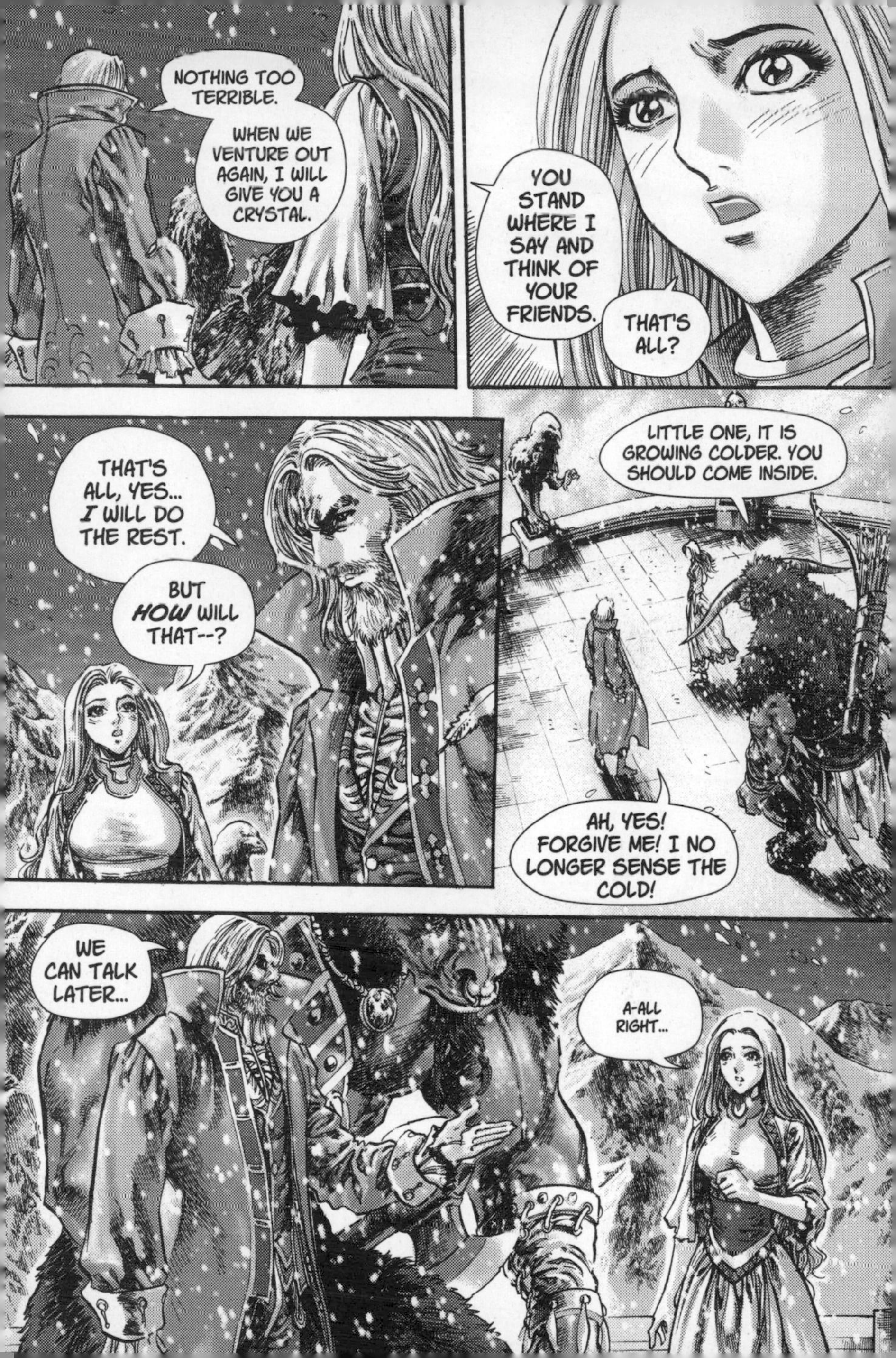
NOTHING TOO TERRIBLE.
WHEN WE VENTURE OUT AGAIN, I WILL GIVE YOU A CRYSTAL.
YOU STAND WHERE I SAY AND THINK OF YOUR FRIENDS.
THAT'S ALL?
THAT'S ALL, YES... *I* WILL DO THE REST.
BUT ***HOW*** WILL THAT--?
LITTLE ONE, IT IS GROWING COLDER. YOU SHOULD COME INSIDE.
AH, YES! FORGIVE ME! I NO LONGER SENSE THE COLD!
WE CAN TALK LATER...
A-ALL RIGHT...

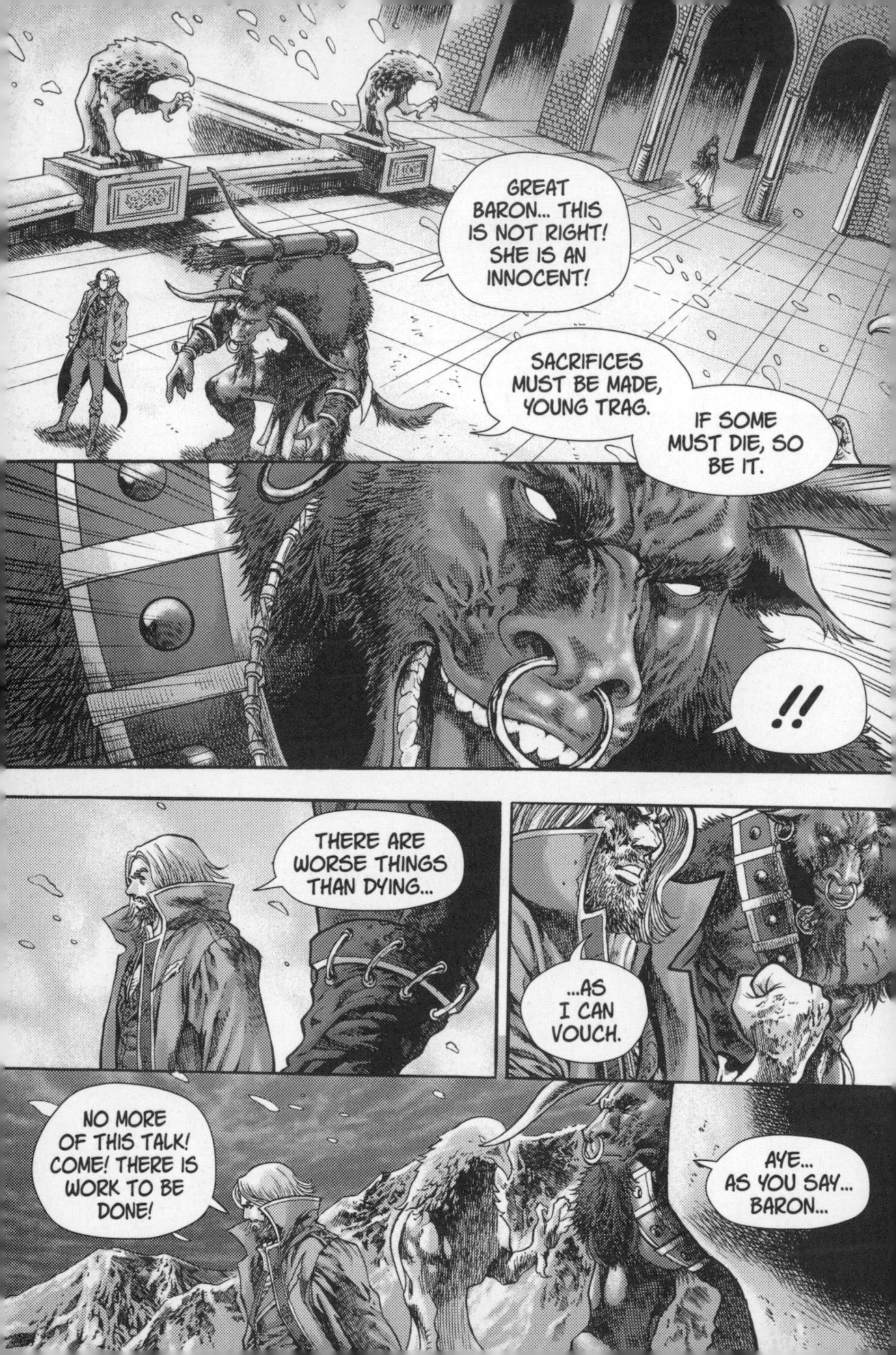
GREAT BARON... THIS IS NOT RIGHT! SHE IS AN INNOCENT!
SACRIFICES MUST BE MADE, YOUNG TRAG.
IF SOME MUST DIE, SO BE IT.
!!
THERE ARE WORSE THINGS THAN DYING...
...AS I CAN VOUCH.
NO MORE OF THIS TALK! COME! THERE IS WORK TO BE DONE!
AYE... AS YOU SAY... BARON...

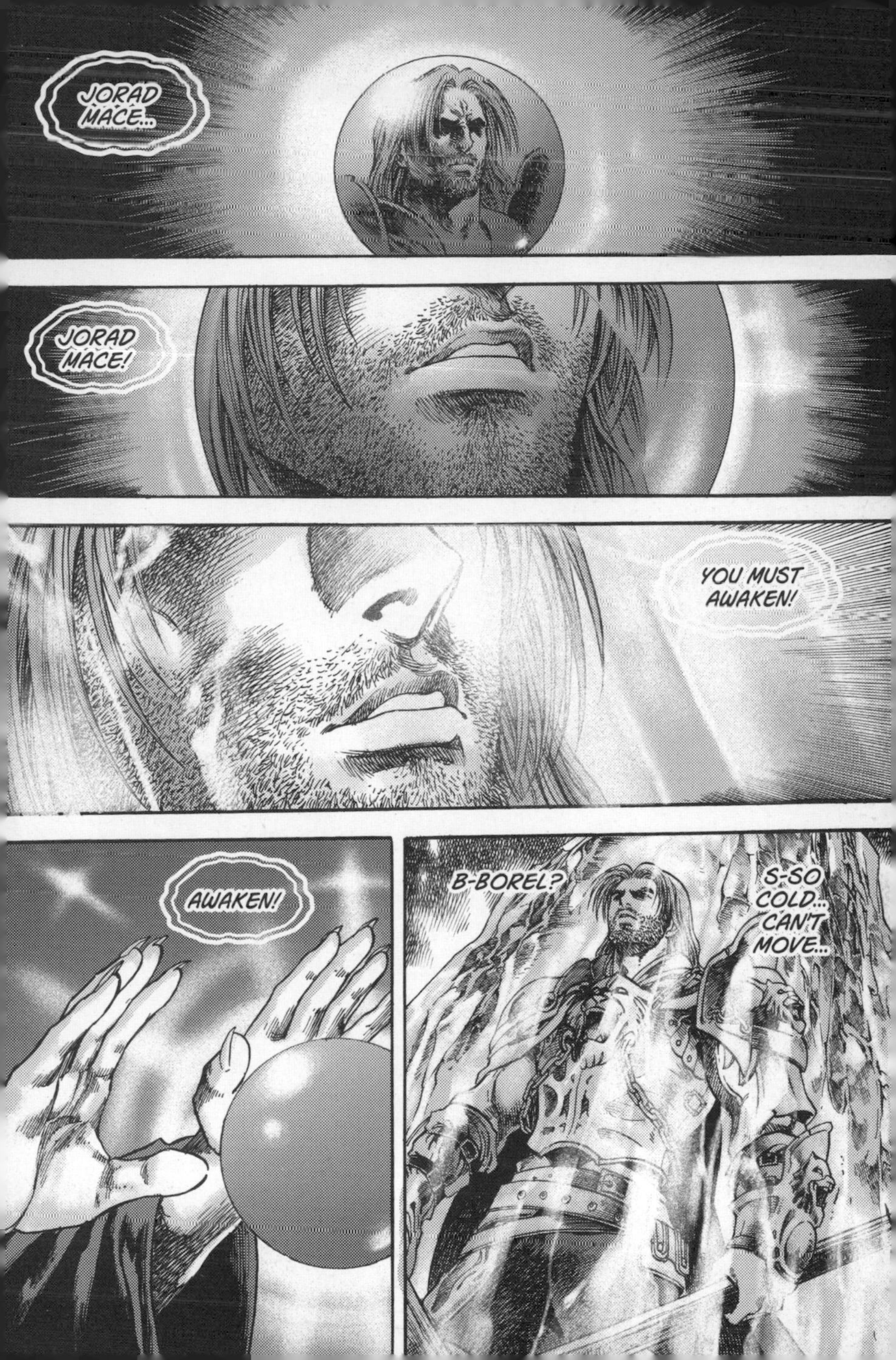
JORAD MACE...
JORAD MACE!
YOU MUST AWAKEN!
AWAKEN!
B-BOREL?
S-SO COLD... CAN'T MOVE...

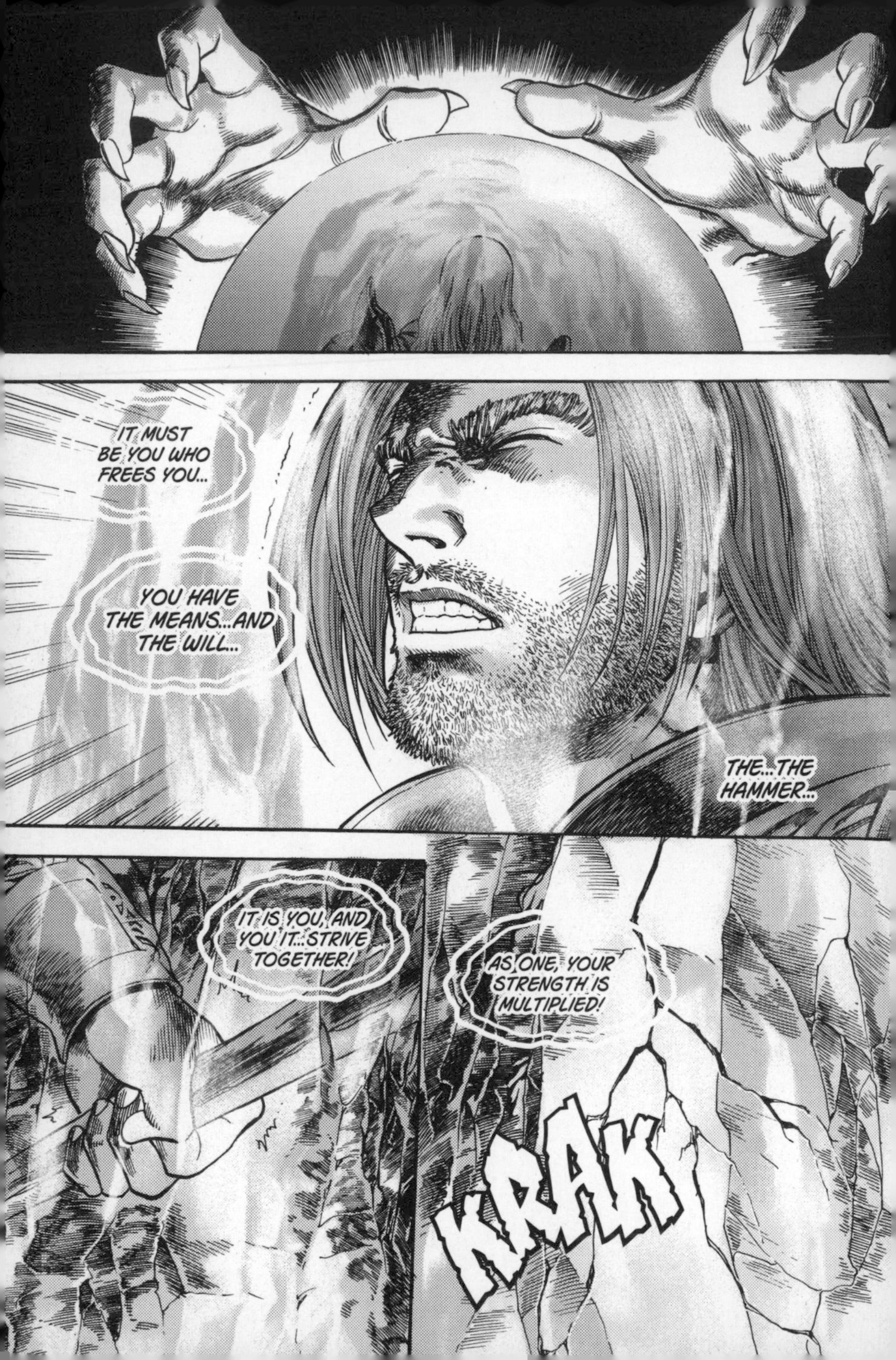
IT MUST BE YOU WHO FREES YOU...
YOU HAVE THE MEANS...AND THE WILL...
THE...THE HAMMER...
IT IS YOU, AND YOU IT...STRIVE TOGETHER!
AS ONE, YOUR STRENGTH IS MULTIPLIED!
KRAK

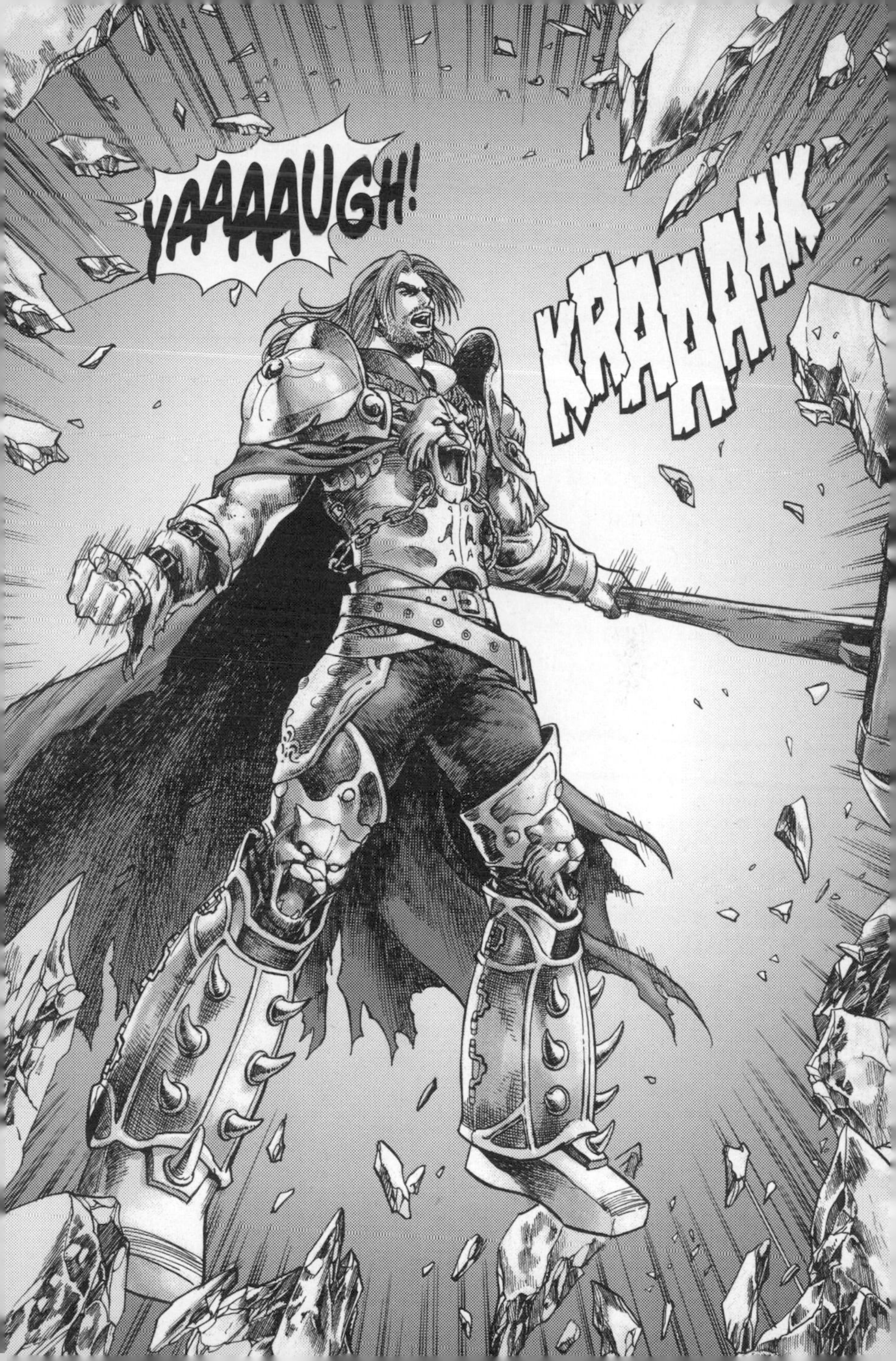
YAAAAUGH!
KRAAAAK

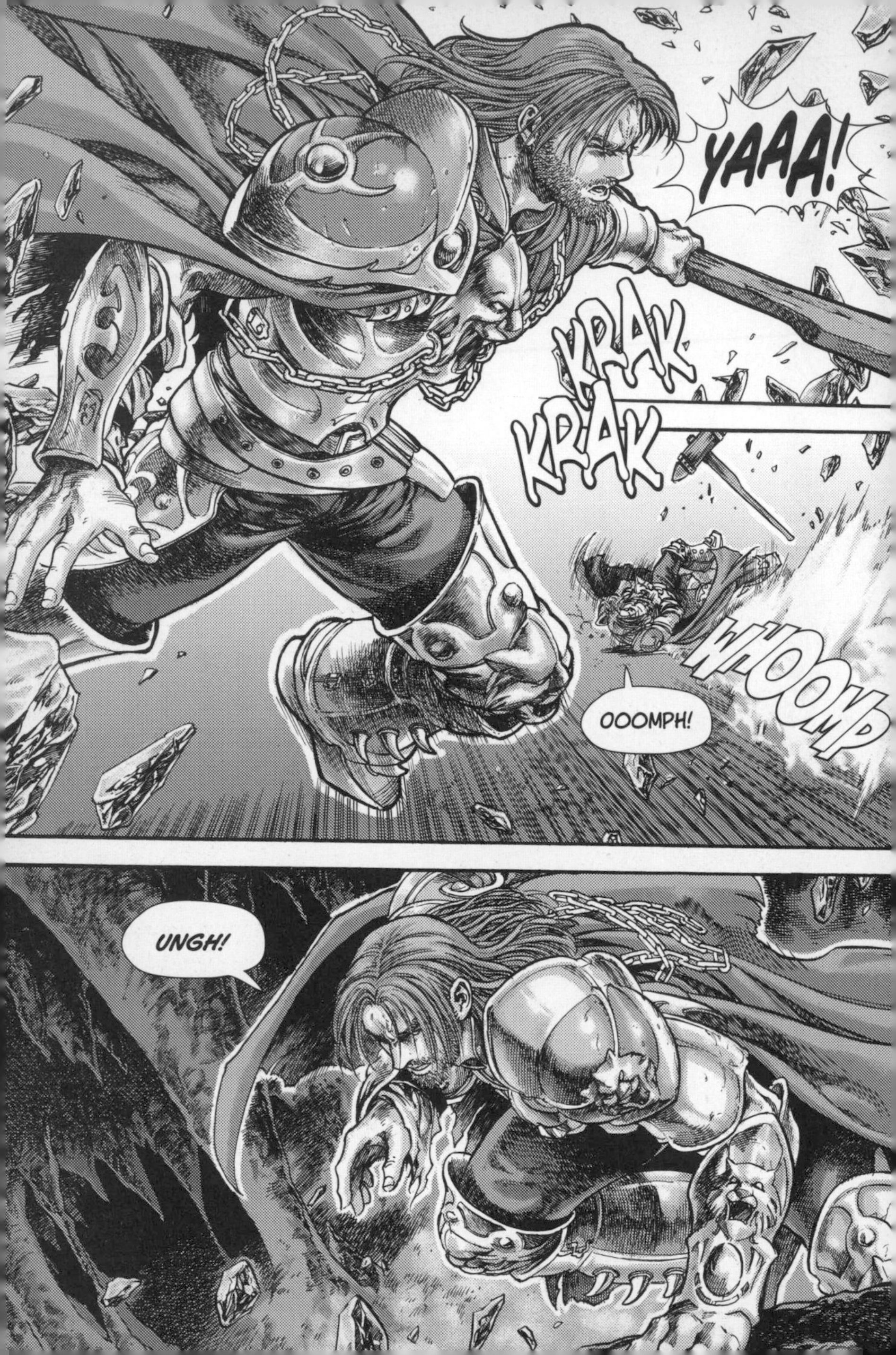
YAAAA!
KRAK
KRAK
WHOOMP
OOOMPH!
UNGH!

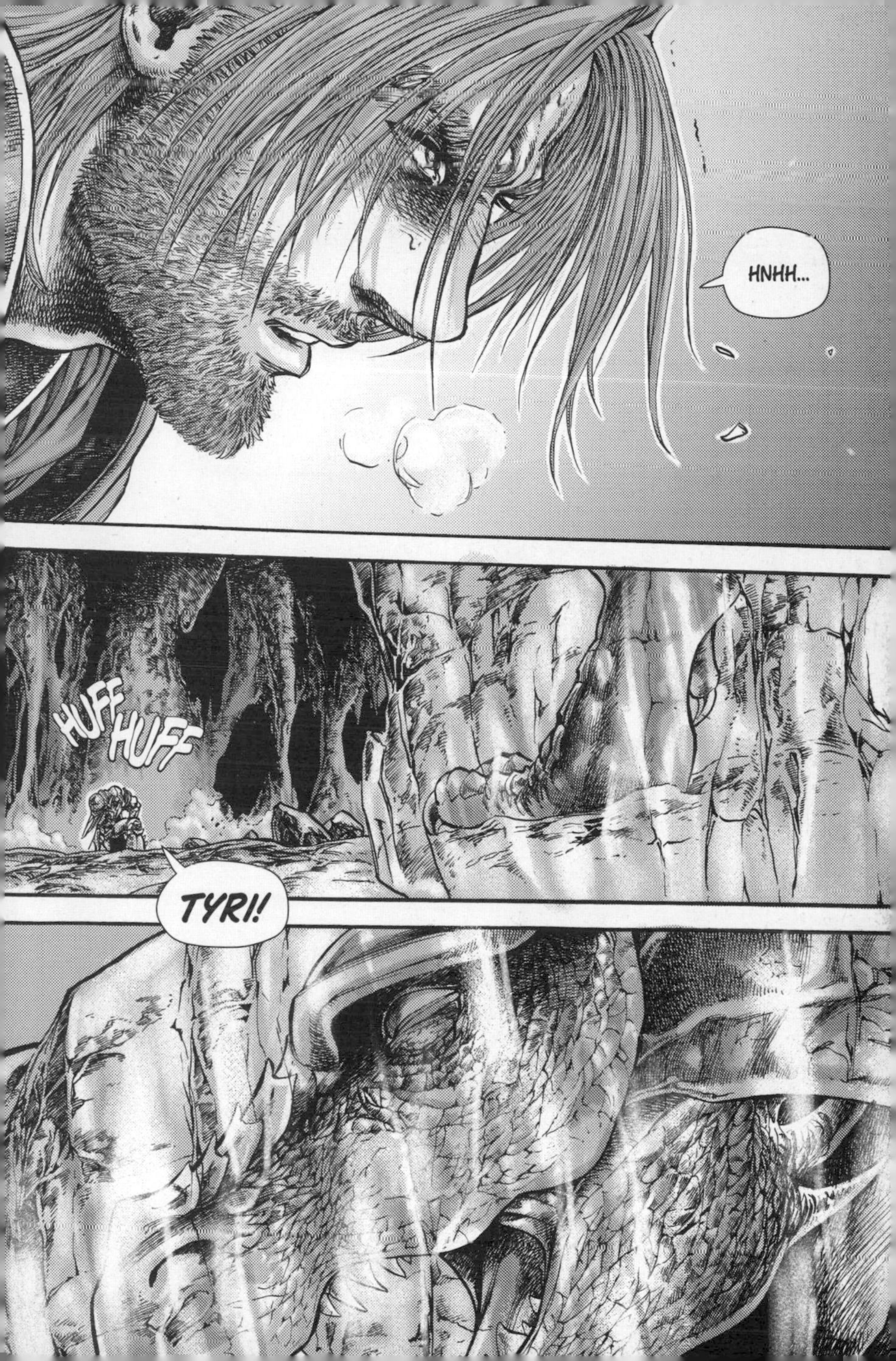
HNHH...
HUFF HUFF
TYRI!

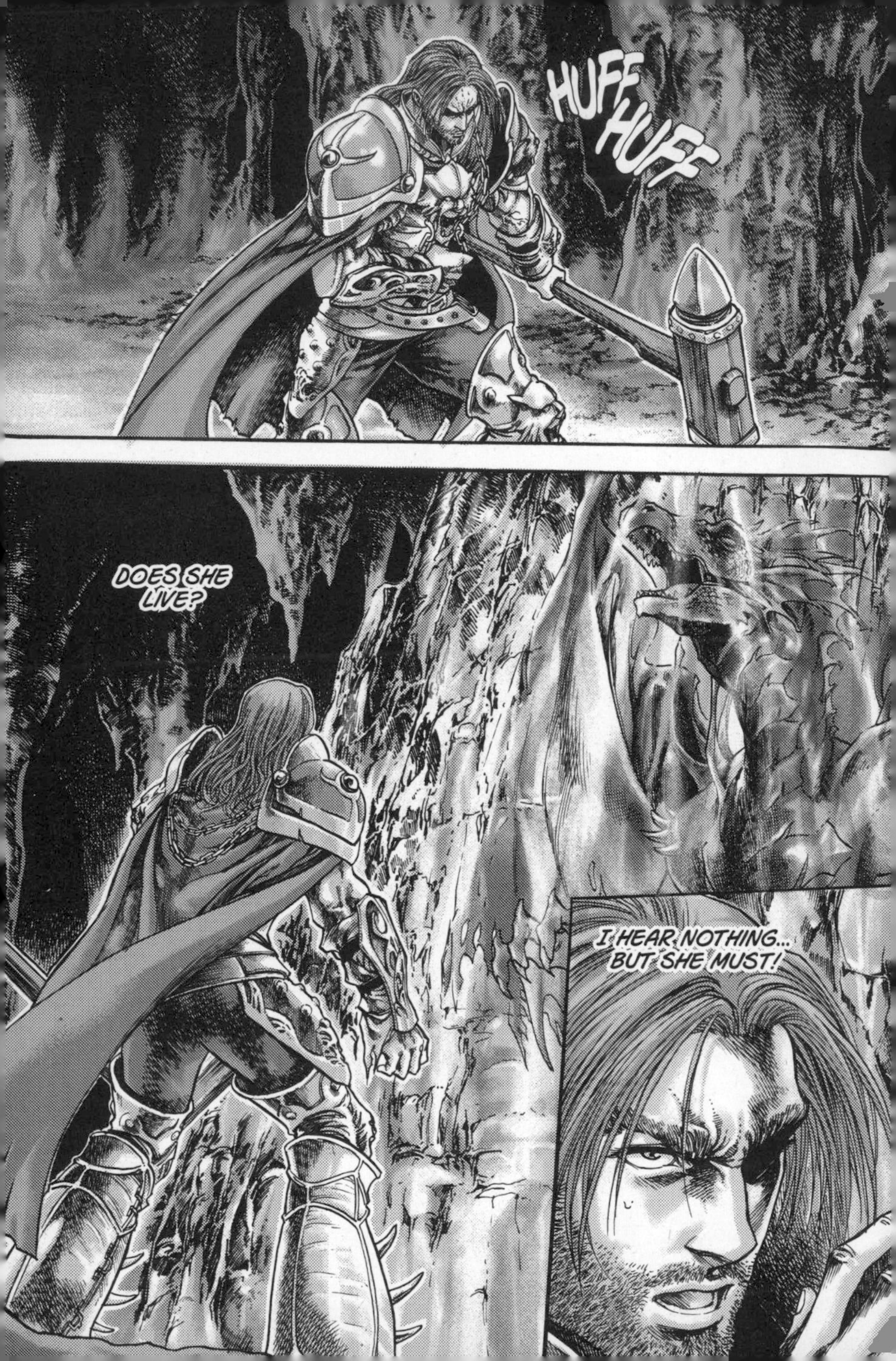
HUFF HUFF
DOES SHE LIVE?
I HEAR NOTHING... BUT SHE MUST!

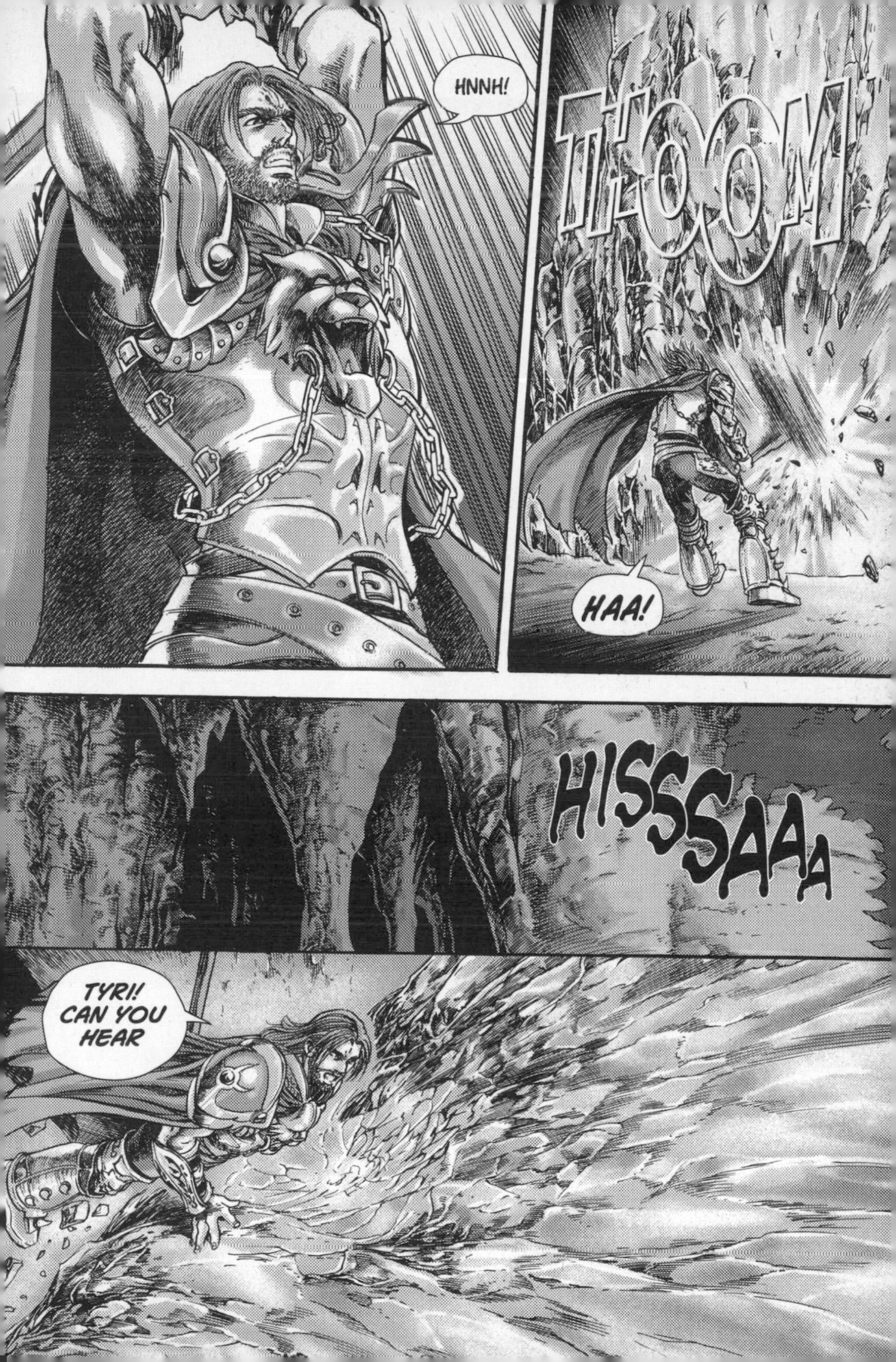
HNNH!
THOOM
HAA!
HISSSAAAA
TYRI! CAN YOU HEAR

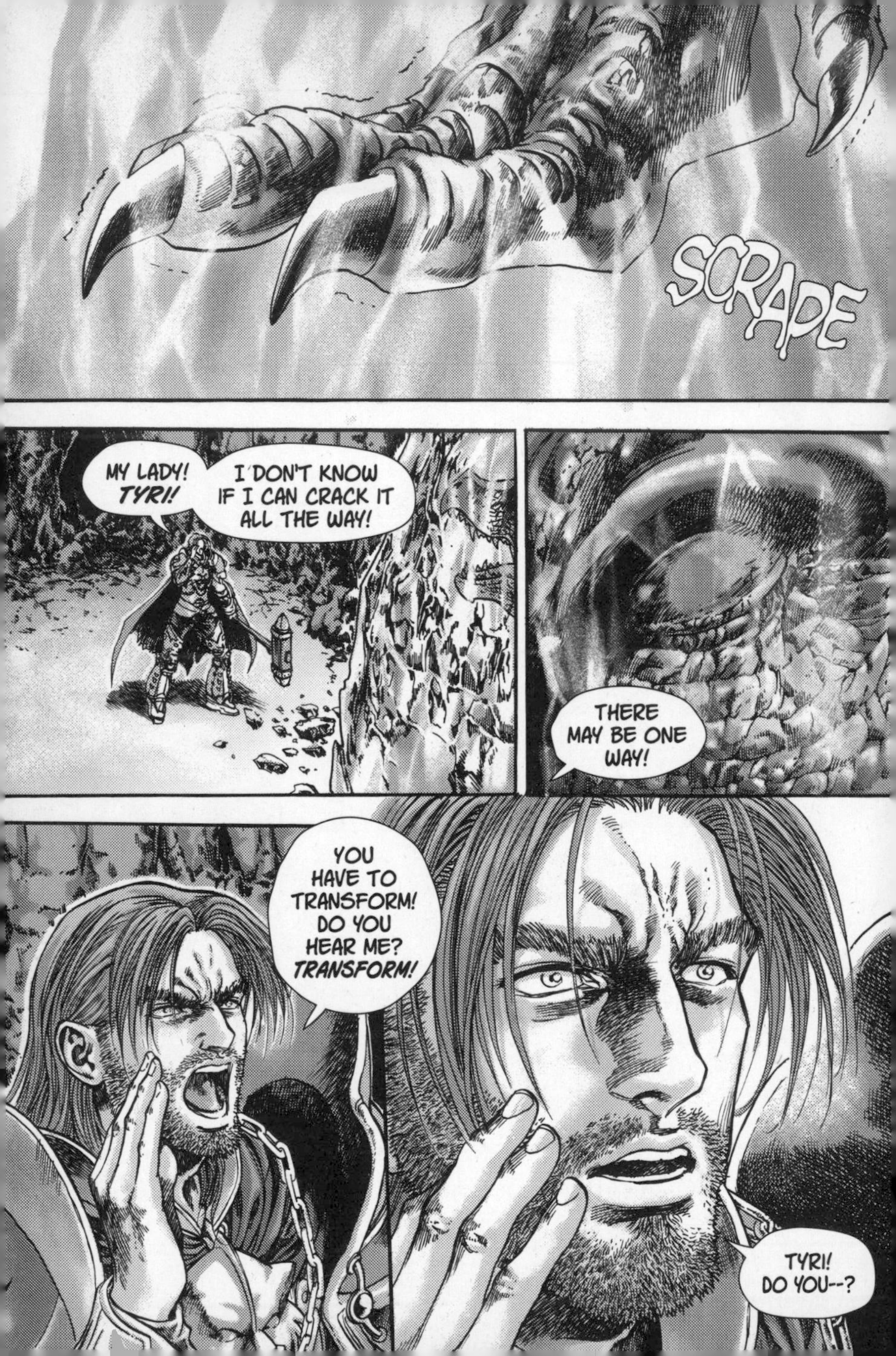
SCRAPE
MY LADY! TYRI!
I DON'T KNOW IF I CAN CRACK IT ALL THE WAY!
THERE MAY BE ONE WAY!
YOU HAVE TO TRANSFORM! DO YOU HEAR ME? TRANSFORM!
TYRI! DO YOU--?

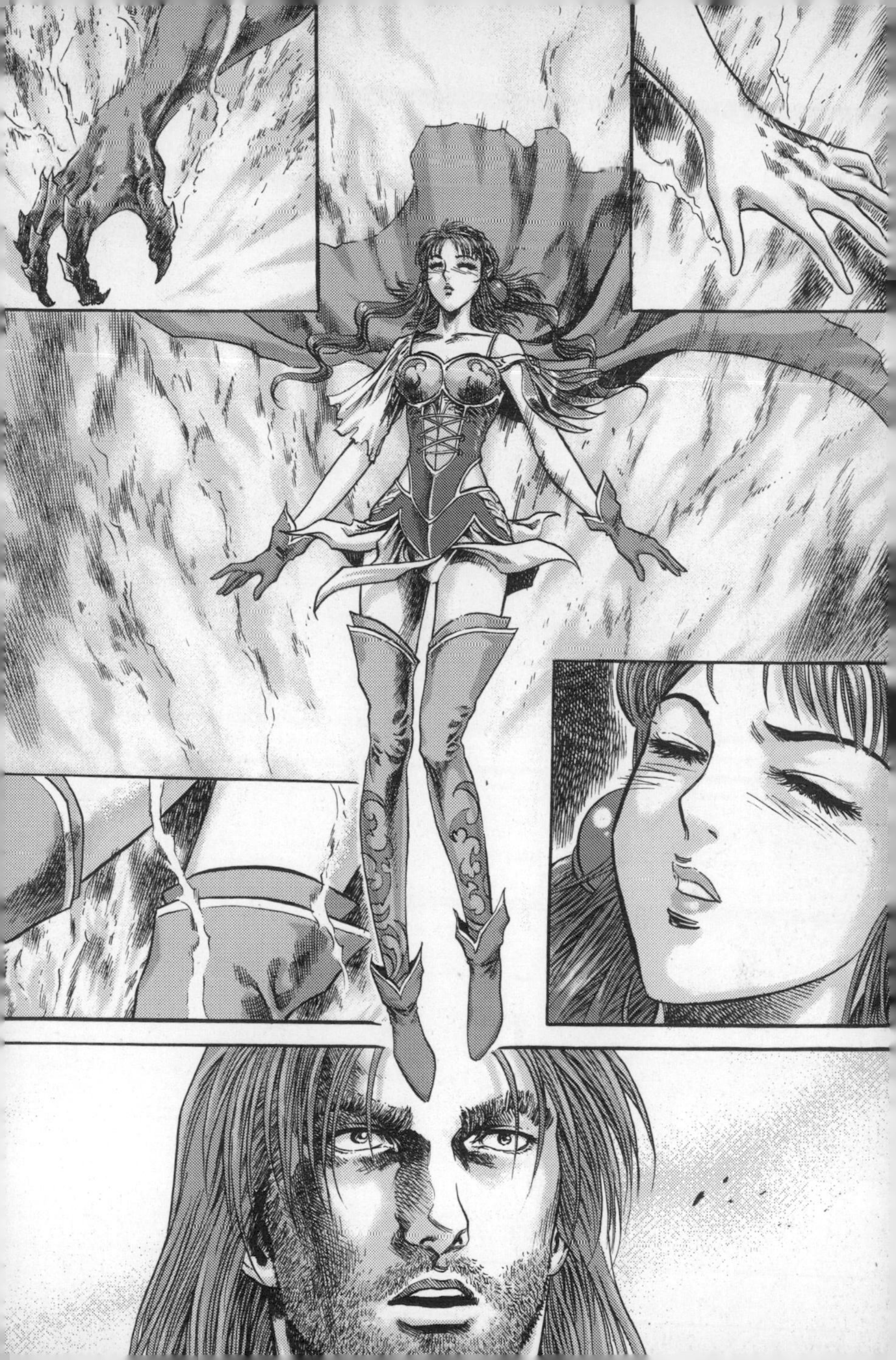

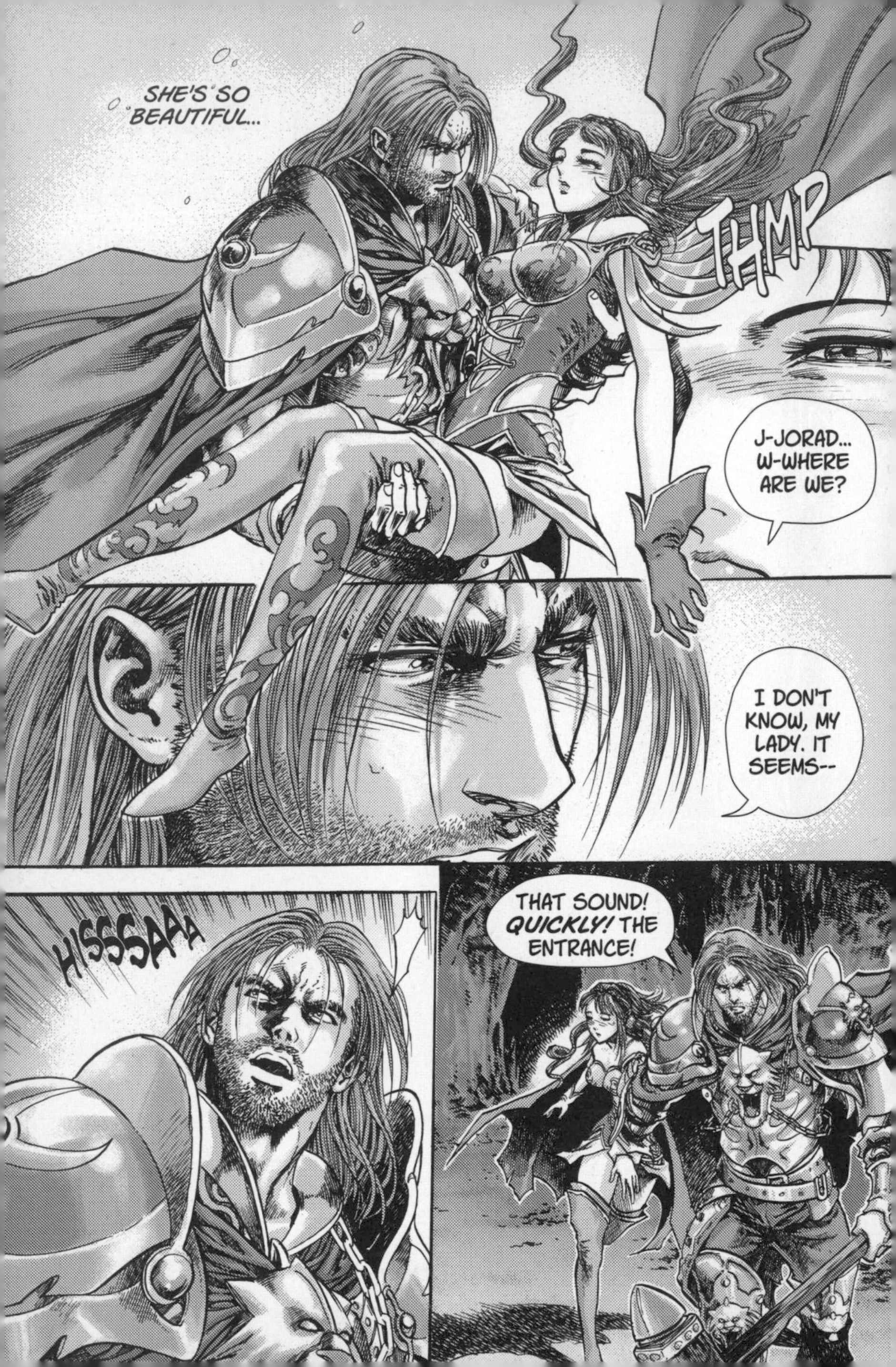
SHE'S SO BEAUTIFUL...
THMP
J-JORAD... W-WHERE ARE WE?
I DON'T KNOW, MY LADY. IT SEEMS--
HISSSAAA
THAT SOUND! *QUICKLY!* THE ENTRANCE!

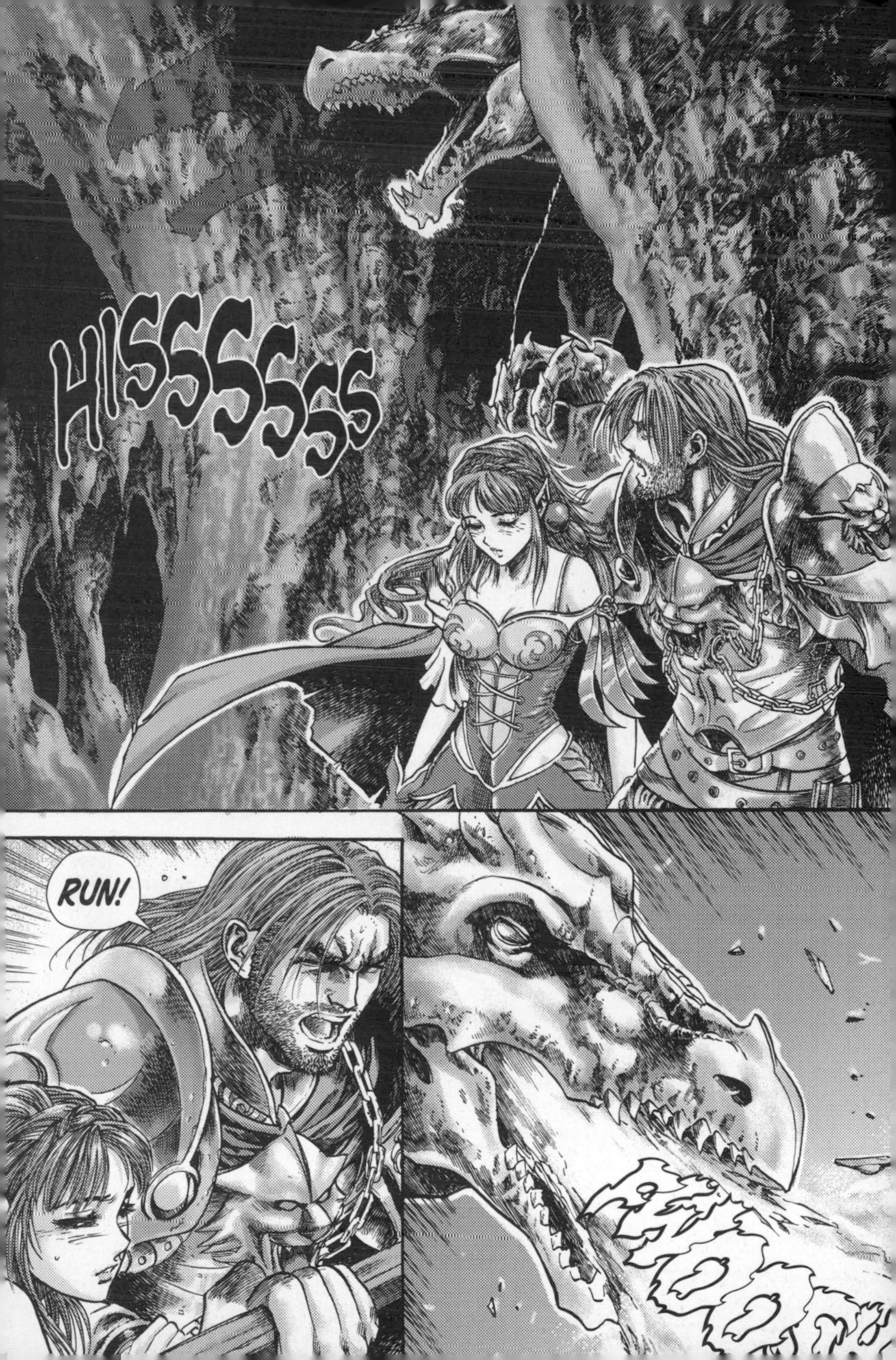
HISSSSSSS
RUN!

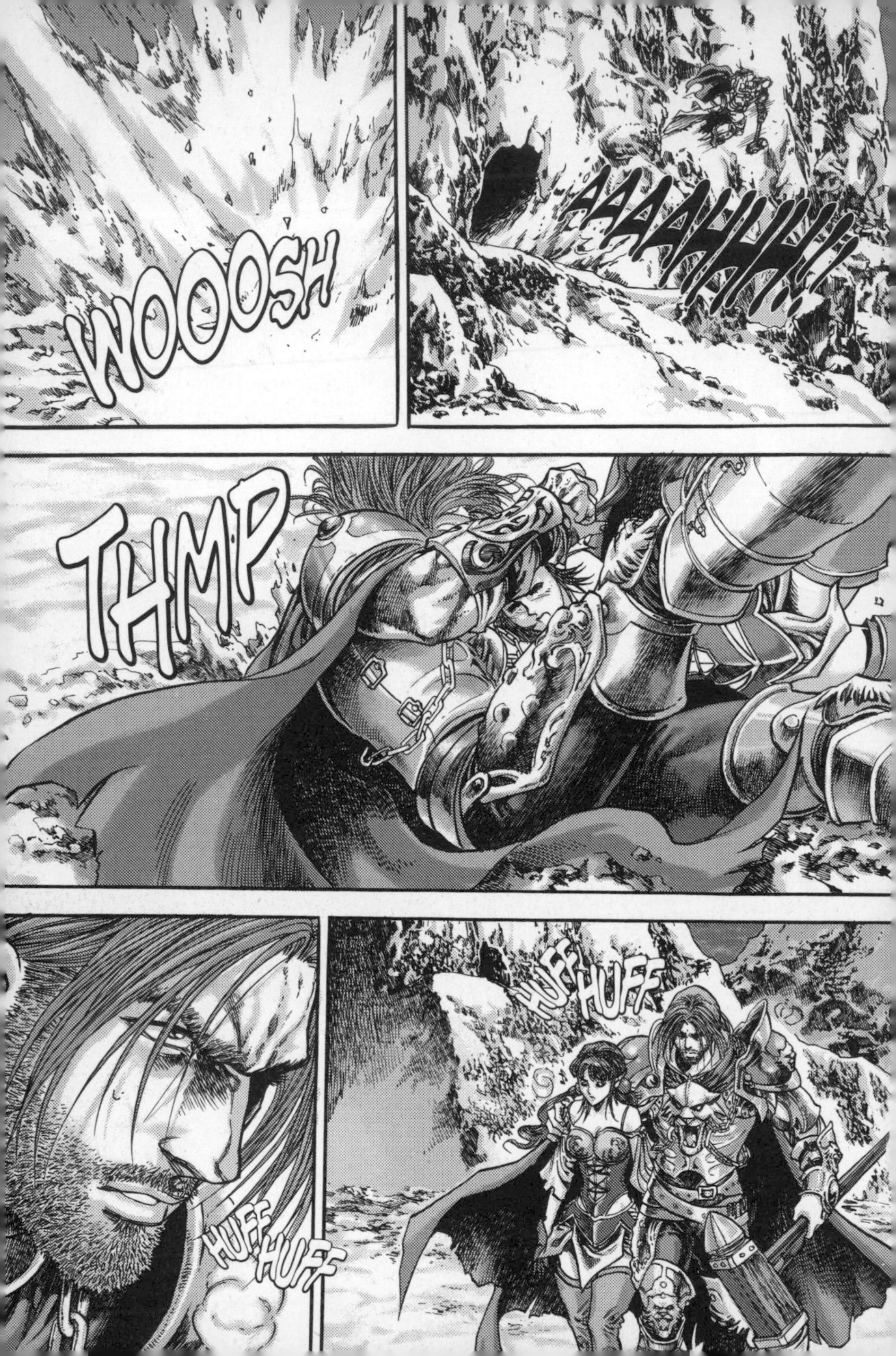
WOOOSH
AAAAHHH!!!
THMP
HUFF HUFF
HUFF HUFF

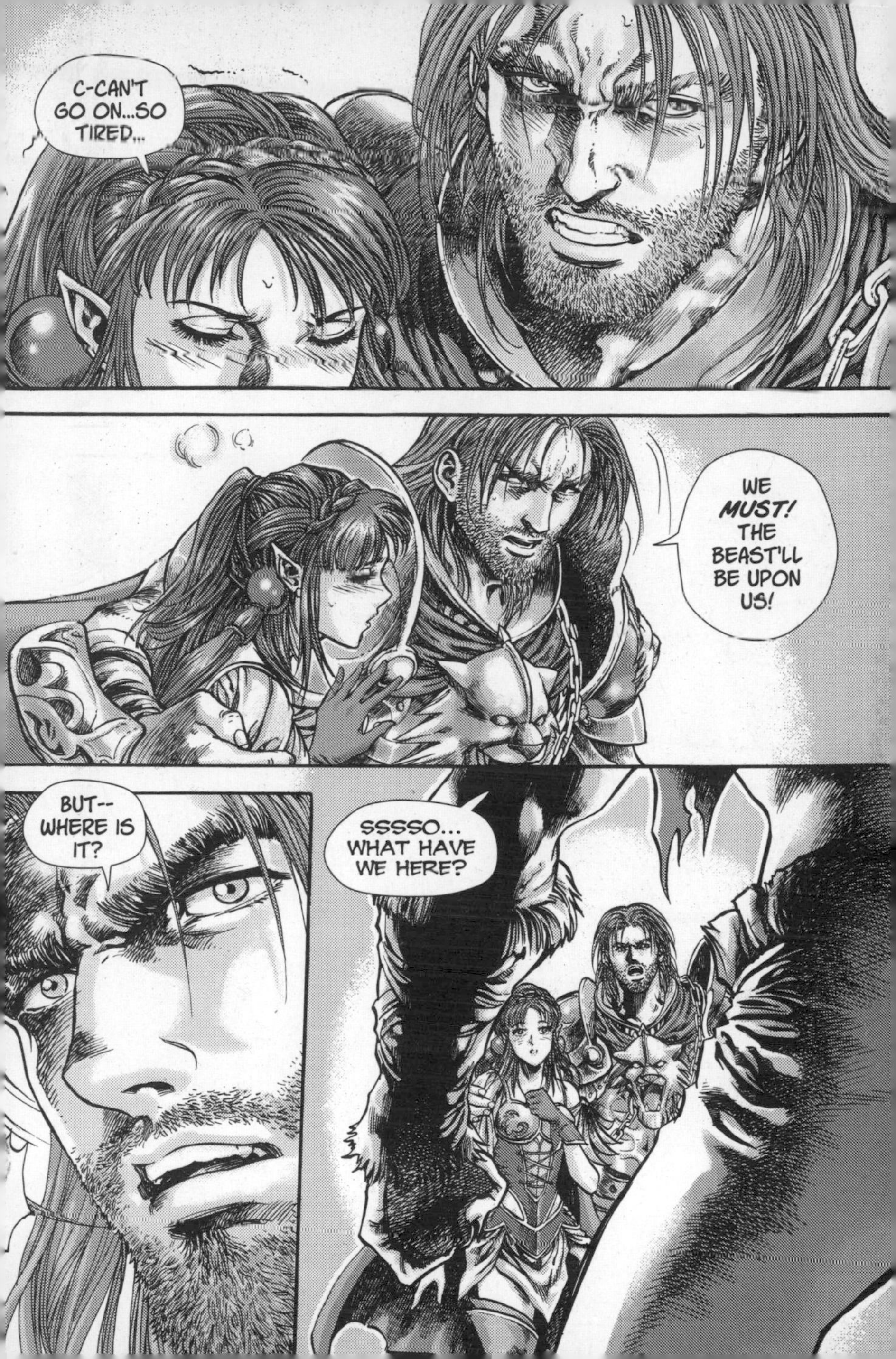
C-CAN'T GO ON...SO TIRED...
WE *MUST!* THE BEAST'LL BE UPON US!
BUT-- WHERE IS IT?
SSSSO... WHAT HAVE WE HERE?

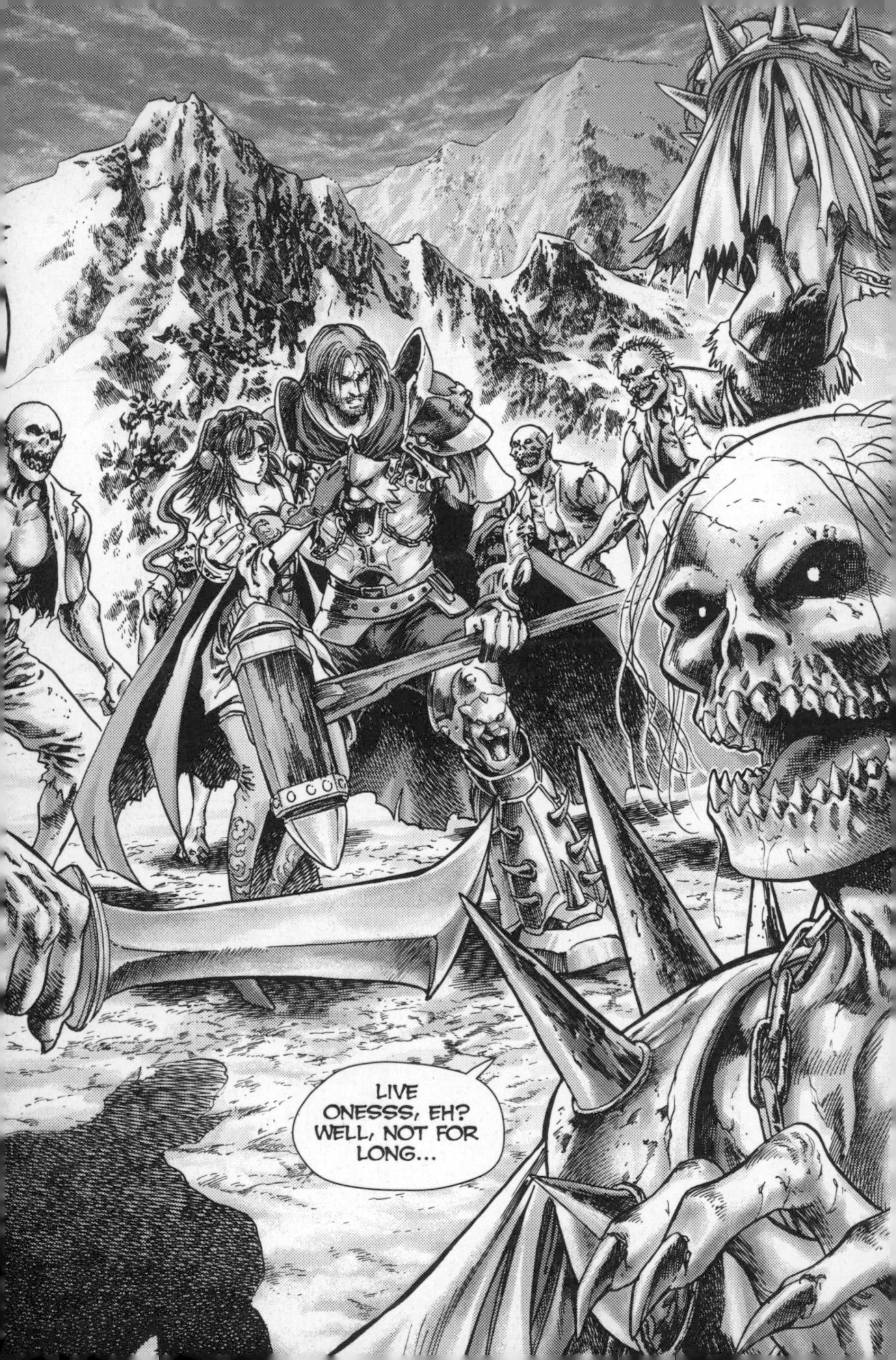
LIVE ONESSS, EH? WELL, NOT FOR LONG...

CHAPTER FOUR The Dwellers Beneath

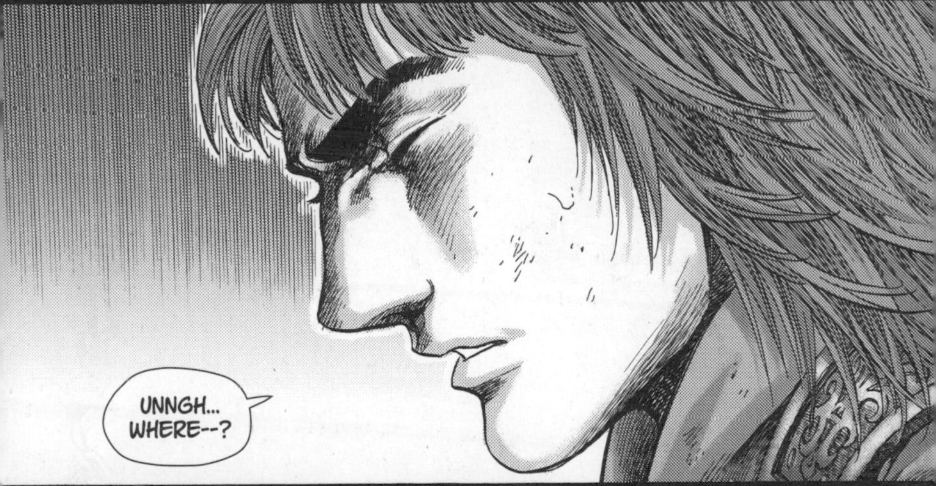
UNNGH... WHERE--?

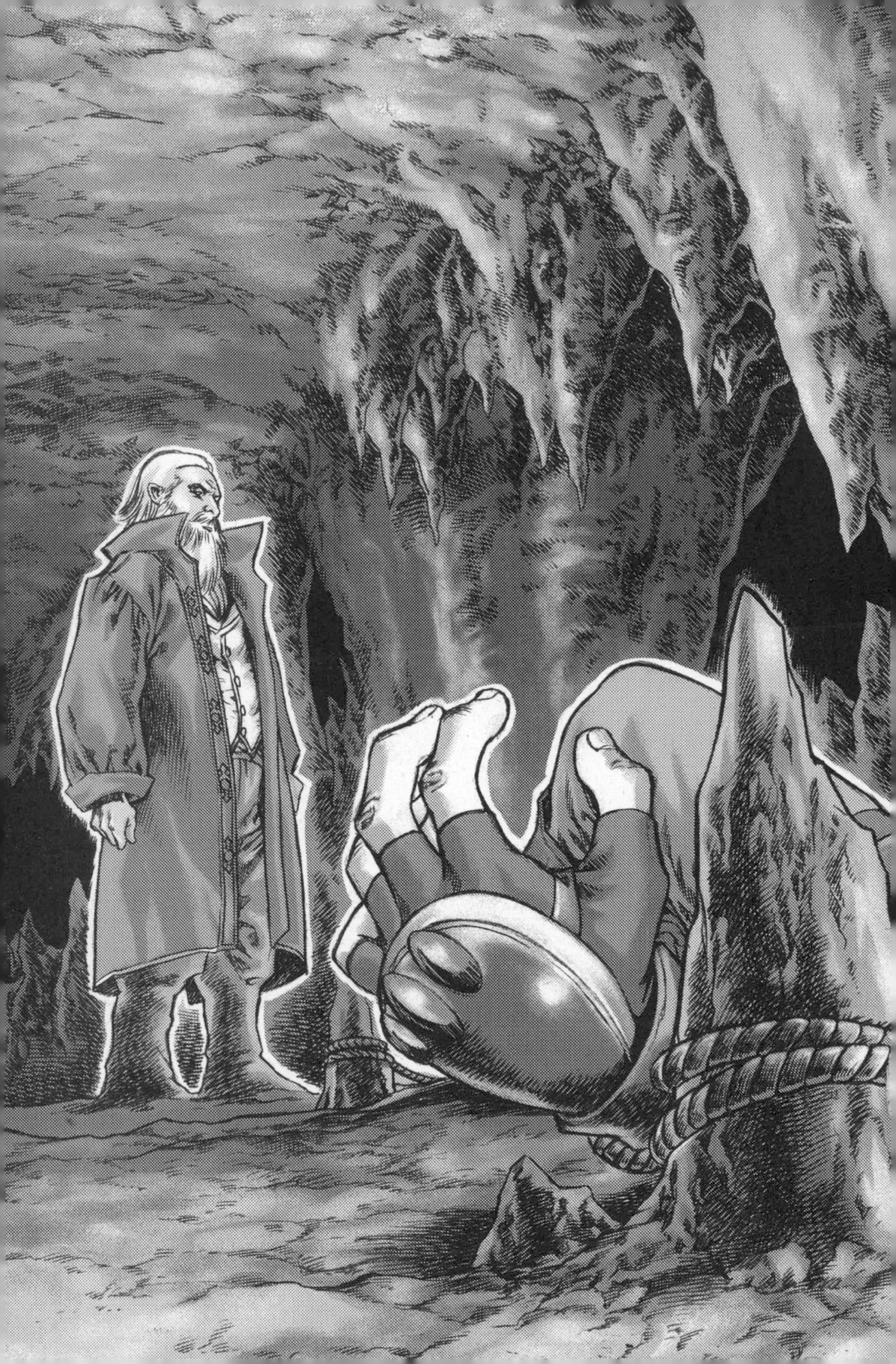

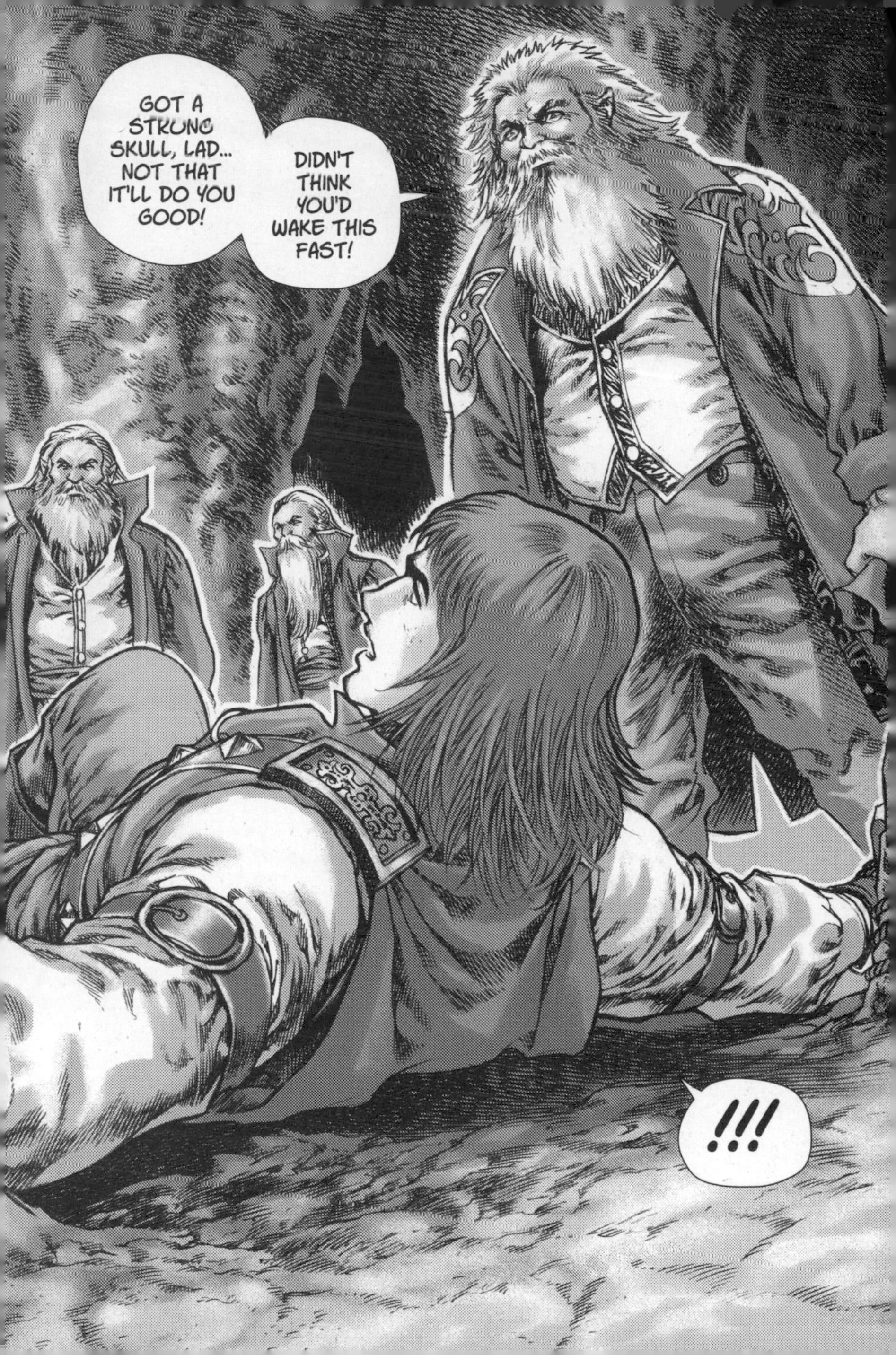
GOT A STRONG SKULL, LAD... NOT THAT IT'LL DO YOU GOOD!
DIDN'T THINK YOU'D WAKE THIS FAST!
!!!

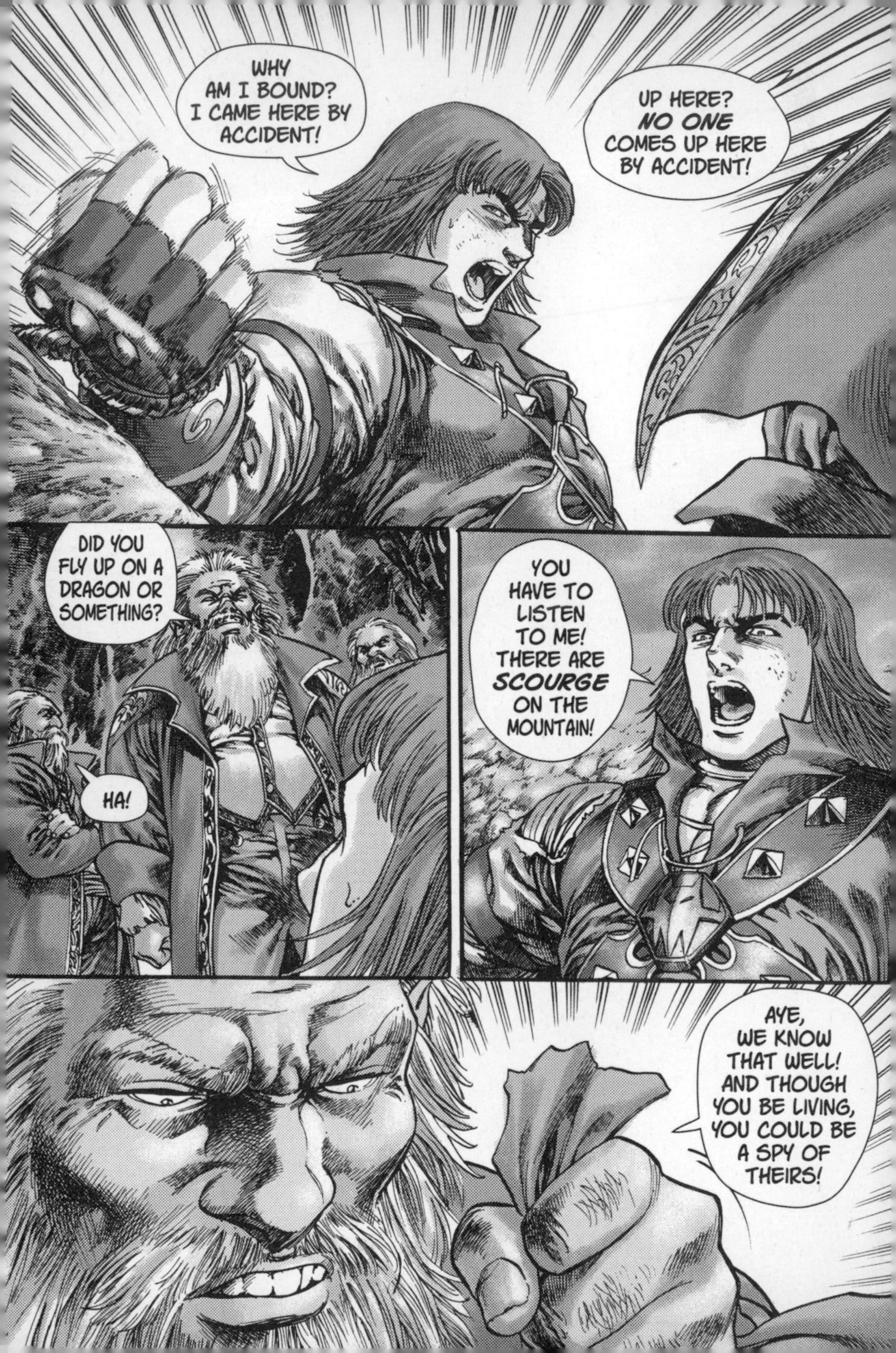
WHY AM I BOUND? I CAME HERE BY ACCIDENT!
UP HERE? *NO ONE* COMES UP HERE BY ACCIDENT!
DID YOU FLY UP ON A DRAGON OR SOMETHING?
HA!
YOU HAVE TO LISTEN TO ME! THERE ARE *SCOURGE* ON THE MOUNTAIN!
AYE, WE KNOW THAT WELL! AND THOUGH YOU BE LIVING, YOU COULD BE A SPY OF THEIRS!

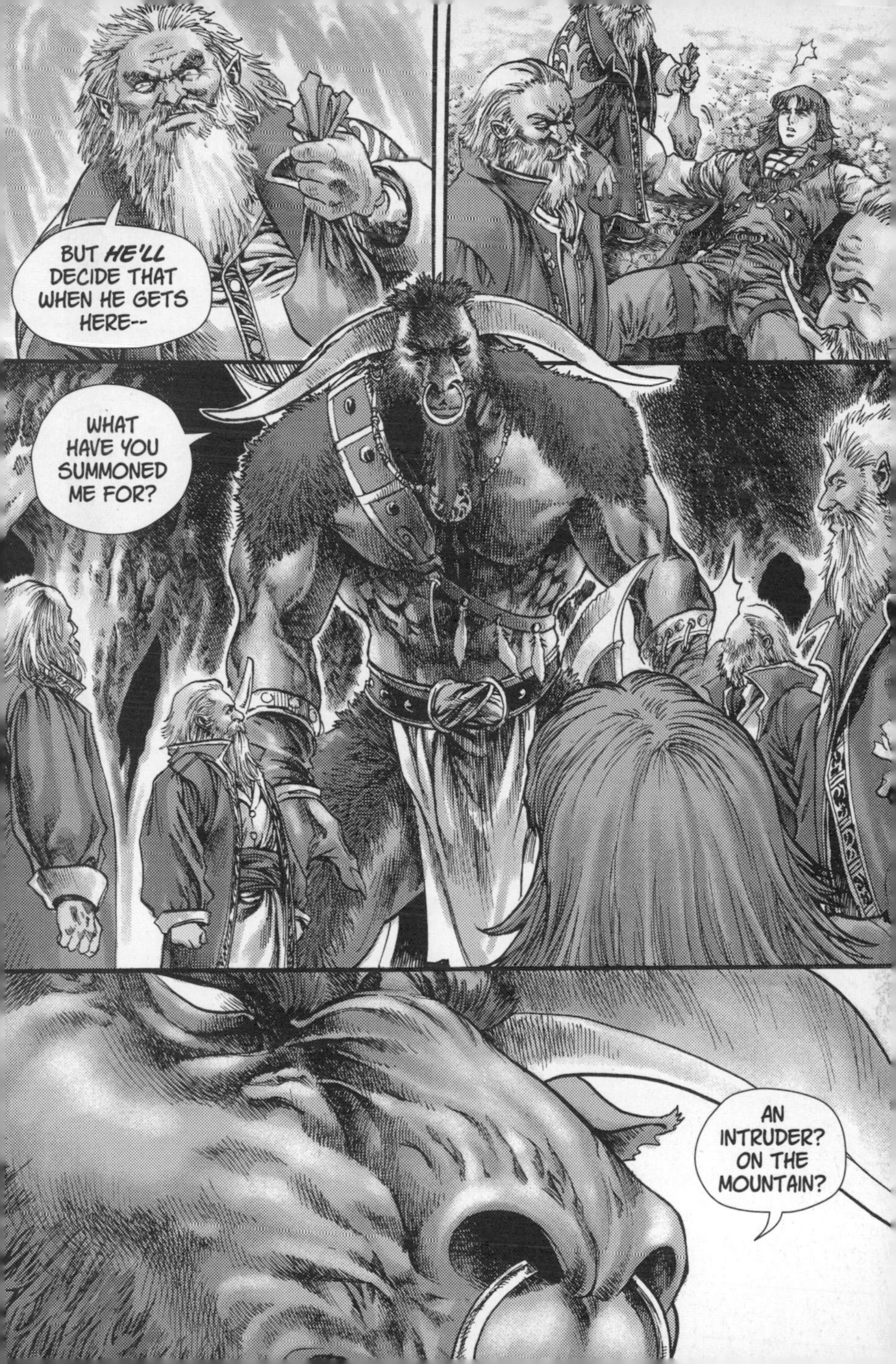
BUT ***HE'LL*** DECIDE THAT WHEN HE GETS HERE--
WHAT HAVE YOU SUMMONED ME FOR?
AN INTRUDER? ON THE MOUNTAIN?

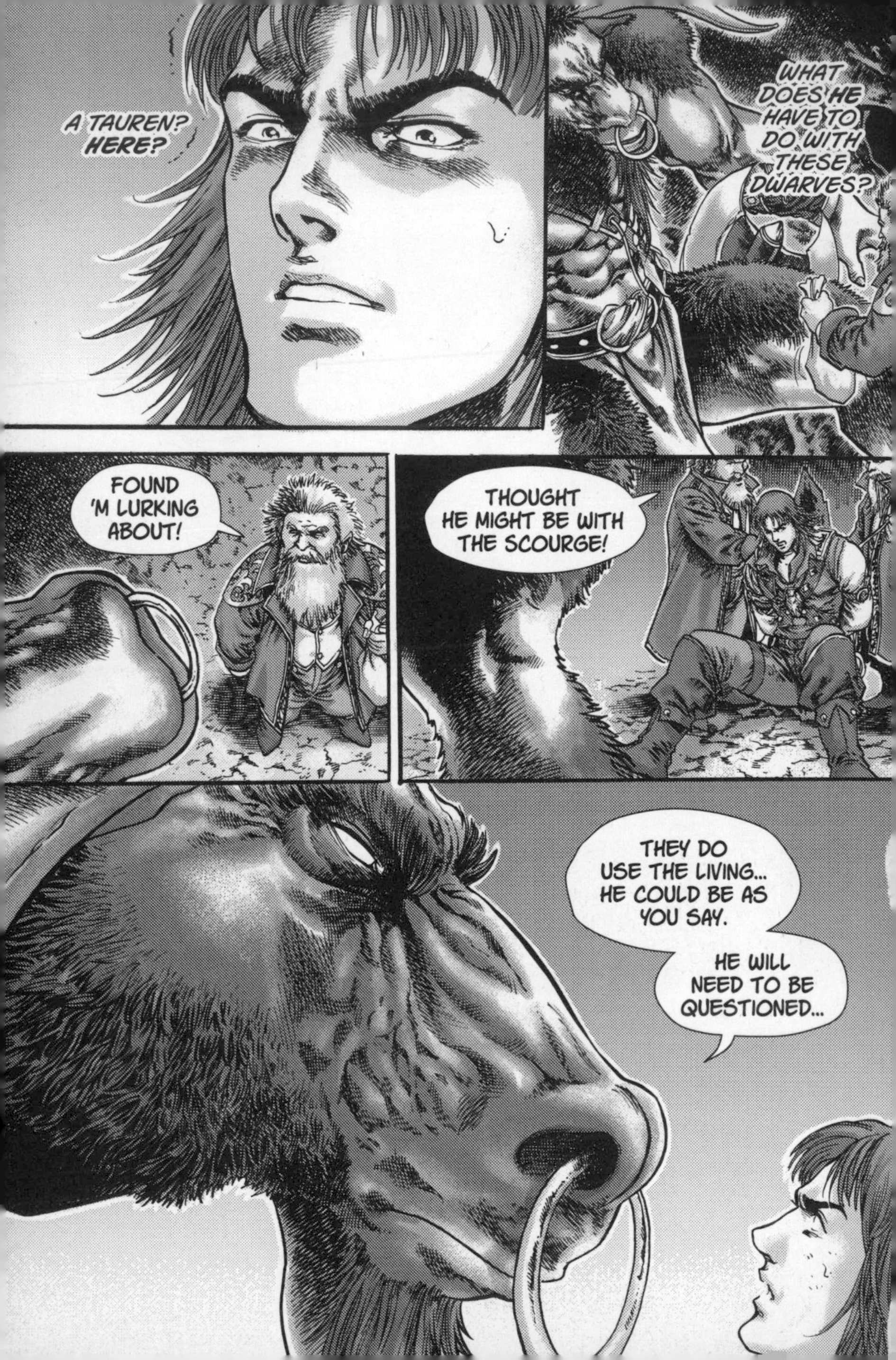
A TAUREN? HERE?
WHAT DOES HE HAVE TO DO WITH THESE DWARVES?
FOUND 'M LURKING ABOUT!
THOUGHT HE MIGHT BE WITH THE SCOURGE!
THEY DO USE THE LIVING... HE COULD BE AS YOU SAY.
HE WILL NEED TO BE QUESTIONED...

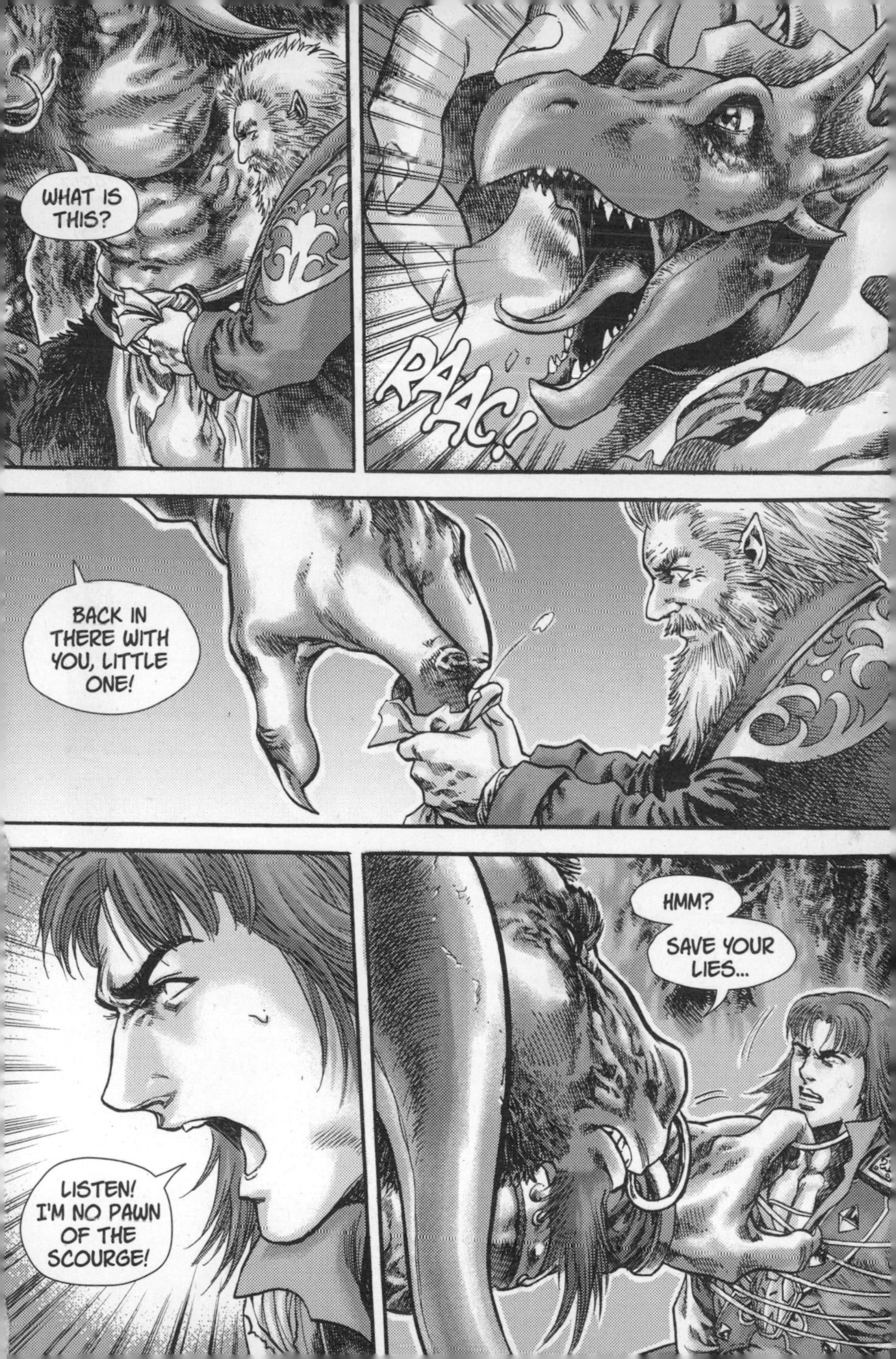
WHAT IS THIS?
RAAC!!
BACK IN THERE WITH YOU, LITTLE ONE!
LISTEN! I'M NO PAWN OF THE SCOURGE!
HMM?
SAVE YOUR LIES...

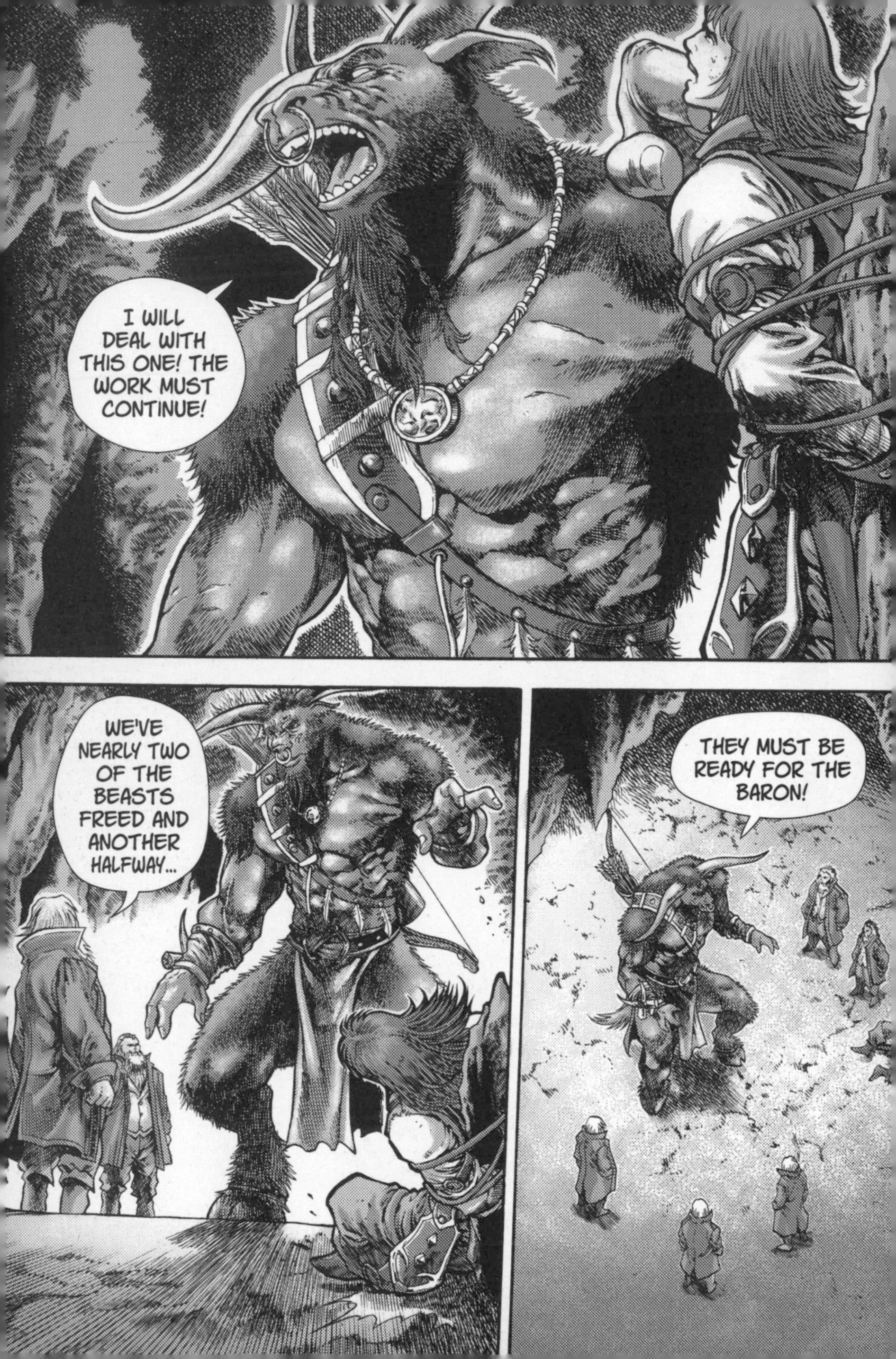
I WILL DEAL WITH THIS ONE! THE WORK MUST CONTINUE!
WE'VE NEARLY TWO OF THE BEASTS FREED AND ANOTHER HALFWAY...
THEY MUST BE READY FOR THE BARON!

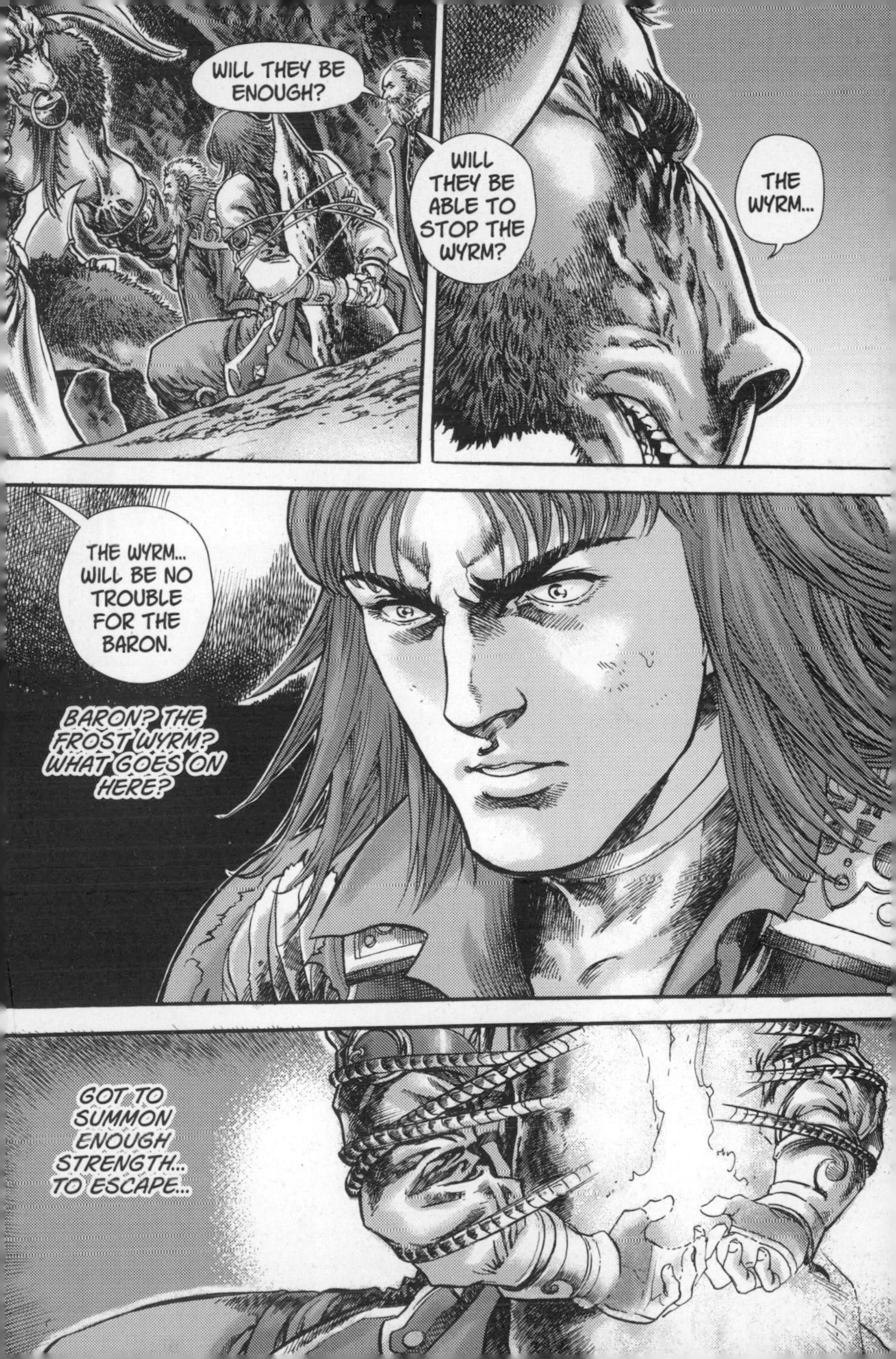
WILL THEY BE ENOUGH?
WILL THEY BE ABLE TO STOP THE WYRM?
THE WYRM...
THE WYRM... WILL BE NO TROUBLE FOR THE BARON.
BARON? THE FROST WYRM? WHAT GOES ON HERE?
GOT TO SUMMON ENOUGH STRENGTH... TO ESCAPE...

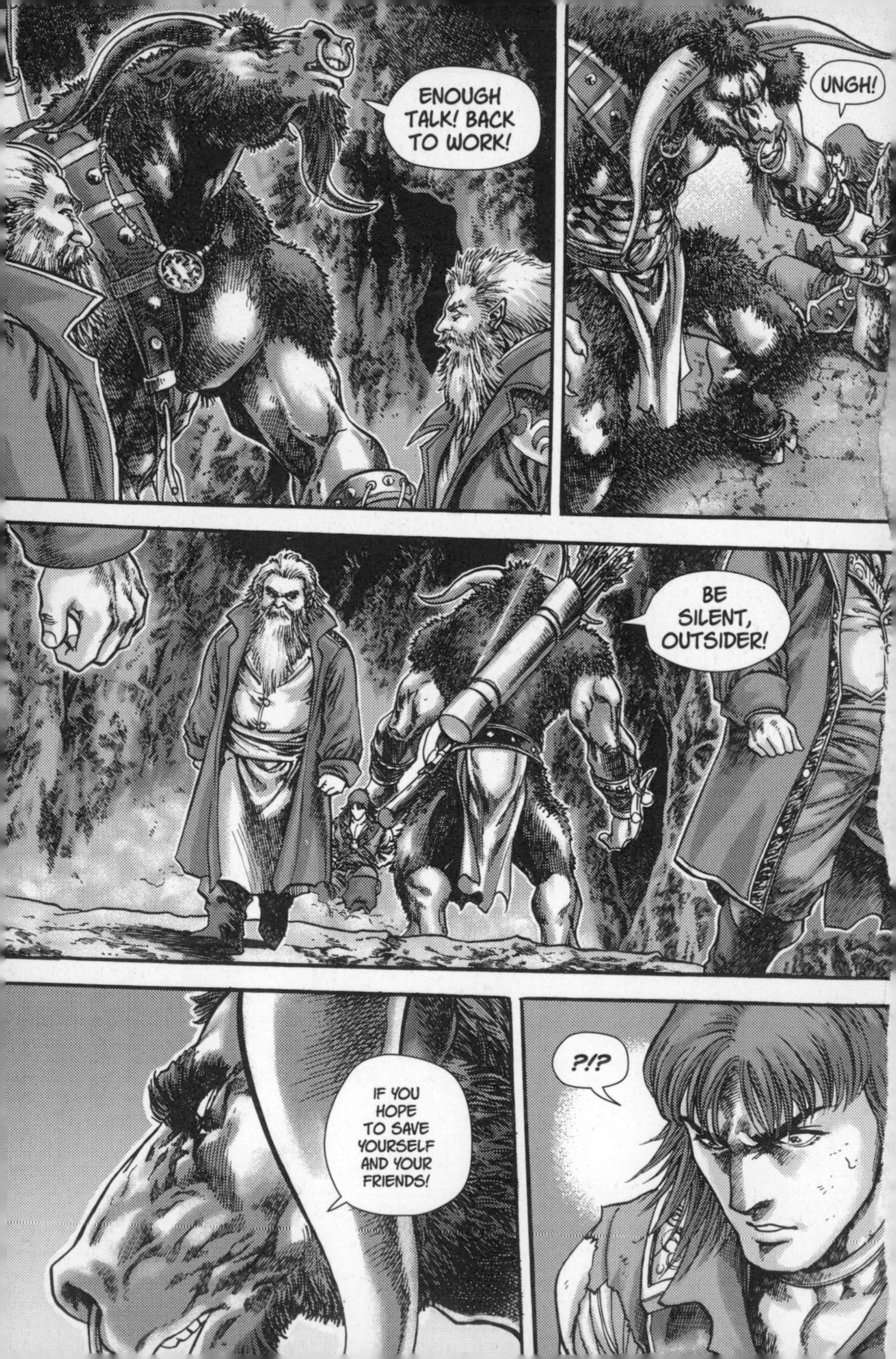
ENOUGH TALK! BACK TO WORK!
UNGH!
BE SILENT, OUTSIDER!
IF YOU HOPE TO SAVE YOURSELF AND YOUR FRIENDS!
?!?

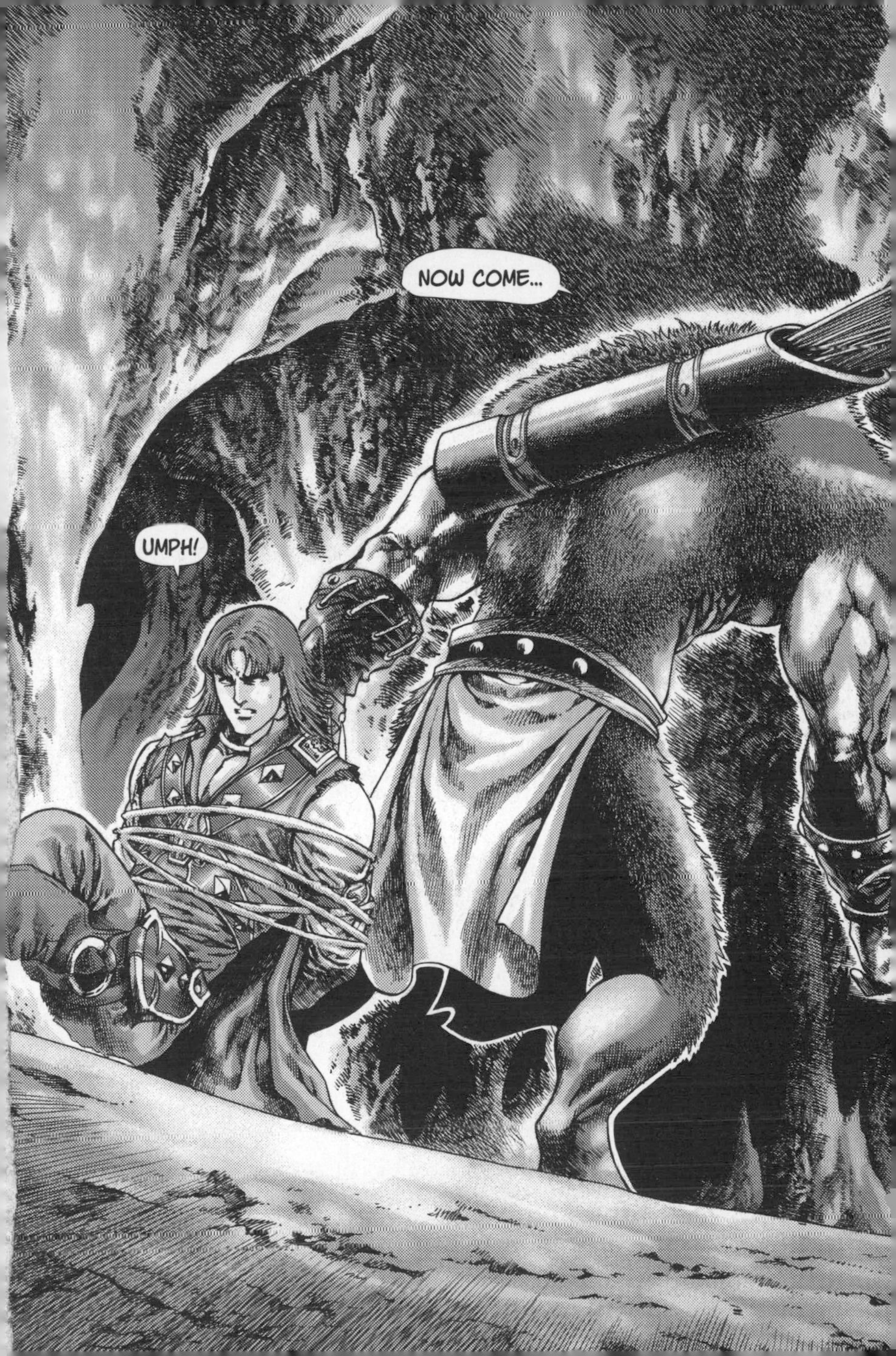
NOW COME...
UMPH!

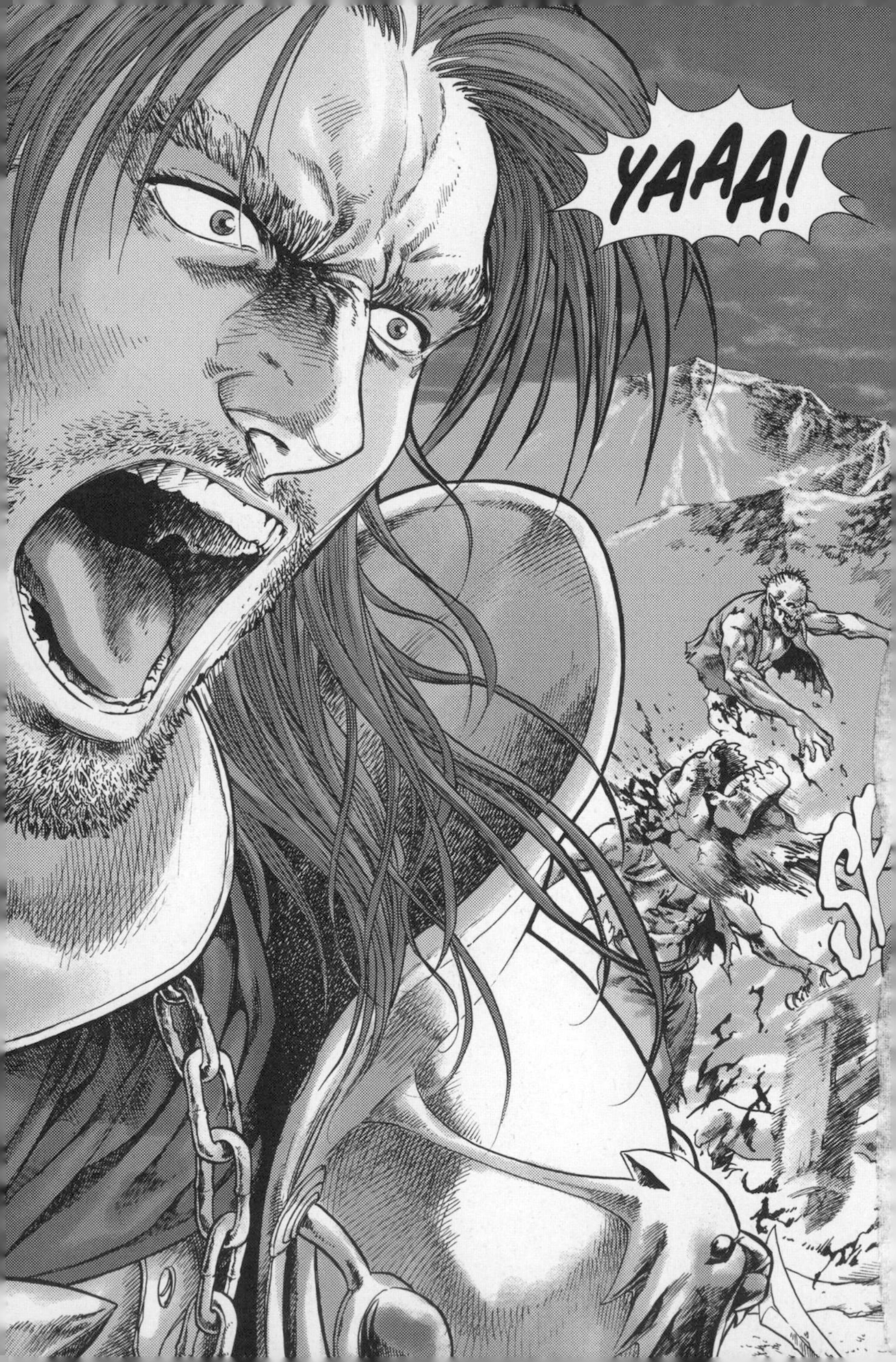
YAAA!

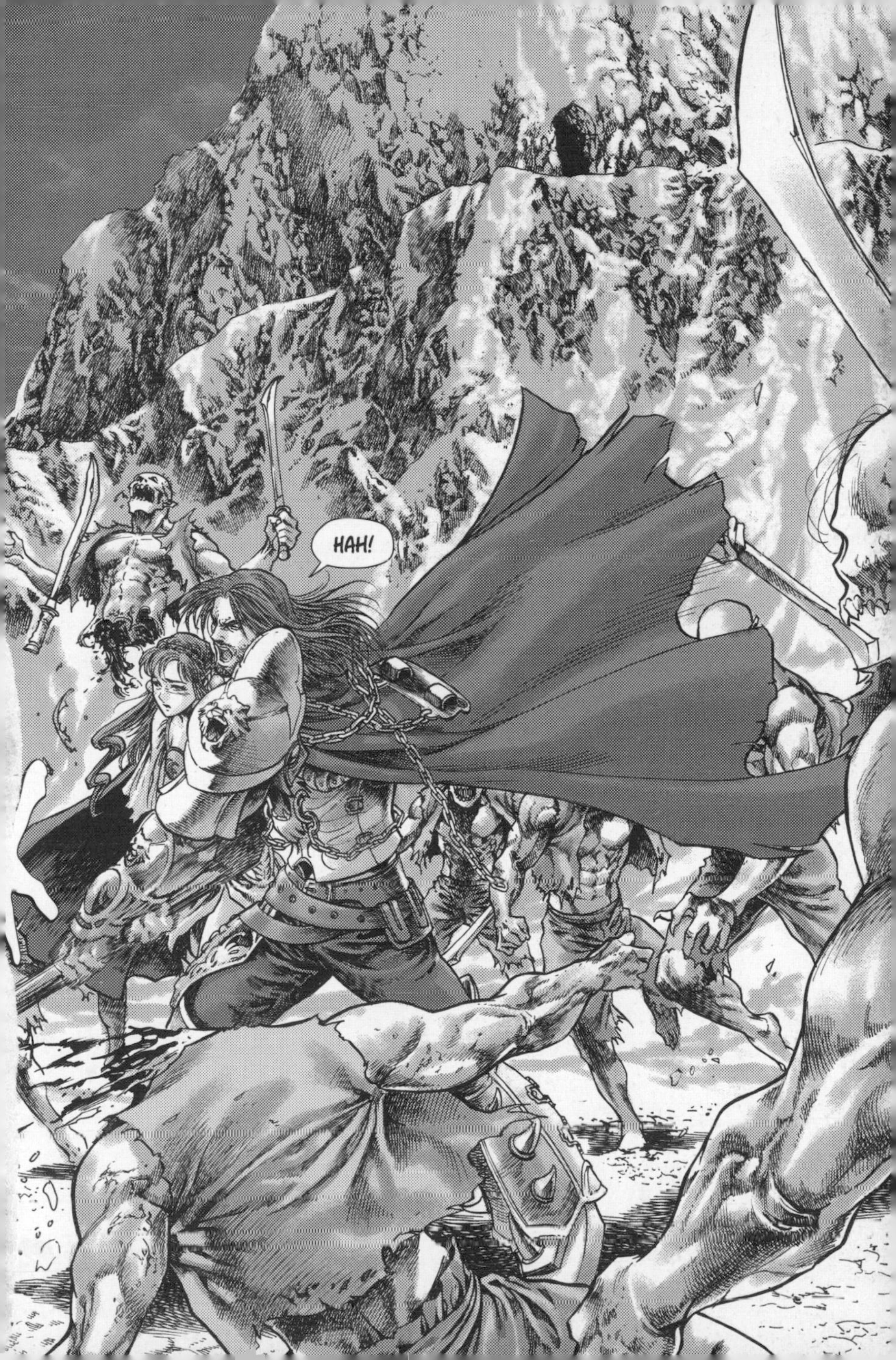
HAH!

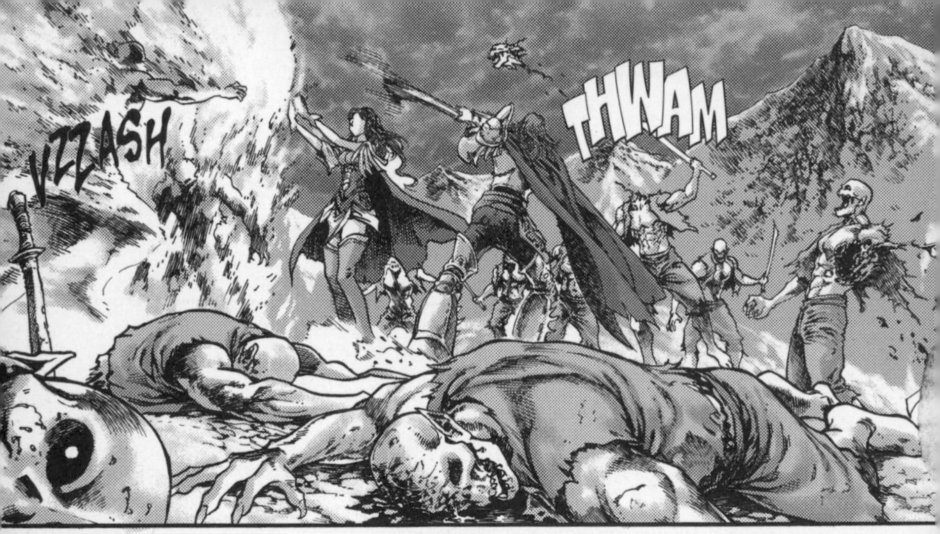
VZZASH
THWAM
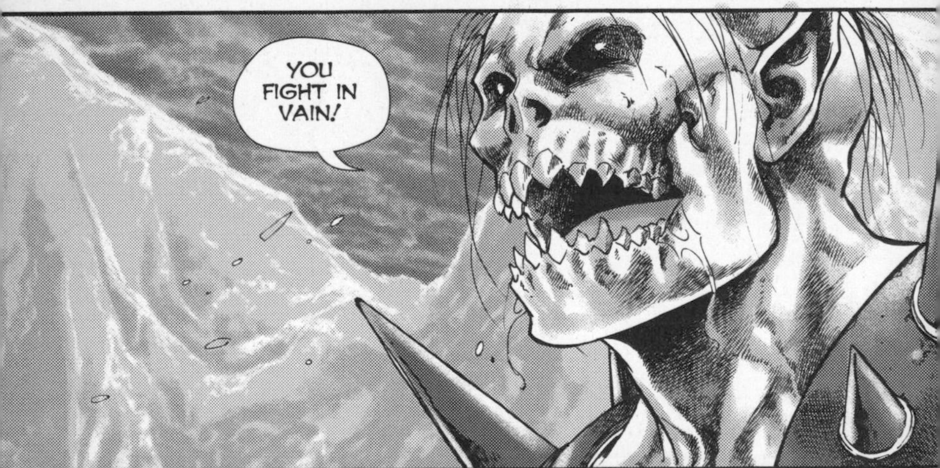
YOU FIGHT IN VAIN!
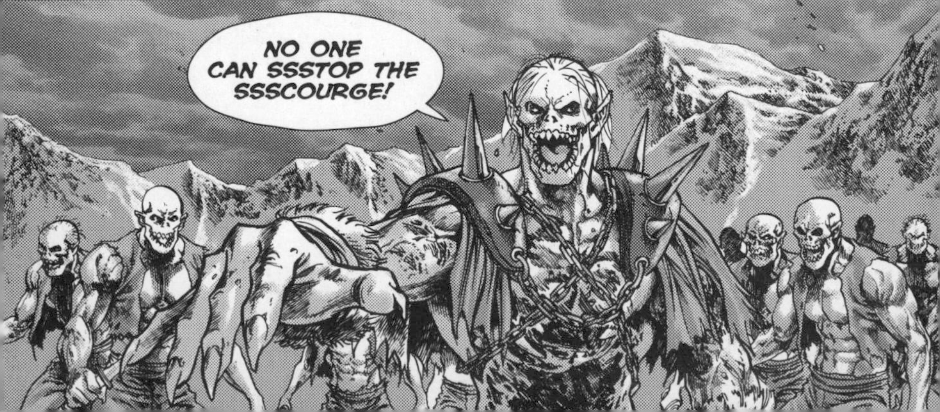
NO ONE CAN SSSTOP THE SSSCOURGE!

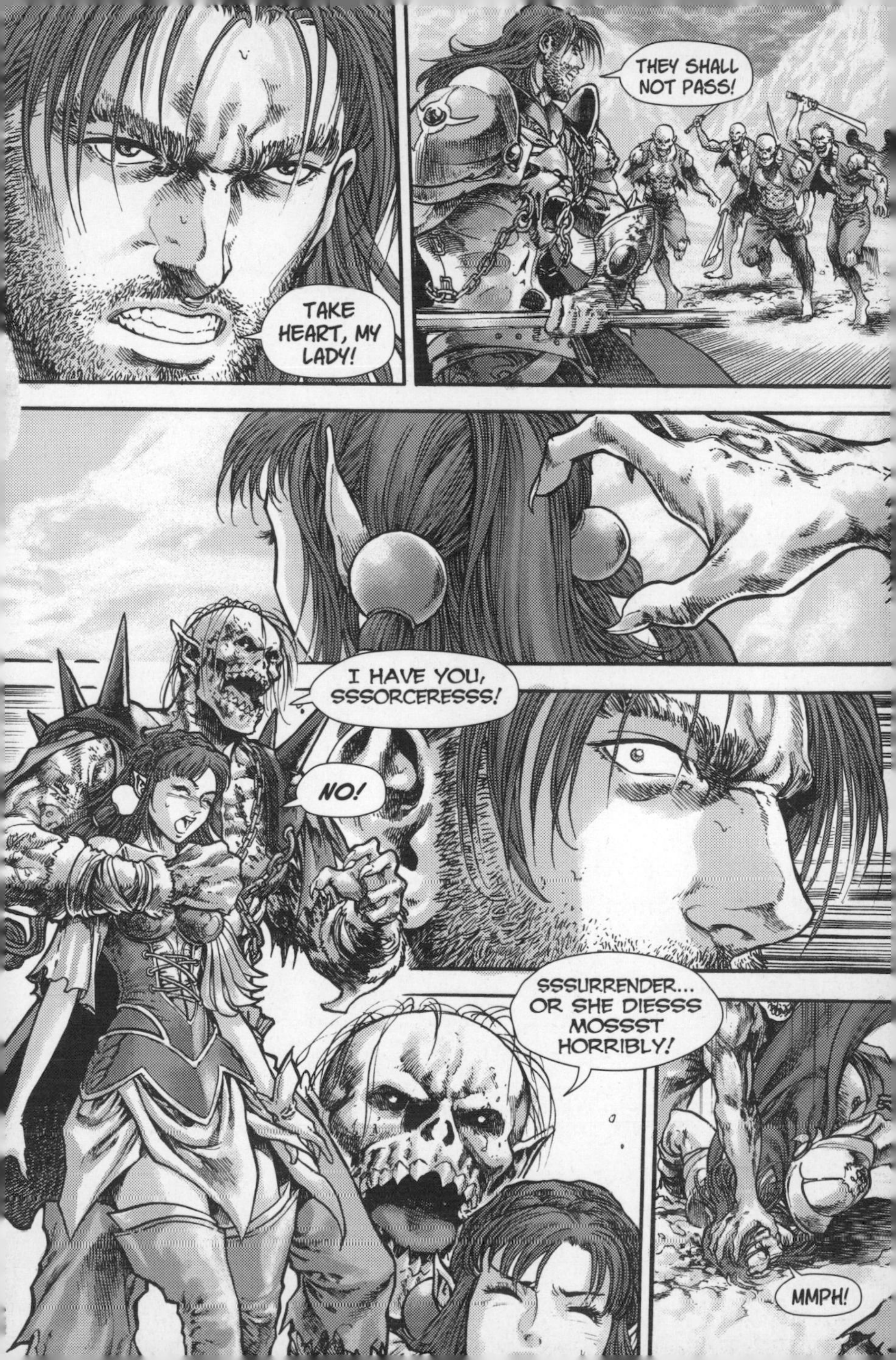
TAKE HEART, MY LADY!
THEY SHALL NOT PASS!
I HAVE YOU, SSSORCERESSS!
NO!
SSSURRENDER... OR SHE DIESSS MOSSST HORRIBLY!
MMPH!

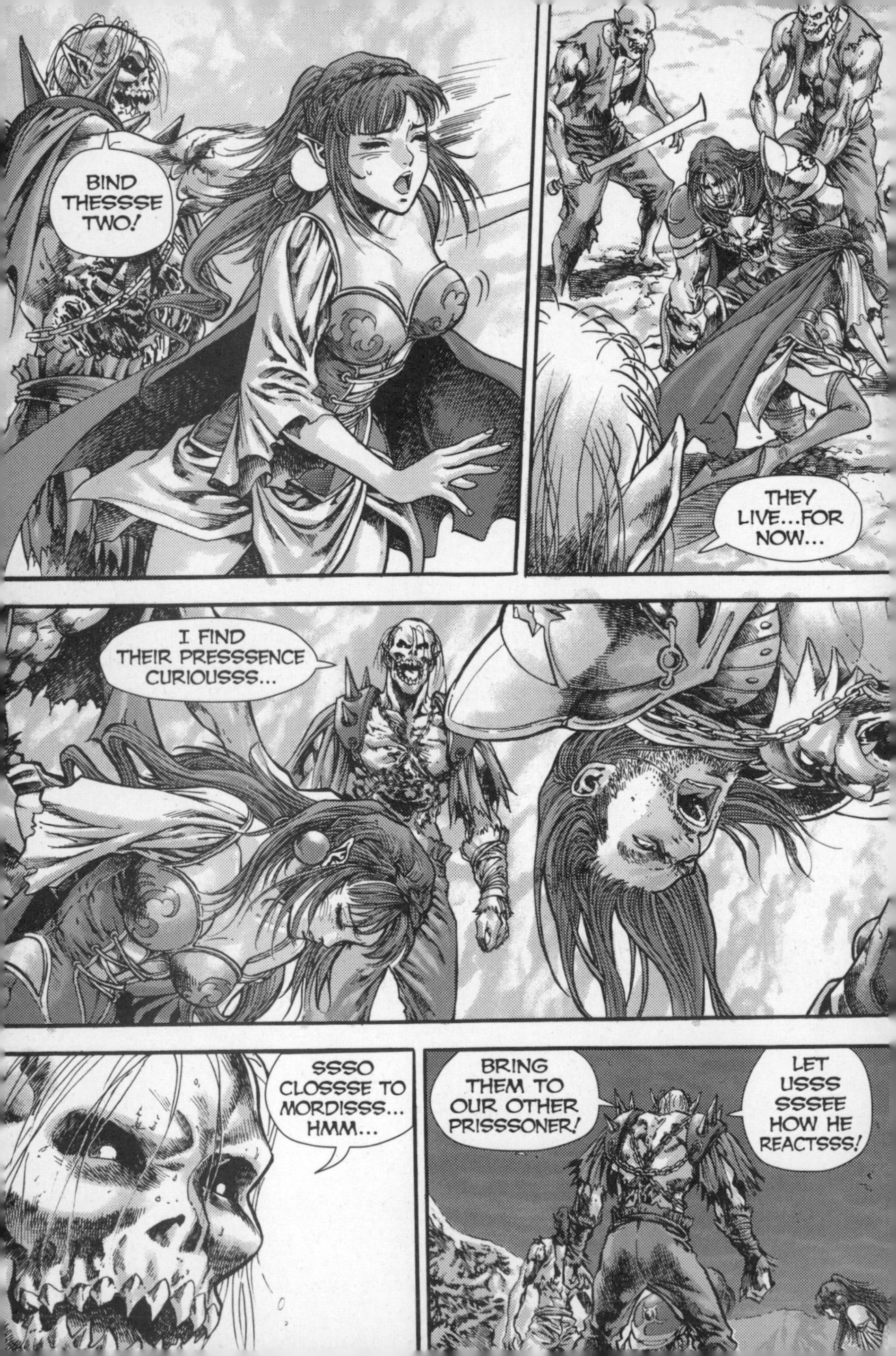
BIND THESSSE TWO!
THEY LIVE...FOR NOW...
I FIND THEIR PRESSSENCE CURIOUSSS...
SSSO CLOSSSE TO MORDISSS... HMM...
BRING THEM TO OUR OTHER PRISSSONER!
LET USSS SSSEE HOW HE REACTSSS!

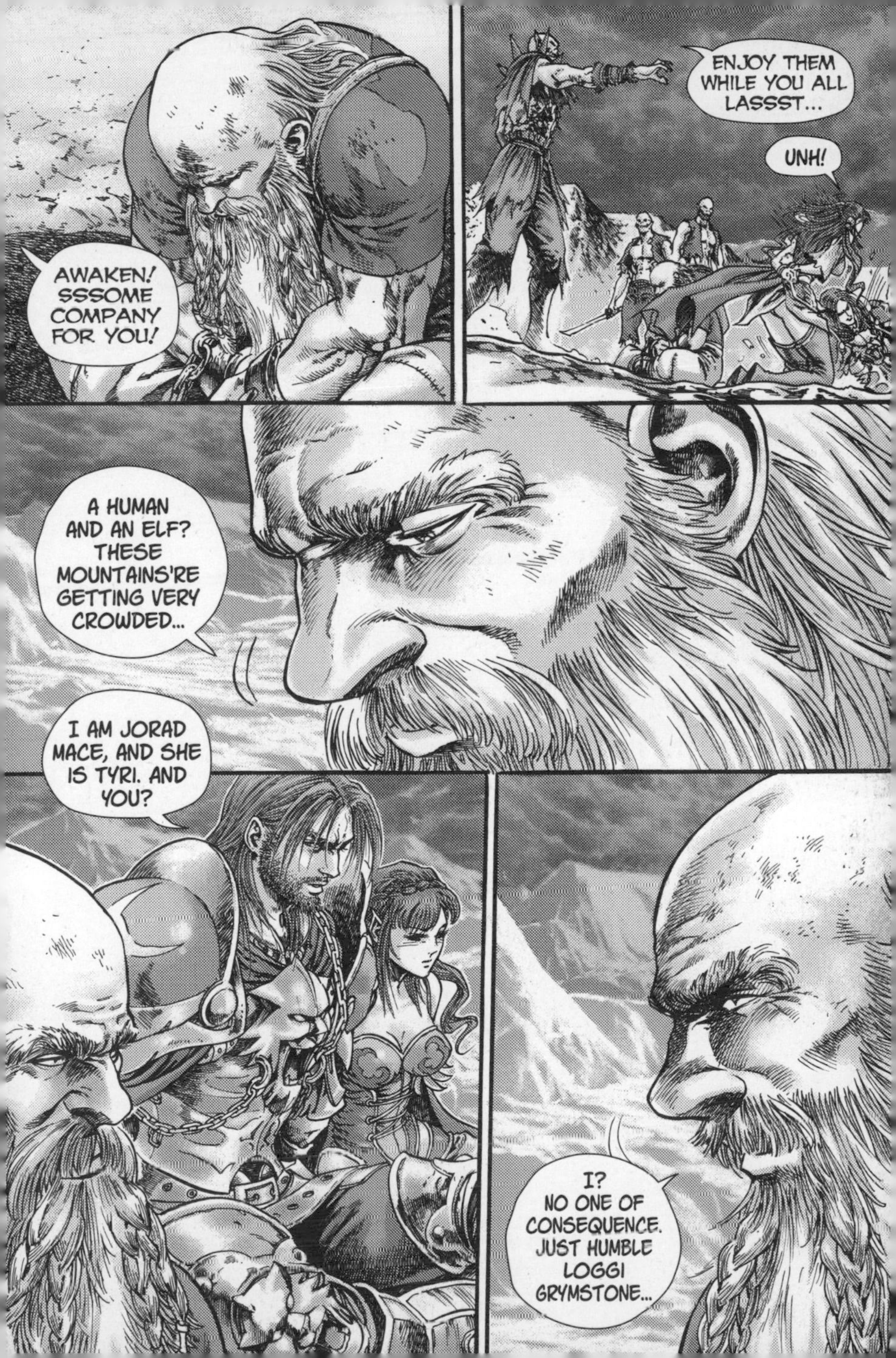
AWAKEN! SSSOME COMPANY FOR YOU!
ENJOY THEM WHILE YOU ALL LASSST...
UNH!
A HUMAN AND AN ELF? THESE MOUNTAINS'RE GETTING VERY CROWDED...
I AM JORAD MACE, AND SHE IS TYRI. AND YOU?
I? NO ONE OF CONSEQUENCE. JUST HUMBLE LOGGI GRYMSTONE...

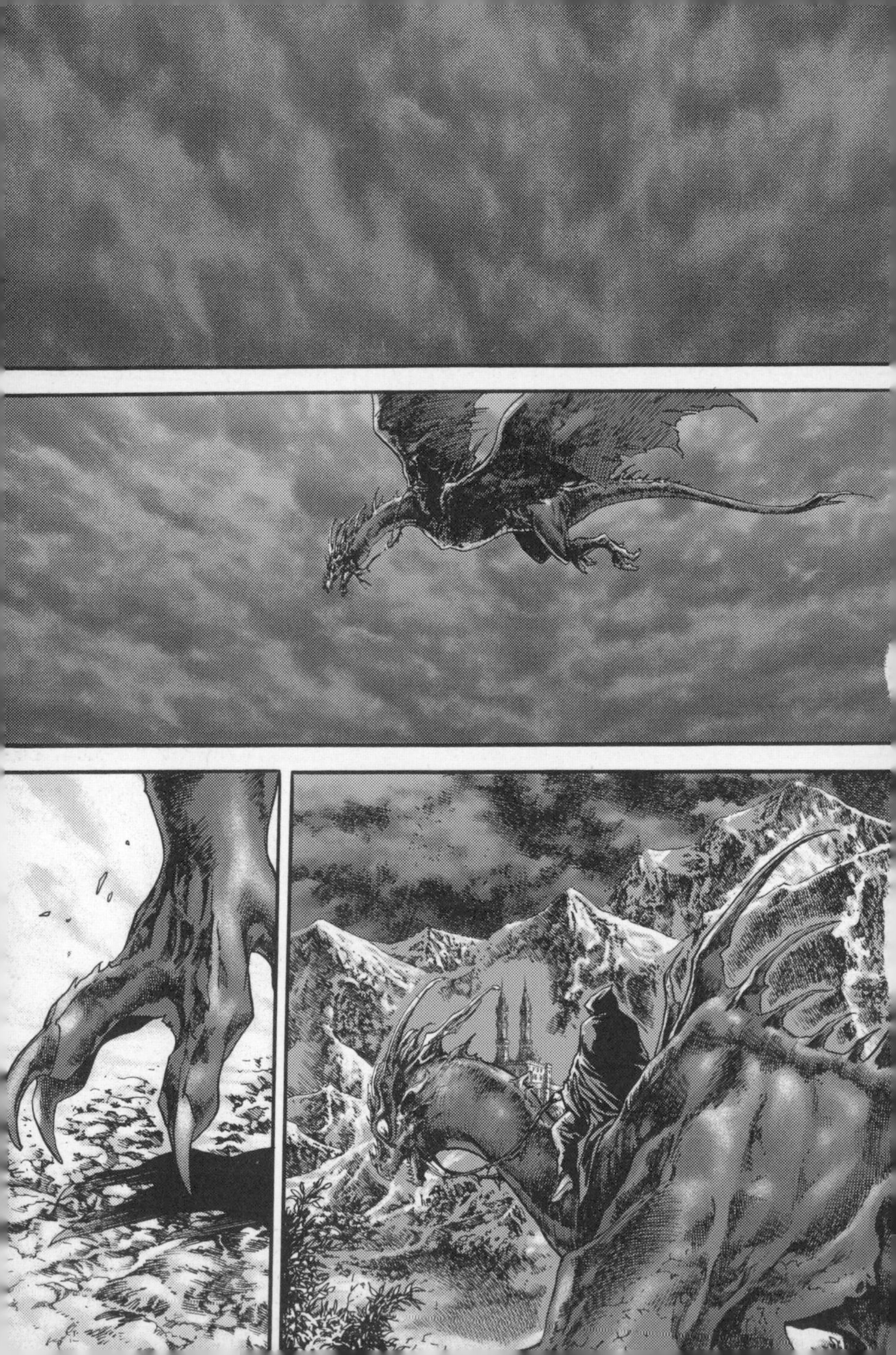

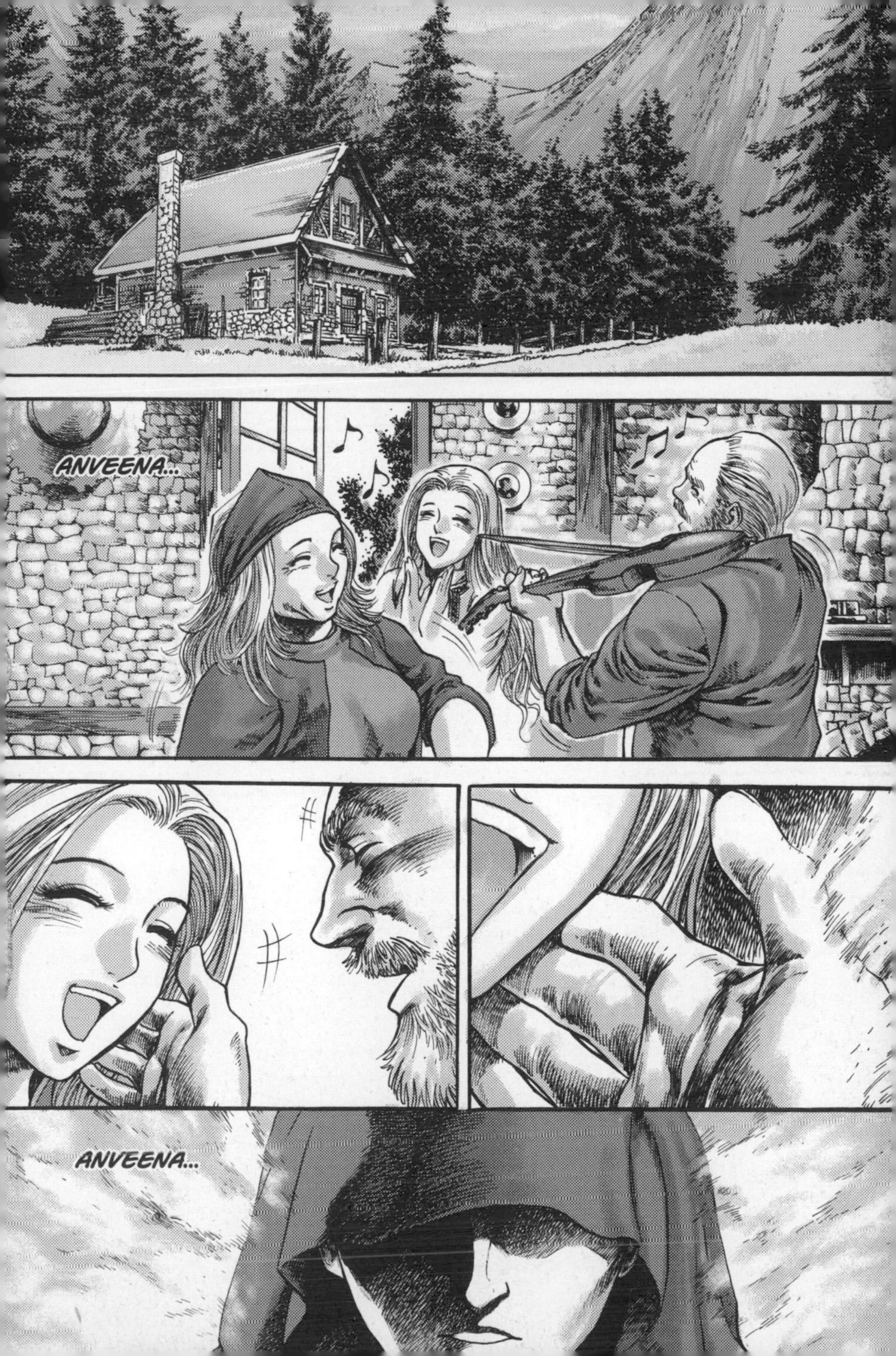
ANVEENA...
ANVEENA...

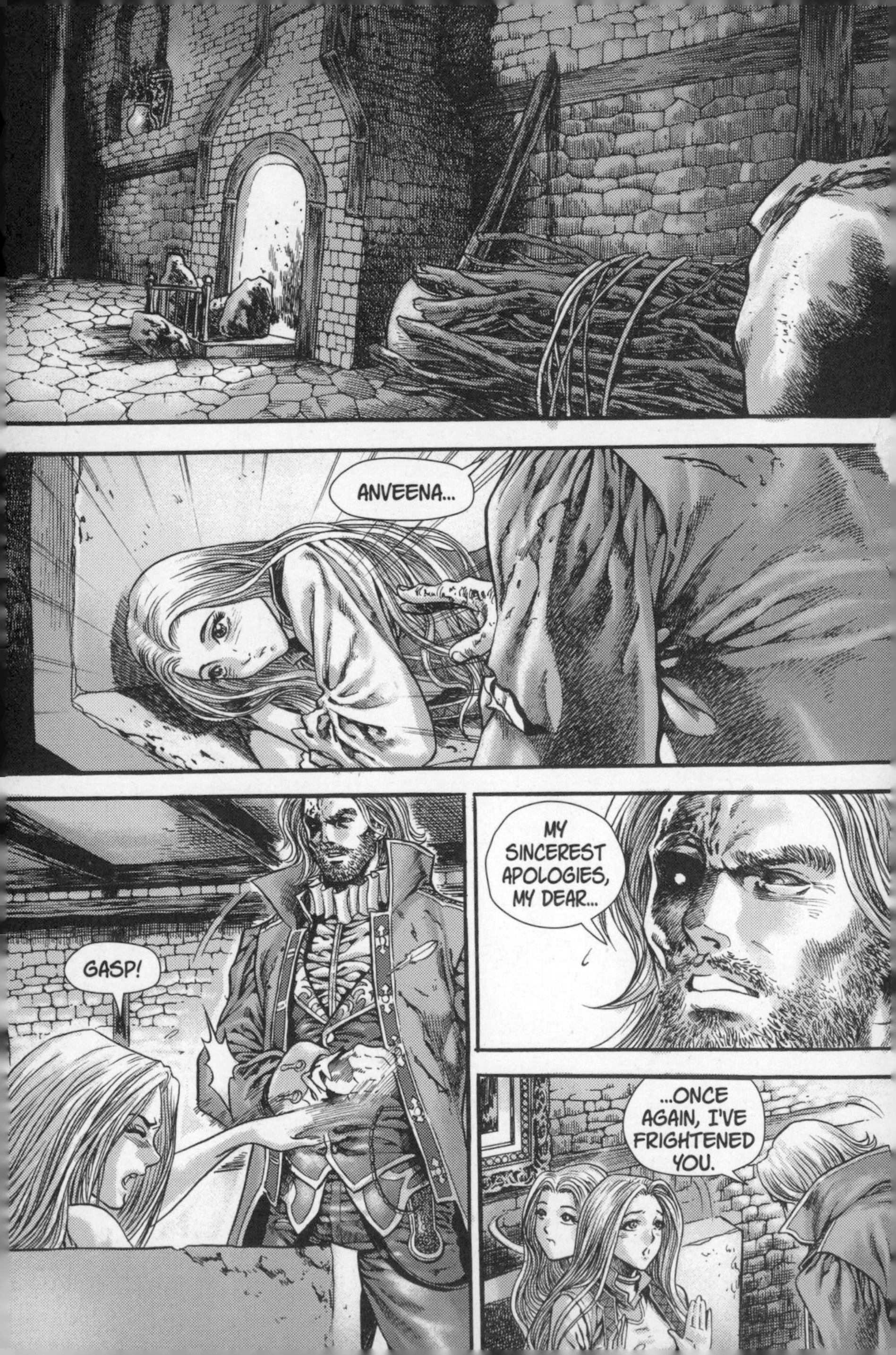
ANVEENA...
GASP!
MY SINCEREST APOLOGIES, MY DEAR...
...ONCE AGAIN, I'VE FRIGHTENED YOU.

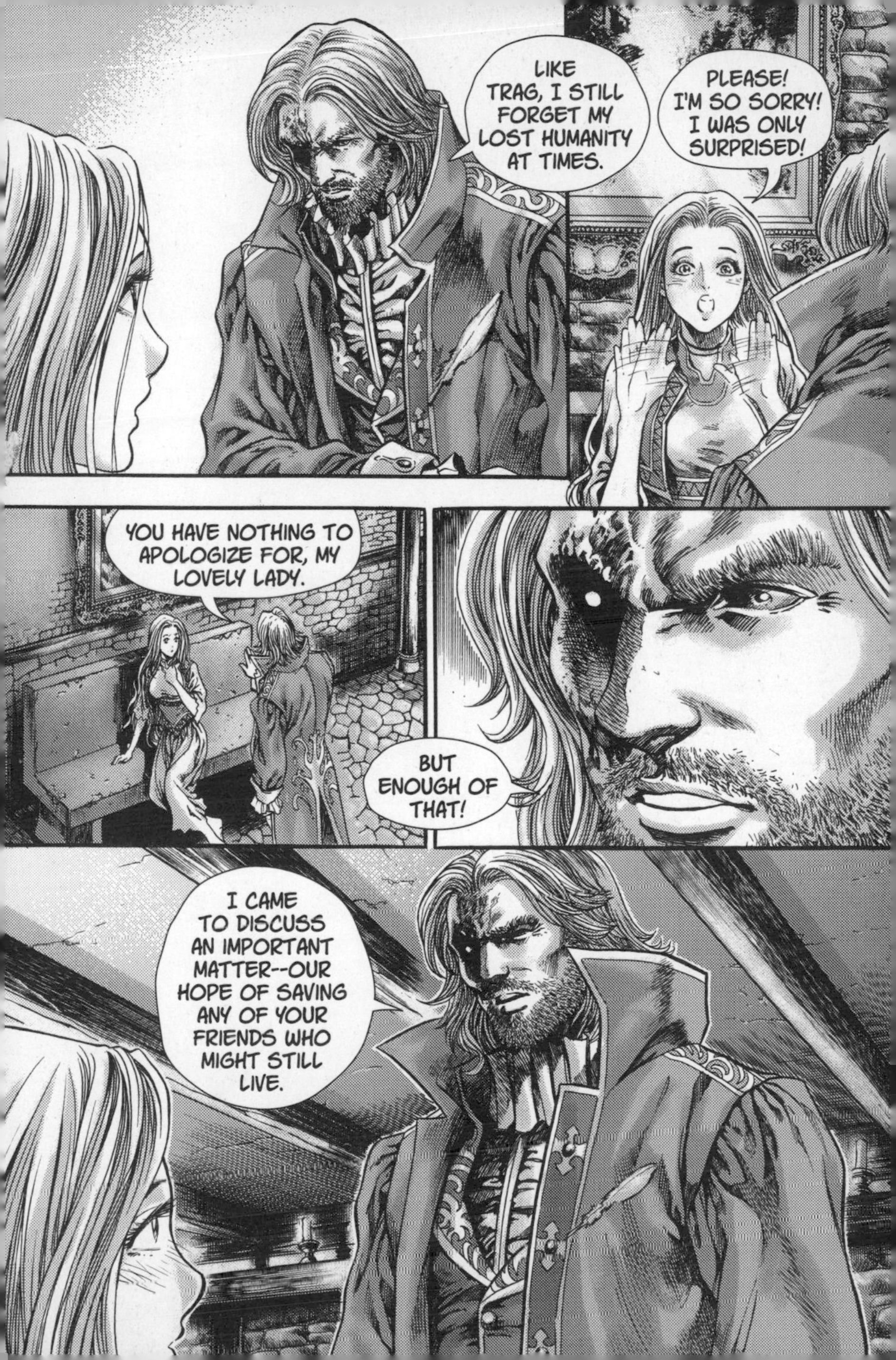
LIKE TRAG, I STILL FORGET MY LOST HUMANITY AT TIMES.
PLEASE! I'M SO SORRY! I WAS ONLY SURPRISED!
YOU HAVE NOTHING TO APOLOGIZE FOR, MY LOVELY LADY.
BUT ENOUGH OF THAT!
I CAME TO DISCUSS AN IMPORTANT MATTER--OUR HOPE OF SAVING ANY OF YOUR FRIENDS WHO MIGHT STILL LIVE.

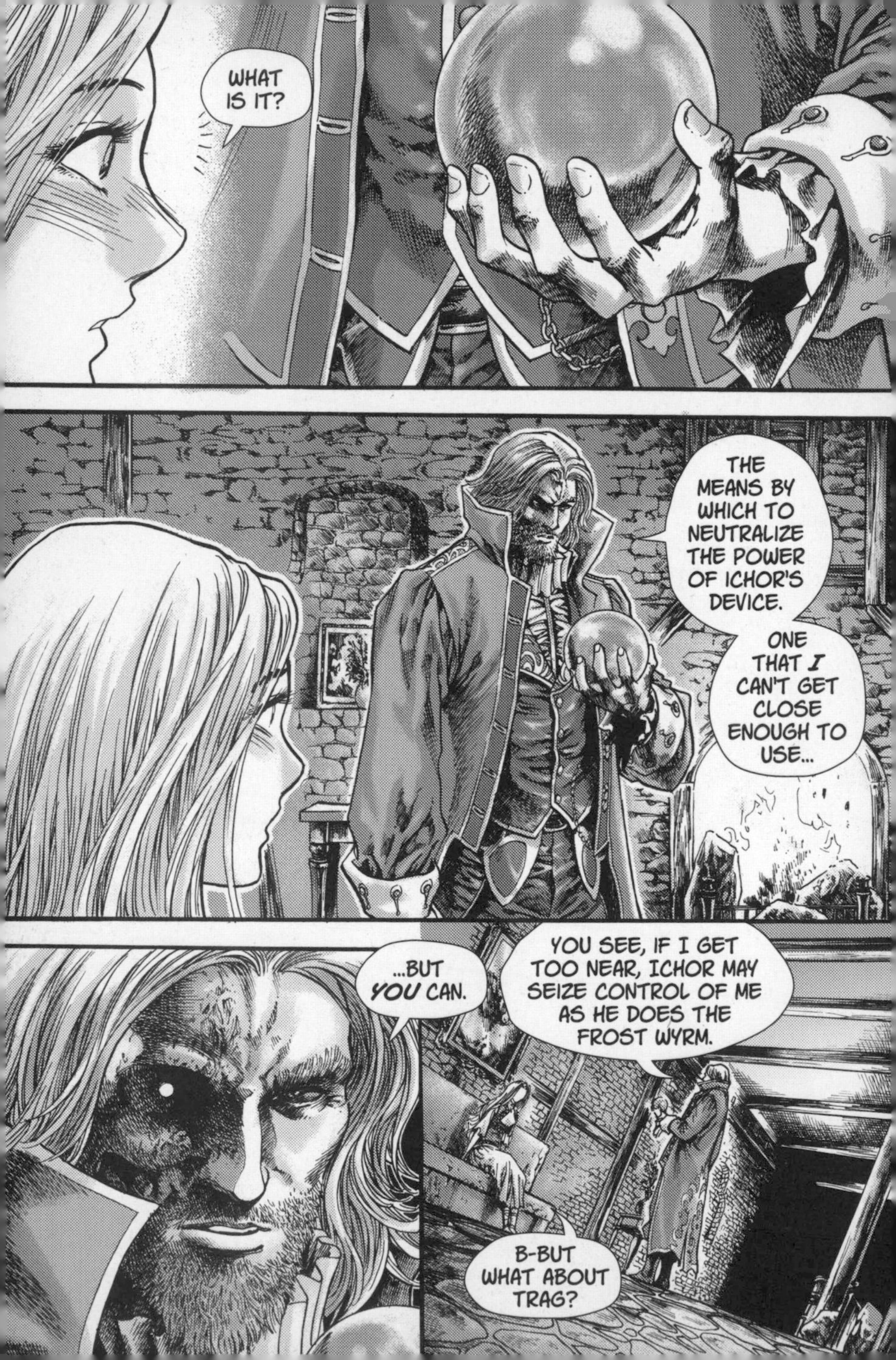
WHAT IS IT?
THE MEANS BY WHICH TO NEUTRALIZE THE POWER OF ICHOR'S DEVICE.
ONE THAT I CAN'T GET CLOSE ENOUGH TO USE...
...BUT YOU CAN.
YOU SEE, IF I GET TOO NEAR, ICHOR MAY SEIZE CONTROL OF ME AS HE DOES THE FROST WYRM.
B-BUT WHAT ABOUT TRAG?

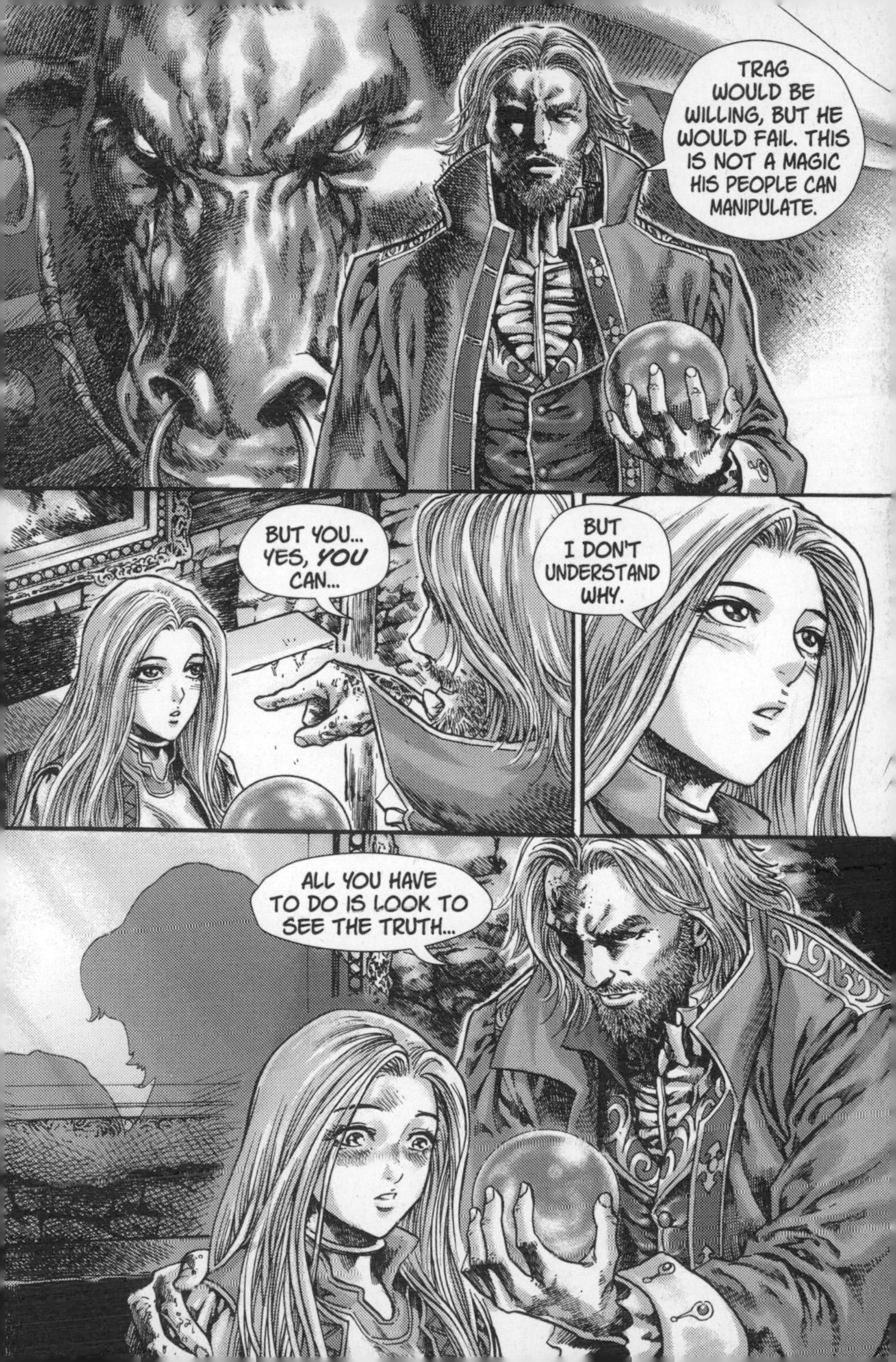
TRAG WOULD BE WILLING, BUT HE WOULD FAIL. THIS IS NOT A MAGIC HIS PEOPLE CAN MANIPULATE.
BUT YOU... YES, *YOU* CAN...
BUT I DON'T UNDERSTAND WHY.
ALL YOU HAVE TO DO IS LOOK TO SEE THE TRUTH...

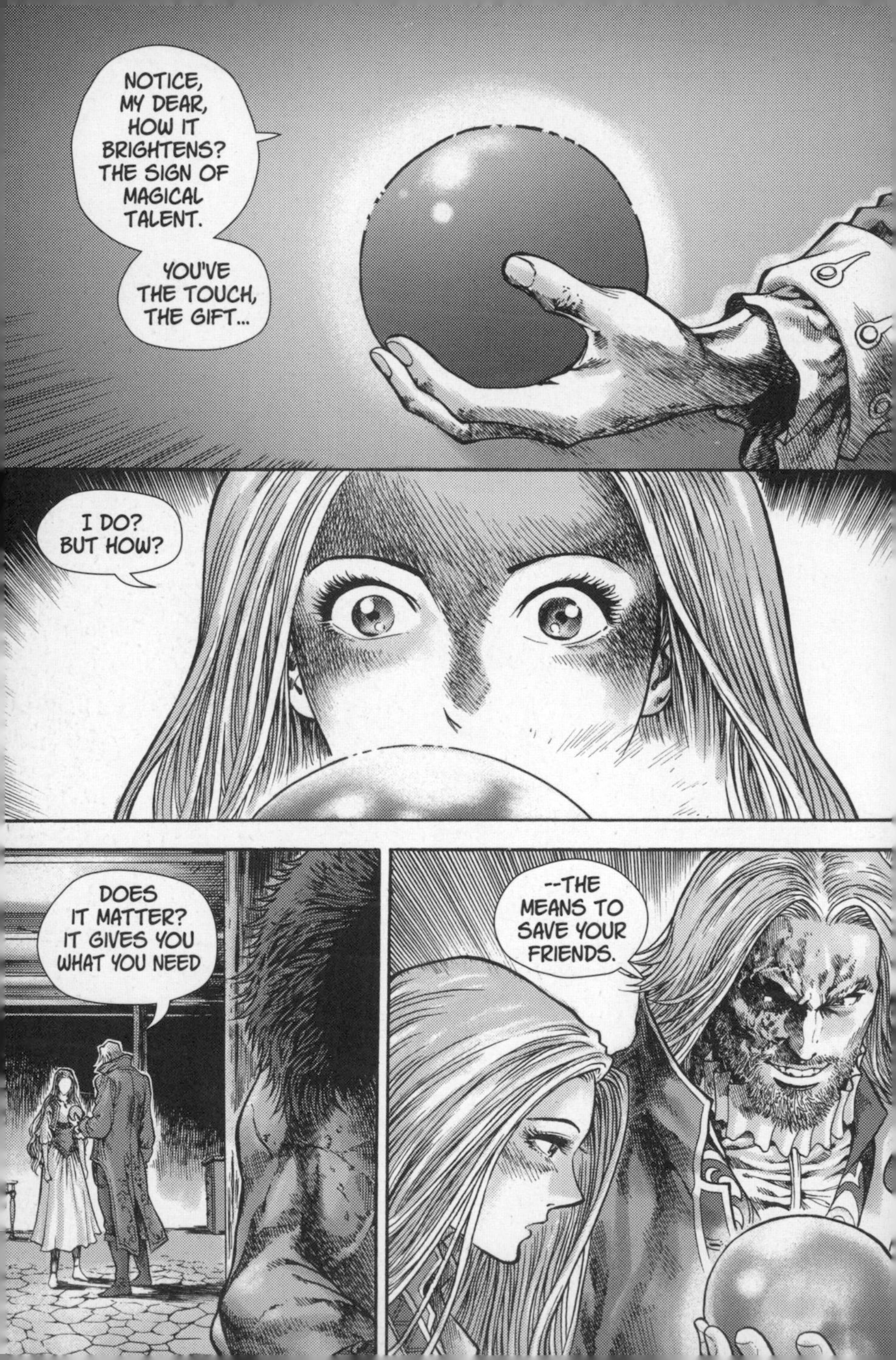
NOTICE, MY DEAR, HOW IT BRIGHTENS? THE SIGN OF MAGICAL TALENT.
YOU'VE THE TOUCH, THE GIFT...
I DO? BUT HOW?
DOES IT MATTER? IT GIVES YOU WHAT YOU NEED
--THE MEANS TO SAVE YOUR FRIENDS.

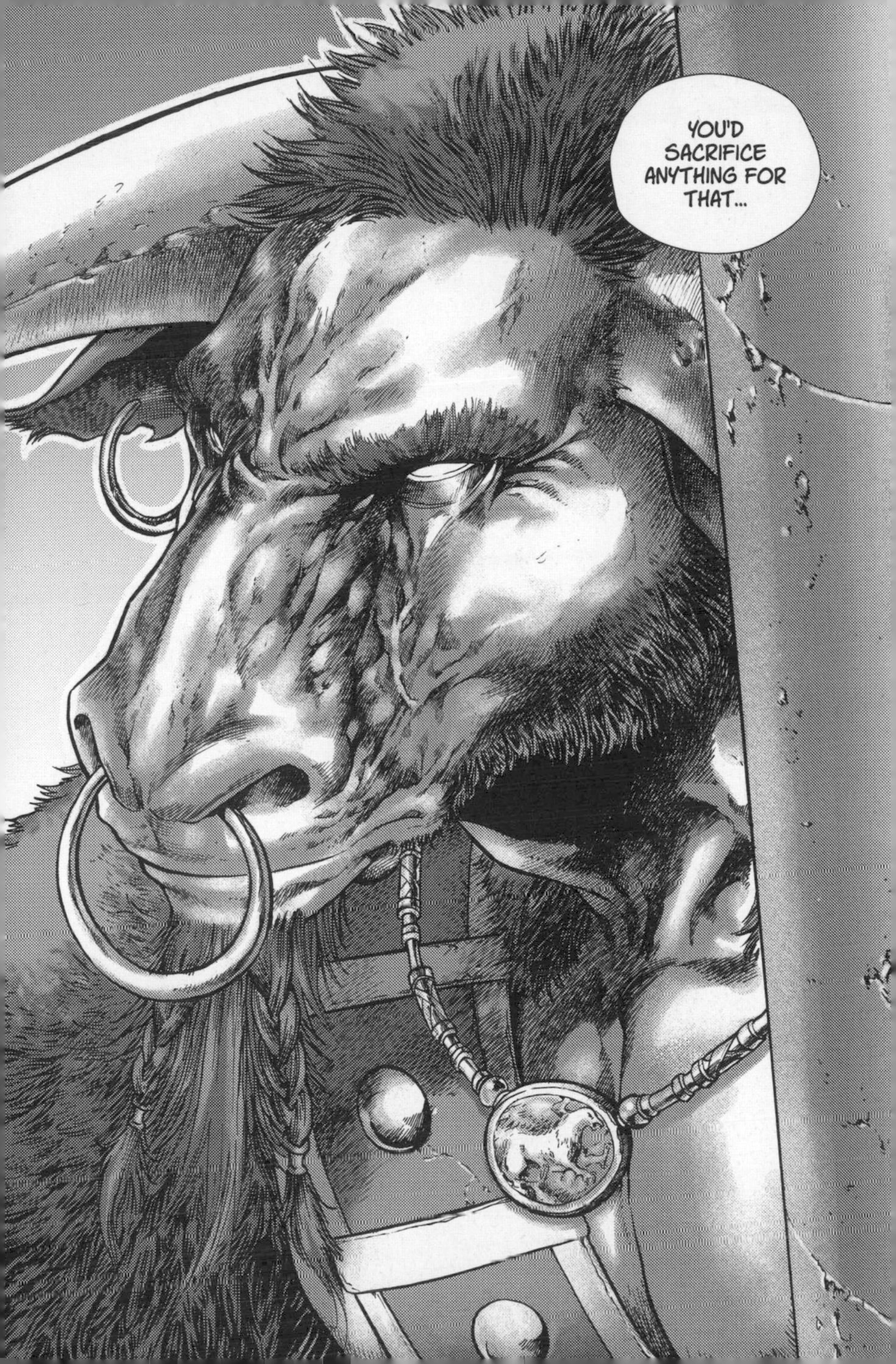
YOU'D SACRIFICE ANYTHING FOR THAT...

...WOULDN'T YOU?

CHAPTER FIVE
The Orb of Ner'zhul

YES, STARE DEEP, VERY DEEP...

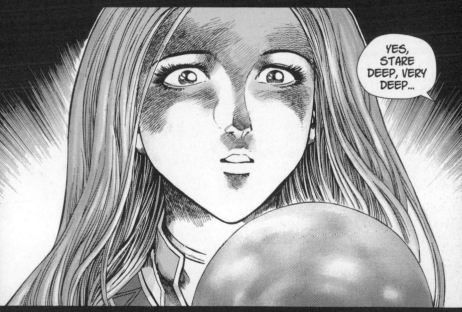

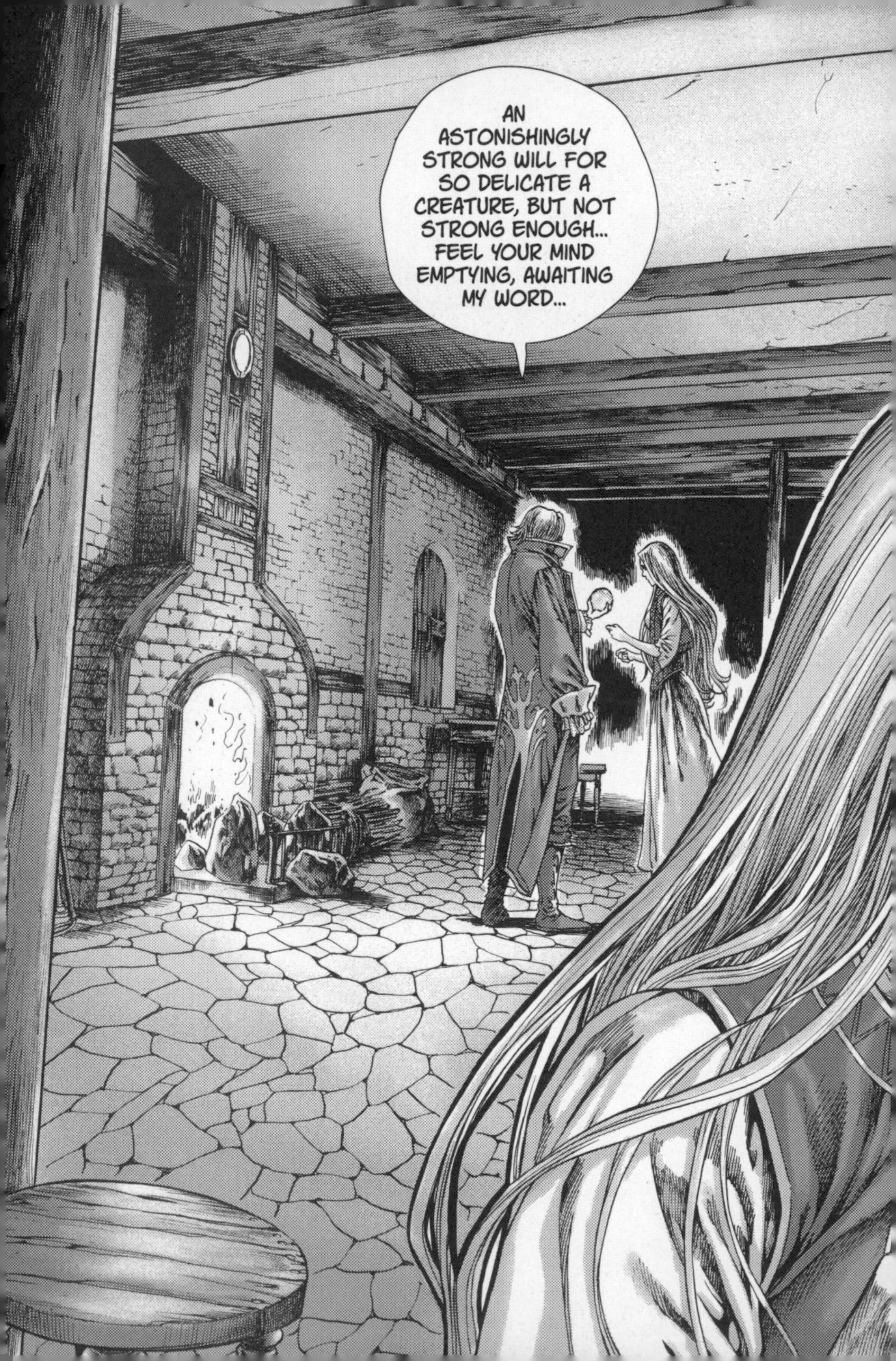
AN ASTONISHINGLY STRONG WILL FOR SO DELICATE A CREATURE, BUT NOT STRONG ENOUGH... FEEL YOUR MIND EMPTYING, AWAITING MY WORD...

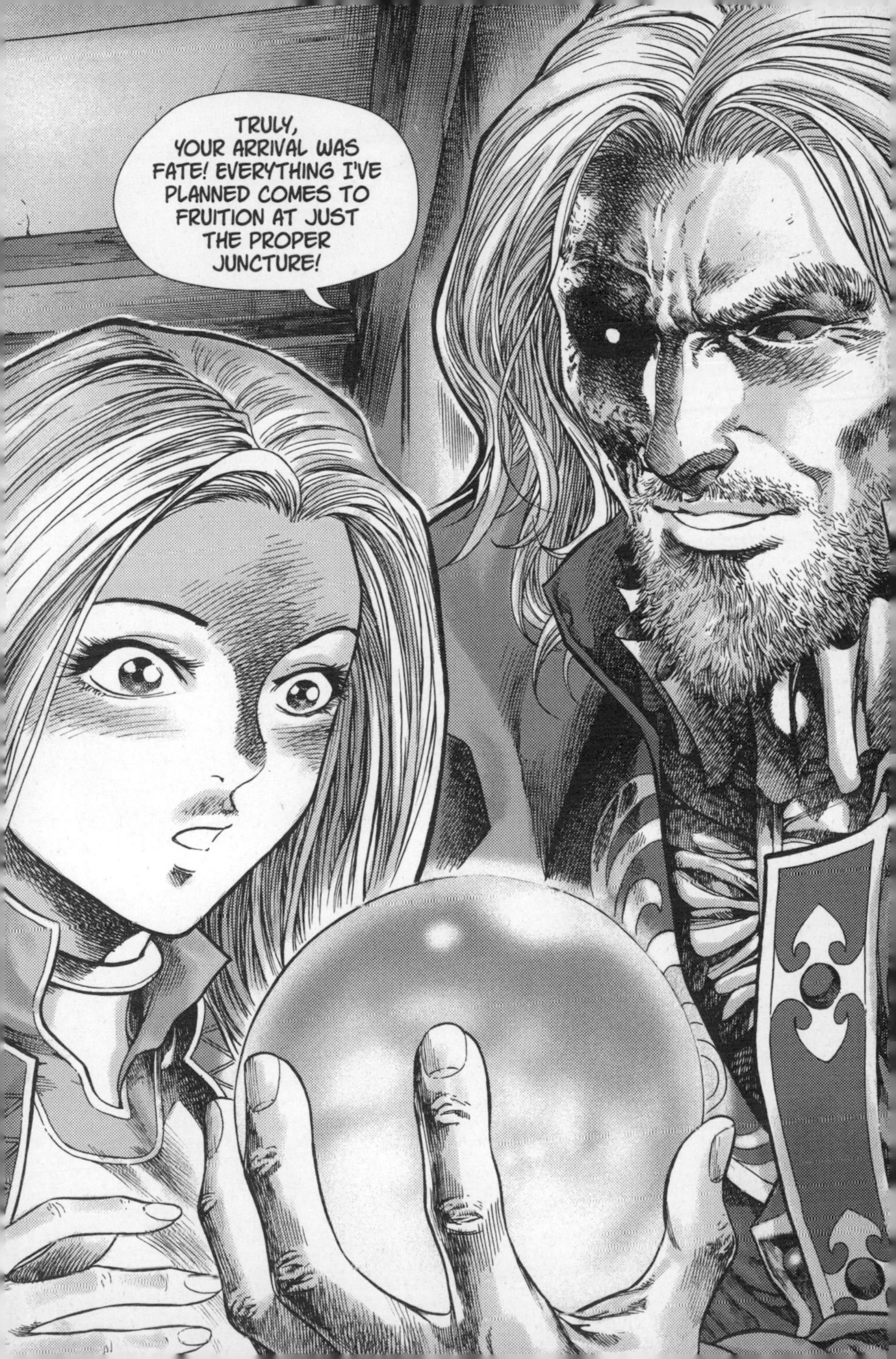
TRULY, YOUR ARRIVAL WAS FATE! EVERYTHING I'VE PLANNED COMES TO FRUITION AT JUST THE PROPER JUNCTURE!

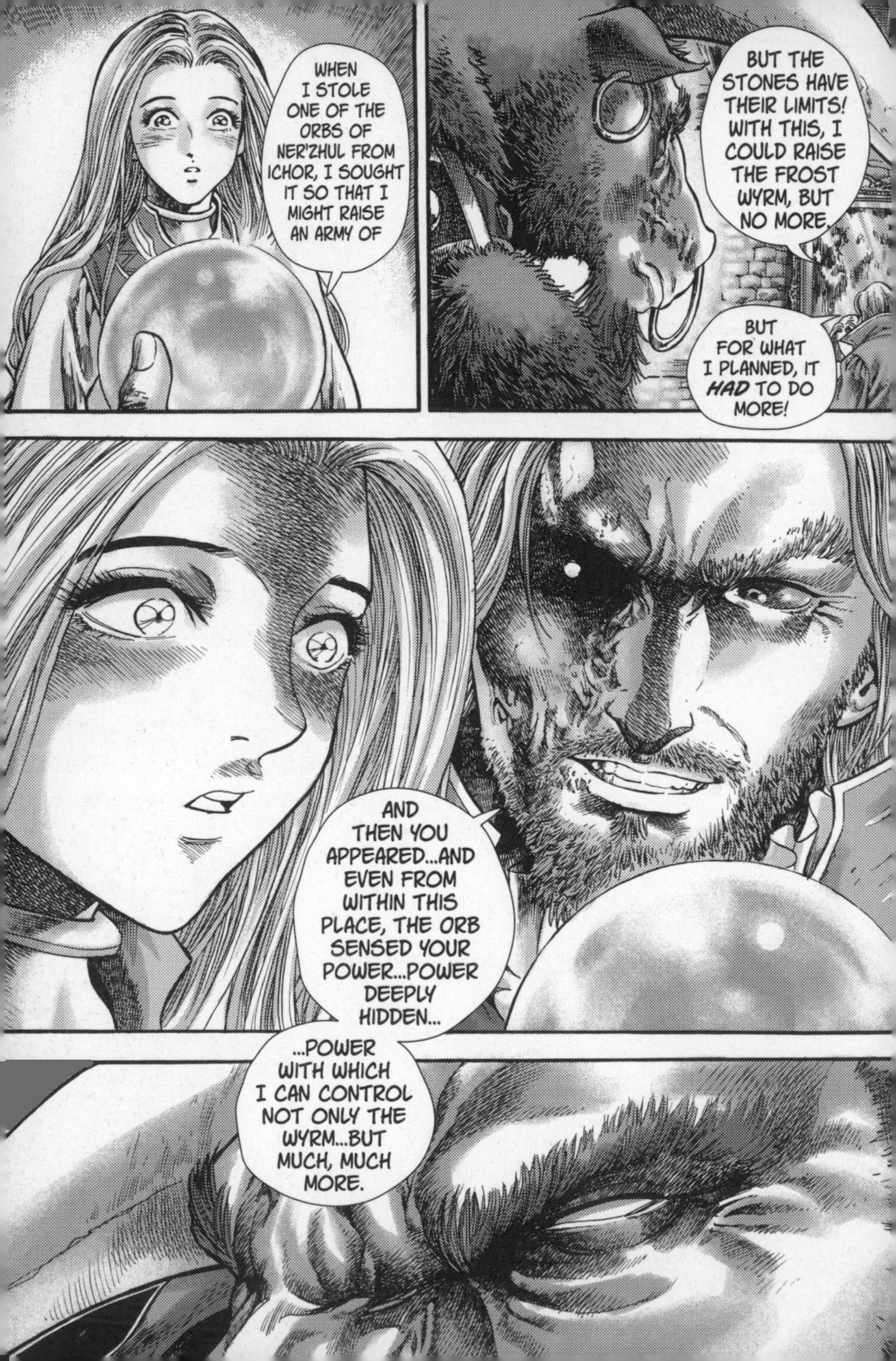

WHEN I STOLE ONE OF THE ORBS OF NER'ZHUL FROM ICHOR, I SOUGHT IT SO THAT I MIGHT RAISE AN ARMY OF
BUT THE STONES HAVE THEIR LIMITS! WITH THIS, I COULD RAISE THE FROST WYRM, BUT NO MORE.
BUT FOR WHAT I PLANNED, IT **HAD** TO DO MORE!
AND THEN YOU APPEARED...AND EVEN FROM WITHIN THIS PLACE, THE ORB SENSED YOUR POWER...POWER DEEPLY HIDDEN...
...POWER WITH WHICH I CAN CONTROL NOT ONLY THE WYRM...BUT MUCH, MUCH MORE.

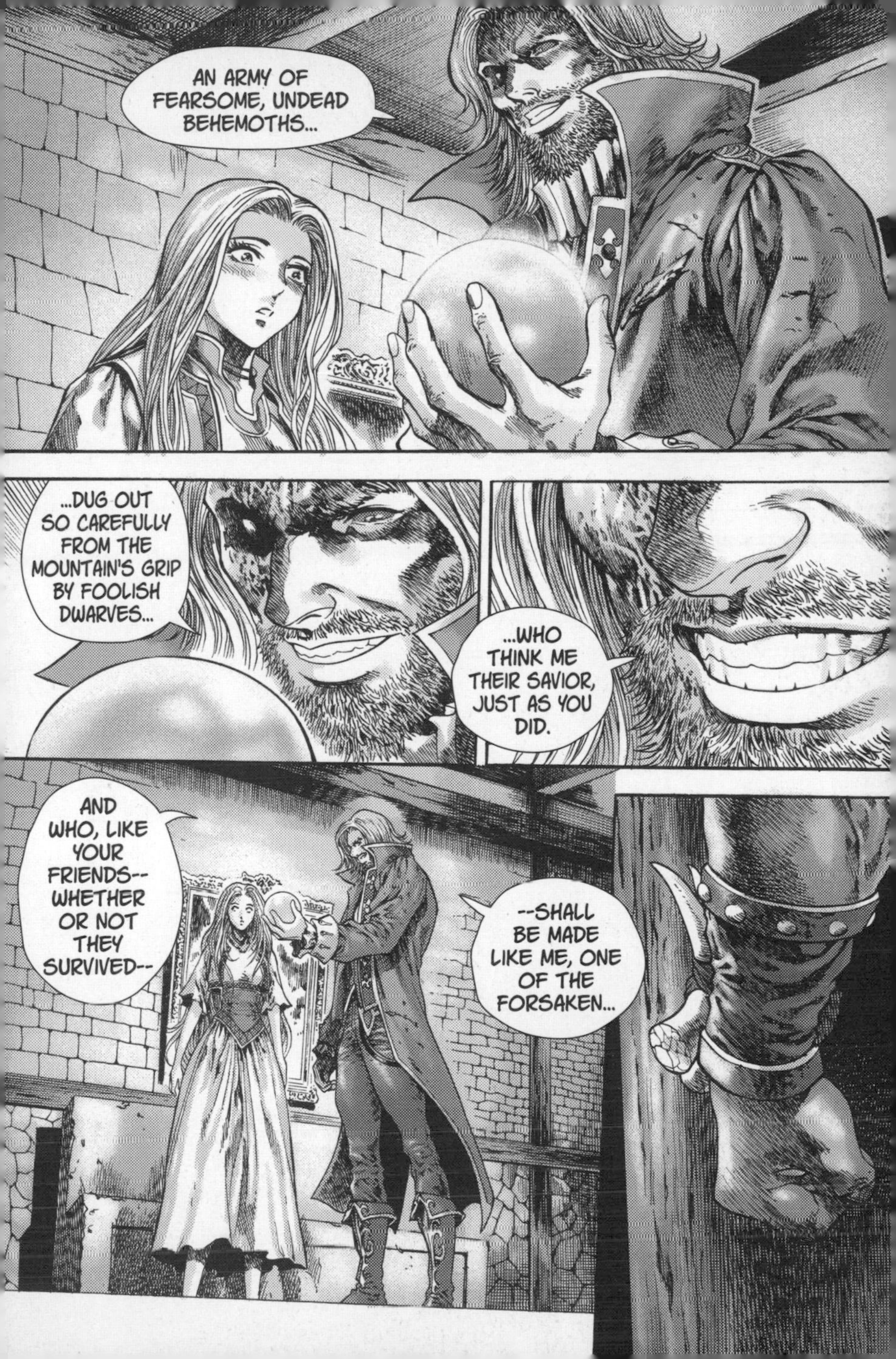
AN ARMY OF FEARSOME, UNDEAD BEHEMOTHS...
...DUG OUT SO CAREFULLY FROM THE MOUNTAIN'S GRIP BY FOOLISH DWARVES...
...WHO THINK ME THEIR SAVIOR, JUST AS YOU DID.
AND WHO, LIKE YOUR FRIENDS-- WHETHER OR NOT THEY SURVIVED--
--SHALL BE MADE LIKE ME, ONE OF THE FORSAKEN...

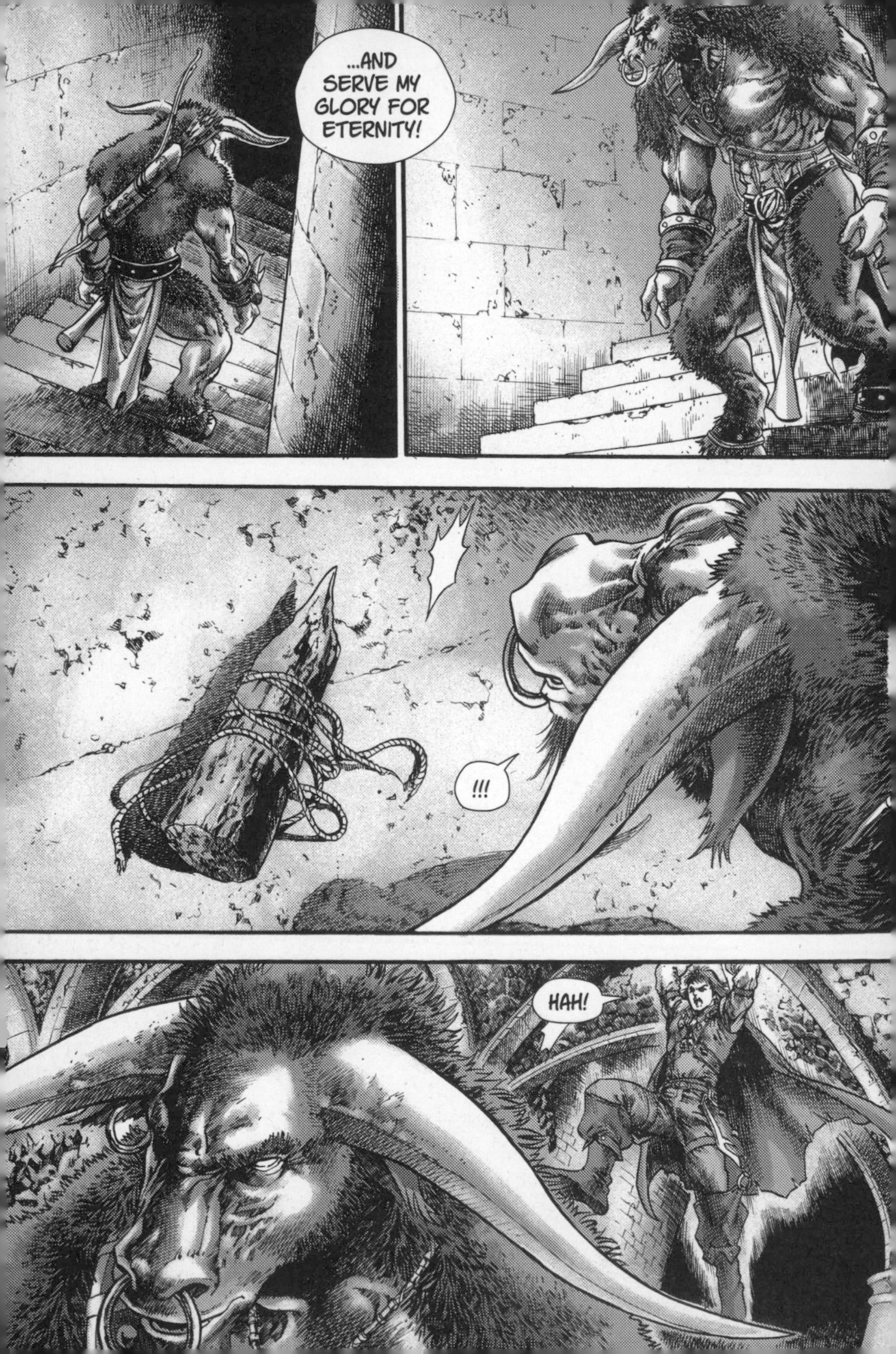
...AND SERVE MY GLORY FOR ETERNITY!
!!!
HAH!

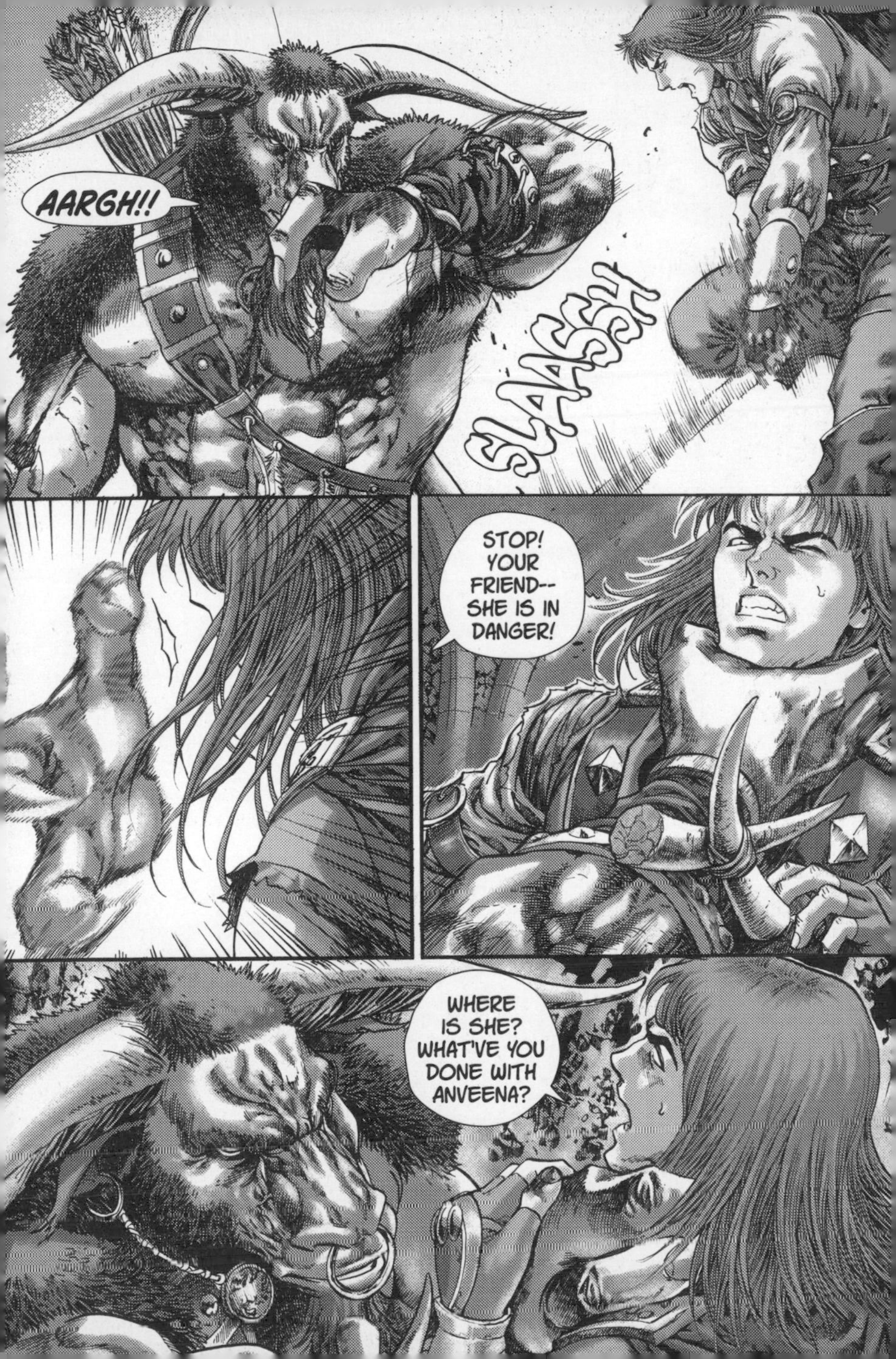
AARGH!!
SLASSSH
STOP! YOUR FRIEND-- SHE IS IN DANGER!
WHERE IS SHE? WHAT'VE YOU DONE WITH ANVEENA?

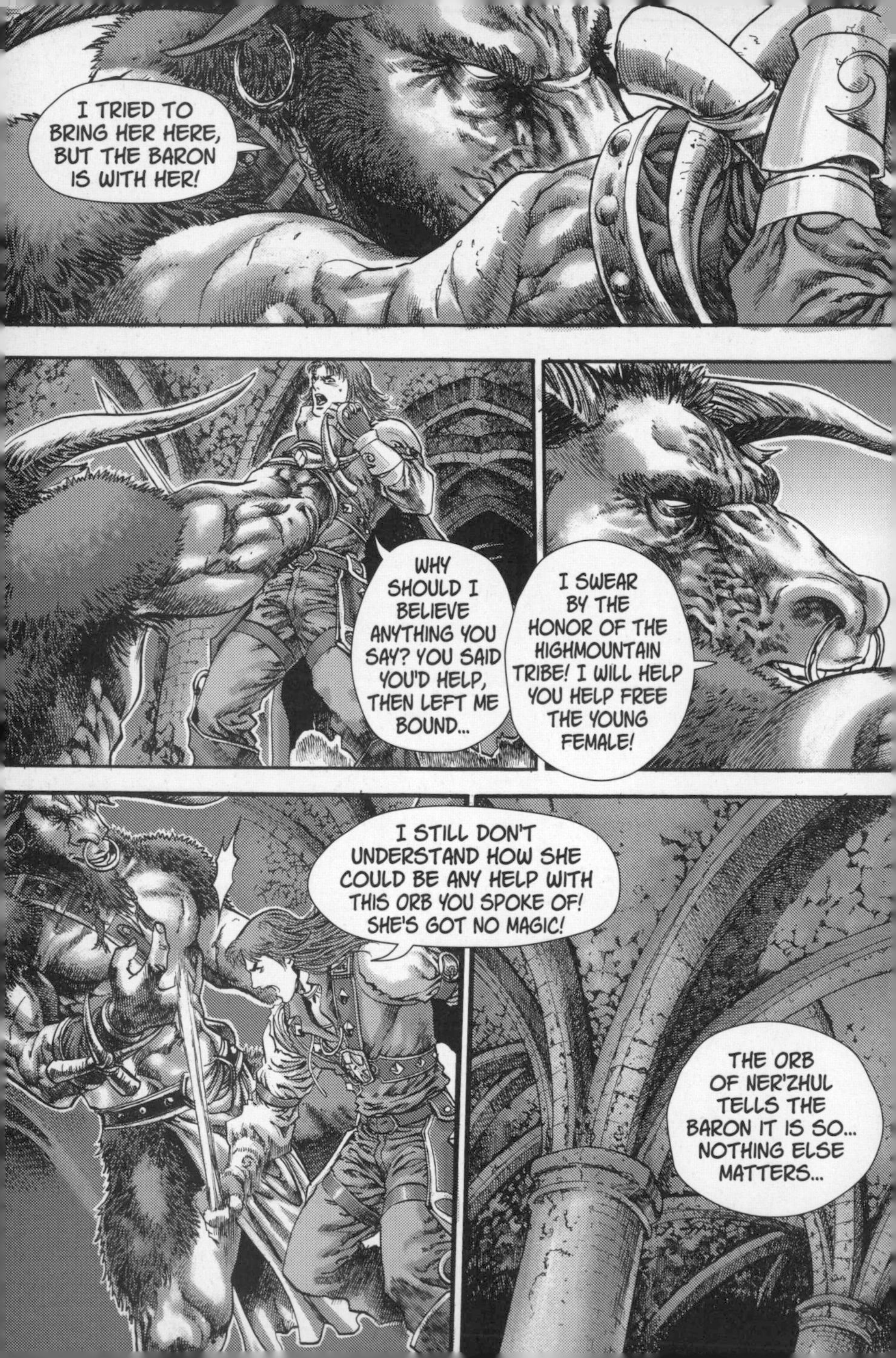
I TRIED TO BRING HER HERE, BUT THE BARON IS WITH HER!
WHY SHOULD I BELIEVE ANYTHING YOU SAY? YOU SAID YOU'D HELP, THEN LEFT ME BOUND...
I SWEAR BY THE HONOR OF THE HIGHMOUNTAIN TRIBE! I WILL HELP YOU HELP FREE THE YOUNG FEMALE!
I STILL DON'T UNDERSTAND HOW SHE COULD BE ANY HELP WITH THIS ORB YOU SPOKE OF! SHE'S GOT NO MAGIC!
THE ORB OF NER'ZHUL TELLS THE BARON IT IS SO... NOTHING ELSE MATTERS...

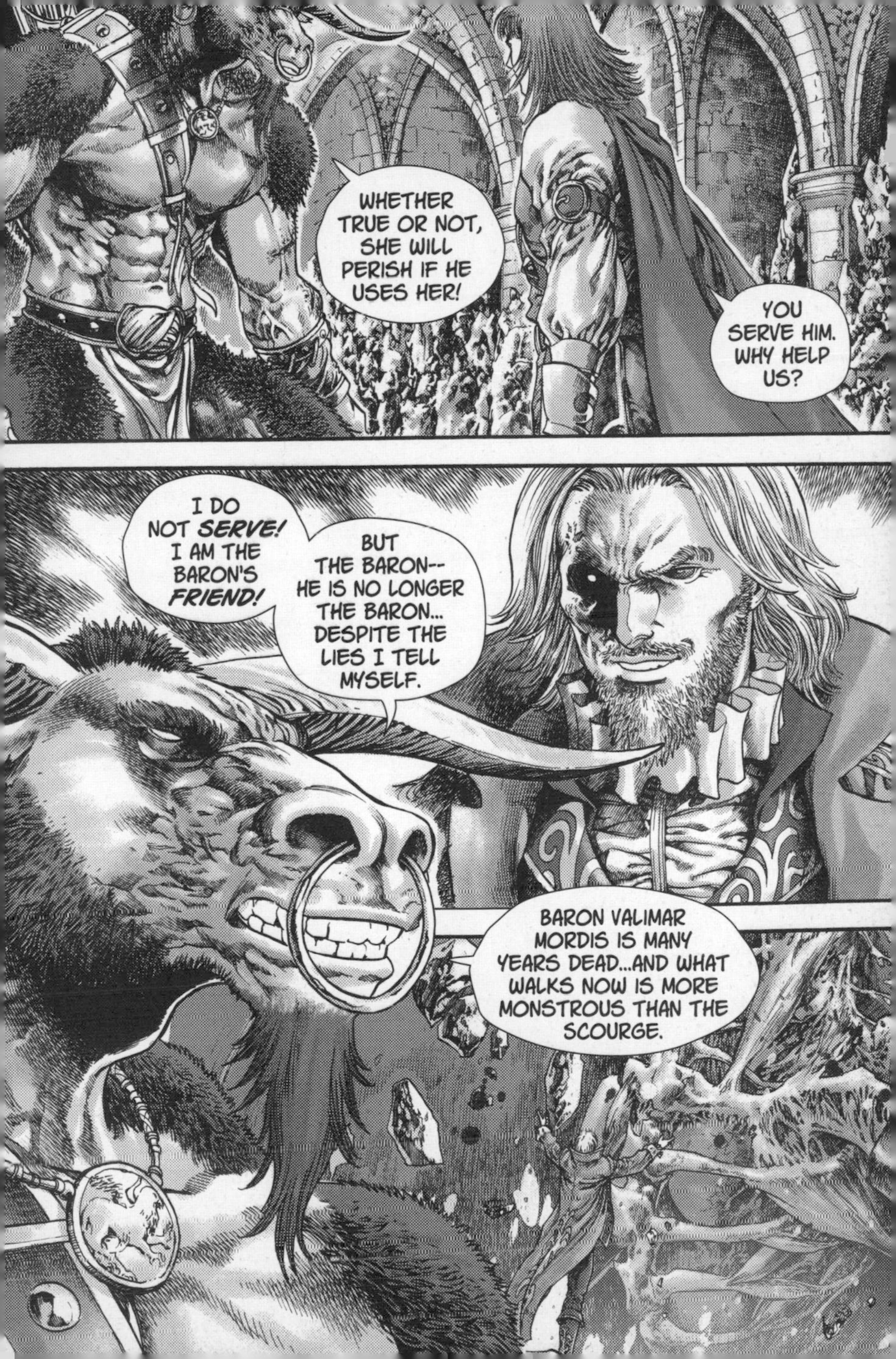
WHETHER TRUE OR NOT, SHE WILL PERISH IF HE USES HER!
YOU SERVE HIM. WHY HELP US?
I DO NOT *SERVE!* I AM THE BARON'S *FRIEND!*
BUT THE BARON-- HE IS NO LONGER THE BARON... DESPITE THE LIES I TELL MYSELF.
BARON VALIMAR MORDIS IS MANY YEARS DEAD...AND WHAT WALKS NOW IS MORE MONSTROUS THAN THE SCOURGE.

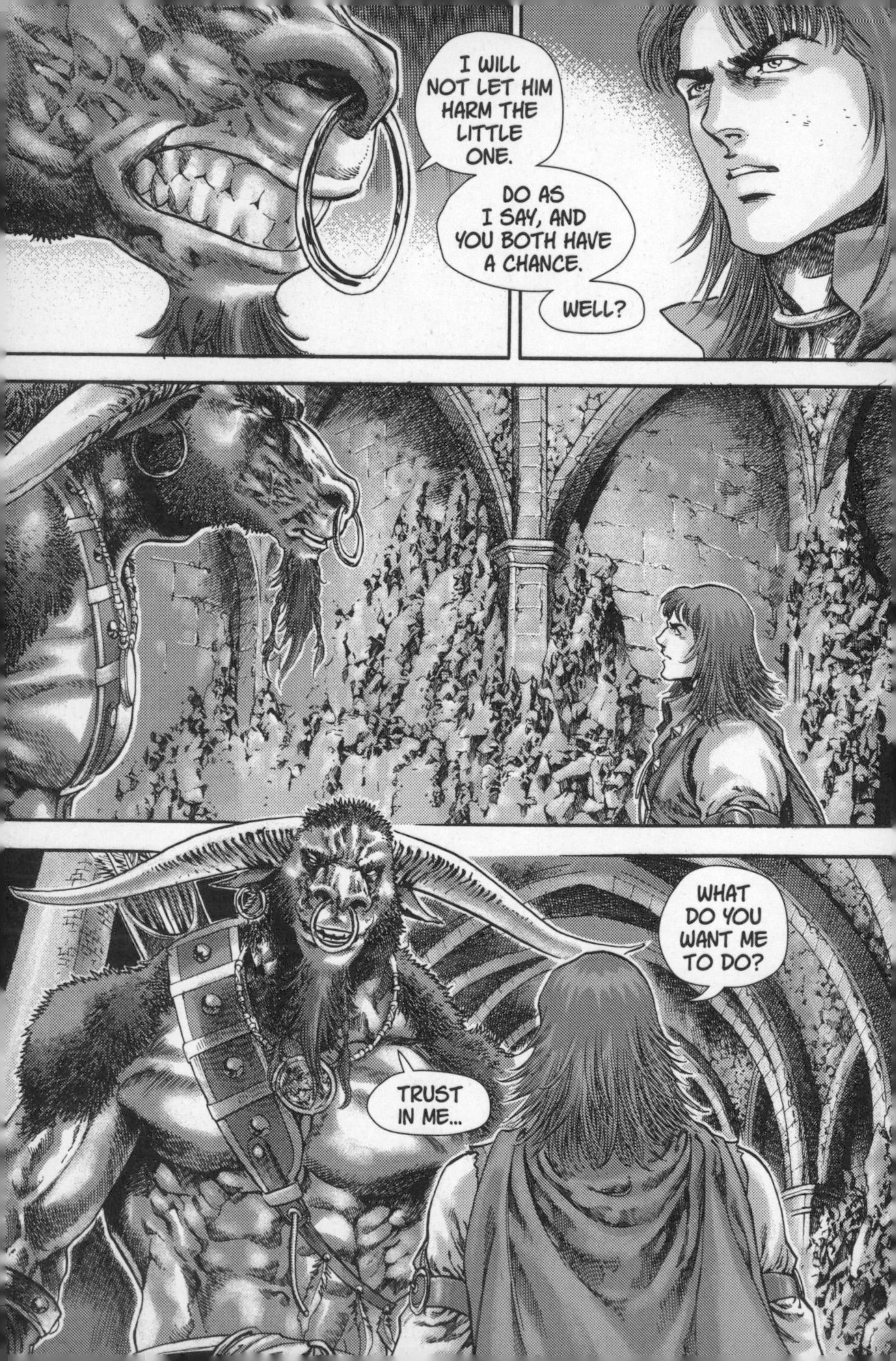
I WILL NOT LET HIM HARM THE LITTLE ONE.
DO AS I SAY, AND YOU BOTH HAVE A CHANCE.
WELL?
WHAT DO YOU WANT ME TO DO?
TRUST IN ME...

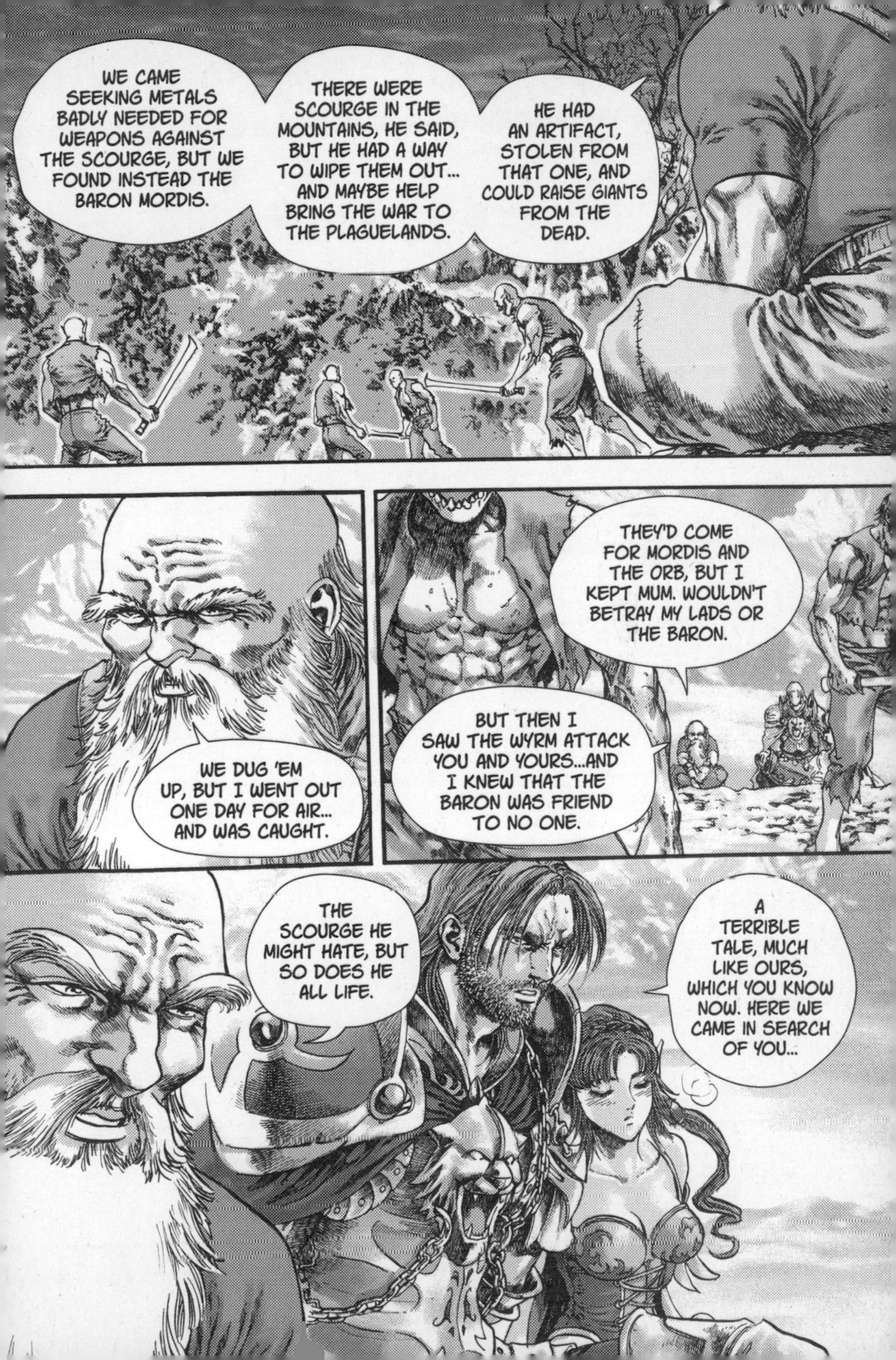
WE CAME SEEKING METALS BADLY NEEDED FOR WEAPONS AGAINST THE SCOURGE, BUT WE FOUND INSTEAD THE BARON MORDIS.
THERE WERE SCOURGE IN THE MOUNTAINS, HE SAID, BUT HE HAD A WAY TO WIPE THEM OUT... AND MAYBE HELP BRING THE WAR TO THE PLAGUELANDS.
HE HAD AN ARTIFACT, STOLEN FROM THAT ONE, AND COULD RAISE GIANTS FROM THE DEAD.
WE DUG 'EM UP, BUT I WENT OUT ONE DAY FOR AIR... AND WAS CAUGHT.
THEY'D COME FOR MORDIS AND THE ORB, BUT I KEPT MUM. WOULDN'T BETRAY MY LADS OR THE BARON.
BUT THEN I SAW THE WYRM ATTACK YOU AND YOURS...AND I KNEW THAT THE BARON WAS FRIEND TO NO ONE.
THE SCOURGE HE MIGHT HATE, BUT SO DOES HE ALL LIFE.
A TERRIBLE TALE, MUCH LIKE OURS, WHICH YOU KNOW NOW. HERE WE CAME IN SEARCH OF YOU...

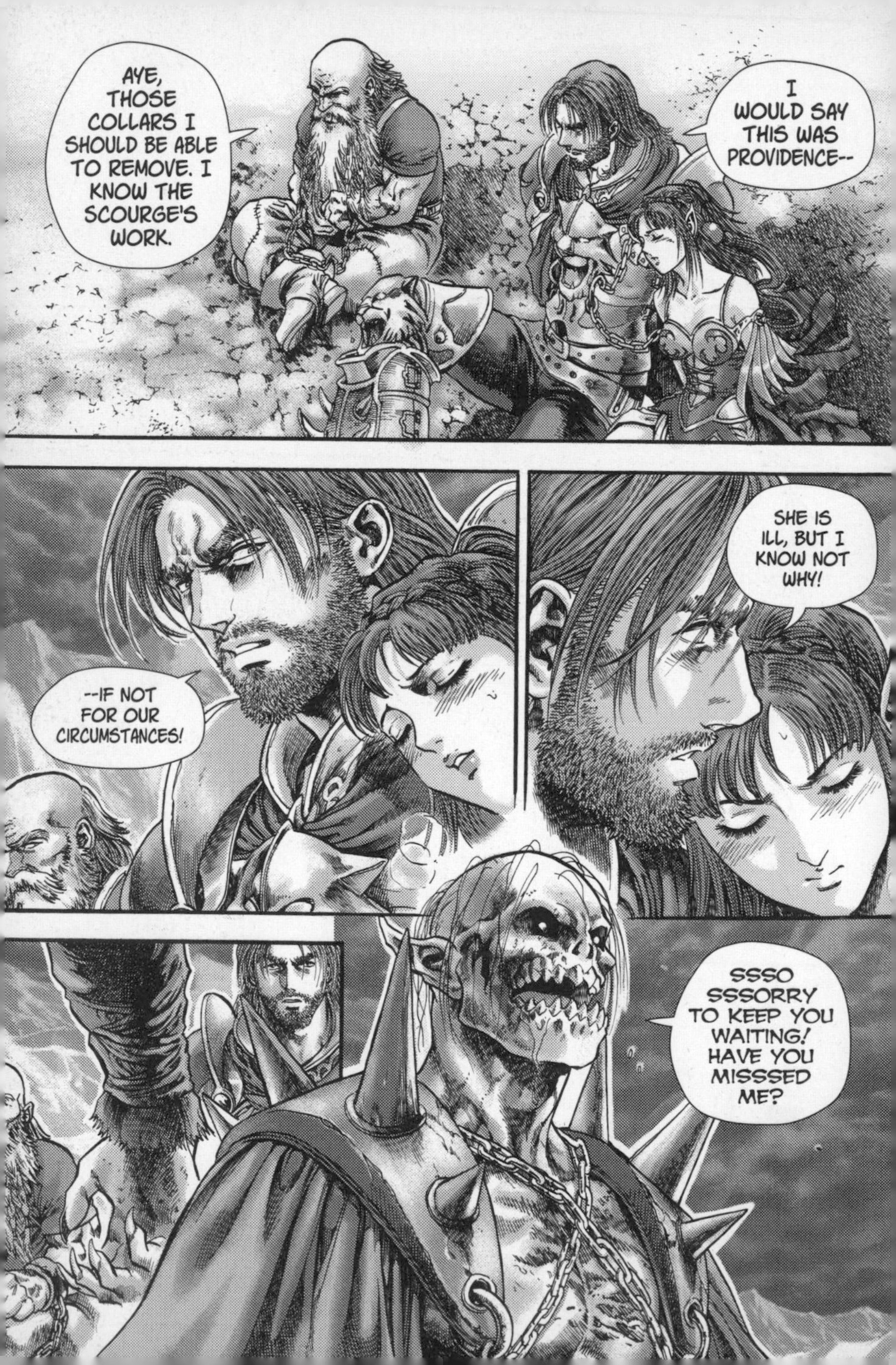
AYE, THOSE COLLARS I SHOULD BE ABLE TO REMOVE. I KNOW THE SCOURGE'S WORK.
I WOULD SAY THIS WAS PROVIDENCE--
--IF NOT FOR OUR CIRCUMSTANCES!
SHE IS ILL, BUT I KNOW NOT WHY!
SSSO SSSORRY TO KEEP YOU WAITING! HAVE YOU MISSSED ME?

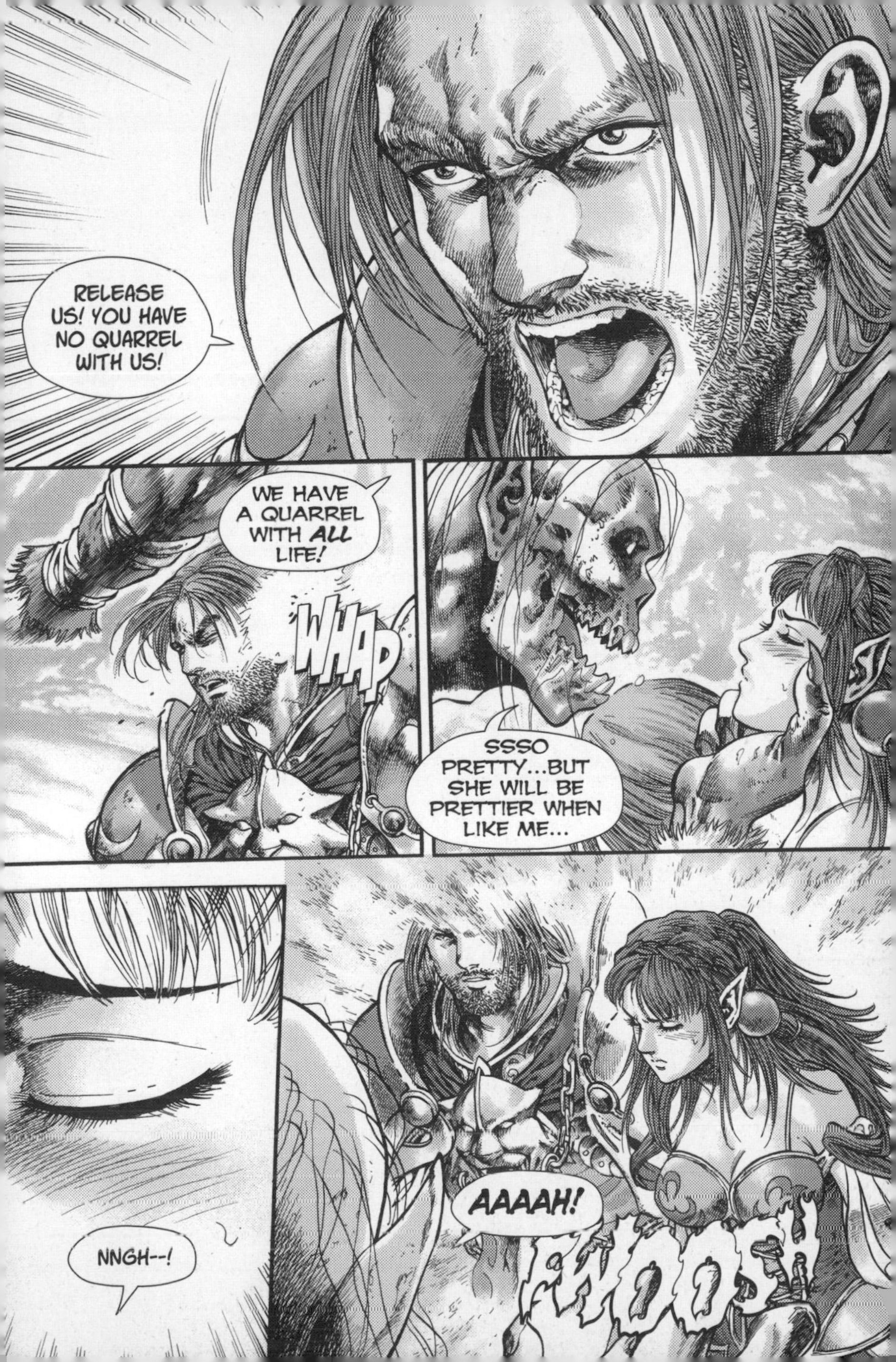
RELEASE US! YOU HAVE NO QUARREL WITH US!
WE HAVE A QUARREL WITH *ALL* LIFE!
WHAP
SSSO PRETTY...BUT SHE WILL BE PRETTIER WHEN LIKE ME...
NNGH--!
AAAAH!
FWOOSH

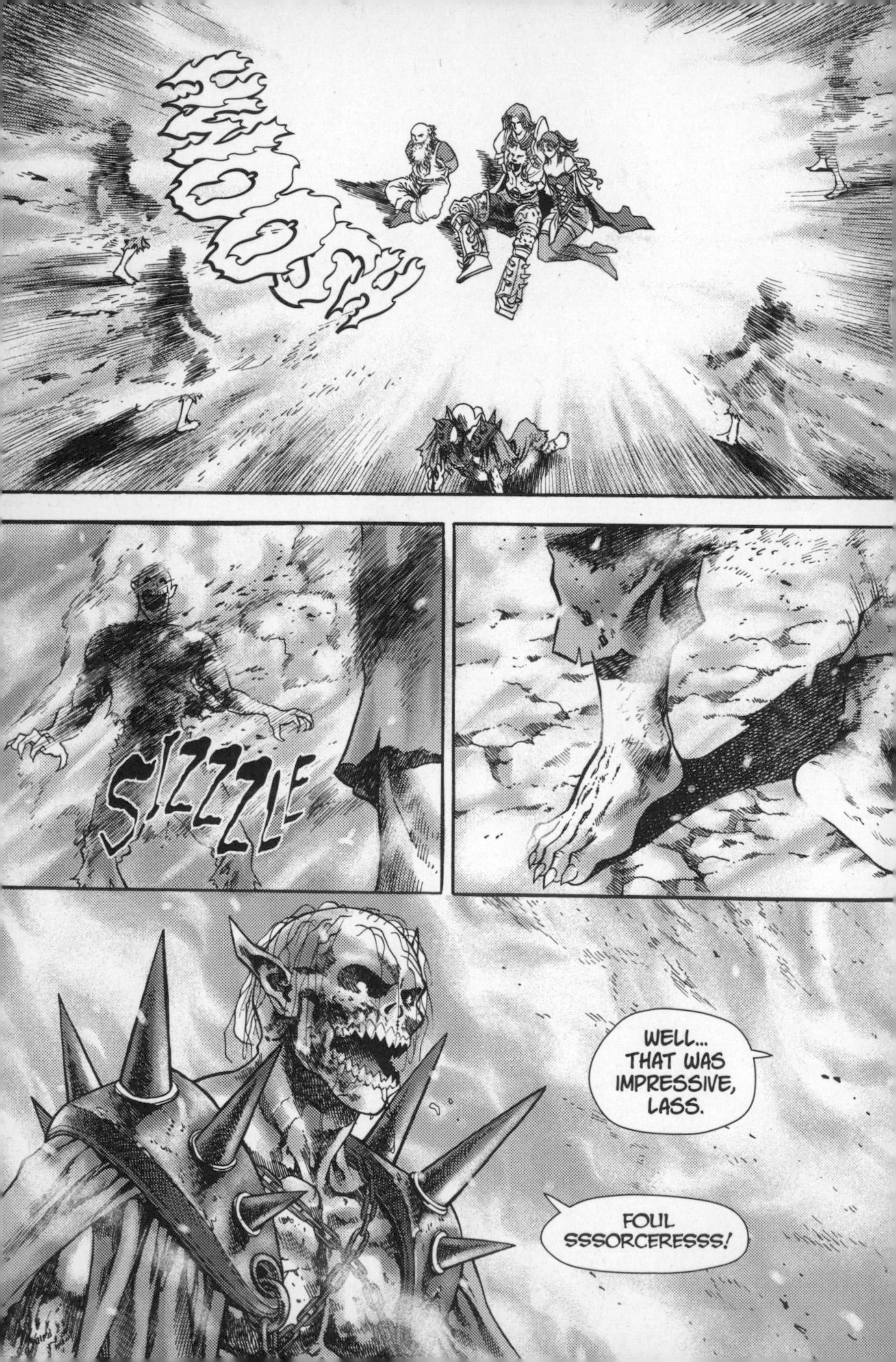
SIZZZLE
WELL... THAT WAS IMPRESSIVE, LASS.
FOUL SSSORCERESSS!

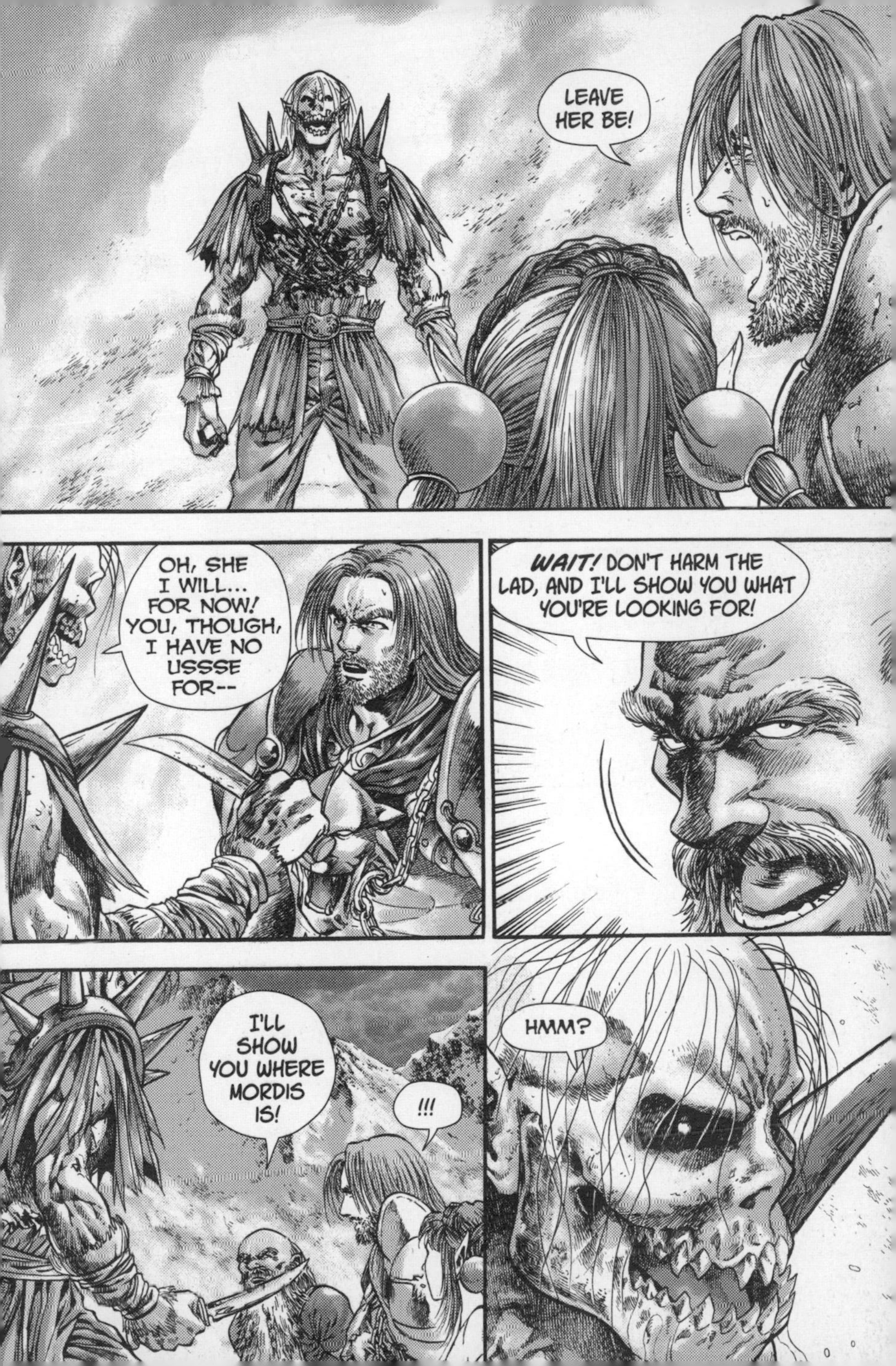
LEAVE HER BE!
OH, SHE I WILL... FOR NOW! YOU, THOUGH, I HAVE NO USSSE FOR--
WAIT! DON'T HARM THE LAD, AND I'LL SHOW YOU WHAT YOU'RE LOOKING FOR!
I'LL SHOW YOU WHERE MORDIS IS!
!!!
HMM?

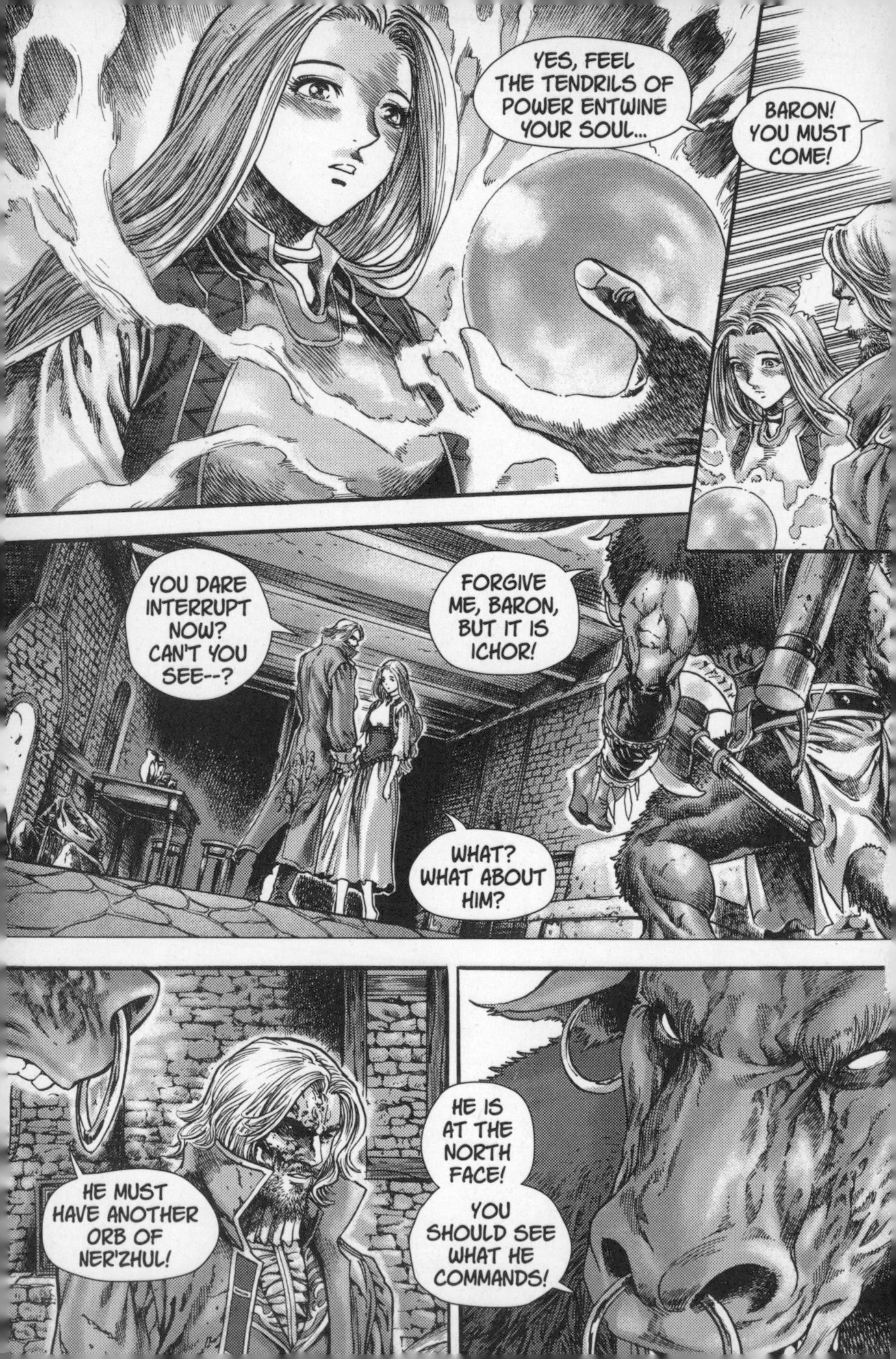
YES, FEEL THE TENDRILS OF POWER ENTWINE YOUR SOUL...
BARON! YOU MUST COME!
YOU DARE INTERRUPT NOW? CAN'T YOU SEE--?
FORGIVE ME, BARON, BUT IT IS ICHOR!
WHAT? WHAT ABOUT HIM?
HE MUST HAVE ANOTHER ORB OF NER'ZHUL!
HE IS AT THE NORTH FACE!
YOU SHOULD SEE WHAT HE COMMANDS!

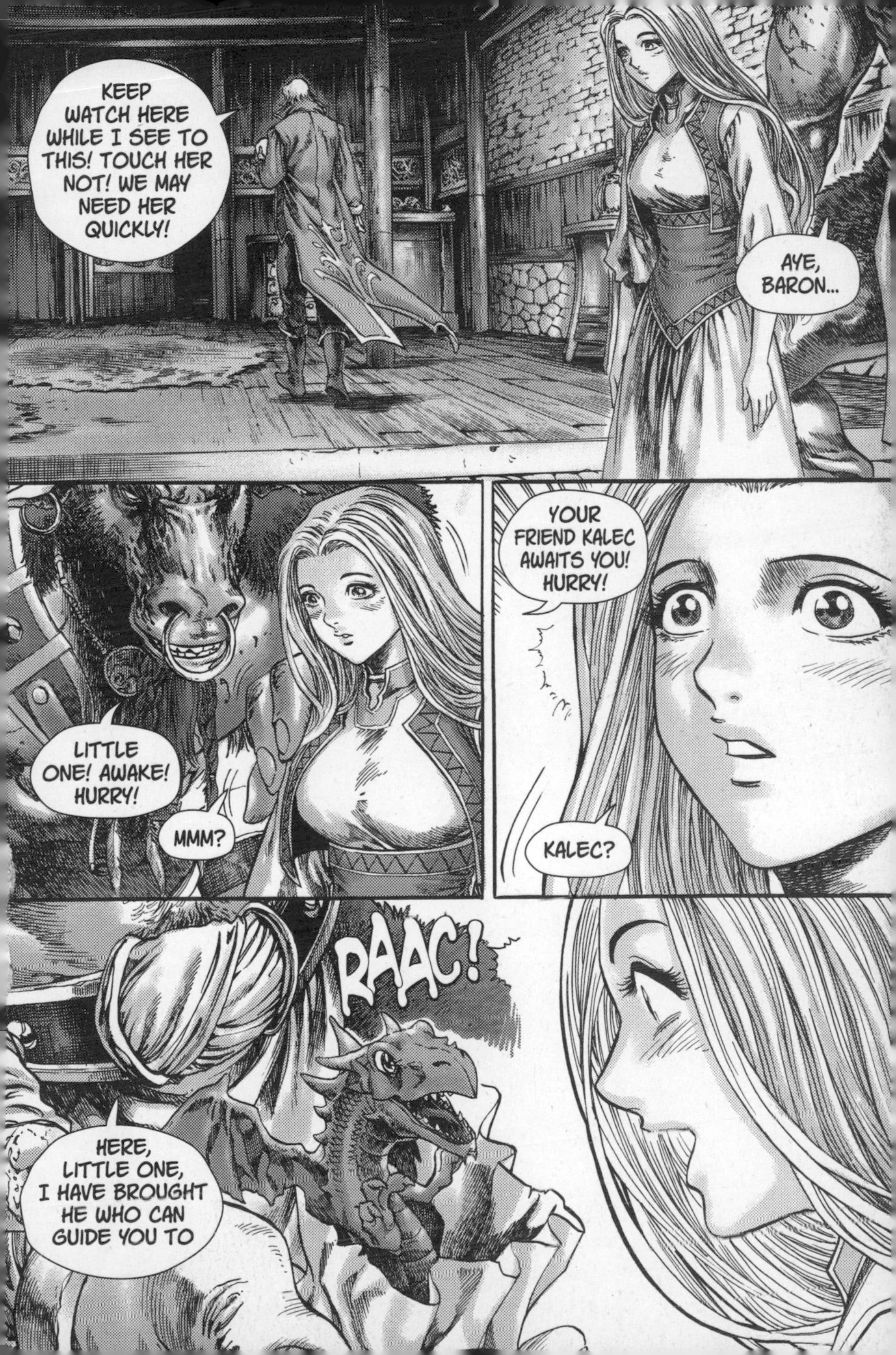
KEEP WATCH HERE WHILE I SEE TO THIS! TOUCH HER NOT! WE MAY NEED HER QUICKLY!
AYE, BARON...
LITTLE ONE! AWAKE! HURRY!
MMM?
YOUR FRIEND KALEC AWAITS YOU! HURRY!
KALEC?
RAAC!
HERE, LITTLE ONE, I HAVE BROUGHT HE WHO CAN GUIDE YOU TO

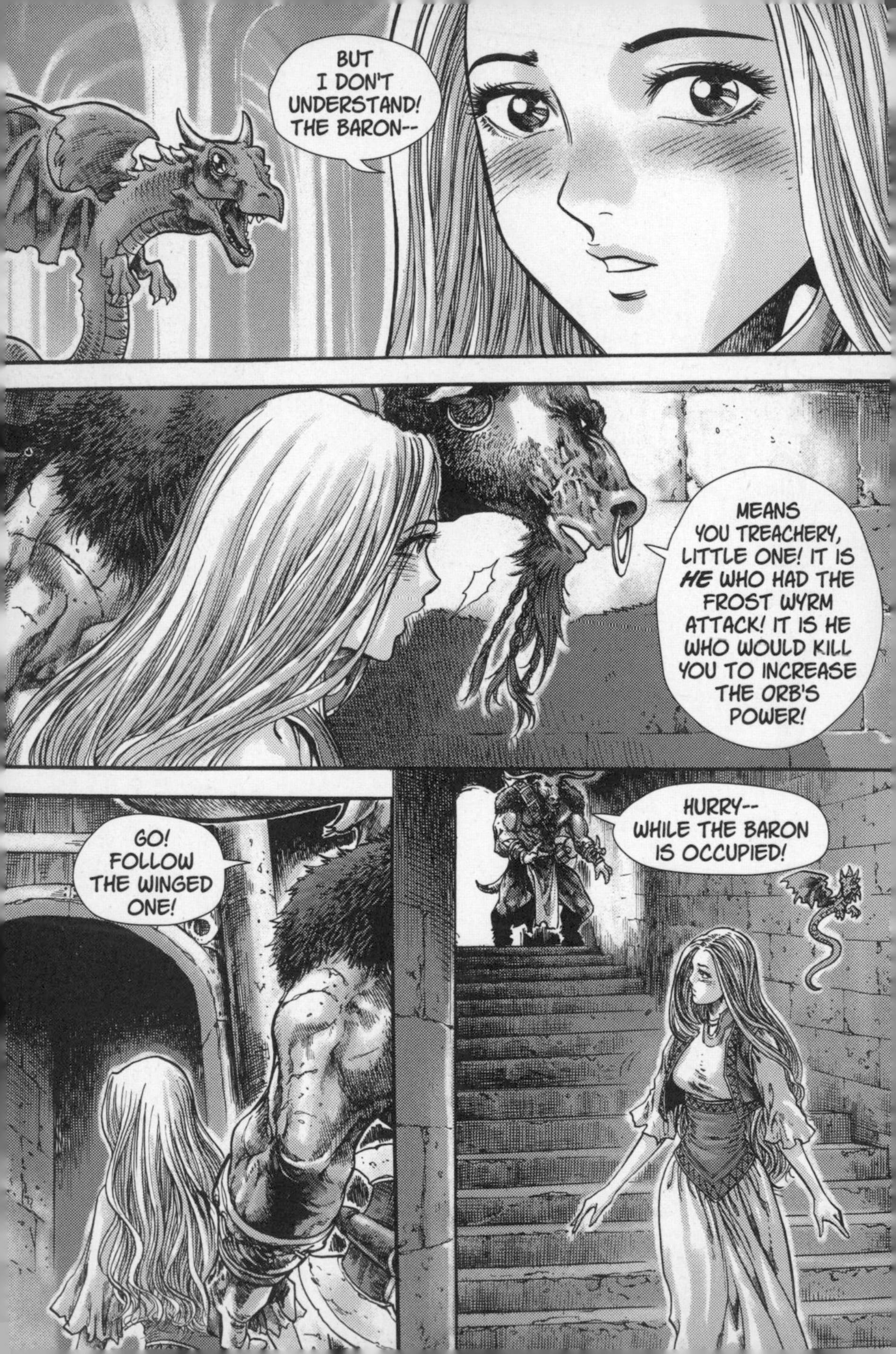
BUT I DON'T UNDERSTAND! THE BARON--
MEANS YOU TREACHERY, LITTLE ONE! IT IS HE WHO HAD THE FROST WYRM ATTACK! IT IS HE WHO WOULD KILL YOU TO INCREASE THE ORB'S POWER!
GO! FOLLOW THE WINGED ONE!
HURRY-- WHILE THE BARON IS OCCUPIED!

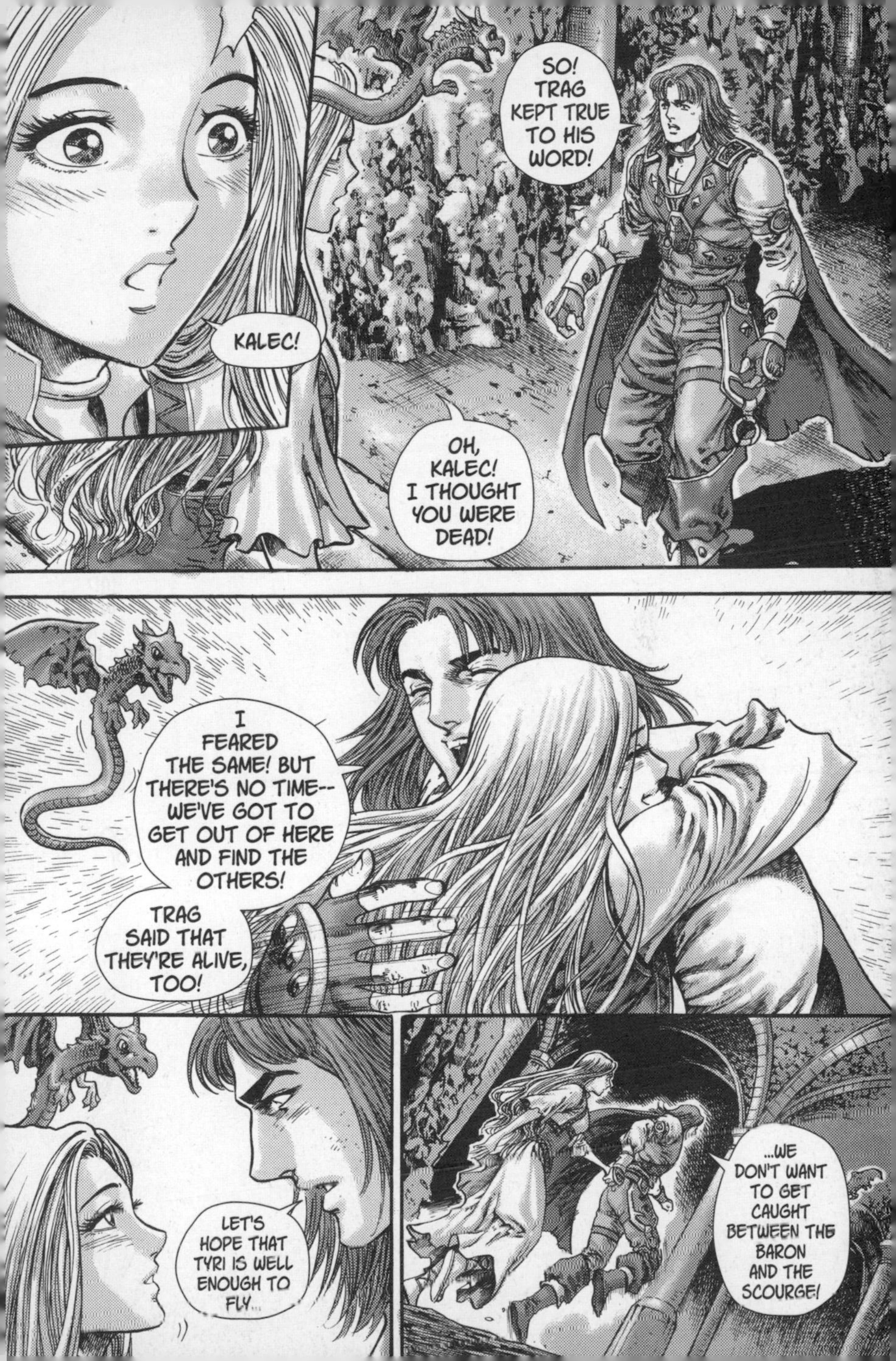
KALEC!
SO! TRAG KEPT TRUE TO HIS WORD!
OH, KALEC! I THOUGHT YOU WERE DEAD!
I FEARED THE SAME! BUT THERE'S NO TIME-- WE'VE GOT TO GET OUT OF HERE AND FIND THE OTHERS!
TRAG SAID THAT THEY'RE ALIVE, TOO!
LET'S HOPE THAT TYRI IS WELL ENOUGH TO FLY...
...WE DON'T WANT TO GET CAUGHT BETWEEN THE BARON AND THE SCOURGE!

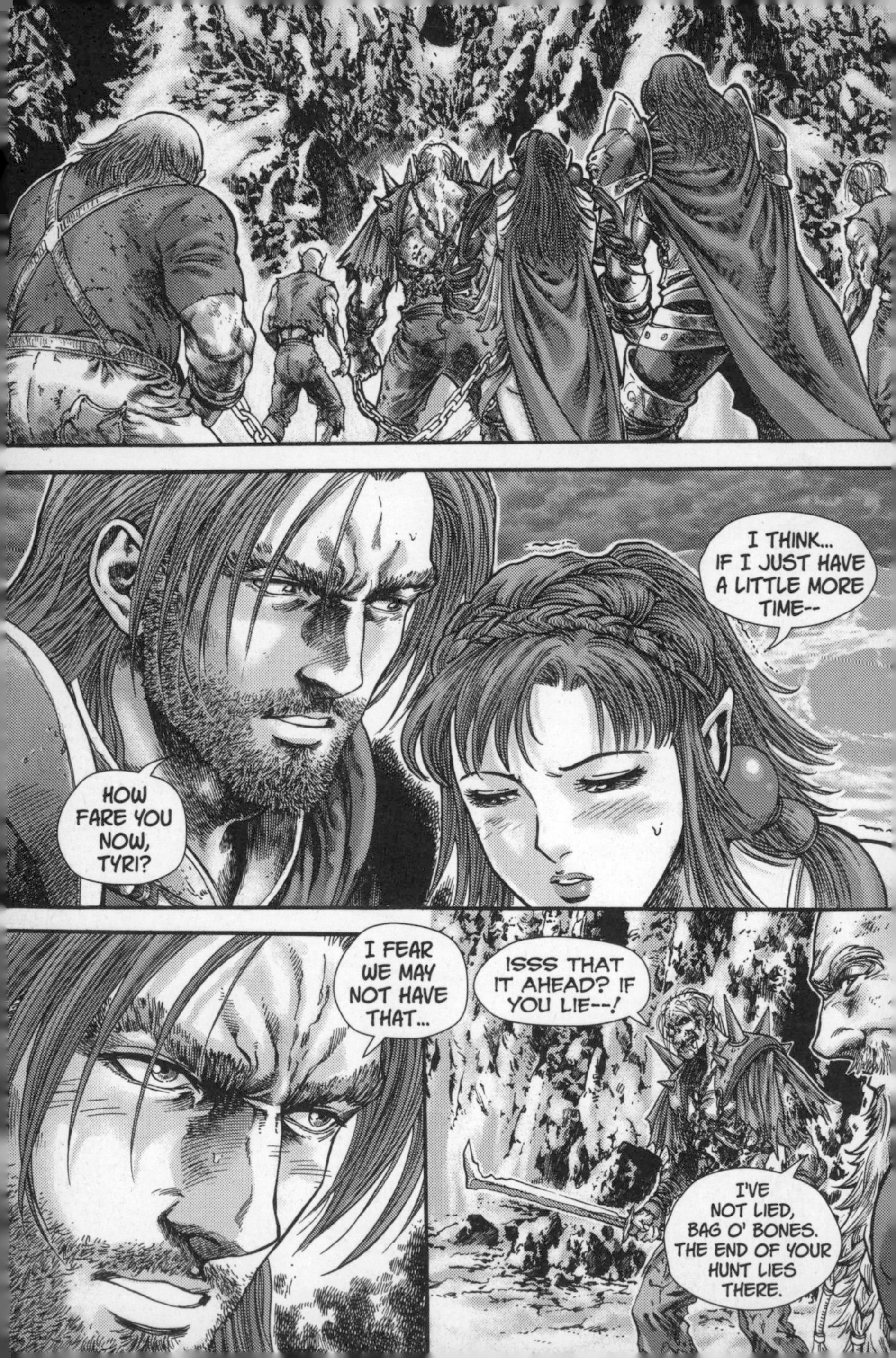
HOW FARE YOU NOW, TYRI?
I THINK... IF I JUST HAVE A LITTLE MORE TIME--
I FEAR WE MAY NOT HAVE THAT...
ISSS THAT IT AHEAD? IF YOU LIE--!
I'VE NOT LIED, BAG O' BONES. THE END OF YOUR HUNT LIES THERE.

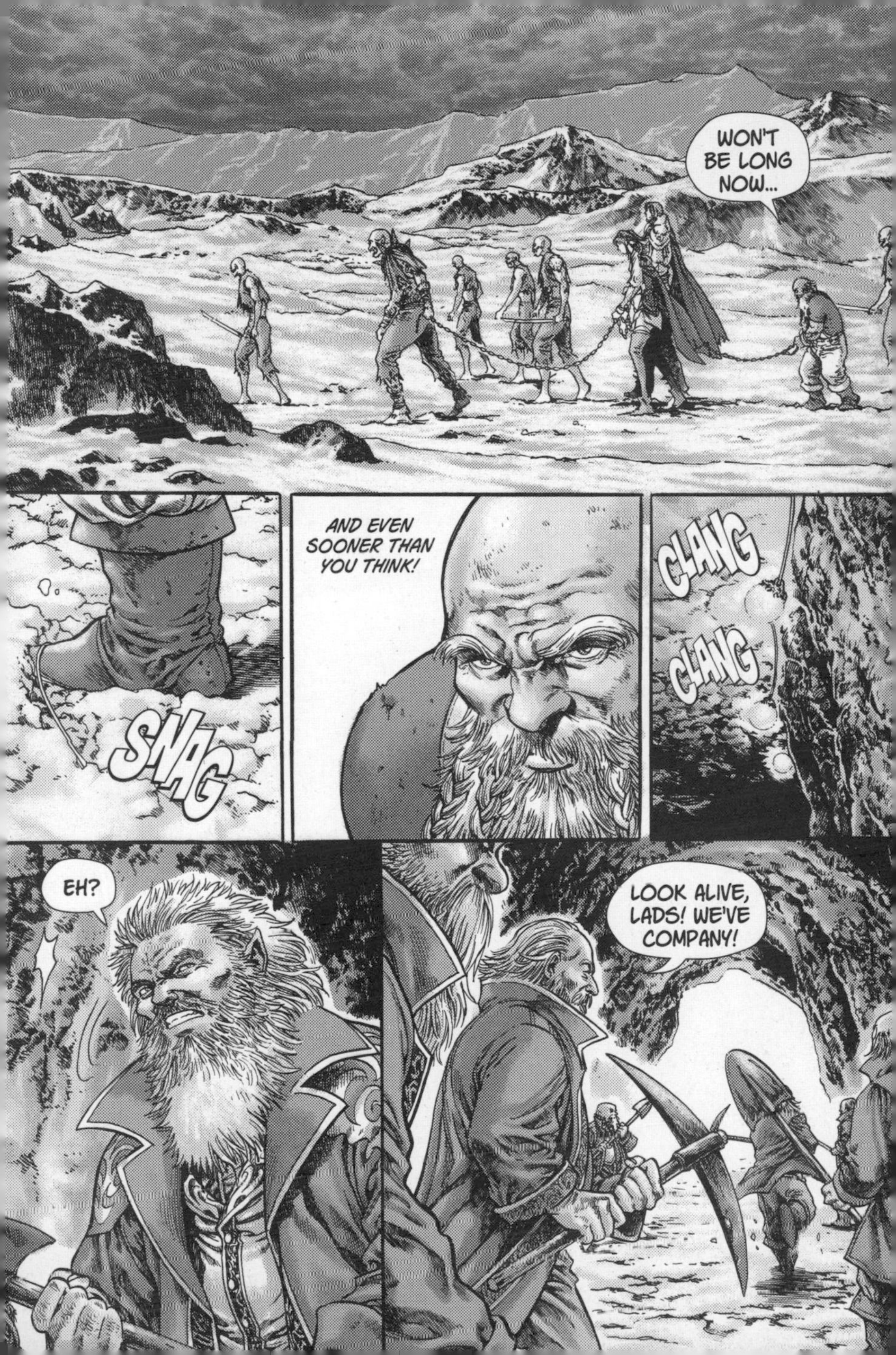
WON'T BE LONG NOW...
SNAG
AND EVEN SOONER THAN YOU THINK!
CLANG
CLANG
EH?
LOOK ALIVE, LADS! WE'VE COMPANY!

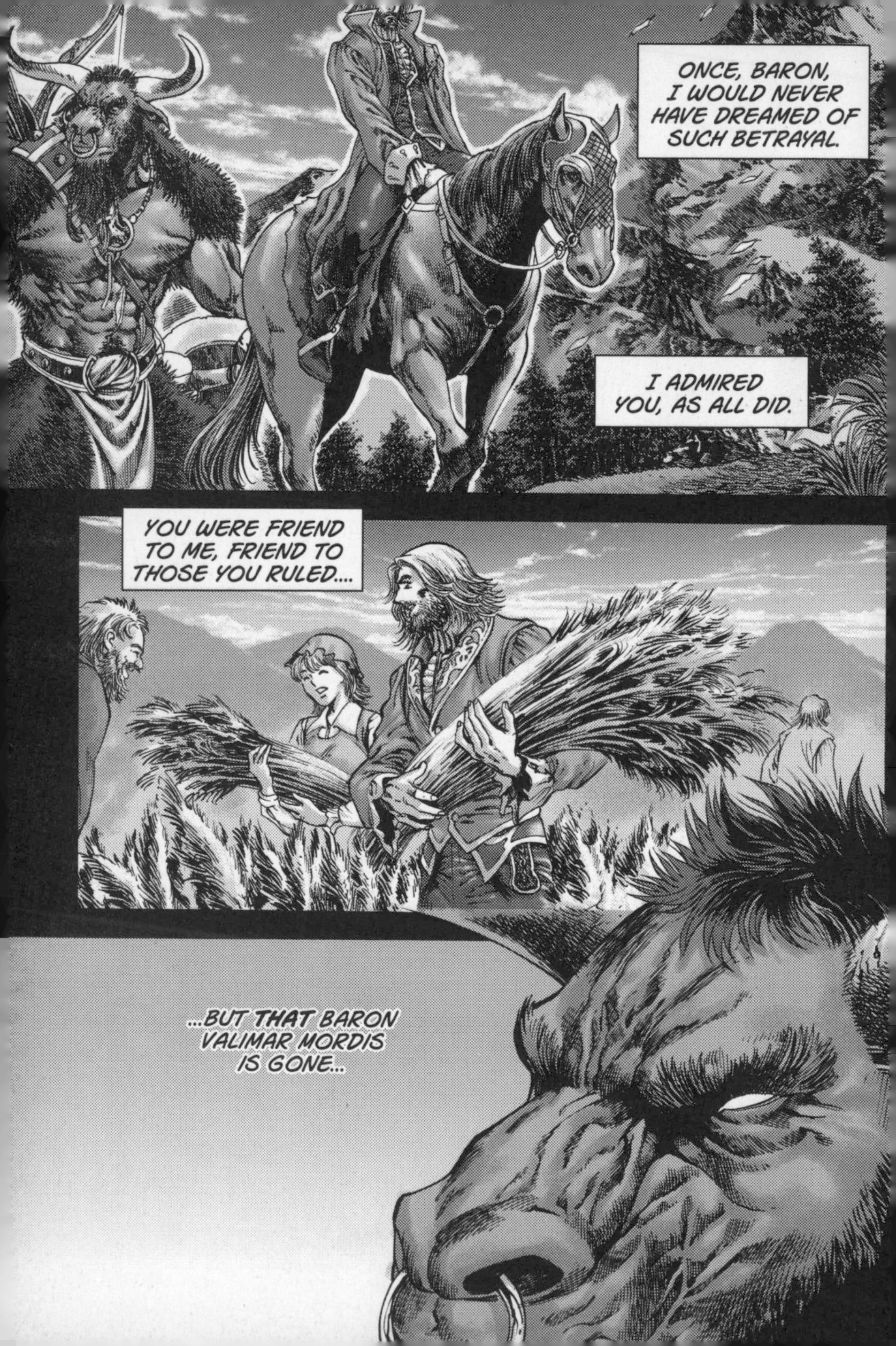
ONCE, BARON, I WOULD NEVER HAVE DREAMED OF SUCH BETRAYAL.
I ADMIRED YOU, AS ALL DID.
YOU WERE FRIEND TO ME, FRIEND TO THOSE YOU RULED....
...BUT THAT BARON VALIMAR MORDIS IS GONE...

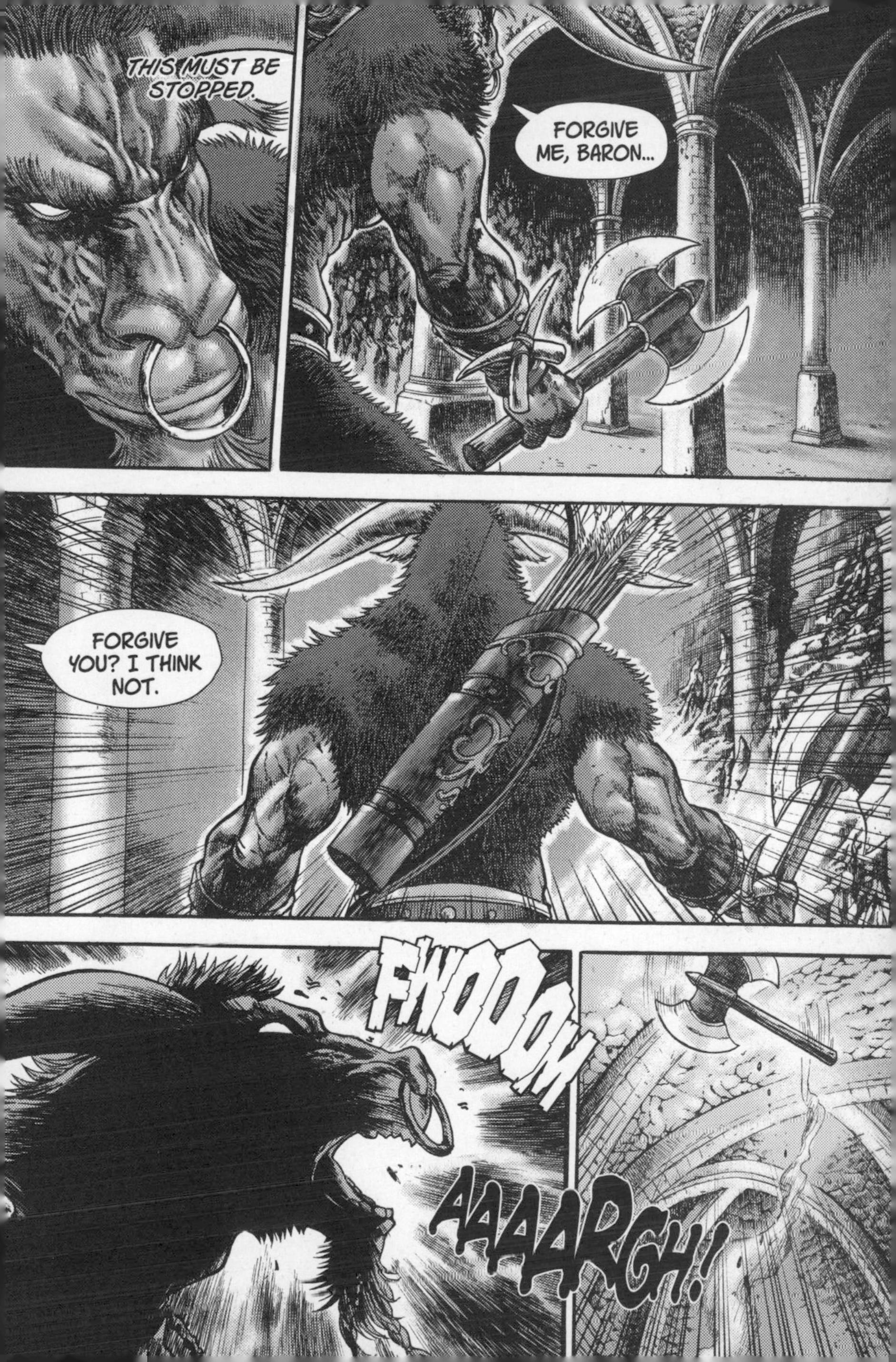
THIS MUST BE STOPPED.
FORGIVE ME, BARON...
FORGIVE YOU? I THINK NOT.
FWOOOM
AAAARGH!

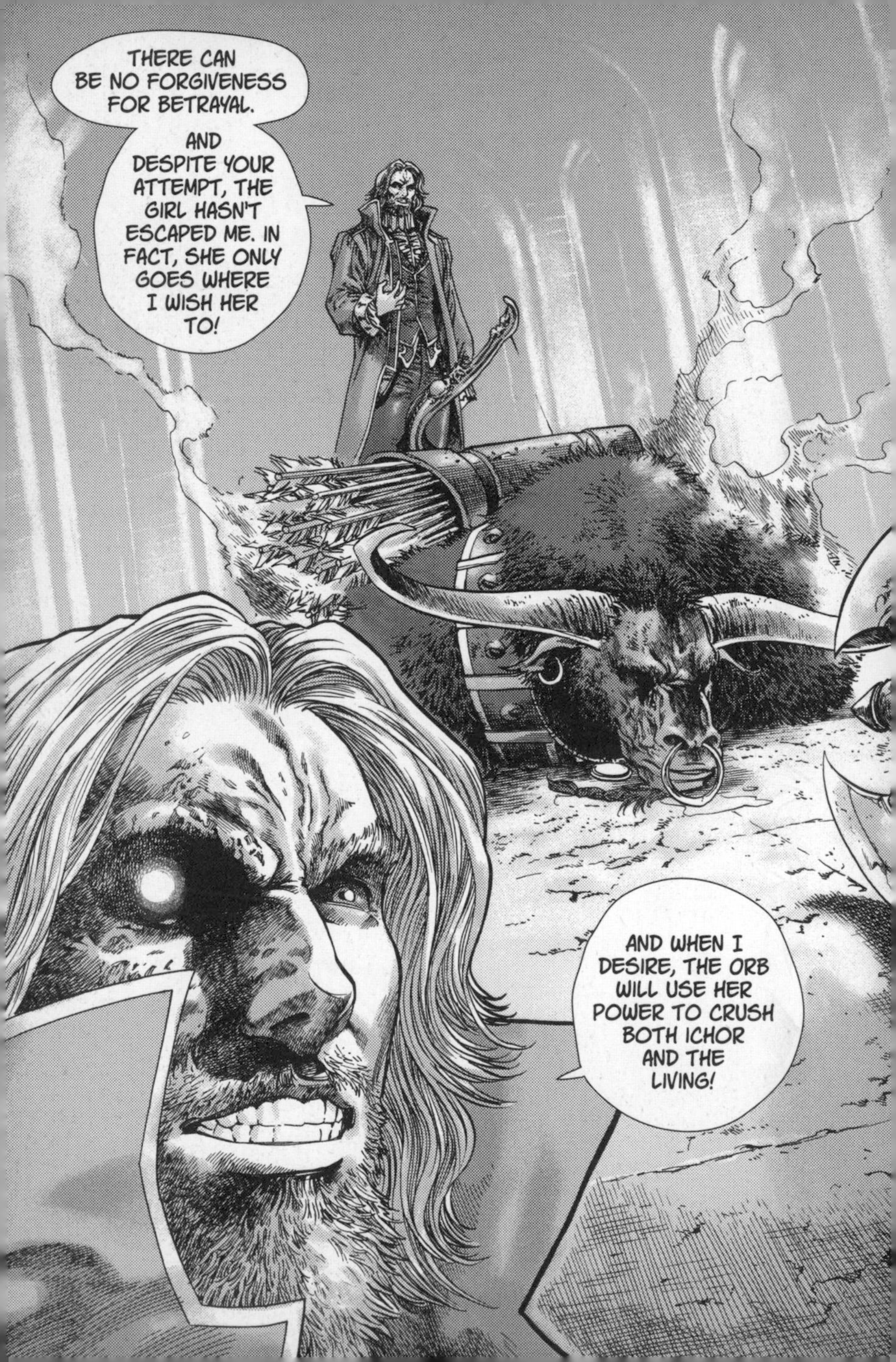
THERE CAN BE NO FORGIVENESS FOR BETRAYAL.
AND DESPITE YOUR ATTEMPT, THE GIRL HASN'T ESCAPED ME. IN FACT, SHE ONLY GOES WHERE I WISH HER TO!
AND WHEN I DESIRE, THE ORB WILL USE HER POWER TO CRUSH BOTH ICHOR AND THE LIVING!

CHAPTER SIX

Death on the Mountain

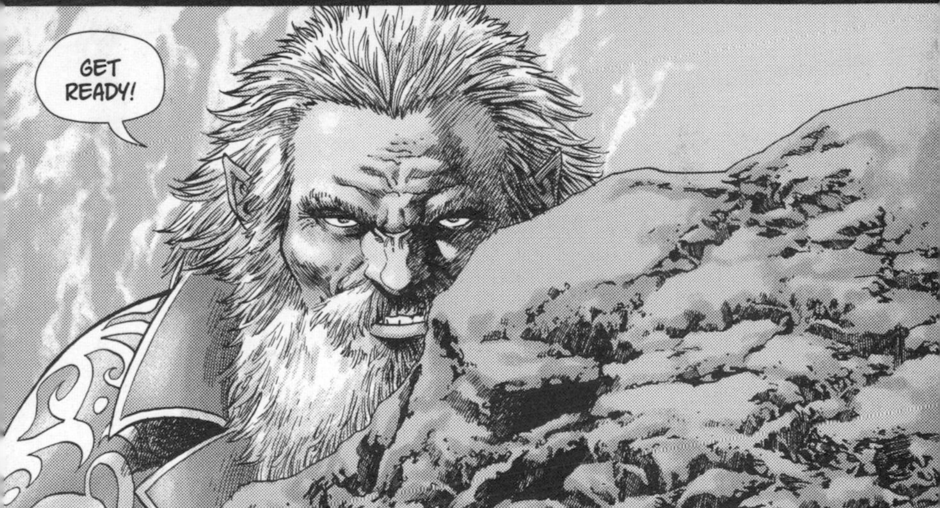
GET READY!

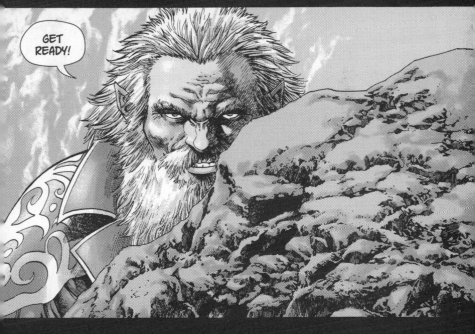

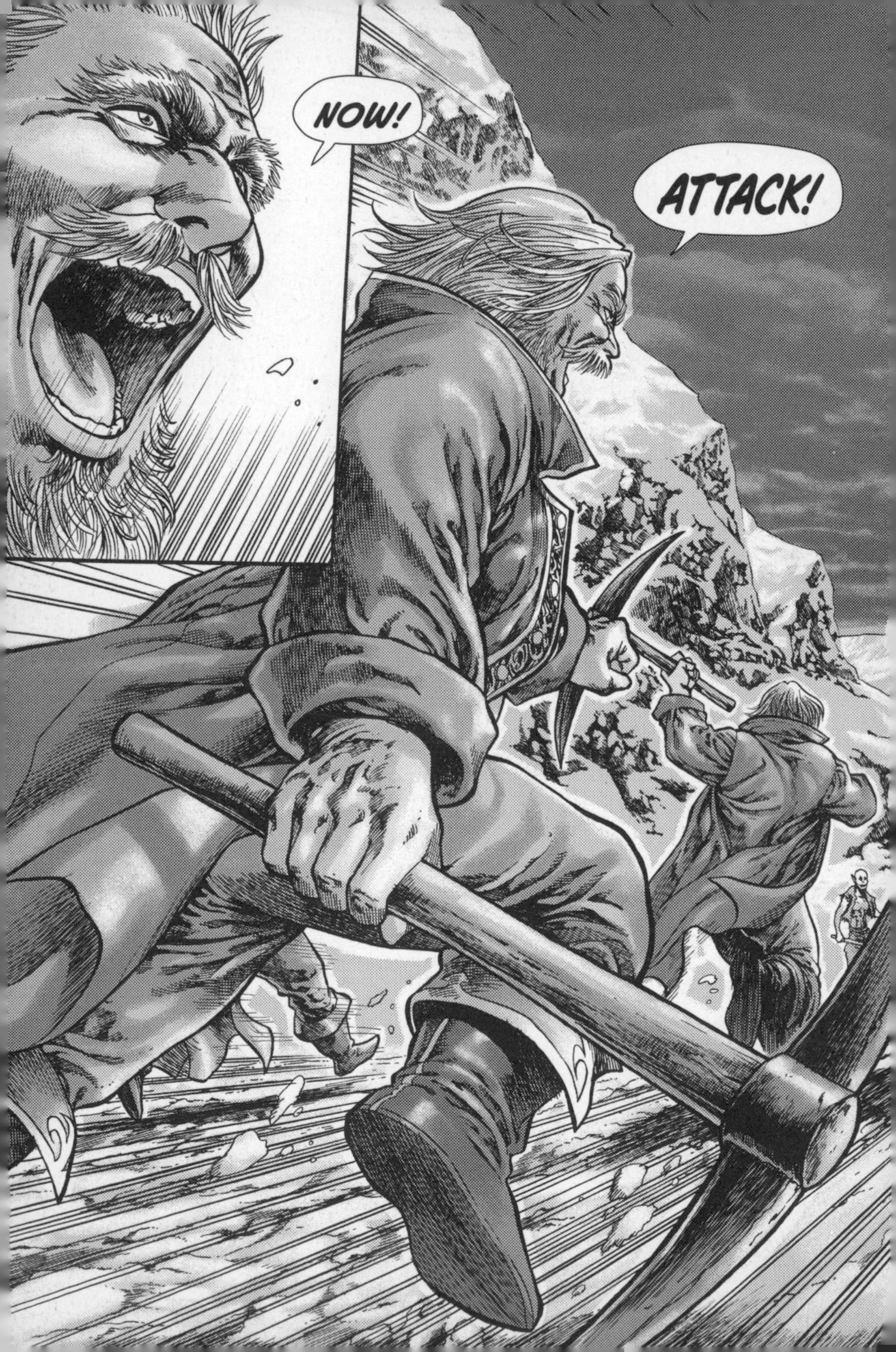
NOW!
ATTACK!

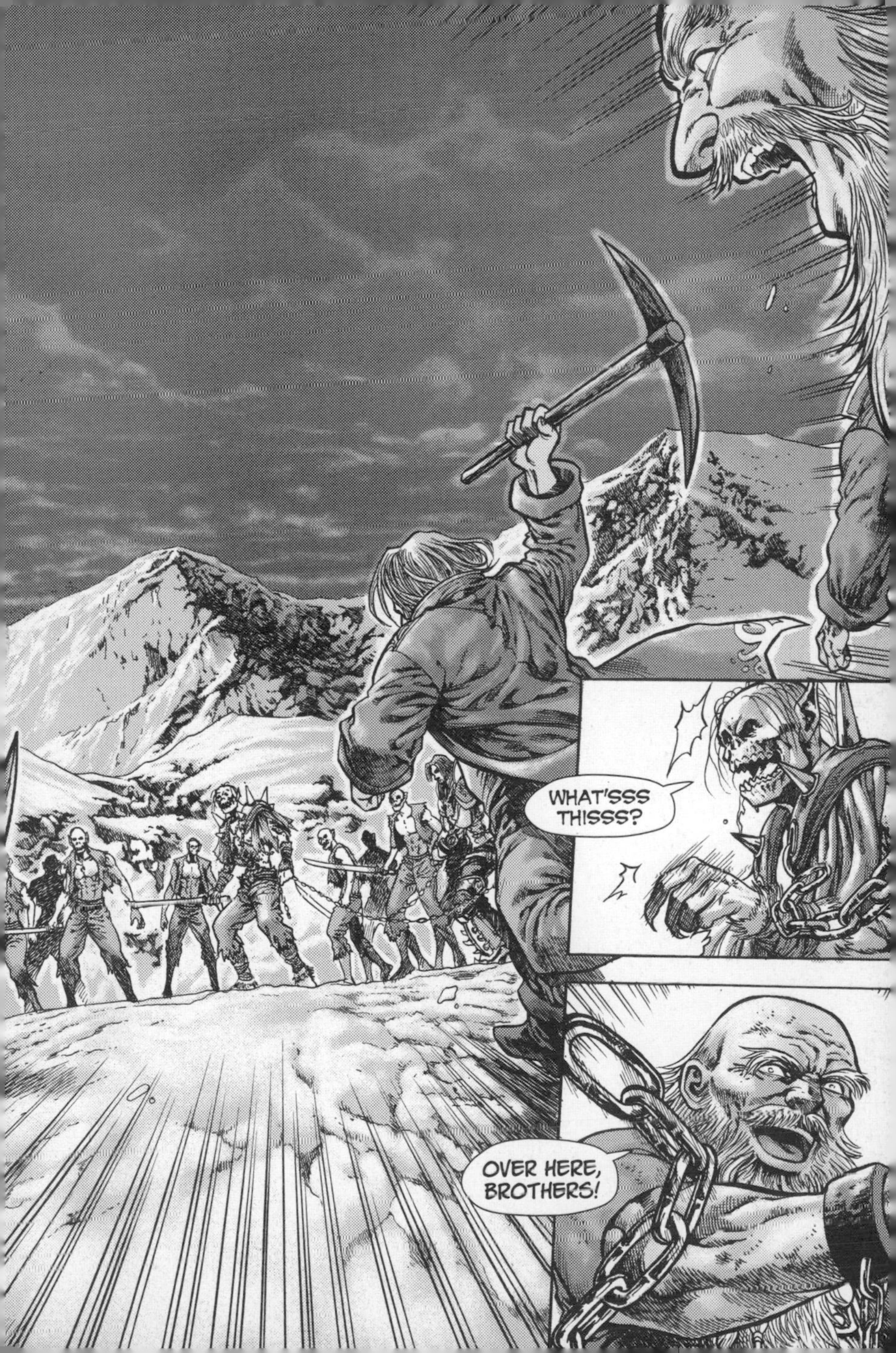
WHAT'SSS THISSS?
OVER HERE, BROTHERS!

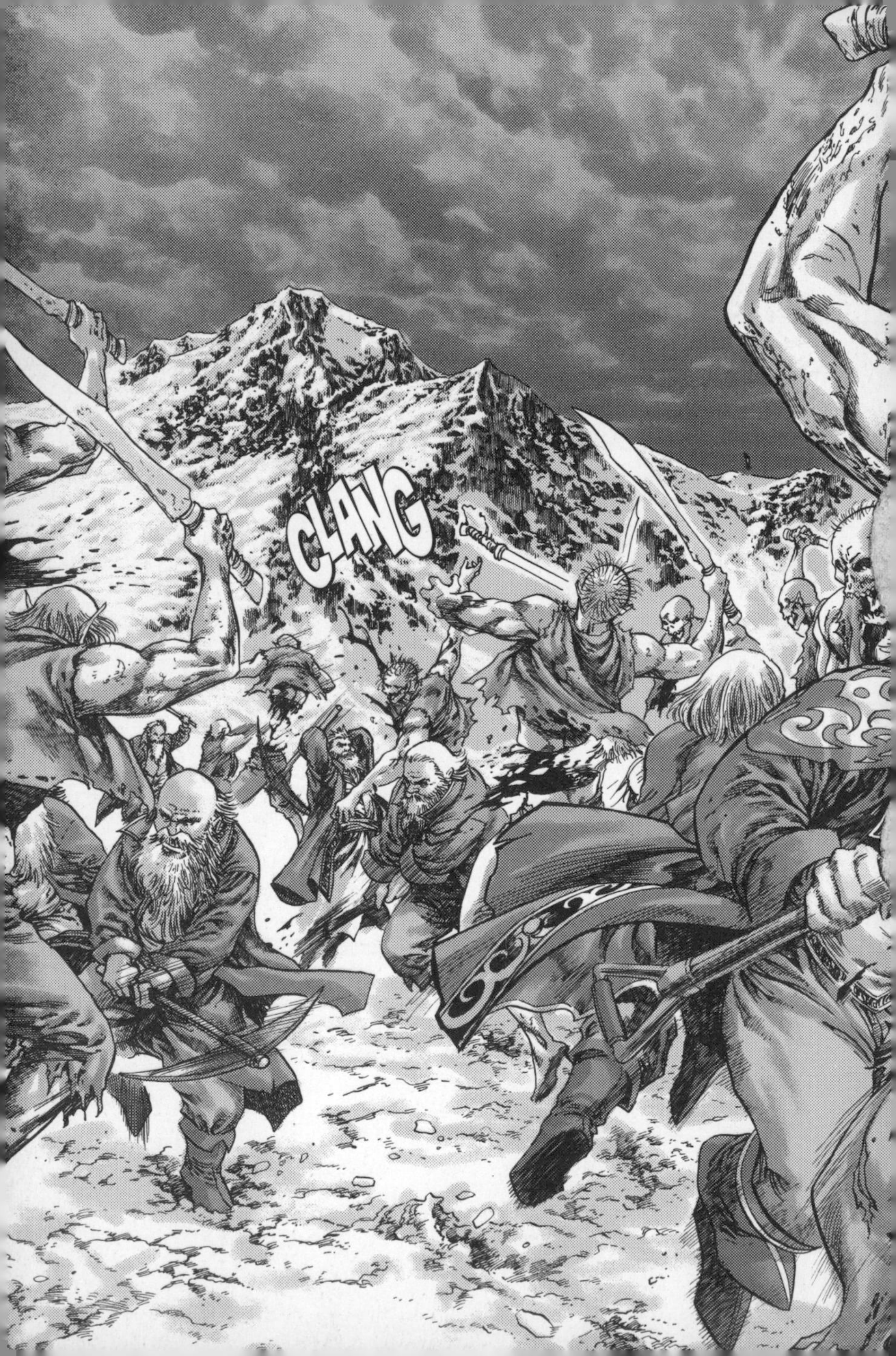
CLANG

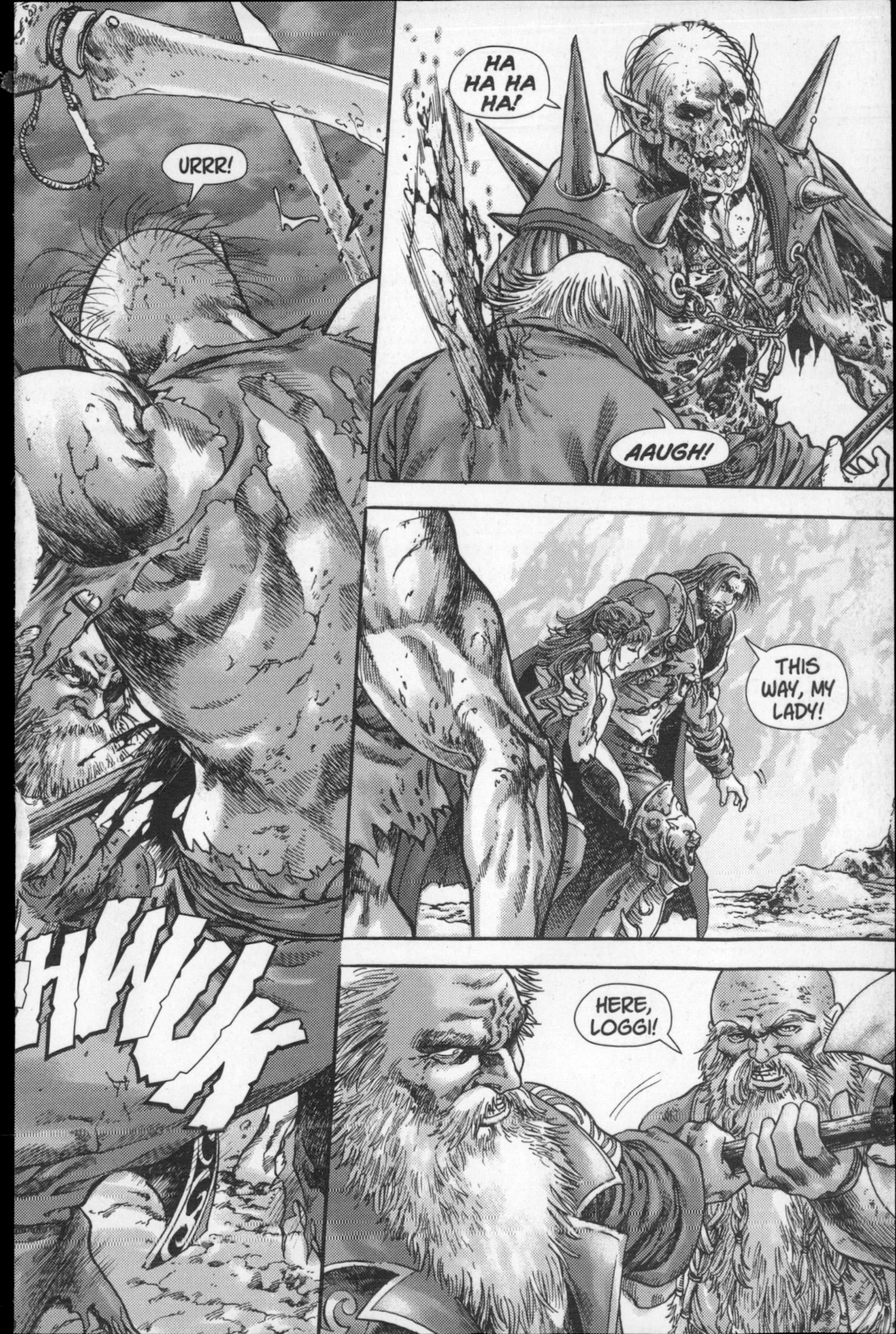
URRR!
HWK
HA HA HA HA!
AAUGH!
THIS WAY, MY LADY!
HERE, LOGGI!

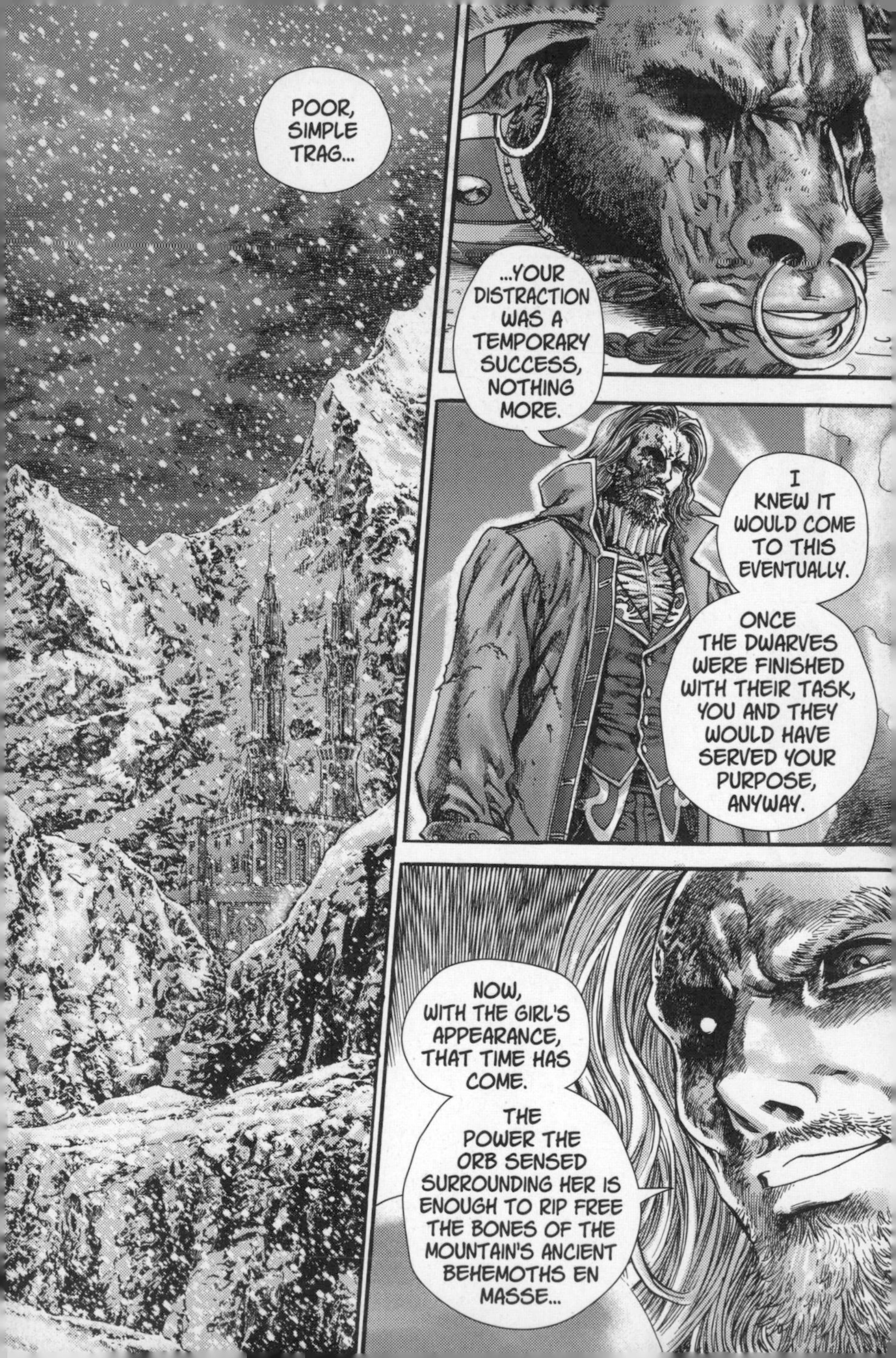
POOR, SIMPLE TRAG...
...YOUR DISTRACTION WAS A TEMPORARY SUCCESS, NOTHING MORE.
I KNEW IT WOULD COME TO THIS EVENTUALLY.
ONCE THE DWARVES WERE FINISHED WITH THEIR TASK, YOU AND THEY WOULD HAVE SERVED YOUR PURPOSE, ANYWAY.
NOW, WITH THE GIRL'S APPEARANCE, THAT TIME HAS COME.
THE POWER THE ORB SENSED SURROUNDING HER IS ENOUGH TO RIP FREE THE BONES OF THE MOUNTAIN'S ANCIENT BEHEMOTHS EN MASSE...

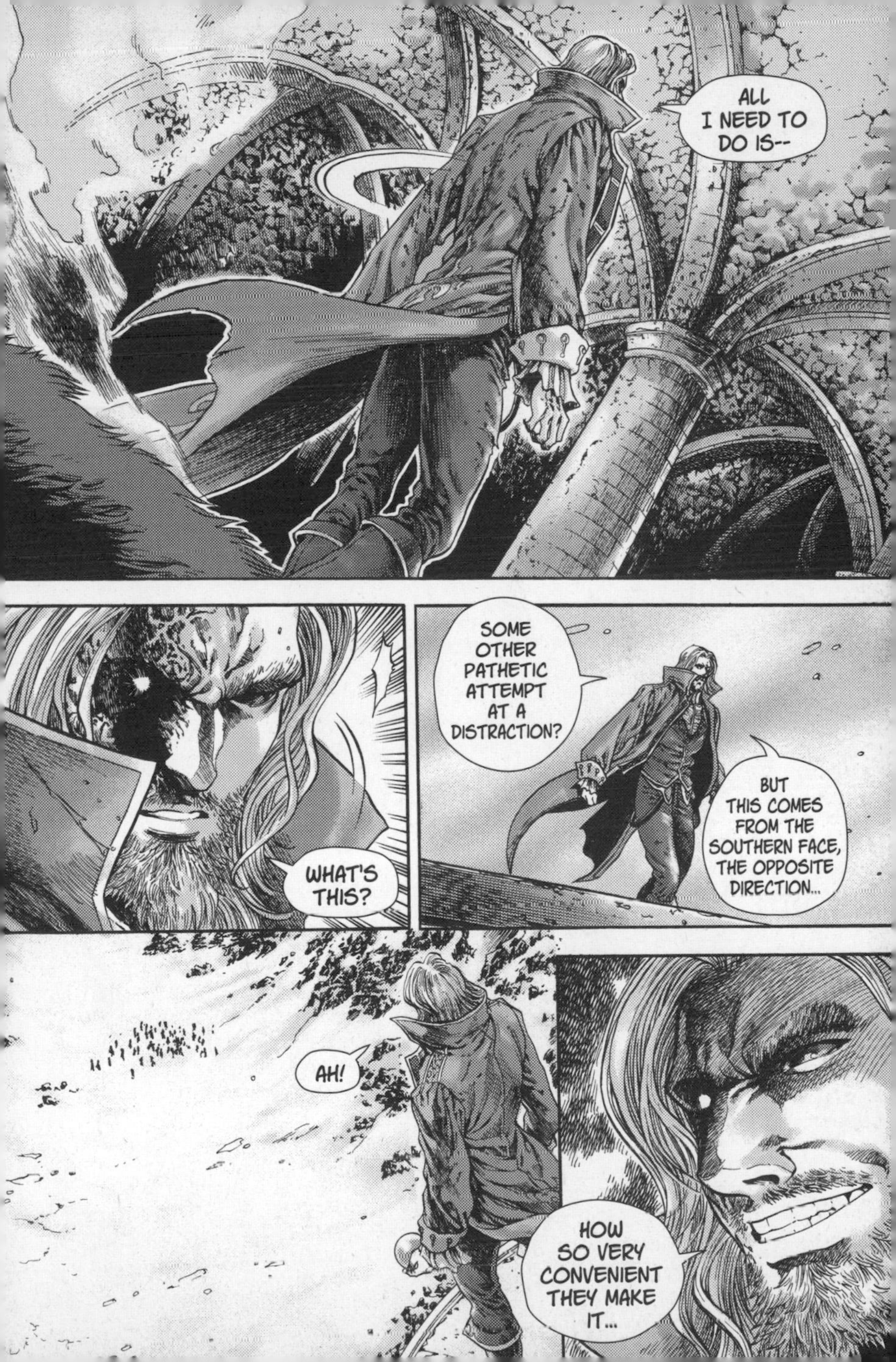
ALL I NEED TO DO IS--
WHAT'S THIS?
SOME OTHER PATHETIC ATTEMPT AT A DISTRACTION?
BUT THIS COMES FROM THE SOUTHERN FACE, THE OPPOSITE DIRECTION...
AH!
HOW SO VERY CONVENIENT THEY MAKE IT...

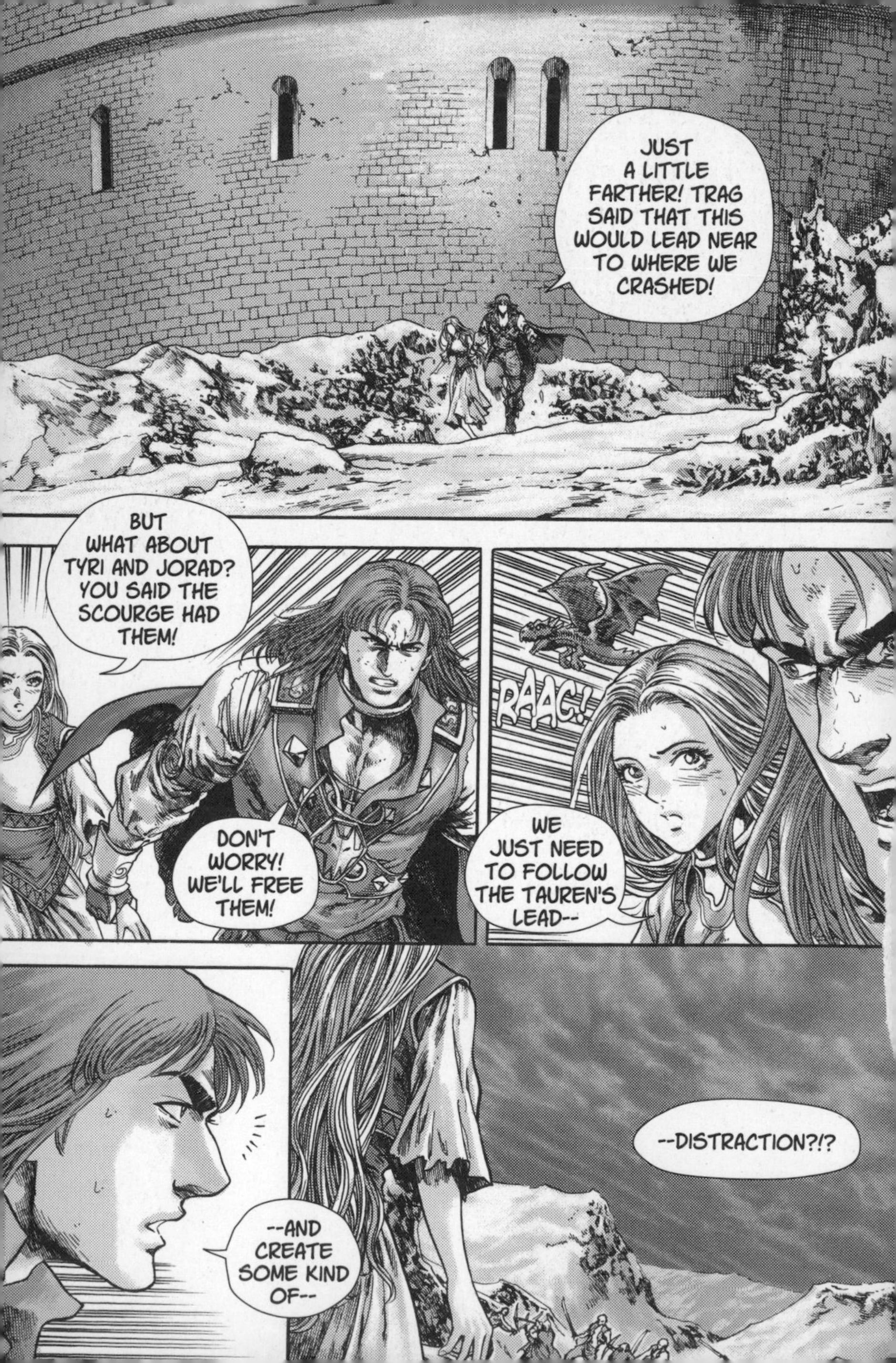
JUST A LITTLE FARTHER! TRAG SAID THAT THIS WOULD LEAD NEAR TO WHERE WE CRASHED!
BUT WHAT ABOUT TYRI AND JORAD? YOU SAID THE SCOURGE HAD THEM!
DON'T WORRY! WE'LL FREE THEM!
RAAC!
WE JUST NEED TO FOLLOW THE TAUREN'S LEAD--
--AND CREATE SOME KIND OF--
--DISTRACTION?!?

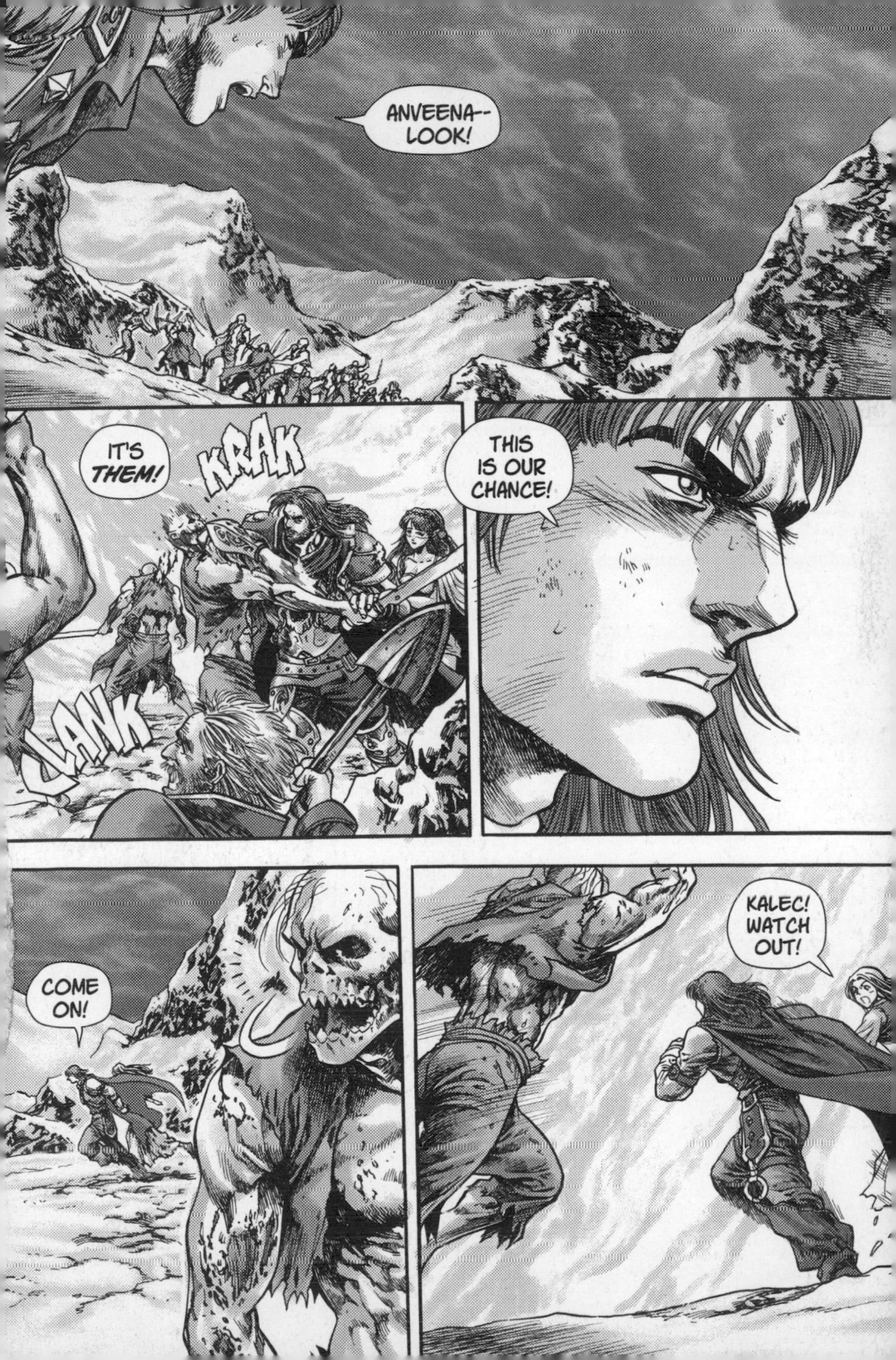
ANVEENA--
LOOK!
IT'S
THEM!
KRAK
CLANK
THIS
IS OUR
CHANCE!
COME
ON!
KALEC!
WATCH
OUT!

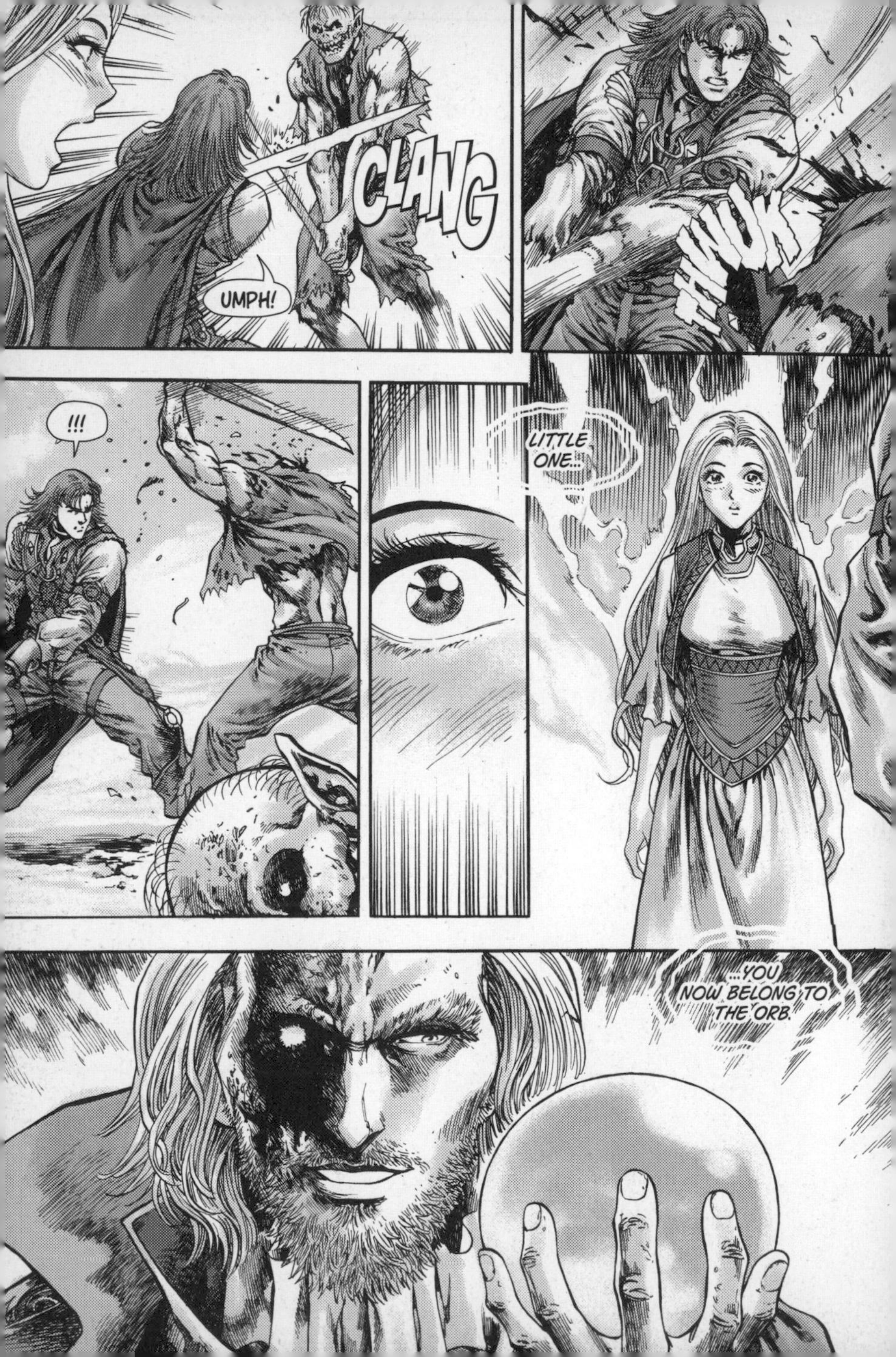
CLANG
UMPH!
THUNK
!!!
LITTLE ONE...
...YOU NOW BELONG TO THE ORB.

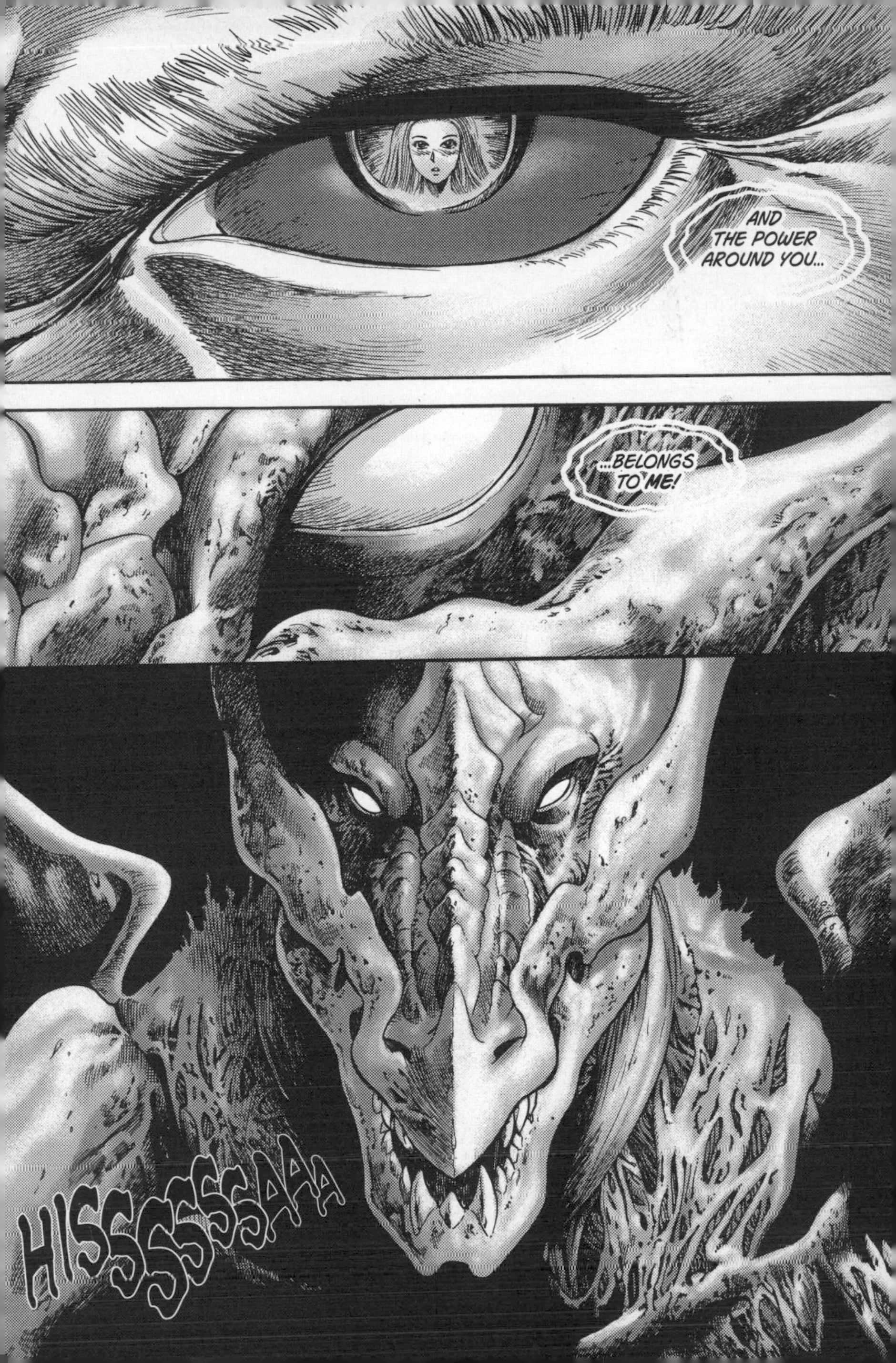
AND THE POWER AROUND YOU...
...BELONGS TO ME!
HISSSSSSAAA

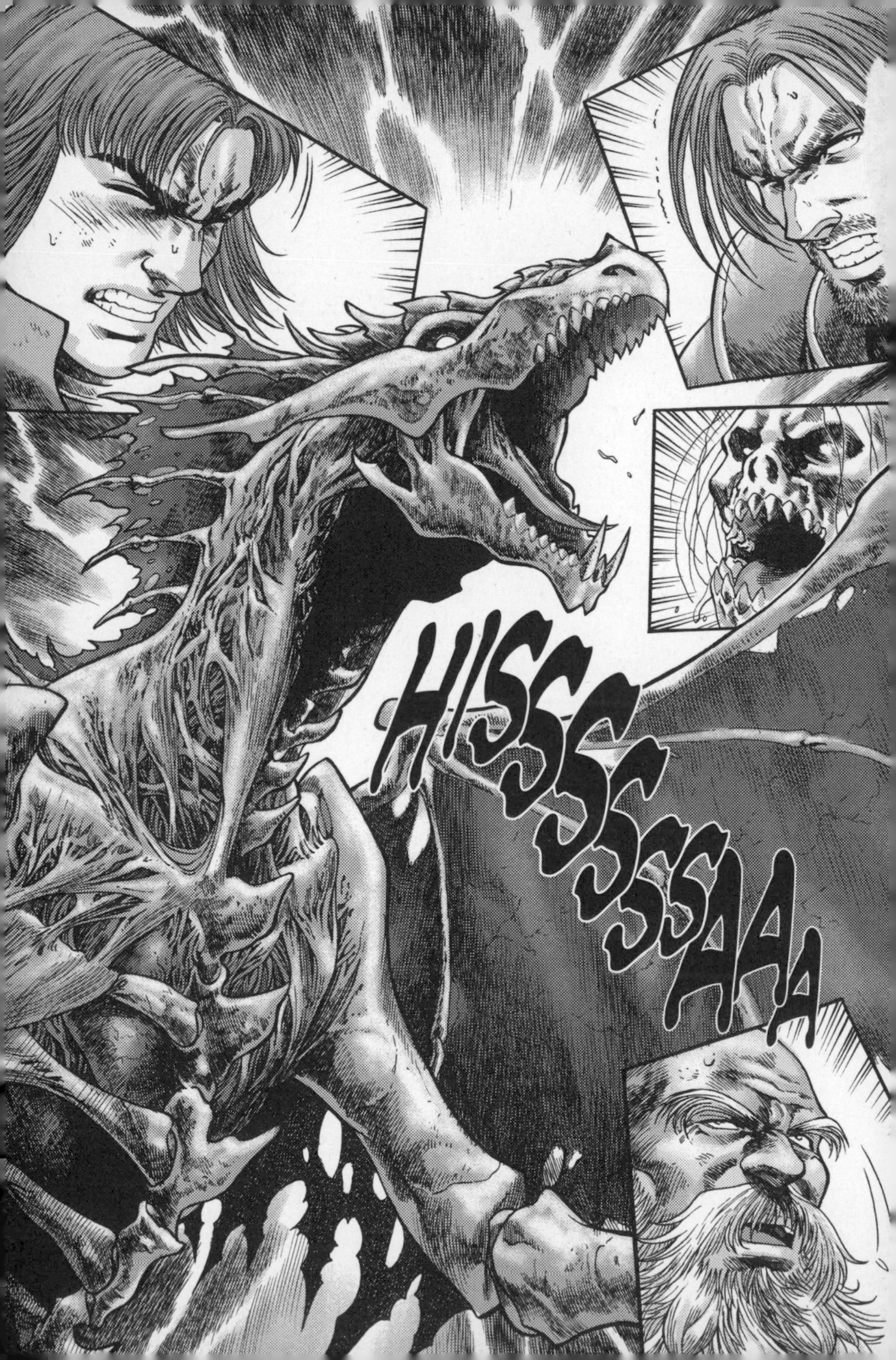
HISSSSSSAAAA

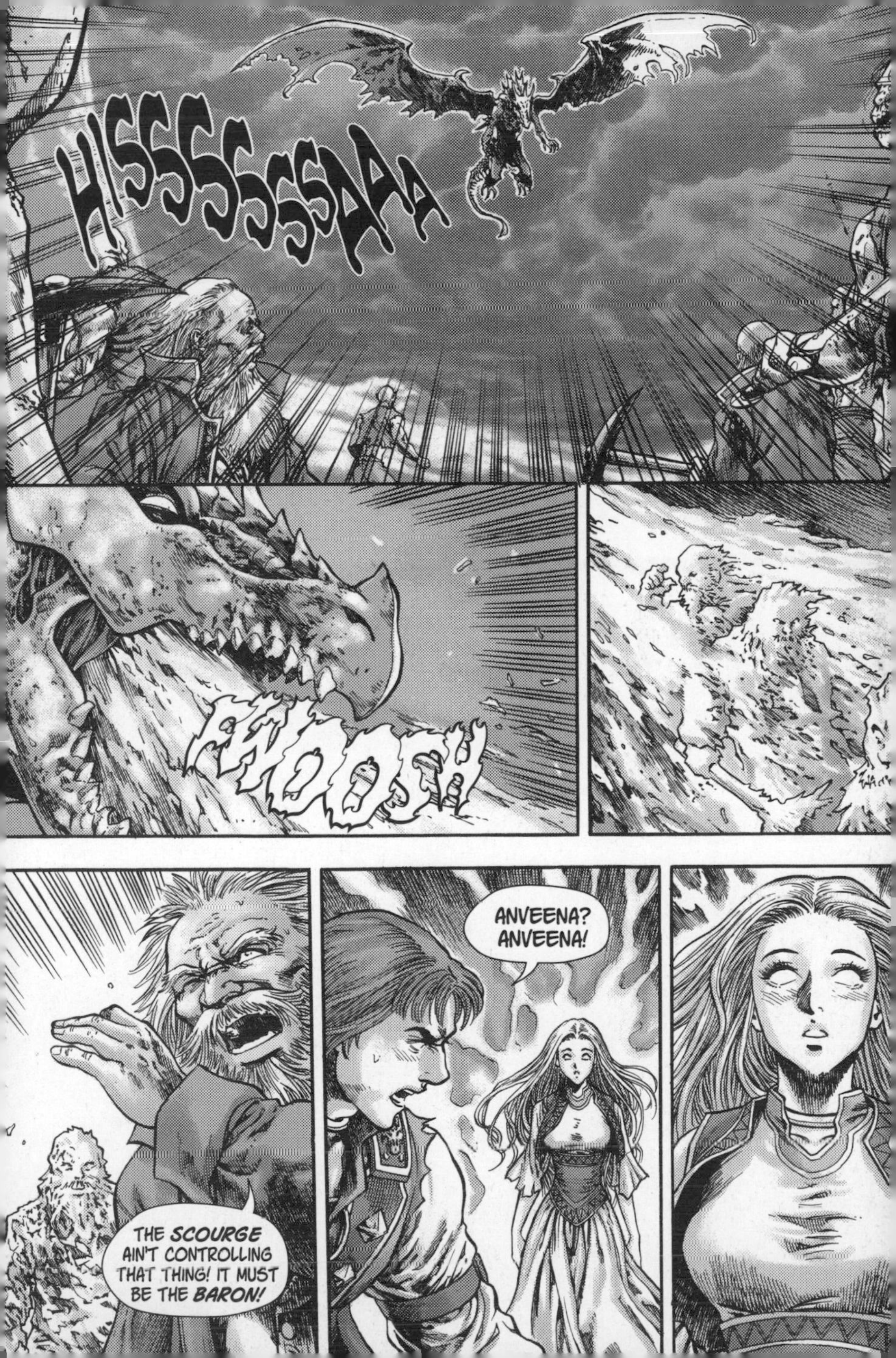
HISSSSSSAAA
WOOSH
THE SCOURGE AIN'T CONTROLLING THAT THING! IT MUST BE THE BARON!
ANVEENA? ANVEENA!

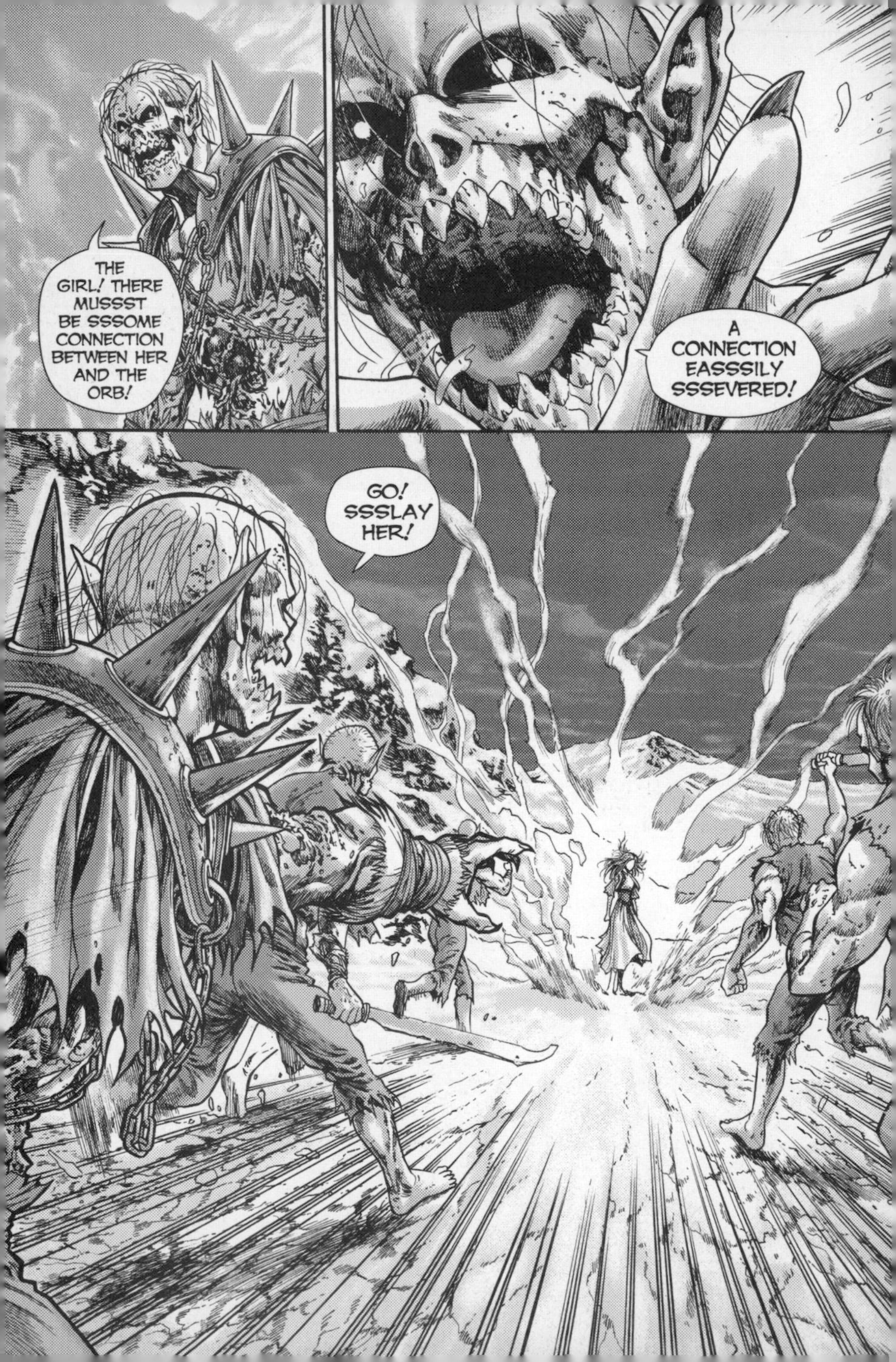
THE GIRL! THERE MUSSST BE SSSOME CONNECTION BETWEEN HER AND THE ORB!
A CONNECTION EASSSILY SSSEVERED!
GO! SSSLAY HER!

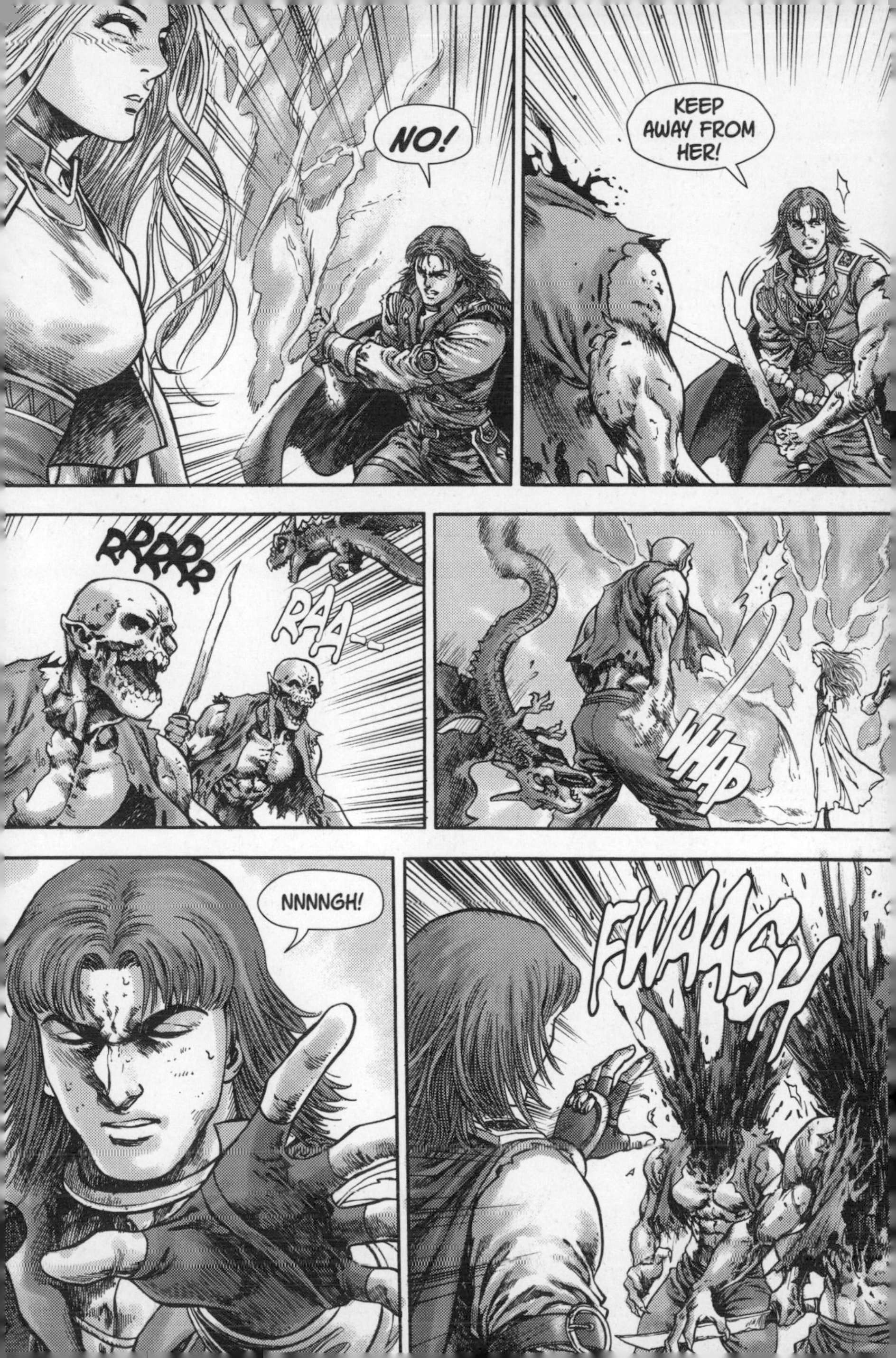
NO!
KEEP AWAY FROM HER!
RRRRR
RAA
WHAP
NNNNGH!
FWAASH

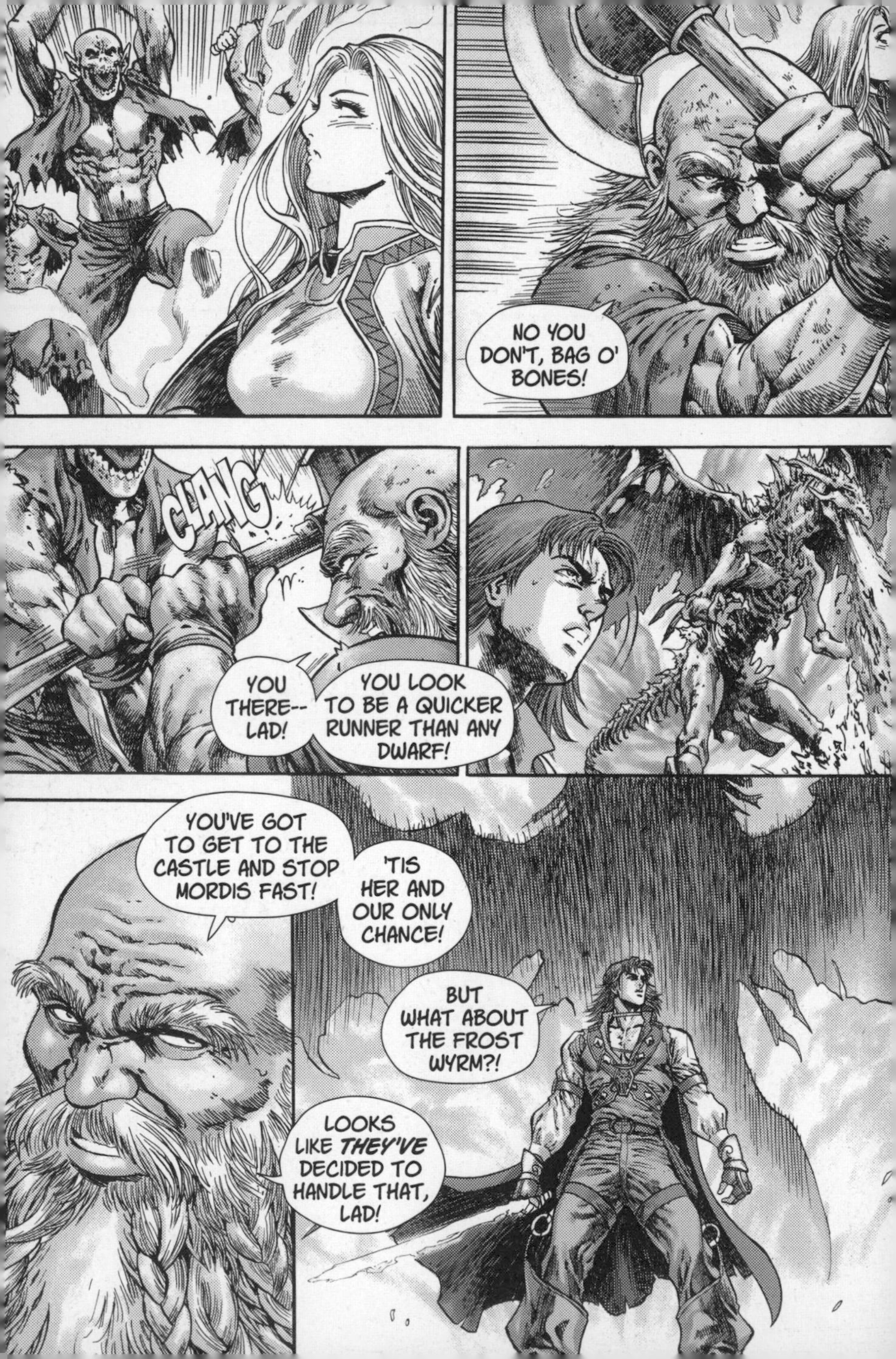
NO YOU DON'T, BAG O' BONES!
CLANG
YOU THERE-- LAD!
YOU LOOK TO BE A QUICKER RUNNER THAN ANY DWARF!
YOU'VE GOT TO GET TO THE CASTLE AND STOP MORDIS FAST!
'TIS HER AND OUR ONLY CHANCE!
BUT WHAT ABOUT THE FROST WYRM?!
LOOKS LIKE *THEY'VE* DECIDED TO HANDLE THAT, LAD!

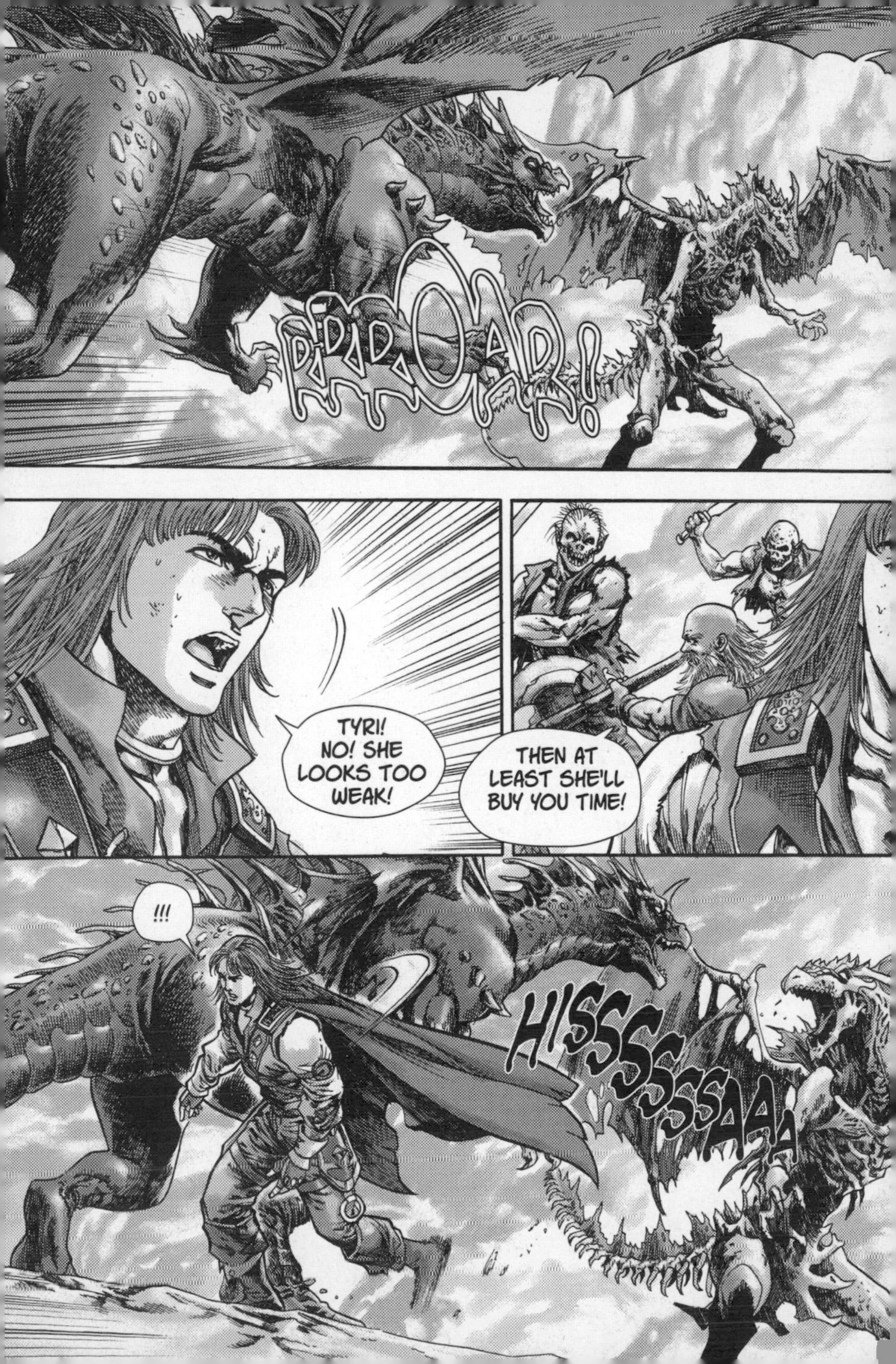
RRRROOAR!
TYRI! NO! SHE LOOKS TOO WEAK!
THEN AT LEAST SHE'LL BUY YOU TIME!
!!!
HISSSSSSSAAA

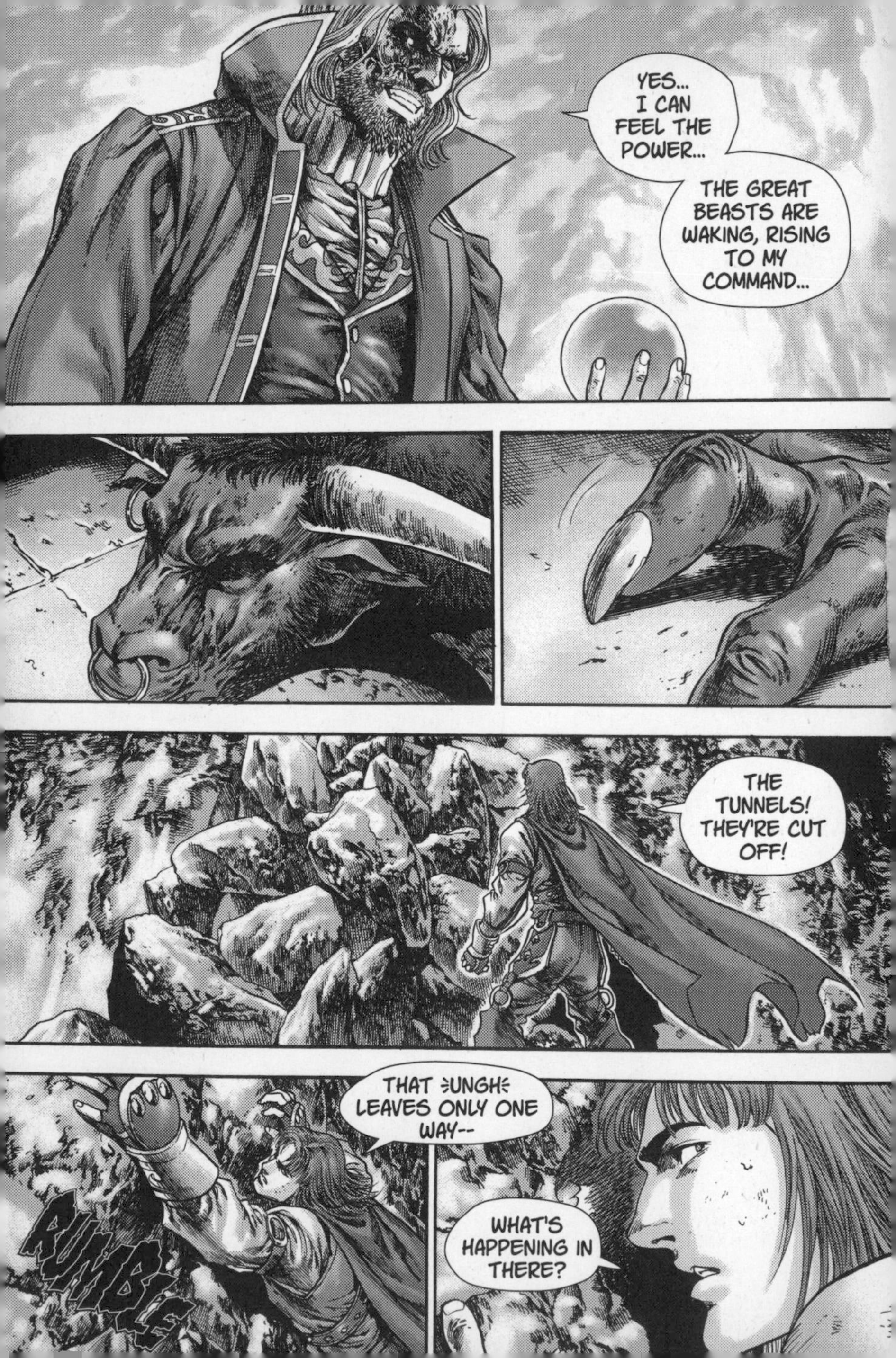
YES... I CAN FEEL THE POWER...
THE GREAT BEASTS ARE WAKING, RISING TO MY COMMAND...
THE TUNNELS! THEY'RE CUT OFF!
RUMBLE
THAT ≑UNGH≑ LEAVES ONLY ONE WAY--
WHAT'S HAPPENING IN THERE?

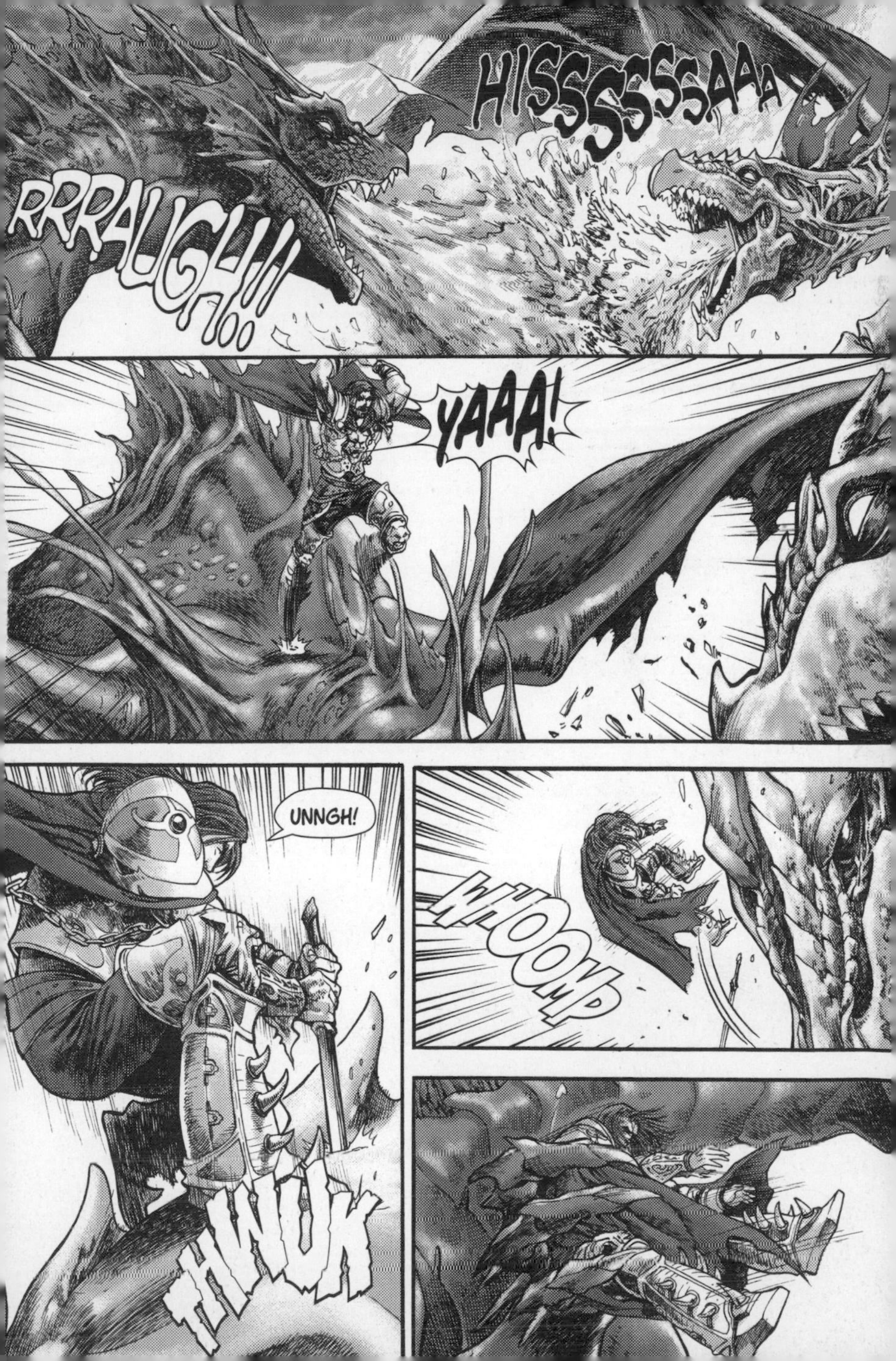
RRRAUGH!!!
HISSSSSSAAA
YAAA!
UNNGH!
THWUK
WHOOMP

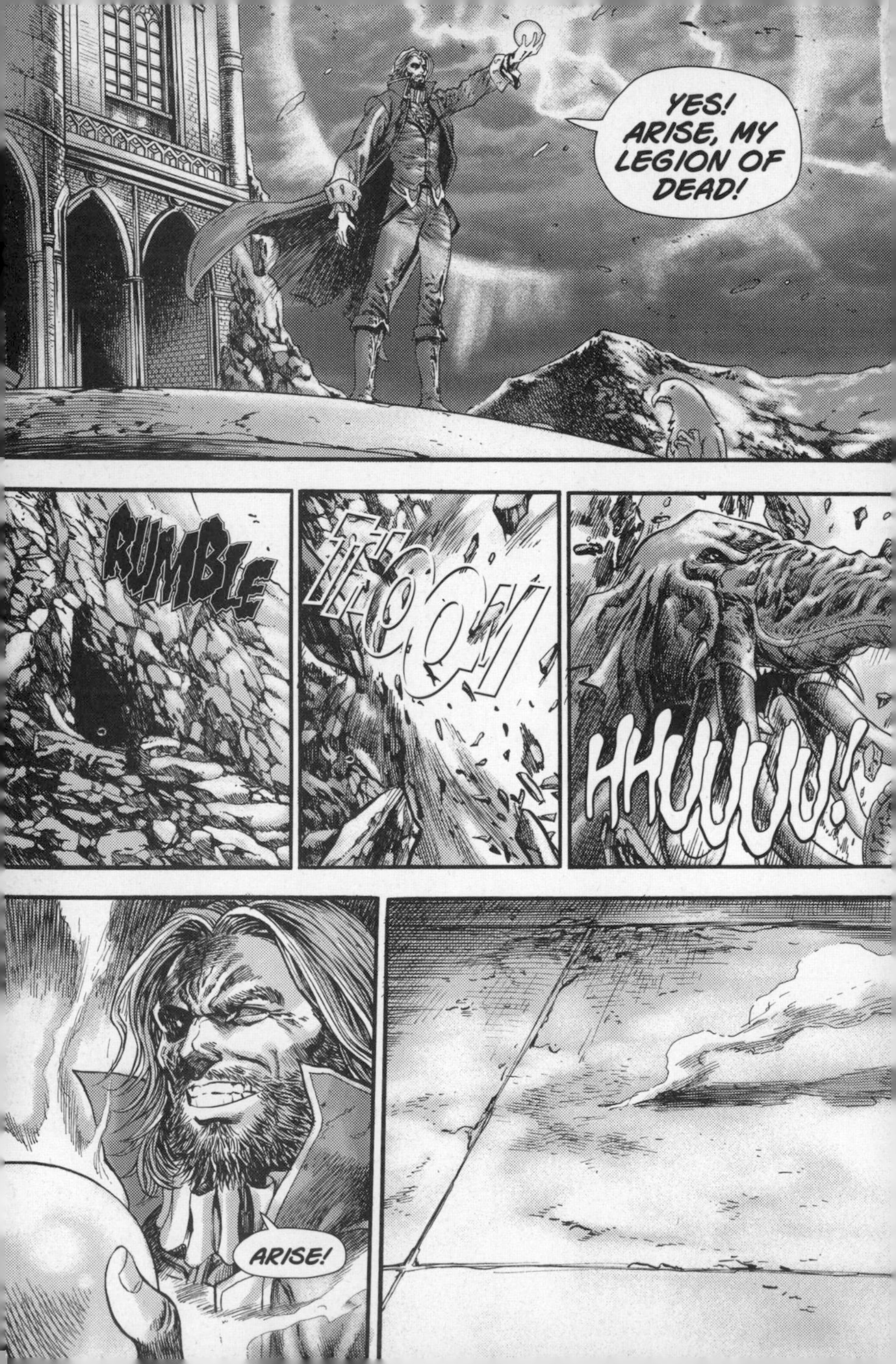
YES! ARISE, MY LEGION OF DEAD!
RUMBLE
HHUUUU!
ARISE!

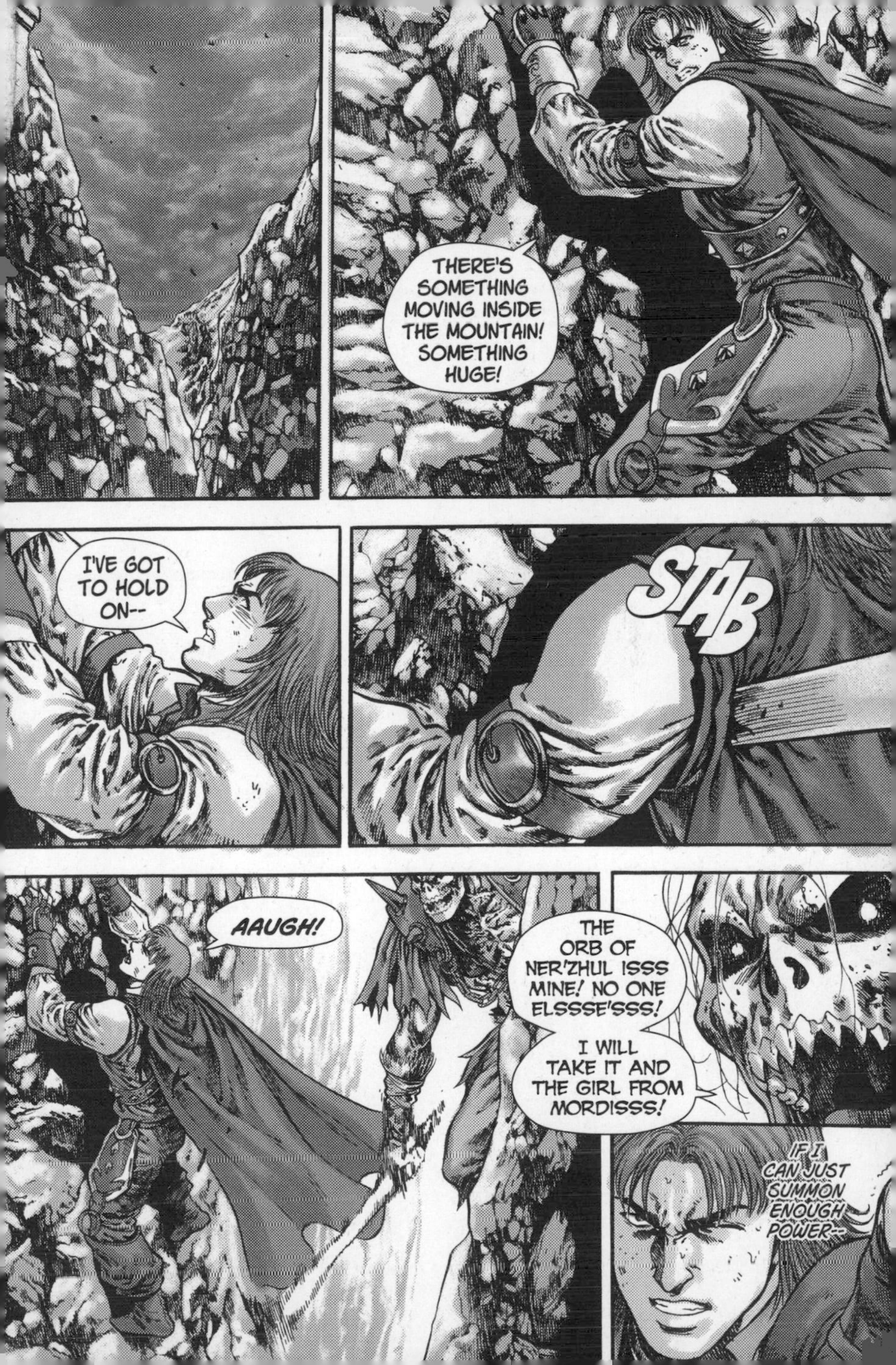
THERE'S SOMETHING MOVING INSIDE THE MOUNTAIN! SOMETHING HUGE!
I'VE GOT TO HOLD ON--
STAB
AAUGH!
THE ORB OF NER'ZHUL ISSS MINE! NO ONE ELSSSE'SSS!
I WILL TAKE IT AND THE GIRL FROM MORDISSS!
IF I CAN JUST SUMMON ENOUGH POWER--

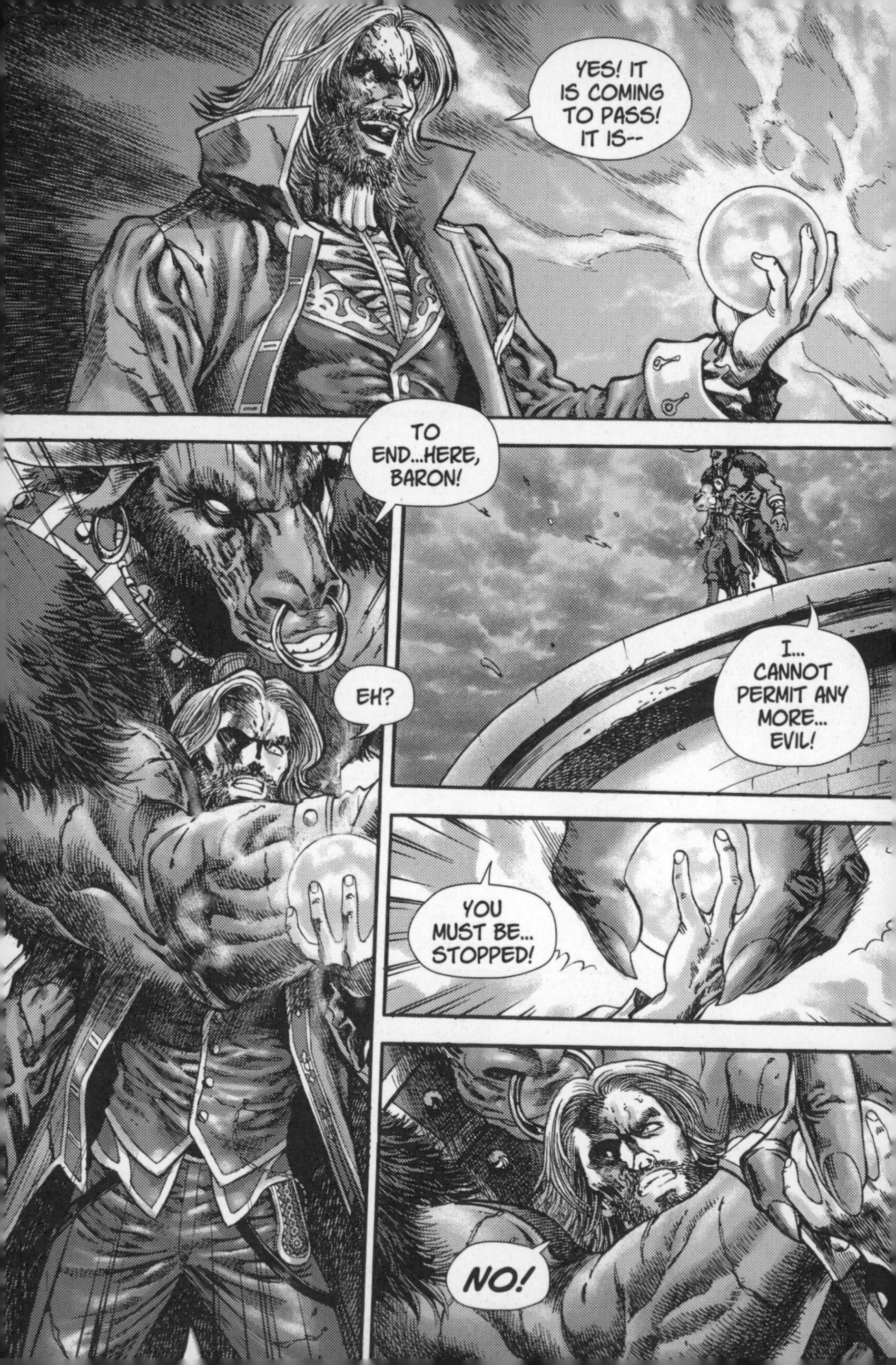
YES! IT IS COMING TO PASS! IT IS--
TO END...HERE, BARON!
EH?
I... CANNOT PERMIT ANY MORE... EVIL!
YOU MUST BE... STOPPED!
NO!

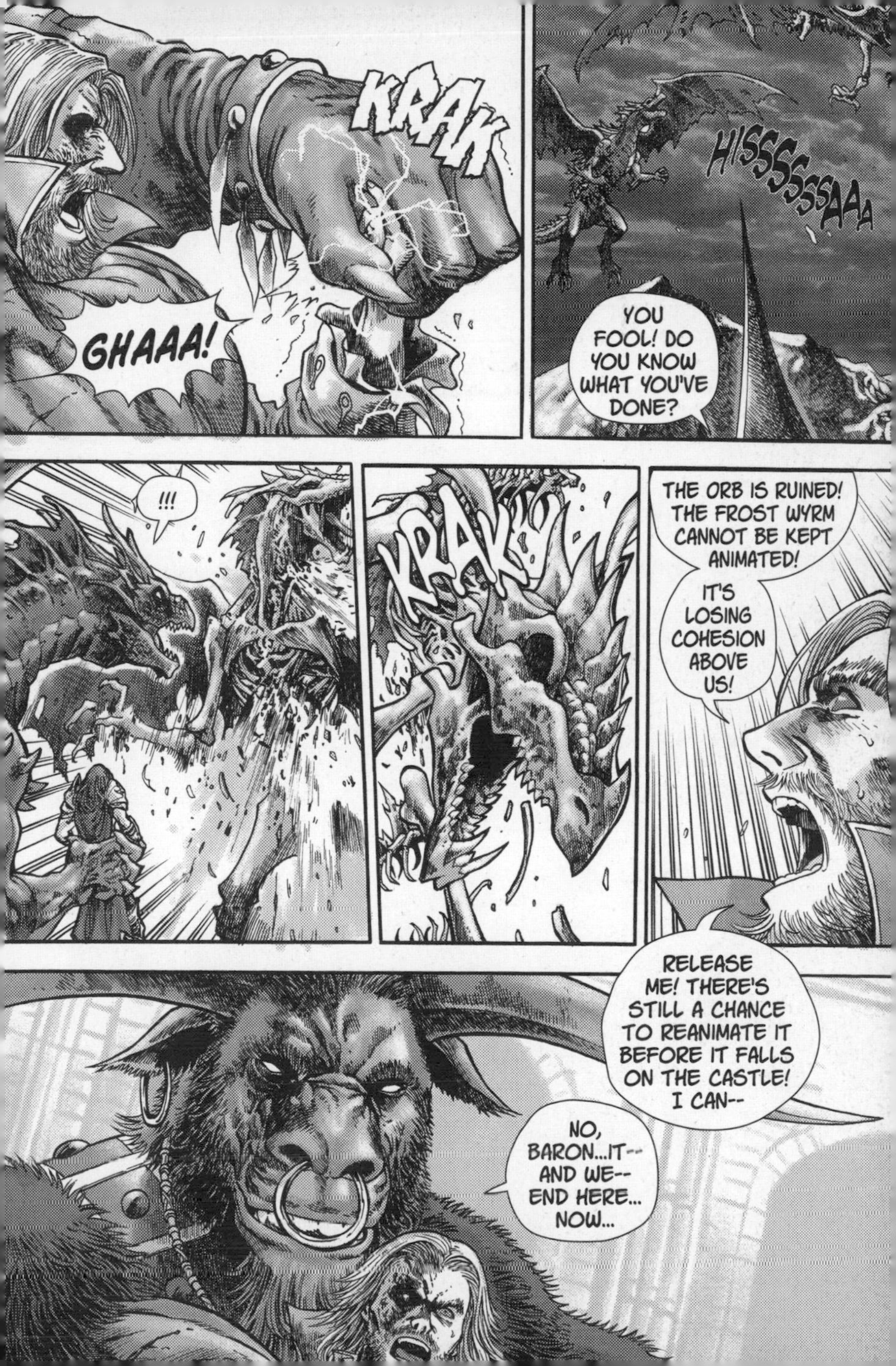
KRAK
GHAAA!
HISSSSSSSAAA
YOU FOOL! DO YOU KNOW WHAT YOU'VE DONE?
!!!
KRAK
THE ORB IS RUINED! THE FROST WYRM CANNOT BE KEPT ANIMATED!
IT'S LOSING COHESION ABOVE US!
RELEASE ME! THERE'S STILL A CHANCE TO REANIMATE IT BEFORE IT FALLS ON THE CASTLE! I CAN--
NO, BARON...IT--AND WE--END HERE... NOW...

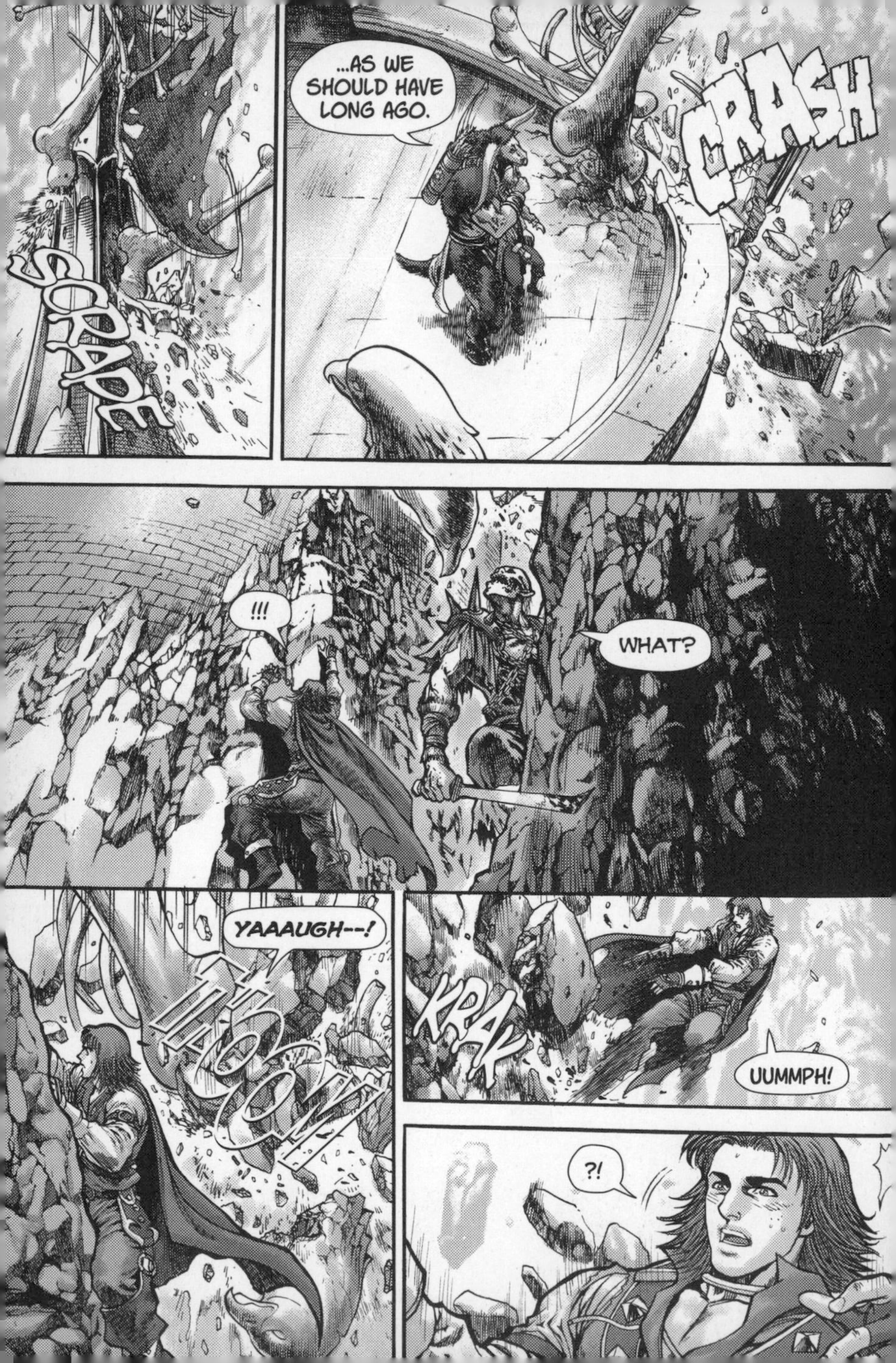
SCRAPE
...AS WE SHOULD HAVE LONG AGO.
CRASH
!!!
WHAT?
YAAAUGH--!
THOOM
KRAK
UUMMPH!
?!

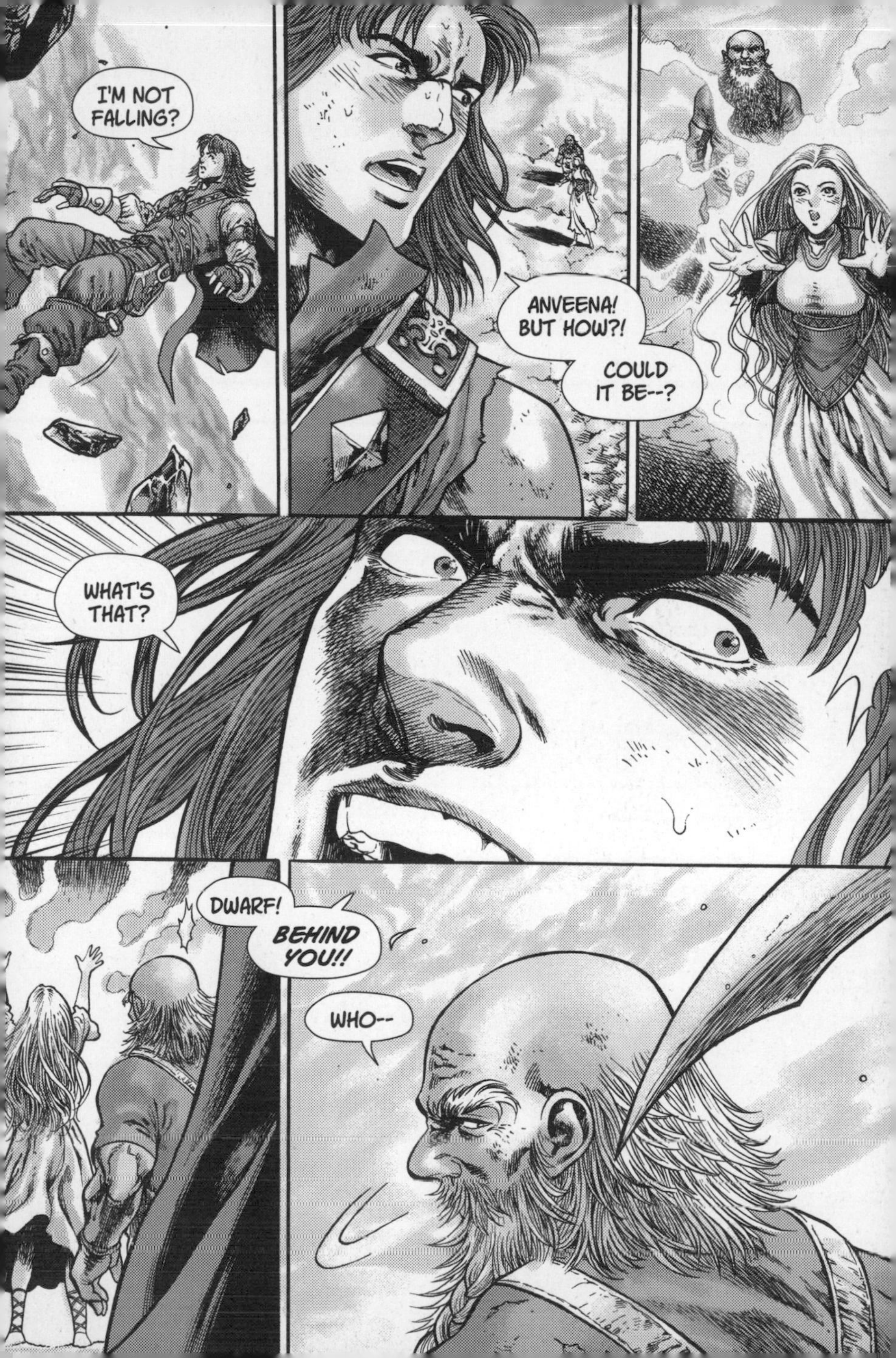
I'M NOT FALLING?
ANVEENA! BUT HOW?!
COULD IT BE--?
WHAT'S THAT?
DWARF!
BEHIND YOU!!
WHO--

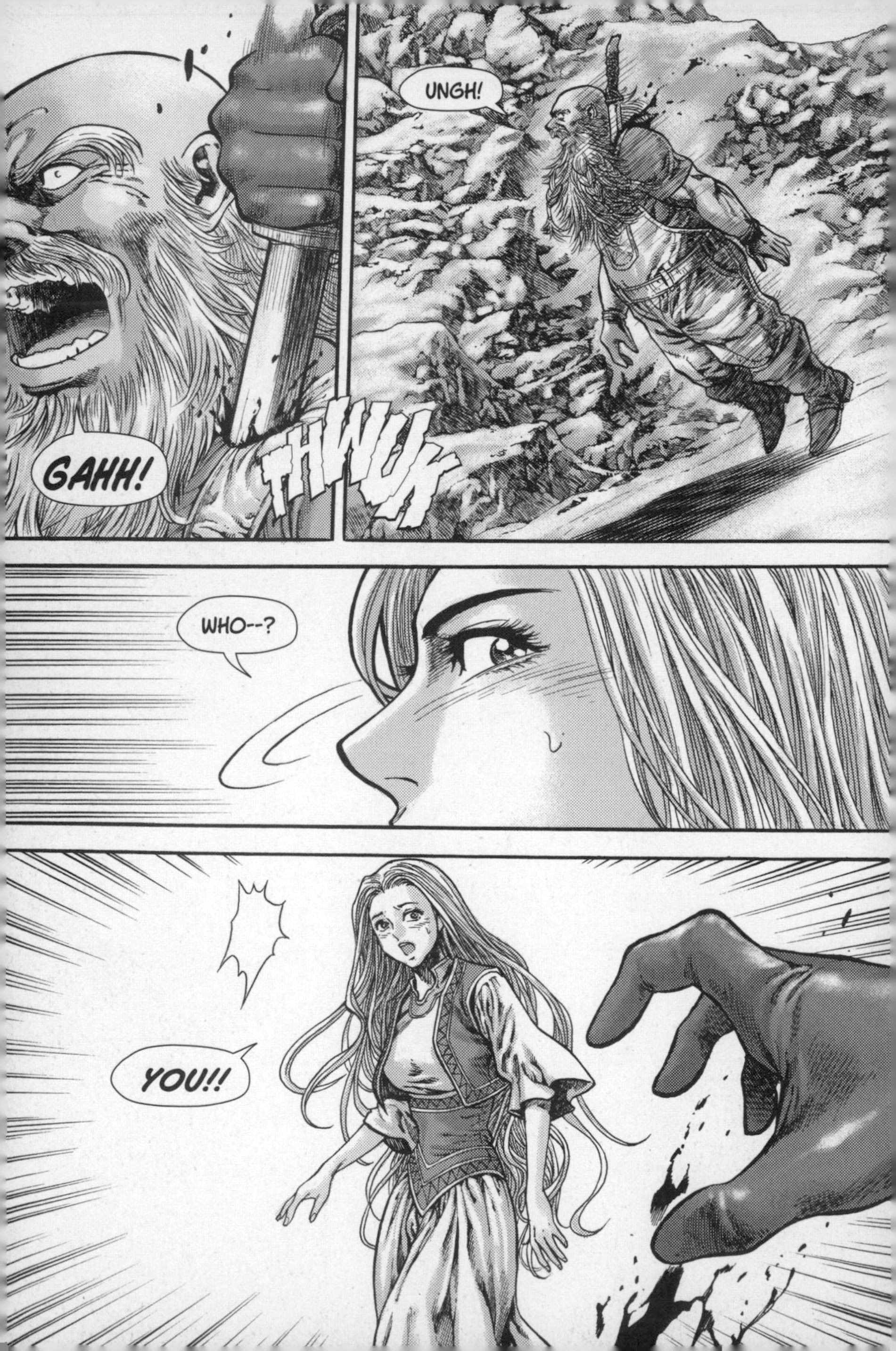
GAHH!
THWUK
UNGH!
WHO--?
YOU!!

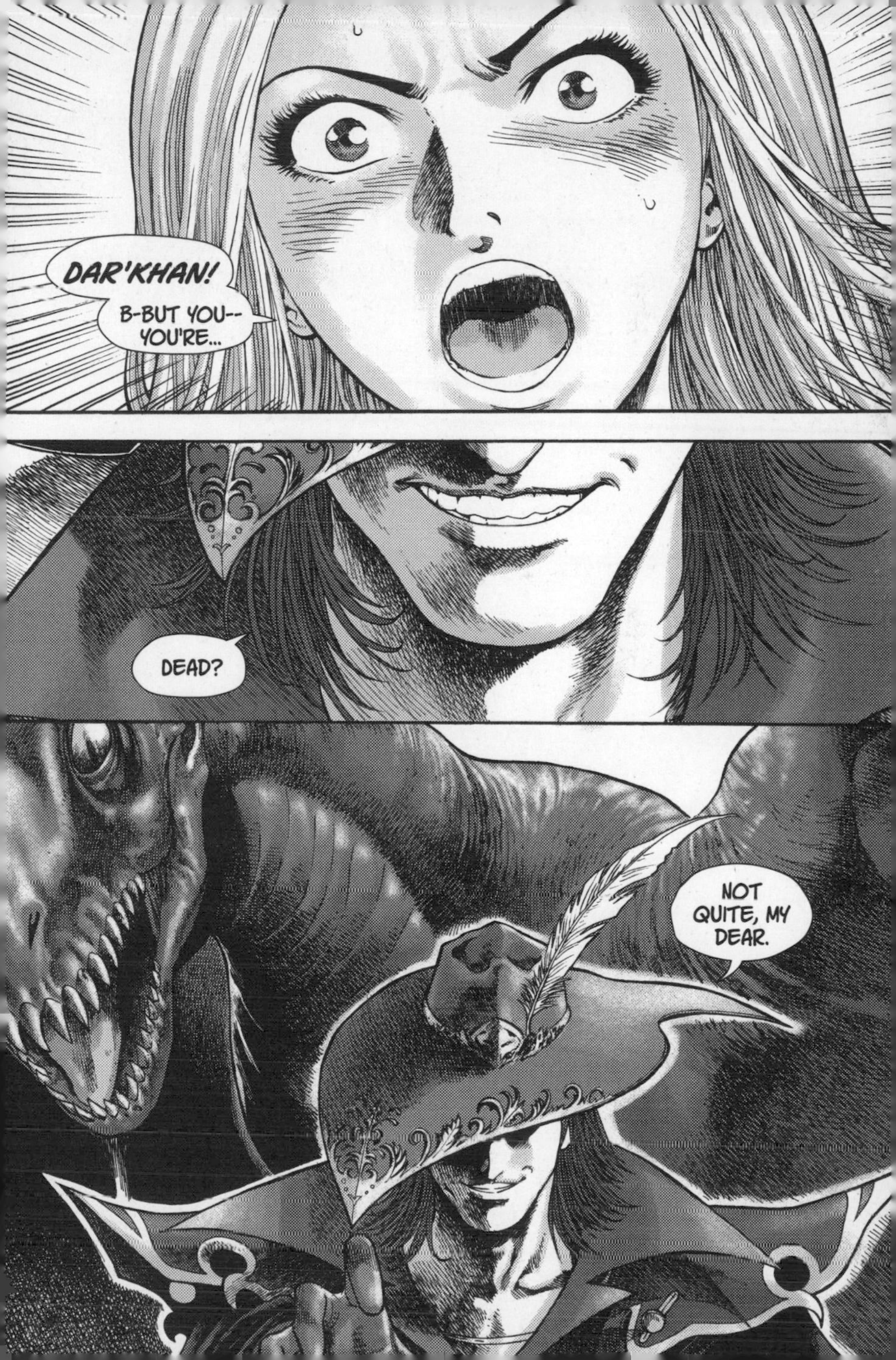
DAR'KHAN!
B-BUT YOU-- YOU'RE...
DEAD?
NOT QUITE, MY DEAR.

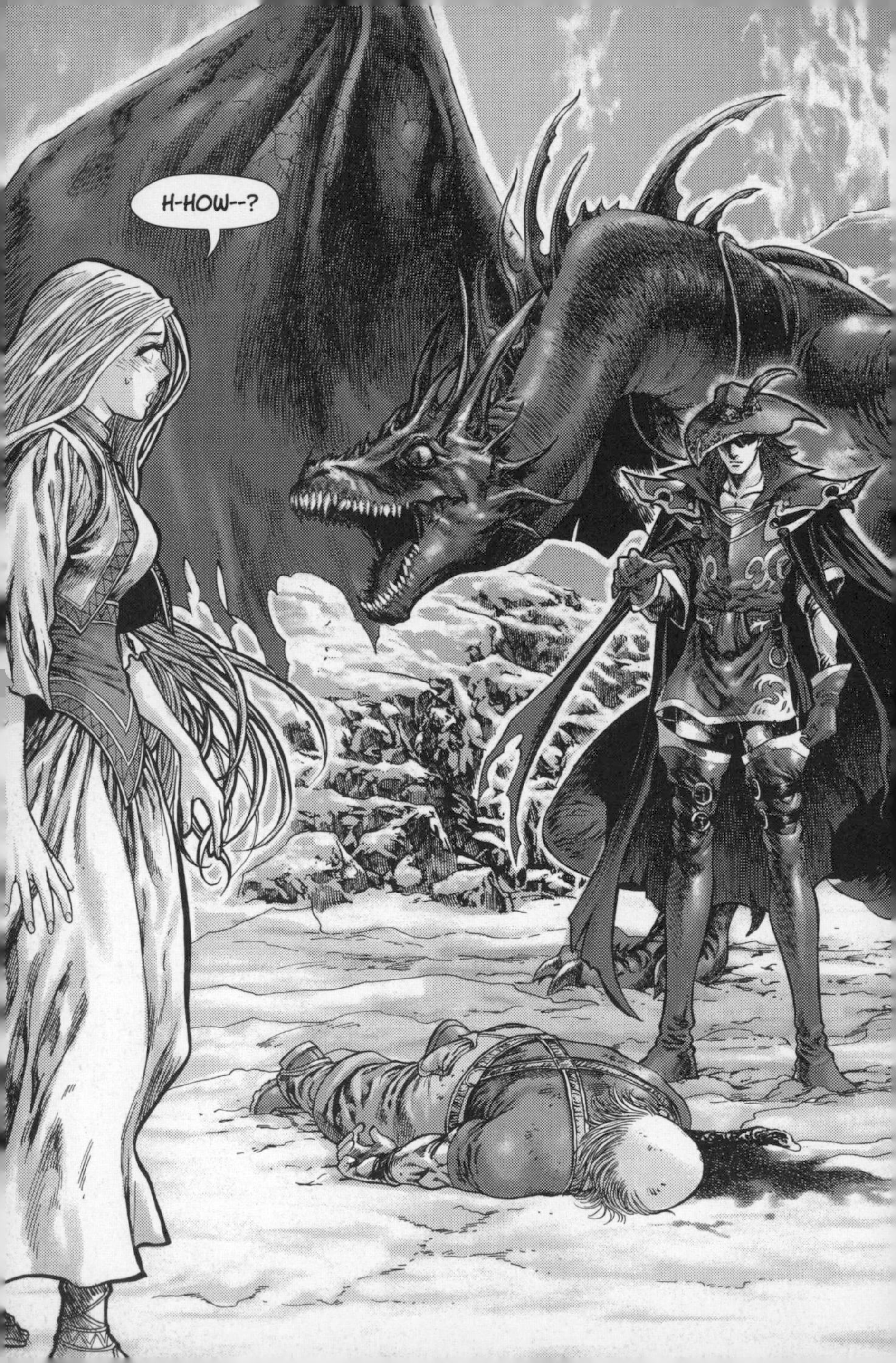
H-HOW--?

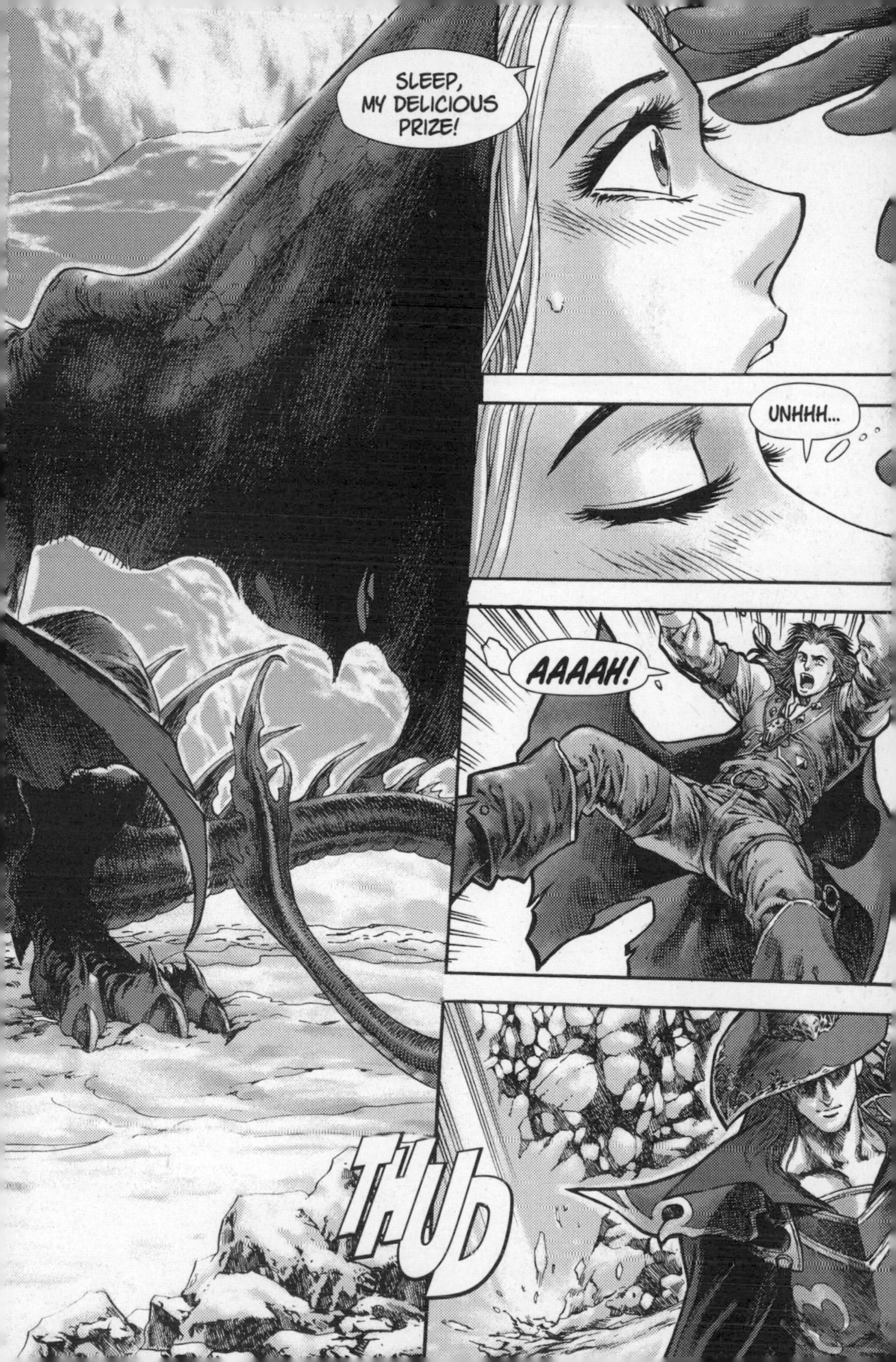
SLEEP, MY DELICIOUS PRIZE!
THUD
UNHHH...
AAAAH!

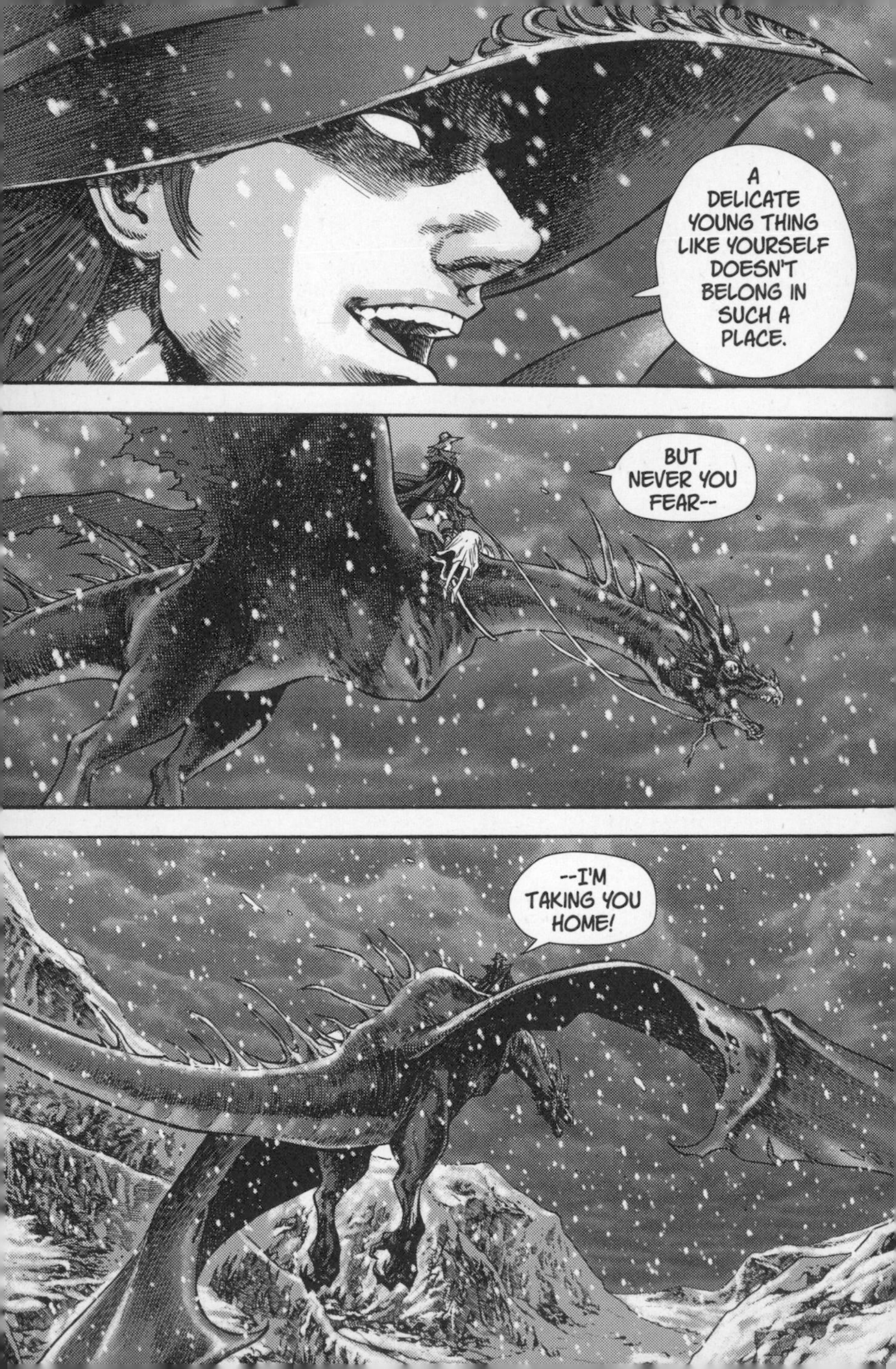
A DELICATE YOUNG THING LIKE YOURSELF DOESN'T BELONG IN SUCH A PLACE.
BUT NEVER YOU FEAR--
--I'M TAKING YOU HOME!

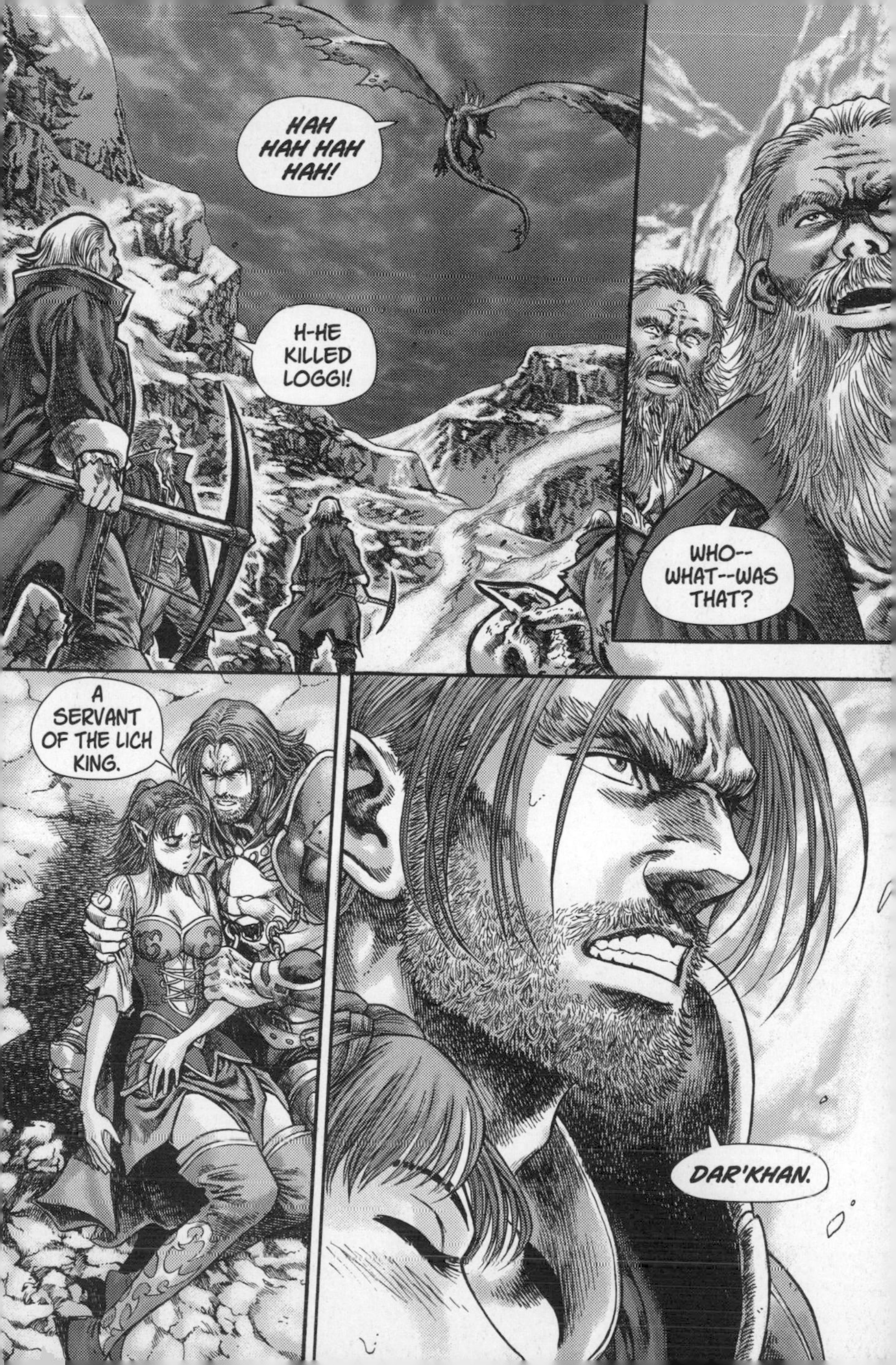
HAH HAH HAH HAH!
H-HE KILLED LOGGI!
WHO-- WHAT--WAS THAT?
A SERVANT OF THE LICH KING.
DAR'KHAN.

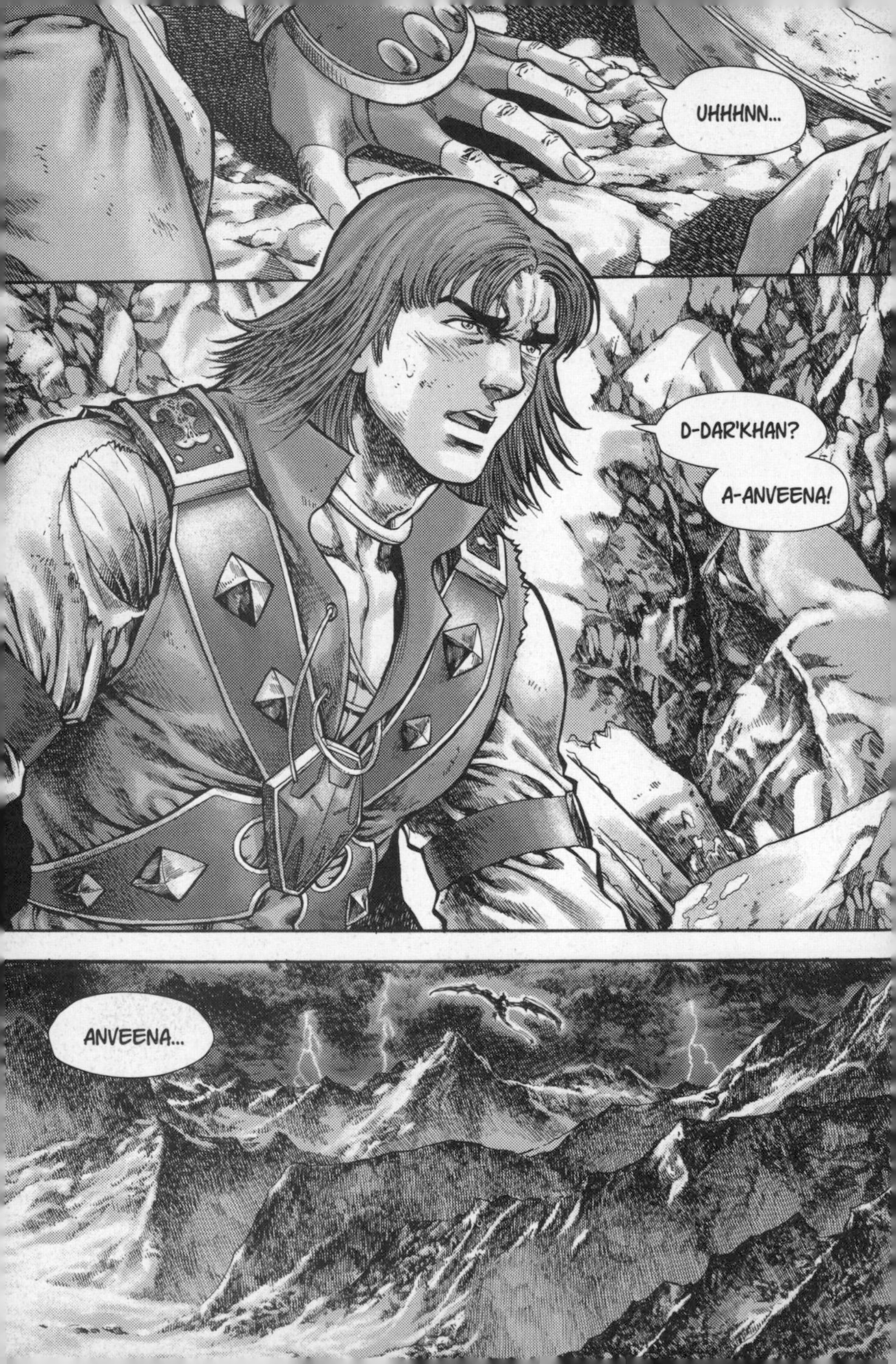
UHHHNN...
D-DAR'KHAN?
A-ANVEENA!
ANVEENA...

To be concluded in

Warcraft
The Sunwell Trilogy

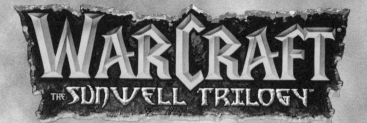

Volume 3

Ghostlands!

DAR'KHAN VENTURES TO THE DESOLATE PLAGUELANDS WHERE ONCE STOOD THE ELVEN CITY OF QUEL'THALAS...AND THE MIGHTY SUNWELL. THE DARK ELF WILL STOP AT NOTHING TO GAIN THE POWER THAT WAS ONCE ALMOST HIS...BUT WHAT ROLE COULD ANVEENA PLAY IN HIS MAD QUEST?

KALEC, TYRI, JORAD MACE AND RAAC ARE HOT ON THEIR TRAIL, BUT THERE ARE OTHER FORCES IN THE RUINS OF QUEL'THALAS--INCLUDING A CERTAIN DARK BANSHEE QUEEN--THEY MUST CONTEND WITH BEFORE THEY CAN HOPE TO THWART DAR'KHAN.

THE MYSTERIES OF RAAC, THE SUNWELL AND KALEC'S QUEST WILL ALL BE LAID BARE...AND WHEN ALL IS REVEALED, NOTHING WILL BE THE SAME!

ABOUT THE CREATORS

In addition to his work on *Warcraft: The Sunwell Trilogy* and *Ragnarok* (also by TOKYOPOP), Richard A. Knaak is the New York Times bestselling fantasy author of 27 novels and over a dozen short pieces, including *The Legend of Huma* and *Night of Blood* for Dragonlance and The Demon Soul for Warcraft. He has also written the popular Dragonrealm series  and several independent pieces. His works have been published in several languages, most recently Russian, Turkish, Bulgarian, Chinese, Czech, German, and Spanish.

Those wishing to find out more about his projects or who would like to join his e-mail list for announcements should visit his website at http://www.sff.net/people/knaak

Jae-Hwan Kim was born in 1971 in Korea. His best-known manga works include *Rainbow, Combat Metal HeMoSoo*, and *Majeh*.

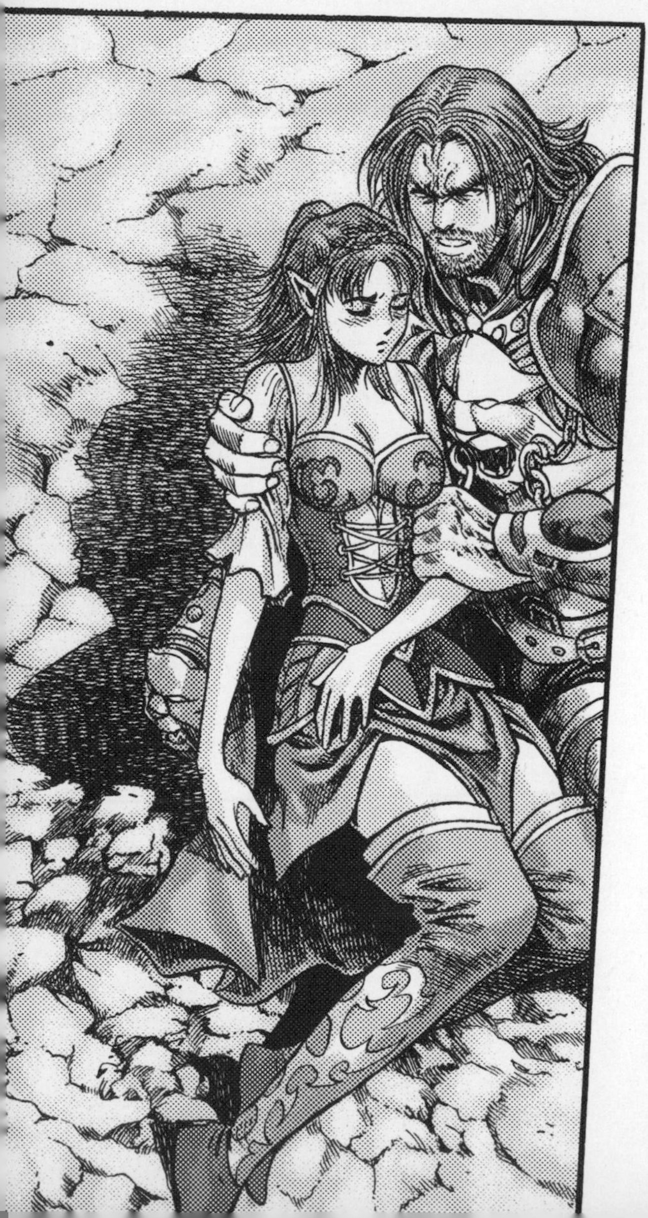

AVAILABLE NOW

WORLD OF WARCRAFT®
CYCLE OF HATRED

by Keith R.A. DeCandido

A new novel from Pocket Books
Available wherever books are sold

Also available as an eBook
www.SimonSays.com

TURN THE PAGE FOR A PREVIEW!

B yrok never imagined that the happiest time in his life would be when he went fishing.

On the face of it, it didn't seem to be the life for an orc. Fishing involved no battle, no glory, no challenging combat, no testing of one's mettle against an equal foe. No weaponry was involved, no blood was shed.

But it was less what he did than why he did it. Byrok went fishing because he was free.

As a youth, he had heard the false promises of Gul'dan and his Shadow Council who promised a new world where the sky was blue and the inhabitants easy prey for superior orc might to conquer. Byrok, along with the others of his clan, followed Gul'dan's instructions, never knowing that he and his council did the bidding of Sargeras and his foul demons, never realizing that the price for this new world would be their very souls.

It took a decade for the orcs to be defeated. Either they were enslaved by the demons they thought were their benefactors, or they were enslaved by the humans, who proved to have more fight in them than the demons imagined.

Demon magic had made Byrok's memories of his life in the orcs' native land dim. A lack of interest in remembering had had a similar effect on his recollections of his life in human bondage. He recalled mainly that the work was backbreaking and menial, and it destroyed what little of his spirit the demons had left intact.

Then Thrall came.

Everything changed then. The son of the great Durotan—whose death had, in many ways, been the end of the orcs' former way of life—Thrall had escaped his overseers and used the humans' own tactics against them. He reminded the orcs of their long-forgotten past.

On the day that Thrall and his growing army liberated Byrok, he swore that he would serve the young orc until one of them died.

So far, that death had not come, despite the finest efforts of human soldiers or demon hordes. One lesser member of the Burning Legion did, however, claim Byrok's right eye. In exchange, Byrok removed the demon's entire head.

When the fighting ended, and when the orcs settled in Durotar, Byrok requested that he be relieved of his service. Should the call to battle be sounded, Byrok promised he would be the first in line to take up the mantle of the warrior once again, even with one eye missing, but now he wished to make use of the freedom he had fought so hard for.

Thrall naturally granted it to him, and to all those who requested it.

Byrok did not need to fish, of course. Durotar included some excellent farmland. Since the human lands were located in the marshy territory to the south, humans could not grow crops, and so turned most of their energy to fishing. They would trade their surplus to the orcs in exchange for their surplus crops.

But Byrok wanted no fish caught by humans. He wanted nothing to do with humans if he could possibly avoid it. Yes, the humans had fought at the orcs' side against the Burning Legion, but that was an alliance of necessity. Humans were monsters, and Byrok wanted nothing to do with such uncivilized creatures.

So it was rather a shock to the one-eyed orc to find six humans in his usual fishing spot on Deadeye Shore.

For starters, the area surrounding Byrok's fishing hole was high grassland. Byrok's tracking skills had been reduced a bit by the lack of a good right eye, but he still saw no indication that any but he had traversed through the grasses—especially not any humans, who, for such small, lightweight creatures, were pathetically overt in their movements. Nor did Byrok see any airships nearby, nor any boats on the water within sight of the fishing spot.

How they arrived, though, was of considerably less concern to Byrok than the fact that they *had* arrived. Setting down his fishing gear, he unstrapped the morningstar from his back. The weapon had been a gift from Thrall after the Warchief had freed him from bondage, and Byrok went nowhere without it.

Were these fellow orcs in Byrok's spot, he would have questioned their presence, but humans—particularly human trespassers—deserved no such consideration. He would find out their intent by stealthier means. At best, they might simply be fools who strayed too far north and did not realize they were invading. Byrok had lived a long time, and had come to understand that stupidity was a far more common explanation than malice.

But at worst, these might be true invaders, and if they were, Byrok would not let them walk out of his fishing hole alive.

Byrok had learned the human language during his time in captivity, and so was able to understand the words of these six—at least those he could hear. From where he was crouched down amid the tall grass, he could hear only a few words.

The words he did hear, however, were not encouraging. "Overthrow" was one, "Thrall" another. So was "greenskin," a derogatory human term for orcs.

Then he caught the phrase, "We'll kill them all and take this continent for ourselves."

Another asked a question, the only word of which Byrok caught was "troll." The one who wished to take the continent then said, "We'll kill them, too."

Pushing aside the grass, Byrok looked more closely at the humans. He didn't notice anything particularly distinguishing about them—all humans looked alike to Byrok—but the old orc did notice that the two closest to him had the image of a burning sword on their person: one as a tattoo on his arm, the other as an earring.

His blood running cold, Byrok remembered where he'd seen that symbol before. It was long ago, when the orcs first came to this world at Gul'dan's urging: they called themselves the Burning Blade, and their armor and flags carried the same symbol that these two humans wore.

The Burning Blade were among the fiercest devotees of the Shadow Council. They were later wiped out, and none of that demon-loving clan remained.

Yet here were *humans* wearing their symbol, and speaking of killing Thrall.

His blood boiling, Byrok got to his feet and started running toward the sextet, twirling the morningstar over his head. Even with his bulk, the only noise he made as he approached was the whizzing sound of the morningstar's chain as it pivoted on the handle in Byrok's fingers and rotated along with the large spiked ball on the other end around the orc's head.

That was, unfortunately, enough. Two of the humans—the two with the Burning Blade symbol—whirled around. So Byrok targeted the nearest of those two first, throwing the morningstar right at his shaved head. He wasn't concerned about losing his weapon—no human could lift the thing, so it would be safe until he could grab it again.

"An orc!"

" 'Bout time one showed up!"

"Kill it!"

Since the element of surprise was gone, he let out a huge roar—that always intimidated humans—and leapt at another, this one with a full beard. Byrok's massive fist collided with the bearded one's head.

The one with the shaved head clutched his shoulder—he had managed to avoid being hit in the head, to Byrok's disappointment—and tried to lift the morningstar with his other hand. Had he time, Byrok would have laughed.

However, he was too busy grabbing another human's head in his right hand and preparing to throw the invader into one of his comrades. That did not happen, however, as another human attacked from the right.

Cursing himself for forgetting to account for the fact that he was now blind on that side, Byrok flailed out with his right arm, even as pain sliced into his side.

Two more humans piled on top of him, one punching him, the

other going at him with a blade. Byrok managed to step on one attacker's leg, breaking it instantly. The screams of his victim served to goad the orc, and he redoubled his attack. But there were simply too many of them. Even though two of them were badly injured, they continued to pile on him, and even Byrok could not defeat six humans while unarmed.

Realizing that he needed his weapon, he inhaled deeply and then let out a huge roar even as he punched both fists outward with all his strength. It only knocked his foes off him for an instant, but an instant was all he needed. He dove for his weapon, his fingers closing around the handle.

Before he could lift it, however, two of the humans pounded on his head, and another drove a dagger through his left thigh. Byrok flailed his arm outward, the morningstar's ball sailing through the air, just missing the humans.

Then, much as he loathed himself for being forced to do it, Byrok ran.

It was a hard thing for him, and not just because the dagger that was still protruding from his thigh slowed his gait. To run from battle was shameful. But Byrok knew he had a higher duty to perform—the Burning Blade had returned, only this time they were humans. And *all* the attackers, not just the two he'd noticed before, wore that flaming sword image somewhere on them: a necklace, a tattoo, *something*.

This was information that needed to get back to Thrall.

So Byrok ran.

Or, rather, he hobbled. His wounds were taking their toll. It became a struggle even to breathe.

But still he ran.

Dimly, he registered that the six humans were giving chase, but he couldn't afford to pay attention to that. He had to get back to Orgrimmar and tell Thrall what was happening. Even with his injury, his strides were greater than those of the humans, and he could outrun them. Once he pulled far enough ahead, he would lose them in the underbrush of this land that he knew better than any outsider possibly could. Besides, they only seemed to want to beat up an orc. They probably did not realize that Byrok understood their gutter tongue, and therefore they did not know that Byrok knew who they were. They would not chase him past the point where it would be useful to them.

Or so he hoped.

No longer were there any thoughts in Byrok's mind. He cleared his head of all save the critical imperative of putting one foot down in front of the other, the ground slamming into his soles. He ignored the pain in his leg, and in all the other places they'd beat or cut him, ignored the fact that his one good eye was getting foggy, ignored the fatigue that drained the strength from his limbs.

Still he ran.

Then he stumbled. His left leg refused to lift as it was supposed to—but his right leg continued to run, and so he crashed to the ground, high grass and dirt getting in his nose and mouth and eye.

"Must . . . get . . . up . . ."

"You ain't goin' nowhere, monster." Byrok could hear the voice, hear the humans' footfalls, and then feel the pressure when two of them sat on his back, immobilizing him. " 'Cause, here's the thing—your time is over. Orcs don't belong in this world, and so we're gonna take you out of it. Got me?"

Byrok managed the effort of lifting his head so he could see two of the humans. He spat at them.

The humans just laughed. "Let's do it, boys. *Galtak Ered'nash!*"

The other five all replied in kind: *"Galtak Ered'nash!"* Then they started beating the orc.

WARCRAFT®

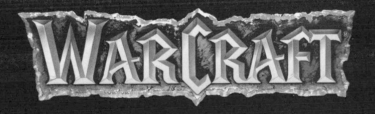

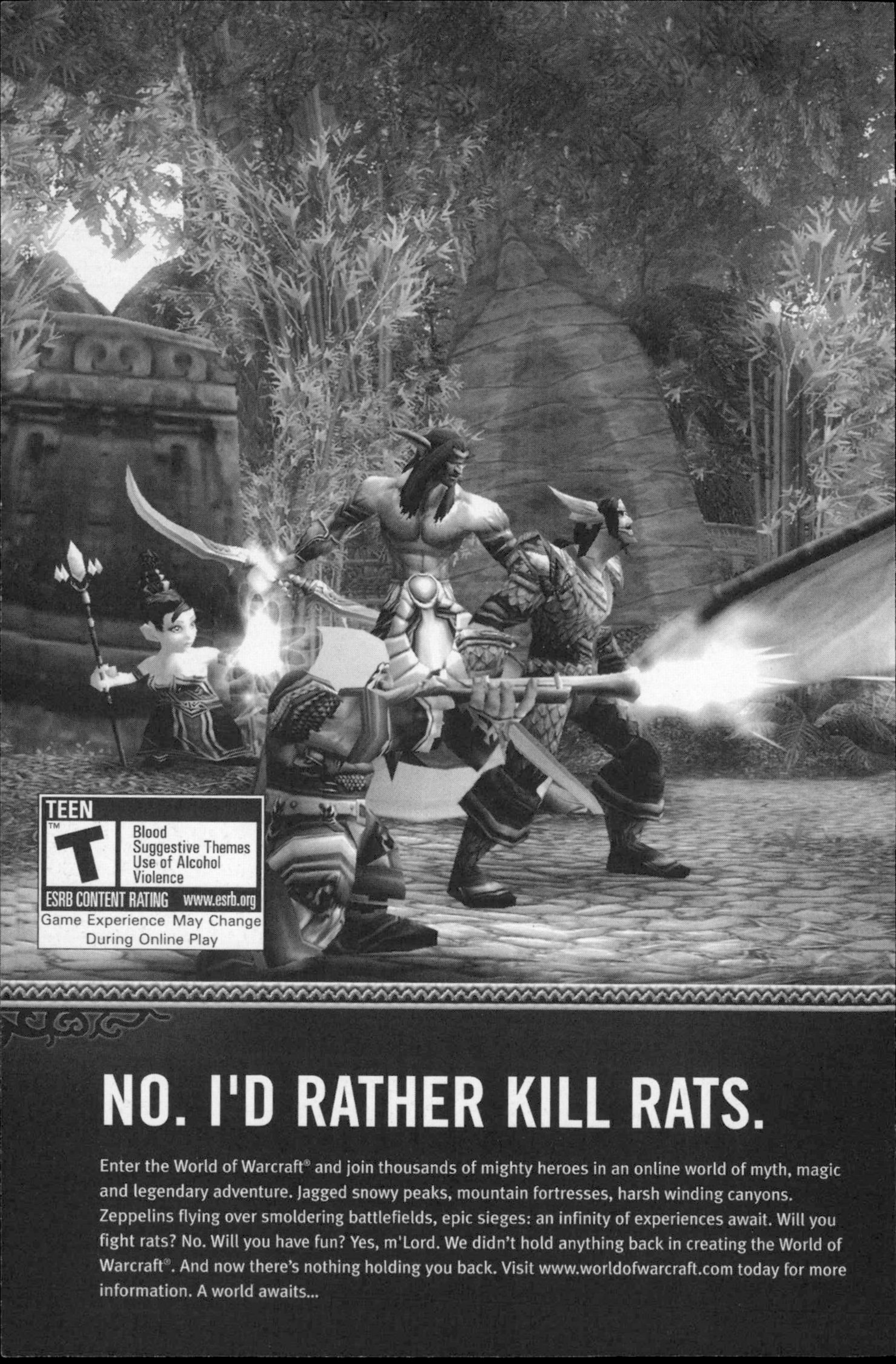
TEEN
T
Blood
Suggestive Themes
Use of Alcohol
Violence
ESRB CONTENT RATING www.esrb.org
Game Experience May Change During Online Play
NO. I'D RATHER KILL RATS.
Enter the World of Warcraft® and join thousands of mighty heroes in an online world of myth, magic and legendary adventure. Jagged snowy peaks, mountain fortresses, harsh winding canyons. Zeppelins flying over smoldering battlefields, epic sieges: an infinity of experiences await. Will you fight rats? No. Will you have fun? Yes, m'Lord. We didn't hold anything back in creating the World of Warcraft®. And now there's nothing holding you back. Visit www.worldofwarcraft.com today for more information. A world awaits...

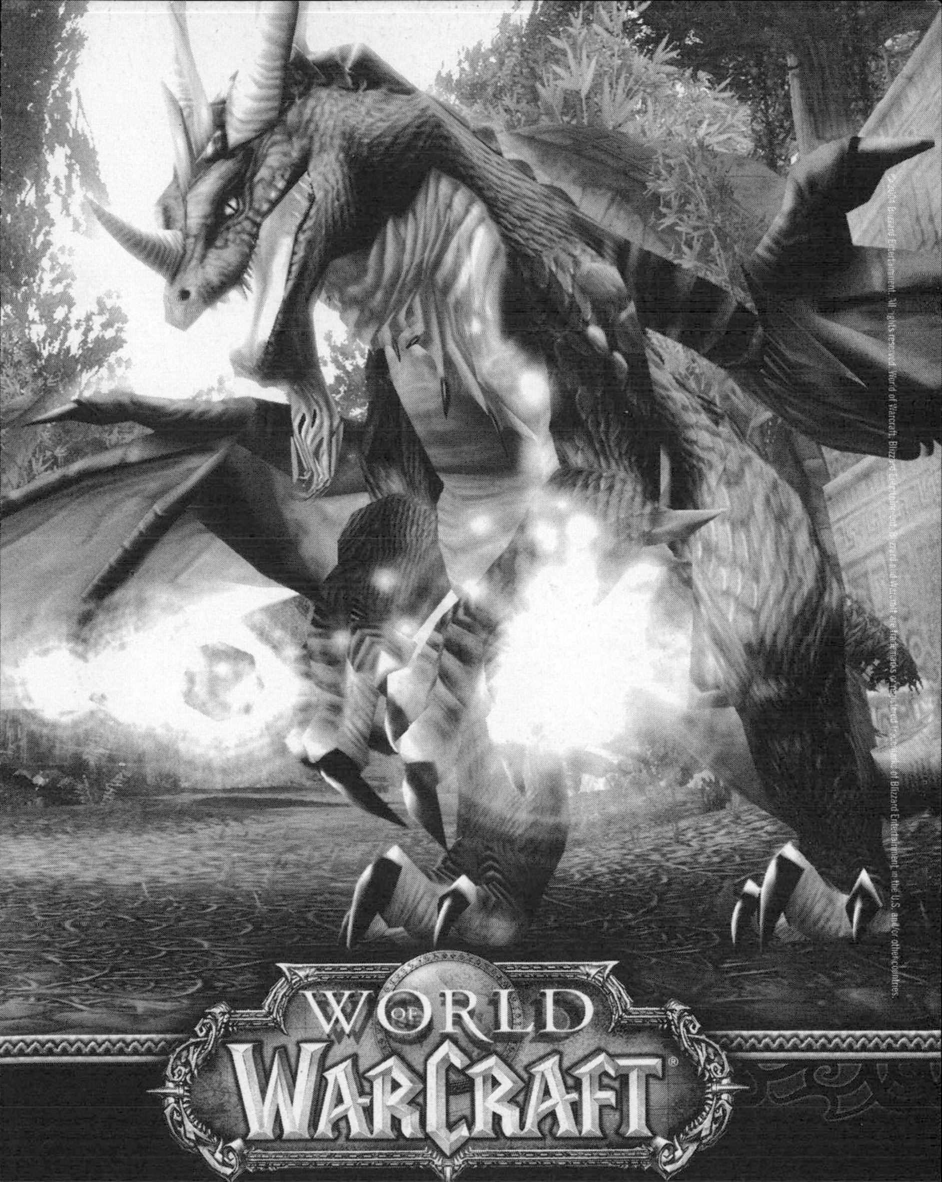
©2007 Blizzard Entertainment. All rights reserved. World of Warcraft, Blizzard Entertainment, Blizzard and Warcraft are trademarks or registered trademarks of Blizzard Entertainment in the U.S. and/or other countries.
WORLD OF WARCRAFT®

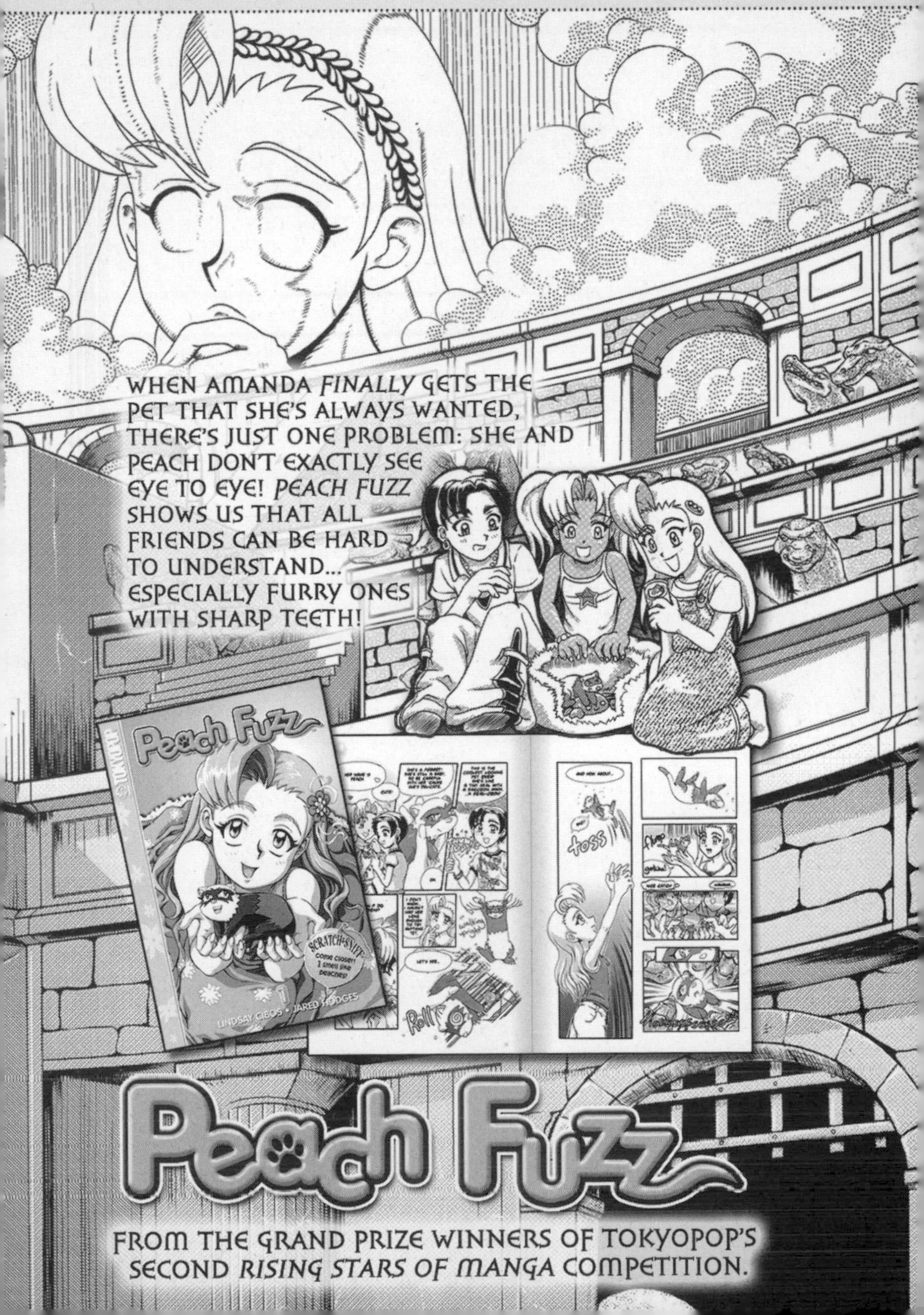
WHEN AMANDA *FINALLY* GETS THE PET THAT SHE'S ALWAYS WANTED, THERE'S JUST ONE PROBLEM: SHE AND PEACH DON'T EXACTLY SEE EYE TO EYE! *PEACH FUZZ* SHOWS US THAT ALL FRIENDS CAN BE HARD TO UNDERSTAND... ESPECIALLY FURRY ONES WITH SHARP TEETH!
Peach Fuzz
SCRATCH+SNIFF
Come closer! I smell like peaches!
LINDSAY CIBOS • JARED HODGES
Peach Fuzz
FROM THE GRAND PRIZE WINNERS OF TOKYOPOP'S SECOND *RISING STARS OF MANGA* COMPETITION.

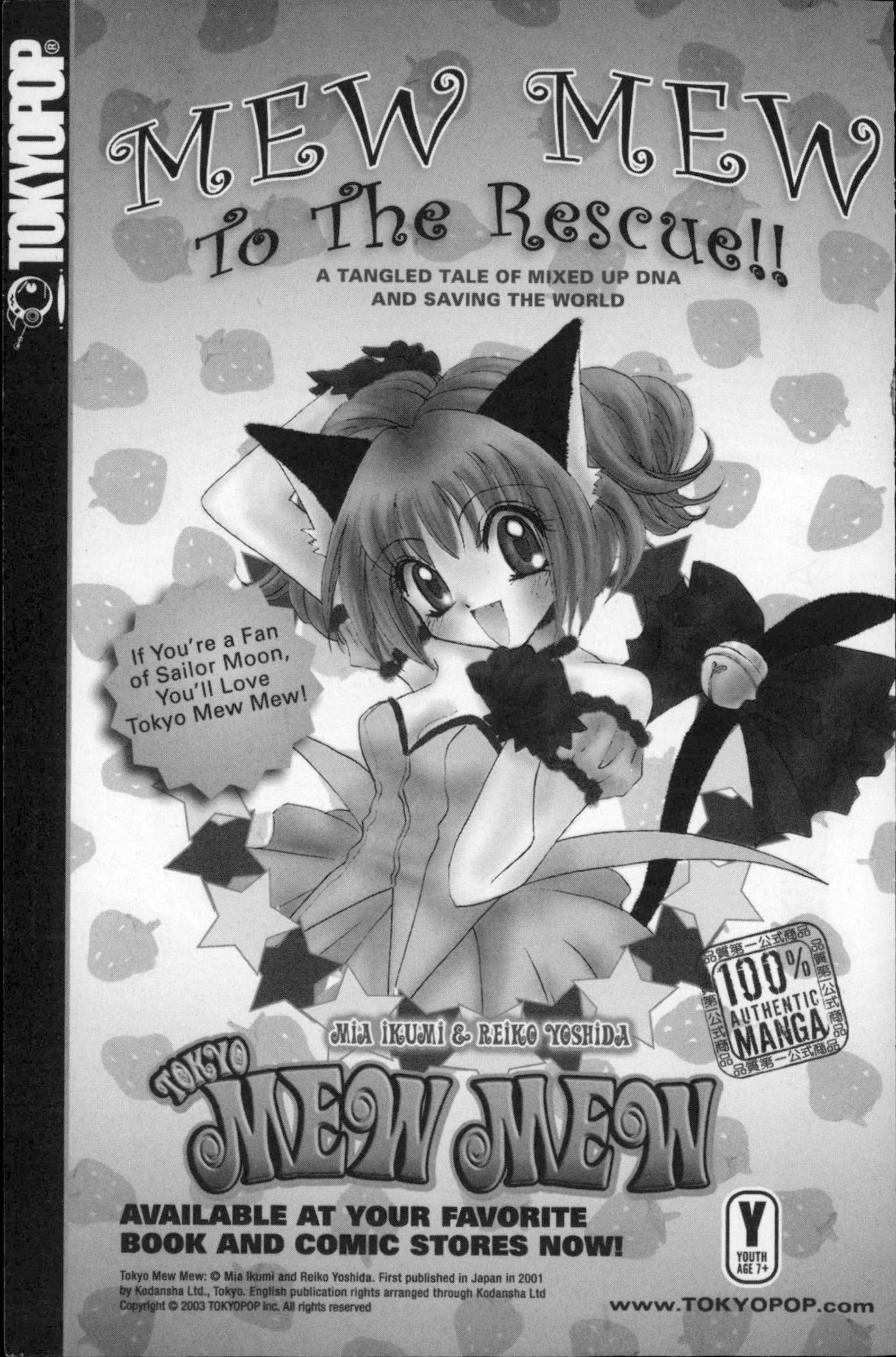
TOKYOPOP
MEW MEW
To The Rescue!!
A TANGLED TALE OF MIXED UP DNA AND SAVING THE WORLD
If You're a Fan of Sailor Moon, You'll Love Tokyo Mew Mew!
100% AUTHENTIC MANGA
MIA IKUMI & REIKO YOSHIDA
TOKYO MEW MEW
AVAILABLE AT YOUR FAVORITE BOOK AND COMIC STORES NOW!
Y YOUTH AGE 7+
Tokyo Mew Mew: © Mia Ikumi and Reiko Yoshida. First published in Japan in 2001 by Kodansha Ltd., Tokyo. English publication rights arranged through Kodansha Ltd
Copyright © 2003 TOKYOPOP Inc. All rights reserved
www.TOKYOPOP.com

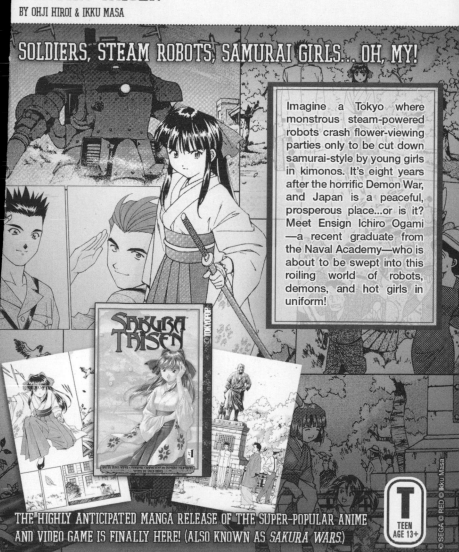

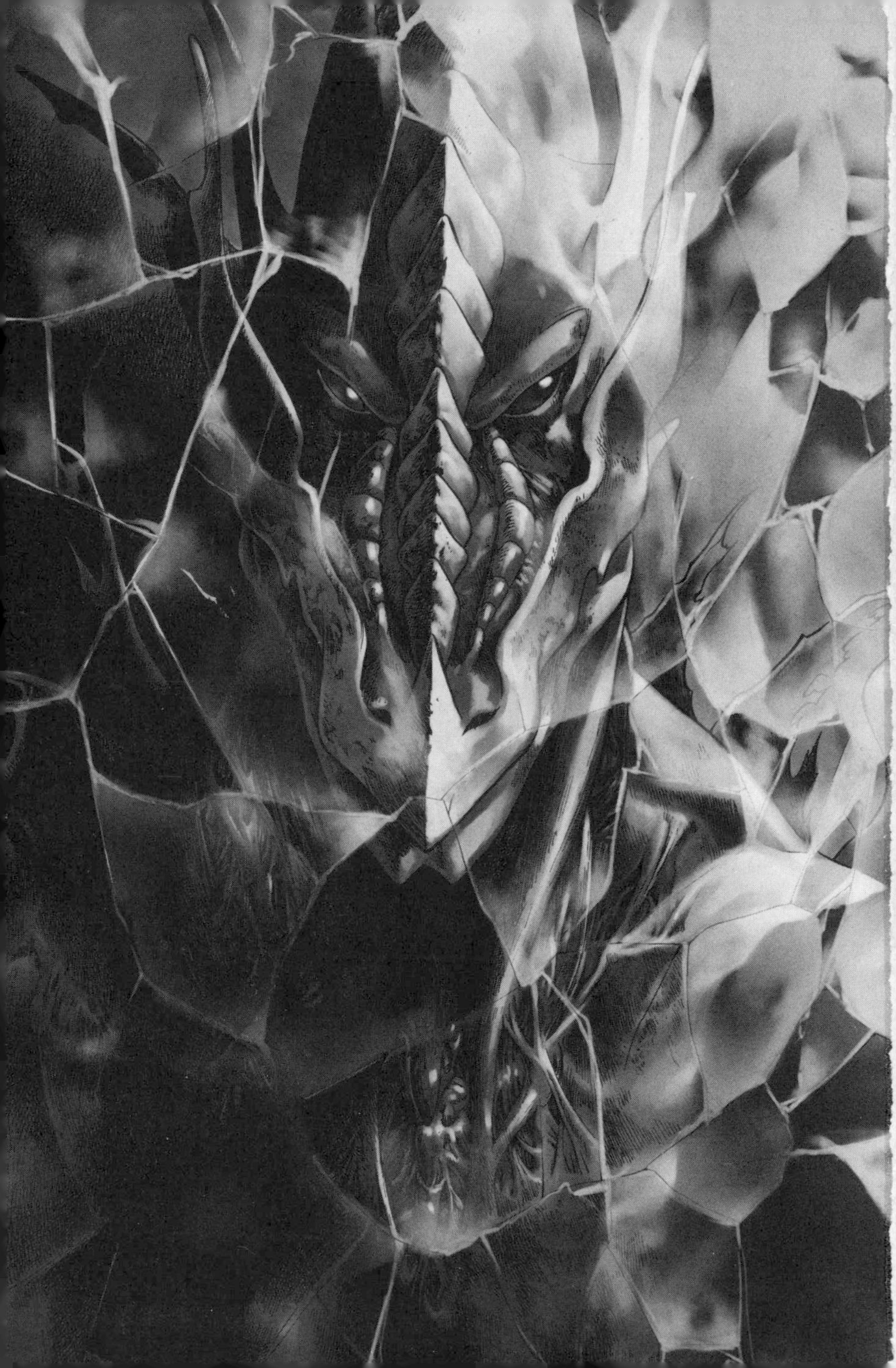